CAMBRIDGE STUDIES IN CRIMINOLOGY XLV
General Editor: Sir Leon Radzinowicz

THE CONTROL OF COMMERCIAL FRAUD

CAMBRIDGE STUDIES IN CRIMINOLOGY

THE CONTROL OF COMMERCIAL FRAUD

L. H. Leigh, B.A., LL.B., Ph.D

*Reader in Law, London
School of Economics and
Political Science*

Heinemann · London

Heinemann Educational Books Ltd
22 Bedford Square, London WC1B 3HH

LONDON EDINBURGH MELBOURNE AUCKLAND
HONG KONG SINGAPORE KUALA LUMPUR NEW DELHI
IBADAN NAIROBI JOHANNESBURG
EXETER (NH) KINGSTON PORT OF SPAIN

First published 1982

Publisher's note: This series is continuous with the
Cambridge Studies in Criminology, Volumes I to XIX,
published by Macmillan & Co., London

British Library Cataloguing in Publication Data

Leigh, Leonard H.
    The control of commercial fraud. (Cambridge studies in criminology; 45)
    1. Fraud
    I. Title
    364.1 '63   HV6771.G7

ISBN 0-435-82519-4

Typeset by Thomson Press (India) Limited, New Delhi, India.
Printed by Biddles Ltd., Guildford, England.

To DMH

Contents

List of Tables

Note to Readers

Numbered references appearing in the text are listed at the end of each chapter, under 'References and Notes'. Other references are given in the text, in abbreviated form and in parentheses. Full details of all the works referred to by the author are included in the bibliography section at the back of the book. An indexed Table of Cases cited is also included for the reader's convenience.

Preface

This is a book about the control of commercial fraud in Britain, primarily in England and Wales, through the medium of the criminal process. It thus treats one aspect of a subject of great contemporary interest and importance. Criminology is a house with many mansions; this book discusses the system of control from several aspects; it does not purport to deal with such matters as the theory of white-collar crime (if such a theory exists), the characteristics of offenders, the learning process in crime, or public perceptions of crime. It does, however, seek to place the law in the context of fraudulent practices engaged in in Britain. Hence the first part of the work discusses the current, or nearly current, patterns of fraud and the recurrent practices which are very often found in fraudulent activities.

The ideal author of this book, someone who understands the subject perfectly in all its facets, would need to be a formidable polymath, equipped to write upon the law, sociology, accountancy and, doubtless, psychology. No one fitting that description has emerged. Certainly this author, all too conscious of the barriers of perception which stood between him as an undergraduate and a well-intentioned accounting department, has no such pretensions. He and his colleagues have learned to use each other's knowledge.

A book about the control of fraud must needs tackle a good deal of law. Some of it can pose difficulties of comprehension for the layman, and even for the sociologically-based criminologist. I have tried to bear this in mind. The great anarchist, Prince Kropotkin, once wrote

> The Great Russian peasant perfectly well understands the educated man's talk, provided it is not stuffed with words taken from foreign languages. What the peasant does not understand is abstract notions when they are not illustrated by concrete examples. But my experience is that when you speak to the Russian peasant plainly, and start from concrete facts...there is no generalization from the whole world of science, social or natural, which cannot be conveyed to a man of average intelligence, if you yourself understand it concretely (1968, p. 105).

It would no doubt be indelicate, even unwise, to draw too close a parallel between the Russian peasant and colleagues in other disciplines who might reasonably reply that lawyers were among the earliest practitioners of unintelligibility. But I have tried to avoid jargon, and a descent into the minutiae of the law, in favour of presenting a broad picture. Some detailed treatment was unavoidable, especially where topics were not well covered in standard legal texts. But, for the most part, I have worked to the rule that obscure details of interpretation ought to be left to legal textbooks or learned journals. The balance between abstract and concrete I have sought to tackle by relating the later parts of the book, so far as possible, to the frauds discussed in the first part.

Inevitably, one incurs debts of gratitude. The greatest is to my colleagues on a working party on fraud offences created by the Attorney-General and chaired by the late W.A.B. Forbes, Q.C. I have benefited from their experience greatly, and only hope I have contributed something of value to their deliberations. They are not to be identified with any of the conclusions in this book. As always, I am grateful to colleagues in the accounting department of my College, and in particular to Professor H. C. Edey and to Mr Duncan Paterson. I owe a debt of gratitude to civil servants and police officers, and to officers of the City institutions, all of whom gave generously of their time and experience. I was privileged to use the law library at Oxford University during a sabbatical year. I am most grateful to the staff of that library for their very great help, as I am to the staff of the British Library of Political and Economic Science. I owe an immeasurable debt as always to Mrs Susan Hunt who typed the entire book.

I have stated the law as it existed on 1 June 1980, save that I have written as though the whole of the Companies Act 1980 were in force. One or two peculiarities of referencing should be noted, the result of a lawyer trying to adapt to another system. For the purposes of the author-date method, I have referred to the Committee to Review the Functioning of Financial Institutions either by that name or as the Wilson Committee, after its chairman. The Department of Trade Report into Ferguson and General Investments Ltd. is referred to by its common name, Dowgate. Department of Trade company investigation reports are listed separately in the bibliography by date. While I have included a table of cases as an additional reference aid, it has not seemed necessary to provide a table of statutes.

I close by thanking my publishers and the general editor of the series, Sir Leon Radzinowicz, for their unfailing courtesy and help. Brickbats are, as always, reserved for the author.

PART I

THE NATURE OF FRAUD

1 Introduction

This book is about the control of commercial fraud in Britain. The phenomenon is timeless and universal, and is found both in the capitalist west and the communist east. The forms which fraud takes are contingent upon the economic system in which they are found; the fact of fraud is not.

In Britain today, there is a lively interest in fraud and its control. There were, of course, major frauds from the South Sea Bubble, to which the government reacted with unparalleled hysteria, through Victorian times to the Second World War, and beyond. Since the war, the expansion and liberation of the economy, in which institutions and procedures of control were demonstrably imperfect, conduced to a series of scandals: ill-conducted insurance ventures, investment schemes in commodities and precious metals, the looting of companies with realisable cash assets, so-called 'cash companies', particularly Malaysian rubber companies and Ceylon tea estates with cash assets derived from payments in compensation for expropriation, wholesale irregularities in the secondary banking sector, bribery of local government officers in order to win construction contracts—an activity particularly associated with the name of John Poulson, exchange-control violations, frauds upon the Common Market and frauds upon the revenue. This list is by no means exhaustive.

Fraud is not only widespread, but it is big business too, and its tentacles spread throughout society. Global figures are unavailable; American estimates put losses through business crime, a loosely descriptive phrase, at $40 billion per annum (Rossum, 1978). In Britain, figures are difficult to find, although occasionally a glimpse is offered. Official sources show that in 1974 the Metropolitan and City Police Fraud Squad had in progress 380 major investigations, with money at risk amounting to £223 million. In 1978, 465 new inquiries were begun. In the year ended 31 March, 1978, tax arrears of Value Added Tax (V.A.T.) amounted to £2,931,398. In the same period the Inland Revenue recovered £37,297,000 by way of tax, interest and penalties. On the other hand, it has not been possible to give accurate figures for revenue loss through evasion by moonlighting, for example. Nor have accurate figures for frauds on the EEC been compiled.

Some idea of the scale of fraud may be conveyed by Table 1.1, showing frauds under active police investigation by the Metropolitan and City Police Fraud Squads as at 1 July 1978. The figure shown in the table necessarily includes only those frauds which were then known to the police and perceived to be frauds. It does not include much questionable business conduct which might be subject to prosecution if barriers of perception, and of evidence and procedure, could be overcome. Nor does it include figures from the provinces. In 1978, however, provincial forces investigated 86,295 cases of which 802 were cases of company fraud. No figures for cash at risk were obtainable for this group. In addition, some categories of fraud are not shown at all. The available figures do not contain information on frauds on the Inland Revenue or on the Customs and Excise. The figure for these is likely to be a high one.

The importance of fraud is not sufficiently explained by reference to figures, which in any event are sufficiently imprecise to serve as no more than polemical devices. Fraud battens on trust. Trust in the institutions of commerce, in their integrity and efficiency, is fundamental to the operation of any advanced economic system. The importance of this point is overlooked by those criminologists who see economic crime not only as endemic in capitalism, but who also see it as 'institutionalized, regular and widespread among the powerful' (Taylor, Walton and Young, 1975, p. 30). The problem with this analysis is that it fails adequately to discriminate between different forms of criminal conduct, some of which can be accommodated within the system, and others of which are ultimately destructive of it. An example of the former would be breaching the sanctions which used to apply to trading with Rhodesia, now Zimbabwe; an example of the latter is the forgery of bills of exchange and letters of credit, which strikes at the operation of the banking system. The economic damage which the former practice may cause is remote, though foreseeable; that of the latter is so immediate that no society could tolerate it. An advanced industrial society can prosper even though it tolerates cartels, but it cannot prosper if its financial institutions commonly misrepresent their solvency, operate on the margins of liquidity and are fatally vulnerable to general economic downturns. Directors of companies may, with the aid of spurious economic arguments, challenge the validity of criminal laws against insider trading, but hardly of those which strike at fraudulent misrepresentation (Pearce, 1976; Conklin, 1977).

TABLE 1.1   Fraud Cases under Investigation: Metropolitan and City Police,
1 July 1978

Type of fraud	Number of cases	Cash at risk (£)
Long-firm fraud	24	17,030,000
Fraudulent trading	39	4,900,000
Other frauds by directors	88	37,545,000
Protection of depositors	1	80,000
Prevention of fraud (investments)	7	5,650,000
Commodities fraud	5	1,940,000
Frauds by bankrupts	5	49,000
Government subsidy fraud	2	1,250,000
Fraud involving forged or worthless valuable securities (not cheques)	9	68,264,000
Public sector corruption	21	4,900,000*
Offshore bank frauds	9	15,150,000*
Cheque frauds	71	3,327,000
Stock exchange rigging	3	21,400,000
Other frauds	77	14,635,000
Total	361	177,120,000
Add other sundry frauds (including factoring frauds, overseas land frauds, credit card frauds, etc.)	112	19,107,000
Grand Total	473	196,227,000

*Note: Figures marked with an asterisk are preliminary estimates. The final totals are likely to be substantially higher.

This book is not an attempt to argue a particular thesis about the relationship of economic crime to society. It is not an enquiry into the causes of crime or the psychology of offenders. It is an attempt to describe, analyse and evaluate a system of control in the light of the fraudulent practices which arise in society from time to time, and to suggest reforms to it. It is written from the perspective of a reformer, not a revolutionary.

The way in which fraud offences are treated arouses strong emotions. There are allegations of bias which favours the fraud offender and other economic offenders, and these come from persons having quite different political views. When the scandal affecting the Crown Agents broke, it was a Labour government which was obliged to defend its decision not to prosecute the principals involved, against criticisms from both Left and Right. It is well that these views can be aired. One of the least attractive aspects of the enforcement of the criminal law in cases of irregularity and fraud is its unimaginative character. One does not have to share extreme political beliefs to question decisions not to prosecute arrived at because practices, while deplorable, were common among financial institutions of that period.[1] Nor does it seem extravagant to conclude, apropos that affair, that the government was readier to protect individuals than to enforce the law.[2] However fragmentary the evidence may be, it is necessary to assess the workings of the law in fraud cases, in the light of the very real difficulties which complicated business affairs produce.

This is a book about crime. It cannot be emphasised too strongly that the topic cannot be seen as one pertaining exclusively to crime, criminal behaviour, or the agencies which operate the criminal law. In saying this, I do not wish to appeal *ad hominem* to moralistic instincts to which conduct, seemingly unfair, irregular or immoral, gives rise. Equally, however, it would be erroneous to concentrate solely upon cases in which there has been a criminal conviction. Much conduct which appears to fall within the ambit of the criminal law is either not prosecuted or is dealt with civilly or administratively. Social problems do not come in a neatly pre-packaged form labelled civil, criminal or administrative. Phenomena are often tackled in a variety of ways, the means chosen being more often motivated by pragmatic considerations than by ideology. Some are defined as crimes and dealt with as such; some, defined as crimes are dealt with by other means; some are not defined as crimes at all.

This is not to say that the distinction between conduct which is defined by law as criminal and that which is not is unimportant (Taylor, Walton and Young, 1975, pp. 38–40). The very fact of definition may itself influence behaviour. A person may be prepared to indulge in sharp practice, but not in crime. Clearly, one must be alive to this point and beware of lumping together as criminal, or allied to crime, conduct of which one disapproves on moral grounds. But it is clear that the notion of crime and of economic crime has rather a contingent flavour. There is no domain of the criminal law bounded by notions of moral fault. Not all crimes respond to common morality; not all conduct commonly regarded as immoral is criminal. In Lord Atkin's words:[3]

> The criminal quality of an act cannot be discerned by intuition; nor can it be discovered by reference to any standard but one: is the act prohibited with penal consequences?

This, most emphatically, does not mean that the moral dimension of crime is unimportant; it does mean that there is a large area in which the criminal law may operate rather than must operate, and no area from which its operation is excluded.

What is 'Fraud'?

This book is specifically concerned with fraud, rather than white-collar crime or economic crime. Those are concepts which cannot be defined with precision, and nor can the notion of business crime (Conklin, 1977). Most definitions are unsatisfactory because agreed unifying elements are hard to find. Professor Sutherland proposed a definition which would take crime in an extended sense to include conduct made unlawful and punished by civil and administrative, as well as by criminal jurisdictions, committed by a respectable person of higher social class, and directly related to his professional activities (Sutherland, 1940). This definition is certainly not synonymous with fraud, much of which is committed by very ordinary persons. In any event, the notion of social class is elusive. Directors of companies, for example, come from very diverse backgrounds and approach social and business situations in very different ways. That is not to say that the concept of fraud itself is other than elusive. For many years the standard formula was that of Buckley J. in *Re London and Globe Finance Corporation Limited*:[4]

> To defraud is to deprive by deceit: it is by deceit to induce a man to act to his injury. More tersely it may be put, that to deceive is by falsehood to induce a state of mind; to defraud is by deceit to induce a course of action.

That formula, it is now accepted, is not exclusive; fraud can consist in depriving a person of what is his by any other dishonest means, including simple taking.

Even where deception is involved, the matter of definition is not easy. Apart from the case of a wholly mendacious, affirmative misrepresentation of fact, the question whether a misrepresentation is fraudulent requires a value judgement, for the law distinguishes between fraud, an exaggerated commendation (a 'puff'), and failure to disclose a material fact or circumstance, treating such a failure as fraudulent, or at any rate giving rise to legal consequences, only where there was a legal duty to disclose.[5] Whether, therefore, a practice is fraudulent, less culpable, or regarded as proper depends upon the mores of the particular society or market place in which it occurs. Commercial morality has advanced considerably since the 1930s, but Thurman Arnold's aphorism sums the matter up: 'Fraud . . . is a difficult thing to define in the ethics of trading, which are essentially the ethics of deceiving the other side' (Arnold, 1937, p. 232).

The maxim *caveat emptor* is ingrained in our law, even though its application is steadily being eroded. In effect, there is a spectrum, from affirmative misrepresentation, made knowing the representation to be false, to misrepresentation made negligently, to non-disclosure in circumstances where there is a duty imposed by law to disclose, to cases where there is no such legal duty. Thus there is a progression to fraud from the problem of inequality in contract, and where for the purposes of definition the line is to be drawn is obscure. Furthermore, fraud also owes its protean character to the fact that it is used in different contexts, in some of which it signifies not moral fault, but rather, for example, that a practice favours one group of creditors over another and thus cannot be allowed to stand. One of the great purposes of bankruptcy law is to prevent an insolvent debtor from preferring one creditor to another. All must share equally in the debtor's estate. The law considers such a preference to be a fraudulent preference, but that does not imply that the debtor acted fraudulently. Moral fault hardly provides us with a key to the definition of fraud, for each of the situations indicated above is apt to engender hostile moral reactions. What varies is the generality of the response and the extent to which it is reprobated by the law.

No definition can adequately comprehend fraud. We are, accordingly, forced back to the position that fraud is what the law recognises as fraud, and that the nature of fraud varies according to the context in which it is used. Even within the area readily recognised as fraud, there are frauds with which this book does not deal. It is not, for example, concerned particularly with frauds upon consumers, important as these are. Its principal concern is with those manifestations of fraud which involve abuses of the forms, facilities and institutions of commerce. The matter is one of emphasis. Admittedly, frauds upon consumers blend into the sort of frauds dealt with in this book, but nevertheless there is a rough line of demarcation, and I have sought to work within it. I have, for example, been interested in the regulation of the securities markets, which certainly affects consumers as investors, but not with consumer protection in general. I have been concerned with company frauds, but not with pyramid selling schemes. I have, however, gone somewhat beyond the area indicated above by dealing with some aspects of tax and customs and excise frauds, since these occupy a central position in the control of fraud. Many company frauds involve a substantial element of tax fraud, for example.

The Ambit of the Law

It is manifestly impossible to construct a thesis which holds that those practices that are regarded as most immoral or most disruptive to the current of commerce are punished criminally, while those that are purely venial are dealt with civilly or administratively, or at any rate before the magistrates' courts. Practices which are morally reprehensible or commercially disruptive are demonstrably not always brought within the criminal law.

In part, the problem is historical. English criminal law progressed, broadly speaking, from prohibited taking, committed openly, to various forms of clandestine taking, to taking by misrepresentation (Fletcher, 1978). The object of the taking was something tangible. Much of our legislation owed its enactment to particular problems. Admittedly, Victorian legislation, for example the Larceny Act 1861, grappled, surprisingly effectively, with forms of conduct which misled creditors and members of companies. Nevertheless, the structure of the law of theft and property offences reflected *ad hoc* legislative and judicial responses to particular problems. Not until the Theft Act 1968, was there a real attempt to look consistently at the structure and coverage of property offences. However, some offences dealt with in special legislation, for instance that which deals with investment fraud, were left untouched. Certain phenomena, rigging the stock exchange, for example, were left to consideration by other bodies.

All this has not meant that the law fails to cover fraud. It does so fairly effectively. But the emphasis of the reformers was upon recasting the existing law, improving its wording, reducing anomalies and eliminating overlap. An attempt was made to overcome problems of interpretation caused by technical minutiae (Stuart, 1967). Piecemeal law reform of this character inevitably left contemporary problems unrecognised and untouched. For example, problems relating to the abstraction of intangibles such as computer based information were not considered. Without a widely based offence of conspiracy to defraud, the system, bereft of reserve powers, would have broken down. Again, there are minor gaps which are explicable on the basis that they appeared in the original statute and their anomalous character was not spotted in the revision. Why, for example, should a company director be criminally liable for a written, but not an oral, false statement made with intent to deceive?[6]

English law also contains much overlap despite the attention given to this issue by law reform bodies. It is probably not a matter of much moment. The important thing is to have adequate controls. Furthermore, it is often desirable to have a particular, self-contained piece of legislation having criminal, civil and administrative components, and particular in its terms, where it is to regulate commerce in a particular milieu. For example, a licensed dealer in securities is likely to know the criminal provisions of the Prevention of Fraud (Investments) Act 1958 far better than he would ever know the Theft Act, because the former act governs his dealings with the world generally.

History and convenience afford only some of the answer as to why the coverage of the law is partial only. One must also recognise that practices once tolerated come to be condemned as a result of the evolution of business morality. This morality may well progress to a point where it is recognised that a given practice must be regulated, limited or stopped. It does not follow, however, that all would agree that it must be dealt with in all its manifestations or that it must be controlled by the criminal law. For example, many countries strike at monopolistic practices by the criminal law, as does the E.E.C. (Tiedemann, 1980). Both Britain and Australia choose to deal with the matter civilly, imposing penalties, if necessary, by contempt of court procedure.

Perhaps the most striking example of a practice ceasing to be tolerated is insider trading. Indeed, in Britain and some continental jurisdictions it is treated as a crime, whereas in America, which has much better developed civil procedures to enable individuals to claim redress, civil or administrative procedure is used (Yontef, 1979). Very broadly, the vice is that of a person who, because of his connections with a company, has price-sensitive information which is not available to the general public and who trades on the strength of it. This often occurs in take-over situations, but it is not restricted to them. If the insider trades, he makes a profit or avoids a loss which others, less fortunately circumstanced, cannot make or avoid. This prevents the market from operating on a basis of rough equality as between buyer and seller. At the same time, the other party does not actually lose more than a contingent advantage. For this reason, among others, the problem was for long thought either not to merit legislation or criminal legislation.

Indeed, insider trading has been defended by economists and others as a means of rewarding hard-pressed executives (Manne, 1966; Slater, 1977). Thurman Arnold notes that in the 1930s Senator Hayden defended the practice as an inherent right of American citizenship (Arnold, 1937), while an American executive summed the matter up briskly, thus: 'Let the buyer beware: that covers the whole business' (Loss, 1970). Evolving morality, and a desire to coax the small investor back into the securities market, induced the City institutions to press for legislation. The response was ambivalent, making the practice illegal, but in terms which bid fair to prevent adequate enforcement. If ever a topic afforded material for an abusive Marxist thesis, insider trading does.

These latter problems are discussed more fully later in this work. Suffice it to say that once the use of the law and, for reasons of a pragmatic character, the criminal law, was resolved upon, a host of problems arose for consideration. These included the problem of brokers dealing innocently for clients, the problem of trustees seeking to liquidate investments and the problems engendered when a financial institution not only acts for a client in a take-over, but acts for other clients in another capacity who are interested in the same securities. These perfectly valid considerations influenced the scope of the legislation.

Many practices, of course, are not dealt with by either the criminal or civil law because, while they are widely regarded as undesirable or unethical, such disapproval is either not general enough or there is a flux of considerations and a conflict of interests which need first to be resolved. The Ayatollahs of criminology can engage in fantasies of simple repression; the real world seldom admits of simple solutions.

As an example, we may take tax avoidance. For a variety of reasons, in particular the need for certainty so that a citizen may know what part of his income the government may take in tax and on what grounds and plan accordingly, the law distinguishes sharply between tax avoidance, which is lawful, and tax evasion, which is not. The distinction between the two is often a fine, but perceptible one, and avoidance manoeuvres, while lawful, some-times attract condemnation on ethical grounds as a result. For example, there was a period when company directors and others arranged for payments of remuneration and commission in sterling tax havens. This was lawful, and could only attract moral censure. Sometimes other directors and company auditors were deceived. This was at least a grave breach of duty on the part of those directors who were privy to the deception. On another occasion, the Crown Agents were castigated for unethical conduct in bargaining with others to avoid United Kingdom tax by themselves and by others, and for a cavalier attitude towards the then system of exchange control (Crown Agents, 1977–8). It was certainly an unlooked-for activity on the part of an emanation of the Crown. Yet, so far as the tax point is concerned, lawful avoidance is the inevitable price of a system which both seeks to define liabilities with precision and rejects as an organising principle the notion that one cannot protect against liability to taxation by adopting schemes which offend against the broad spirit of the Act. These matters are dealt with further in this book. At this juncture it is, perhaps, enough to note that basic questions of principle are involved and that simple moralism is a refuge from analysis and not a substitute for it.

There are other situations which involve a flux of considerations. Take, for example, the vexed question of the duty of a merchant bank when it becomes aware that its clients, company directors, perhaps, are prepared to use the bank's facilities to act to the detriment of their company to which they owe fiduciary duties. The problem arose in Dowgate, (1979). The merchant bank concerned, Keyser Ullman, certainly accepted that a sensible banker would not knowingly have entered into such a transaction. But as to legal or moral duties to abstain from lending, it was less inclined to assume the mantle of the penitent. As two of the bank's directors said (Ferguson & General Investments Ltd., referred to as Dowgate, 1979, p. 252):

> The Bank had no legal obligation of any sort to investigate the commercial prudence of any other party to the transaction entering it on whatever terms it did, whether a public company or not and whether separately advised or not. There is not the slightest support by the authorities for any such duty, and indeed the wheels of commerce would grind to a halt if each party was the other's keeper.

The inconsistencies hardly need emphasis. If the wheels of commerce would be impeded by such a duty, whatever its extent, there seems no reason to insist that a sensible banker, adequately secured, would not have entered into such a transaction. Nor does the invocation of the law do more than state the current position. The extent to which duties can be imposed consistent with the free flow of commerce or, at any rate, with that freedom which at any given time is considered necessary, is, however, a consideration which needs to be explored. So too is the extent to which the practice of lending in such circumstances is disapproved of. And there is the question, who is to be protected: no borrowers, all borrowers, or only those not competently advised? And should shareholders be protected by bankers against their own directors when the shareholders and the bank are not in a direct relationship with each other?

Dowgate also provides an example of a practice which caused disquiet but which it would be difficult to regulate by the criminal law. Dowgate facilitated the takeover of G. Ltd. by a firm called CST, the latter being a Dowgate subsidiary. The directors of G. Ltd. had reservations about the bid and, according to their evidence, determined to take no action over a particular weekend before deciding whether to recommend the offer to the shareholders. The directors testified that they agreed that they would hold their shares to the order of the board. One director, D., whose evidence differed from that of his fellows, insisted that no such undertaking was sought or given and sold his shares during that period to the bidder. This had the effect of undermining the board's resistance, and the take-over went through (Dowgate, 1979, pp. 105–33).

Suppose that the account given by G. Ltd.'s directors was right. D. committed neither a crime nor a tort nor a breach of contract in selling his shares. He owed no duty to the company or to other shareholders not to sell his shares; he plainly did not purport to give them advice. When the Inspectors concluded that the question was not whether D. was in breach of his duty to the company, but only the extent of that breach, they were presumably expressing themselves in terms wider than strictly legal propositions. Only if there were a clandestine bribe might a sale of shares to a bidder in such circumstances be criminal.

The problem with taking a wider view of the matter, and of suggesting a criminal offence, is that a crime which consisted solely in a breach of an undertaking, however morally reprehensible such a breach might be, would be very nebulous. Many people make promises and many promises are broken. Directors owe duties to their company as directors, not, broadly speaking, as shareholders.[7] Thus their status as shareholders cannot serve as a peg upon which to hang a duty. That is not to suggest that a duty could not be imposed but, again, limits would have to be worked out. To what extent should management responsibilities preclude dealing in one's private share interests? The City institutions have begun to consider such matters, especially in respect of insider dealing, but we have not yet reached a stage at which any comprehensive set of rules can be said to have evolved.[8]

Clearly, therefore, the law is extensive, but it is complicated and sometimes ambiguous. Practices which appear to be undesirable – many would say wrong, or immoral, or akin to crime – are not covered by the criminal law and some are not dealt with civilly either. The legal maxim, *nulla poena sine lege*, that there must be no crime or punishment except in accordance with fixed, predetermined law, is fundamental to English law as to that of all western systems (G. L. Williams, 1961). It inhibits courts from indulging in moralism, creating new offences and extending old ones without regard to the limitations of precedent.

If one considers what has been and might be covered by legislation, one must take account not only of the values embodied in the doctrine of legality, but also of a flux of interests that require to be reconciled. It is too simple to say, as some scholars do, that conduct which is compatible with the interests of a ruling class is tolerated while conduct which strikes at its interests is not (Quinney, 1975). Even accepting the class rhetoric involved, one cannot overlook the fact that interests are differently perceived by persons in the so-called ruling class, that they clash and that homogeneity of interest only looks plausible when it is advanced at an absurdly high level of abstraction.

It would, at the same time, be wrong solely to concentrate on the enforcement of the criminal law as it pertains to fraud. That does not mean denying the importance of the distinction between criminal and non-criminal conduct which has already been stressed. But the institutions and mechanisms of control outside the criminal law extend widely. It is impossible to deal with the structure of control over commercial fraud without dealing in some measure with these wider aspects. Admittedly, this renders the limits to discussion rather nebulous, but that is not an important consideration.

References and Notes

1. Sess. 1977–8, 940 H.C. Deb. (Vth Ser.) cols. 1026–1646.
2. See e.g. *ibid.*, col. 739 *per* Mr. Mendelson.
3. *Proprietary Articles Trade Association* v. *Attorney-General of Canada* [1931] A.C. 310 at p. 324; for an example of the 'domain' view, see *per* Lord Haldane in *In re Board of Commerce Act* [1922] 1 A.C. 191.
4. [1903] 1 Ch. 728 at p. 732.
5. In order to maintain a tort action for deceit, the defendant must have known the representation to be false; *Derry* v. *Peek* (1889), 14 App. Cas. 356.
6. Compare, for example, Theft Act 1968, s. 19 with Criminal Code (Canada) R.S.C. 1970 C-34, s. 358, both of which derive from the same source.
7. *Percival* v. *Wright* [1902] 2 Ch. 421.
8. Wilson Committee, Second Stage Evidence, vol. 4, *The Stock Exchange*, Appendix E (1979).

2 Company Fraud

Police sources have described to me at least twenty-eight different kinds of frauds currently practised in Britain. Not all of these form the subject matter of this book, but many do. This and the two succeeding chapters are devoted to a description of these frauds in order to provide a foundation upon which the later discussion of controls can rest.

This chapter deals with what I have chosen to call company frauds, though most frauds can be committed under the aegis of any form of business organisation. There is no easy way in which to classify company frauds. A company may be the victim of fraud or it may be a vehicle by which frauds are committed or it may be both at the same time. It may have been created for a fraudulent purpose or adapted to that end. The great bulk of fraudulent companies fall into this category (Argenti, 1976, pp. 42–3). It may, on the other hand, have been created in order to carry on a legitimate business but have suffered the depredations of an unscrupulous management which treated it as its fief, disregarding the interests of shareholders, creditors or employees. In a sense, some of this crime can be looked upon as opportunistic or incidental in character, as a manifestation of what Argenti calls 'creative accounting', but that form of words should not conceal the reality, which is that the actions of such managements are very often criminal and that the crimes involved can be very serious in character.

The crimes committed by the controllers of fringe banks which came to light as a result of the slump of 1974 were extremely serious and, from an economic point of view, far more serious than the blatantly criminal looting of non-trading cash companies characteristic of the 1960s, about which more will be said later. The damage done to the interests of creditors and employees when directors seek, often for good motives, to prolong the life of failing companies, concealing their true position by improper accounting manoeuvres, again causes economic losses of some magnitude and may have a distinctly adverse effect upon employees' careers.

Classification of frauds must be somewhat rough and ready in nature. Dr. Hadden lists management frauds, market frauds, trading frauds and subscription frauds (Hadden, 1968). In this work, partly because of its wider perspective, I have allocated company frauds as follows: ordinary theft and fraud upon the public (much of which could be committed whatever type of business organisation was adopted); thefts of assets and corporate looting; subscription and investment frauds; incidental crimes (which in this schema are forms of management frauds); frauds in relation to securities; insurance frauds; and insider trading. Of course, none of these categories is other than descriptive. None is self-contained. They are adopted for the sake of exposition. Similarly, for the sake of exposition, I have limited the examples in each group and have been obliged to simplify the facts. There is a further point also. The examples chosen are not necessarily those which were most prominent in recent years, although some are. Many Department of Trade reports offer valuable insights into deficiencies in management, unsatisfactory accounts, difficult relationships with auditors, and the like. But where the Department of Trade report stops short of affirming fraud, and none has been established by civil or criminal proceedings, both decency and prudence dictate circumspection to the author.

As already stated, many offences of theft and fraud can, of course, be committed whatever the nature of the business organisation adopted by the rogue, whether it be a sole proprietorship, partnership or company. Some frauds, such as insolvent trading, are at present only criminal where the corporate form of business enterprise is adopted. Securities frauds depend on the availability of shares in a listed company. Discount and factoring frauds appear, in practice, to be committed through companies. There are three reasons, fundamentally, for the emphasis on the use of companies as a vehicle for fraud. The first is simply that the company is a very common form of business organisation. One can buy a dormant company, or a company 'off the peg' with constituent documents already drafted, very cheaply. Provided that a private company is chosen and the promoters do not engage in insurance there are no minimum capital provisions; the law prescribes a minimum capital only for public companies and insurance companies.[1] It is not difficult to create a semblance of respectability and prosperity.

A second reason why companies serve as a vehicle for fraud is that a company has perpetual succession. In other words, although all the shares may change hands and the directors change, the company continues to exist under the same name. This makes it possible to deceive the public and even trade protection agencies, for if there is a delay in notifying changes in control to the Department of Trade, a trade supplier may, reasonably, believe that he is still dealing with the same people.

The attribute of limited liability is not always of importance although some fraud investigators believe that directors who take risks with their company might not do so if they were likely to be made personally liable for its debts. The practice of banks and other institutions in taking personal guarantees from directors renders limited liability of less importance as a measure of immunity for losses whether induced by fraud or otherwise. Admittedly, there have been cases where such guarantees have been worthless. In Dowgate, personal guarantees taken from Selmes, a principal actor, proved in the result to be unenforceable, and the merchant bank which took them ultimately released him from liabilities on his personal guarantee of £17,250,000 in return for a sculpture valued at £20,000, shares worth £16,000 and a debt of £14,000 'binding in honour only' (Dowgate, 1979, p. 297). The Crown Agents took personal guarantees from William Stern for loans worth £4 million. These too were worthless (Crown Agents, 1977–8, pp. 98–113). But in general, banks ensure that they are well secured, and limited liability thus does not afford complete protection to directors and members of companies. In any event, limited liability is not a substantial consideration to fraudulent promoters and managers of companies who do not propose to remain to face civil, let alone criminal, proceedings. Most outright frauds involving companies fall into these categories (Argenti, 1976, pp. 42–3).

Ownership in large, and even medium-sized, companies is in some measure divorced from control. As shareholding in such companies is diffused, and as most shareholders do not want to take part in management or oversee its performance with any particularity, companies are run by boards of directors which function as self-perpetuating oligarchies (Berle and Means, 1936; Arnold, 1937). From this it is argued that a critical element of control over management is lacking, thus facilitating fraud (Hadden, 1968).

There are problems with this argument. It is, of course, true that many small shareholders do not wish to participate in or monitor management. But patterns of share ownership are changing. Institutions are taking an increasingly prominent role as shareholders. A recent study shows, for example, that, whereas shareholdings in the personal sector in large companies have fallen steadily from 56.1 per cent in 1963 to 39.8 per cent in 1975, the institutions' share has risen from 30 per cent to 48.1 per cent (Central Statistical Office 1979: Erritt *et al.* It can thus be argued that shareholding is becoming more concentrated. Institutions which come increasingly to dominate the list of investors may well wish to take a more active role in monitoring performance than hitherto.

It would be easy to exaggerate the likely influence of the institutions. Hitherto, they have been content to secure information in order to monitor their investments, rather than play a part in management. Even where lending institutions have placed a director on a board, he has, it is said, been content to take a narrow view of matters, considering primarily the security of his principal's loan (Argenti, 1976). Institutional shareholders nevertheless have an interest in maintaining some distance between themselves and the companies in which they invest. Institutions, it is said, do not wish to constitute themselves as insider traders, which could happen if they came into possession of information which is not publicly available, concerning companies in which they invest. Small shareholders might then have reason to feel aggrieved if they sensed that close links between companies and institutions gave the latter access to price-sensitive information. Furthermore, institutions such as unit trusts and investment trust companies are forbidden to acquire control over companies in which they invest. Thus the move towards concentration of shareholding represented by a shift from small individual investors to big institutions does not premise close control over companies in which they invest.

But while management control is not the function of the institutional investor, one can expect institutions to monitor management performance, and to conduct the monitoring more closely in periods of recession, when it is more difficult for an investor to divest himself or herself of shares without incurring a loss, than in times of prosperity. Conceivably, recent proceedings by the Prudential Assurance Company in relation to alleged misfeasance in Newman Industries Limited signal an increasing willingness on the part of institutions to take remedial and even punitive action where a company is thought to be the victim of misfeasance or fraud.[2]

This possibility apart, in a large company, the real controls are internal management controls, and their deficiencies may not be noticed until disaster strikes. There is, as will be seen, a pattern of fraud which manifests itself in attempts by directors and managing directors to conceal by 'creative accounting' a drift into failure if not insolvency (Argenti, 1976, pp. 141–43). Furthermore, the history of company mismanagement and wrongdoing abounds with cases in which a dominating managerial figure rode roughshod over his fellow directors and the officers of the company. This managerial style is really inimical to the growth and development of proper managerial controls within the company. Many cases do not present a pattern of controllers who commence business with the conscious object of defrauding the public. Many irregularities, even some which might have been prosecuted, had the evidence held up or investigations been completed in time, represented, essentially, incidental criminality. Inflated profit forecasts, over-optimistic directors' reports, sales whose integrity was uncertain, represented not part of a scheme to defraud the public, but rather the reaction of an entrepreneurial chairman endeavouring to box his way out of a tight corner.

This is not, of course, to deny that there have been cases, some notorious, in which management structures have deliberately been kept weak in order to enable fraudulent management manoeuvres to take place. In some of these cases, there was no appreciable institutional shareholding and so no real monitoring took place. Certainly the divorce of ownership from control and the ability of directors to pass control to a new board without consulting shareholders conduced to the looting of 'cash' companies in the 1960s. We will examine one such case in detail, that of Town Centre Properties Ltd. But general weaknesses in management structures seem to be a more important condition.

These, then, are factors which help to explain why the corporate form features so often in fraudulent transactions. Some of the details of fraudulent schemes are developed later at greater length, and some problems of corporate management are illustrated when dealing with controls imposed by company law and in management practices within companies.

Ordinary Theft and Fraud

The great majority of frauds involve either theft from the company or theft or deception perpetrated through the company (Comer, 1977).[3] The most common form of deception perpetrated through the medium of a company is long-firm fraud. The genesis of the name is unknown but it probably derives from buying 'long' on credit and selling 'short' for cash. It is among the oldest known forms of fraud. It is also the most common form of company fraud and it is primarily committed through the medium of the private company. There can be little doubt that the prevalence of dormant or near dormant companies facilitates long-firm fraud. Such companies can be acquired cheaply and put to criminal purposes. Reference to Table 1.1 discloses that at 1 July 1978 the Metropolitan and City Police Company Fraud Squad was dealing with 24 cases, involving £17 million.

The essence of long-firm fraud is credit (Campbell, 1979). A company is either formed or acquired to trade as a wholesaler. The intention of the promoters is usually fraudulent from the outset. It requires careful planning because it requires the criminal to warehouse and dispose of goods often with documentation which makes it possible for a person dealing further with them to claim plausibly that they were not obtained by crime. The object of a long-firm fraud is to obtain goods on credit, to sell them without paying the supplier, and to decamp. This is facilitated if an existing business can be acquired because firms which have traded with it may be unaware of the change in control. The rogue establishes good credit, or acquires a firm with it, ultimately orders easily saleable goods to a considerable value, and then, having disposed of them, makes off without payment.

Borrell and Cashinella offer the following illustration (1975, p. 86). One Dunstance purchased a small wine company. He advertised Scotch whisky at very low prices on terms requiring orders of at least a dozen bottles, cash paid in advance. He received very large sums of money from customers but, after a short period, left for the Continent with the moneys received and without having supplied whisky. Nor had he paid wine suppliers for wine which he sold to customers for cash. When the Official Receiver took charge it was discovered that the company was so heavily indebted that its creditors obtained only 21p in the £.

Goods acquired by means of long-firm fraud are disposed of through various outlets. The most common are street markets and cut-price shops. In the latter category are to be found shops whose proprietors have previously been convicted of fraud and other crimes of dishonesty. Also used are high-turnover businesses which consistently place a number of small orders (Comer, 1977). Ultimately, the rogues, having disposed of large quantities of goods , flee without paying. It would appear that despite increasing trade links with Europe, long-firm frauds are domestic in character. The more widespread such trading becomes, the greater becomes the danger of exposure and therefore detection. Nevertheless, there have been reports of foodstuffs frauds in which lorry-loads of meat, bought on credit in England, have been sold in France, the rogues disappearing with the money.

Another common fraud is insolvent trading, that is, broadly speaking, continuing to do business when the company has no hope of meeting its obligations. This may or may not be criminal, depending upon the type of firm involved and the knowledge which its controllers have of the firm's affairs. If the firm is a partnership, or other unincorporated body, the members will be liable criminally for trading on a false appearance of solvency only where they have either expressly misrepresented the firm's solvency to the person with whom they dealt, or conspired among themselves to trade on a false appearance of solvency. If the firm is a company, there is no need for conspiracy; it is a substantive offence for the directors of a company to trade knowingly on a false appearance of solvency. The position is both anomalous and indefensible, and is likely to be reformed in the near future.

The controllers' expectations are obviously material on the issue of whether there was intent to defraud creditors. The point is dealt with further in connection with the criminal law. However, if criminal liability attached simply to trading while insolvent, the directors of many ordinary companies and of more than one state enterprise would live in peril of conviction. It is very common for directors of companies who realise that the company is sinking to continue to trade, disguising the truth, in the hope and expectation, often ill-founded, that the tide will turn (Argenti, 1976). In these common cases, neither the courts nor the Department of Trade are inclined to move with great severity. The adoption of desperate expedients may result in conduct which could form the basis of a criminal charge, but directors who indulge in such conduct are often seen as not deserving of criminal punishment. As the Departmental Inspectors stated of the directors of Larkfold Holdings Limited, a company formed to take over a tea company which by the date of acquisition was a cash shell and went into the property market and crashed (Larkfold Holdings Limited, 1979, para. 9.51):

> ...it can be said in their defence that they were not trading and were not the first board of directors of an ailing company to have persevered overlong.

In any event, in cases of fraudulent trading, the directors are personally liable civilly for the debts of the company. But the law is deficient both in the conditions for liability relating to companies and in the lacuna which exists in respect of unincorporated associations. These matters are further dealt with in discussing the criminal law.

Looting the Company—Theft

Quite the simplest way to loot a company is to steal from it. Simply to abstract money from the till is crude and invites detection. Whatever is done needs to be disguised in such a way that it will appear to be done regularly, in the company's interests; in other words, it must give the appearance of being a regular transaction. Concealment, an essential ingredient of prolonged frauds involves the manipulation of records and the misrepresentation of transactions in order to conceal a taking or prevent or delay recognition of the true character of a transaction, or to establish a plausible excuse for the transaction. That is, error or impercipience, for example, rather than dishonesty.

Eglinton Hotels (Scotland) Limited (1961) affords an example of the genre. The company owned and managed a series of hotels in Scotland. The majority of shares were held by the Adelphi Hotel company which was controlled by one MacLachlan, whom the Inspectors found to be a vague and unsatisfactory witness. Among the transactions questioned by the Inspectors was the drawing of cheques payable to MacLachlan's relative, Miss Muir, for carpeting for the hotels. The carpeting was never supplied. There is a strong inference that the cheques did not enter or remain in Miss Muir's bank account. Other examples of disbursements for articles never supplied appear in the report, and the Inspectors called for a police investigation into the matter. Similar allegations concern alleged abstractions of large sums of money from the National Liberal Club by raising cheques on the club for the fictitious purchase of carpets from a non-existent company.

Another common device for concealing theft is known as 'teaming and lading' (Comer, 1977, p. 29). This is illustrated by the affair of Grays Building Society (Cmnd. 7557, 1979). Jaggard, its chief executive, stole about £2 million from the Society over many years, and in so doing cost it another £5 millions in lost interest. Jaggard operated the system of teaming and lading, the essence of which was to misappropriate cash from the Society's takings, to cover up the misappropriations by accelerating the banking of cheques received in a subsequent banking period and then, when his misappropriations had reached a point where they might become apparent, to abstract a cheque and use it to fill the gap.

Jaggard himself opened the mail. Jaggard made entries in the mortgage ledger to close accounts. He destroyed correspondence files in cases where he misappropriated the cheques. He falsified passbooks of members whom he could be sure would deal only with him. He never left the office and he never delegated responsibility. He relied on his command of the enterprise and a lack of initiative on the part of the auditors, whose audit proceeded according to the same routine for years. For years Jaggard was able to falsify the totals of year end summaries, to falsify details to agree with these totals, and then, after the auditors had checked the totals, to reinstate the details, allowing them to be checked against the ledgers. Finally, the auditors one day unexpectedly jumped beyond the point where Jaggard had completed his falsifications. He left, went home and committed suicide in the bathroom. His governing passion was gambling, an activity which Grays had subsidised for forty years.

Sir Eric Miller's operations in Peachey Property Corporation Limited were equally theftuous, but more stylish (1979). While the Inspectors, conscious that Miller was by then dead and unable to answer allegations against him, do not use the word 'dishonesty' it is difficult to think of a more suitable word in respect of a number of transactions in which he engaged. The criticisms noted here do not cast aspersions upon Peachey, but rather upon its expansive chief executive and some who dealt with him. Among Miller's misdeeds was the use of company money to cover his own overdrafts, thereafter covering up the transactions by forgeries. Money was advanced to Fulham Football Club, the directors of which acted honestly. It was shown in Fulham's books as an interest-free loan, but in Peachey's as payment for an option. Football was Miller's personal rather than Peachey's corporate enthusiasm.

Some payments were not recorded in the books, or appeared in a disguised form. Miller cooked his expense accounts. He incurred expenses for entertainment in circumstances which could not have benefited Peachey and which could not therefore have been authorised as a valid gift by the company. Whether notional benefit could have accrued to Peachey or not from entertaining Labour party notables, Miller hardly put Peachey in a position to benefit from its largesse. The good and the great were led to understand that Miller was personally footing the bill.

Miller was a generous giver—through Peachey. The Inspectors found that he spent some £250,000 on gifts over a ten-year period. No detailed invoices were ever seen by the company. Where the recipients could be identified, the Inspectors found it difficult to believe that gifts to them would, or could, have been of advantage to the company. Miller used company funds for private purposes. The case of his Ferrari car affords an example. He obtained a Ferrari from a motor dealer, who invoiced AHP, a Peachey subsidiary, for £9,500. The dealer applied the money to the invoice. AHP showed it as a 'deposit'. When, after several years had elapsed and the auditors demanded an explanation, Miller in order to cover his tracks sold to Aspreys the jewellers (who acted honestly throughout) articles which he had previously bought from them with Peachey money and paid £9,500 to the motor dealers. The dealers then obligingly wrote a letter to AHP at Miller's request, which they knew could not be true, regretting their inability to supply the car and returning the 'deposit'. Other missing sums were explained to the auditors as 'introductory commissions' (bribes) paid in connection with property development. The Inspectors concluded that in some instances the notion of 'introductory commissions' provided a potent vehicle for defalcation by Miller which he took.

Miller's life-style depended upon his misuse of company assets. As the Inspectors make clear, this could not have been done without the co-operation of others. Miller ran the company as an autocrat. His board was weak until the arrival of Lord Mais who took vigorous action. Able executives were kept at arm's length from work of real substance and left to wither on the vine. The company appeared to be prosperous and, indeed, weathered the storm. Thus shareholder action was not to be expected. All of these are matters which we shall have occasion to discuss in connection with the duties of management. But some transactions cannot have appeared normal to those engaged in them. The case of the motor dealer's letter is one such instance. That of the Churchill Hotel is another. Miller did a great deal of entertaining there. Ultimately the day came when the auditors needed to be satisfied about these expenditures. Miller covered himself by procuring letters from the hotel after the transaction and by arranging with a manager to prepare cooked accounts which Miller then showed to the auditors as accounts for business guests of Peachey. Taxed by the Inspectors with these accommodations, the hotel manager responsible said that it was difficult to believe that Miller was acting illegally, but the thought that he might be using the vouchers to mislead the Inland Revenue did cross his mind (Peachey Property Corporation Limited, 1979, p. 92). Further comment would be superfluous were it not for the fact that the notion that tax evasion is at most only quasi-criminal is held even by parliamentarians.[4]

Management Frauds and Incidental Crime

I have adopted this description simply because there are cases in which it could not be said that a company was created to perpetrate a fraud, yet the way in which it was managed and the practices engaged in go far beyond the sorts of abstractions engaged in by Sir Eric Miller, and yet are not rightly to be regarded as theft, perhaps.

Roadships Limited falls within this category (Roadships Limited, 1976). The company, originally Ralph Hilton Transport Services Ltd, expanded rapidly, overrunning both the managerial capacities of its autocratic controller and his acolytes, and its primitive accounting system. Indeed, the auditors were forced into the undesirable position of providing some routine accounting assist-ance to the company. Take-overs were engaged in, some unwisely, and in at least one case there was a concealed side-payment to the controller of the target company. Cash was removed from the company as a result of which tax evasion apparently took place. The company paid 'sweeteners' to employees of other companies in order to obtain business. This is bribery, prohibited, as will be seen, by the Prevention of Corruption Act 1906. But the controller, Hilton, behaved no worse than many competitors. The Inspectors summed these aspects up thus (p. 20):

> In fact no consistent pattern of attitudes emerged from the evidence. Some transport operators from fairly rough commercial backgrounds regarded such payments as disgraceful. Some oper-ators—and indeed some professional men—viewed them with equanimity or at least with philosophical acceptance as a necessary evil... [auditors] thought that the scale on which they were practised at HTS was 'not large' for a transport under-taking.

The atmosphere at the company was tough. But the company was not run with a view to defrauding the public. It crashed because, essentially, it expanded beyond the capacities of its controllers. While officers were convicted of conspiracy, falsification of accounts and forgery, and in one case given a suspended sentence and in another a fine, the accountant S, against whom the bulk of convictions was registered, was a person who fundamentally was liable to react dishonestly under pressure. Faced with an authorita-rian and overbearing chairman, S, overworked, persuasive and glib, falsified profit results in connection with a take-over bid, and these were published. Fictitious invoices on customers were raised but never sent. Accounts payable invoices were suppressed. So too were transactions between different companies in the group.

We have noted that none of these categories of fraud is mutually exclusive of the others. Hilton, the controlling figure, used company funds for his private purposes, and he took an expansive view of the relationship between his personal expenditures and the company's benefit. He ran a boat at the company's expense, justifying this by its publicity value to the company. Of this, the Inspectors say (p. 128):

> ... [this is] a view which we feel will be regarded with scepticism by those who are obliged to pay for their recreations out of their taxed income, but with considerable sympathy by many honest and shrewd company directors who are fortunate enough to find

that the interests of their shareholders are consistent with them pursuing their own recreations partly at the expense of the shareholders and partly at that of the taxpayer.

Roadships Limited is not, of course, the only case in which a subordinate reacted to severe pressure from a dominant executive by falsifying accounts in order to turn away wrath, however temporarily (Bernard Russell Limited, 1975). Nor is it the only case in which collateral assurances were given in order to obtain improper advantage. In Blanes Limited the Inspectors found that false invoices were supplied to a Dutch firm so that this firm, by representing that it had been supplied with goods, could obtain additional credit facilities. In turn, the Dutch firm was enabled to repay its outstanding debts to Blanes forthwith (Blanes Limited, 1975). In order to obtain a refund of premium, Blanes falsely represented to an insurance company that it had dismissed a senior employee for dishonesty. The company, however, used the sum thus received to pay compensation to the employee, thus avoiding a civil action by her.

More serious in their consequences were the irregularities engaged in by some insurance companies and secondary banks in the 1970s. The line between irregularity and criminality is often difficult to draw. But both irregularities and crimes played a part. For example, the Vehicle and General debacle in which a motor insurance company crashed owing large sums to third parties and leaving many motorists uncovered, was due primarily to bad management, but some of what was done went far beyond that description (The Vehicle and General Insurance Company Limited, 1976). Under bad management one can group failure to make adequate provision for claims and to maintain adequate reserves, concentrating investments dangerously in a hire-purchase company owned by two of Vehicle and General's controllers, taking profits on the sale of investments to profit and loss account which induced the company to pay dividends in excess of the trading results achieved by the company and its associates. A disastrous Australian venture was undertaken.

Other activities must be viewed less indulgently. The company borrowed money from the Crown Agents on a one day arrangement over the year-end in order to impress brokers by showing high gross cash figures. Whether or not the tactic in the particular circumstances amounted to the emission of a false statement with intent to deceive contrary to the Theft Act 1968 is a point which was not taken. But even if no statute was contravened, the manoeuvre cannot be thought of as entirely honest, and it was certainly imprudent from the point of view of the Crown Agents (Crown Agents, 1977–8, p. 74).

Much worse was done. Profit figures were deliberately inflated and accounts published which, the Inspectors conclude, would give all but the most sophisticated reader an entirely misleading picture of the company's true position. In part it did so by raising swingeing and unjustified management charges against associated companies. In 1969 it showed a profit of £460,164 by understating provision for losses on the motor account and by showing a pre-acquisition capital profit as a trading profit. The Inspectors conclude that four directors (pp. 298–9):

> ...knowingly published or concurred in the publication of consolidated accounts for 1969 which gave a wholly misleading impression of the results of the operations for the year end of the state of affairs of V. & G.

Even when in 1970 interim figures showed a loss, Hunt, the dominant figure, declined to believe them, and a dividend was declared.

The damage which the crash of Vehicle and General caused was considerable, though mitigated by the facility of the Motor Insurers Bureau to cover losses. But not only were members of the public hurt; the effect of the mis-statements was to disarm the Department of Trade, the body responsible for regulating the insurance business. Happily, the Department, while in some measure inept, was not corrupt, and the system of control was thereafter strengthened (The Vehicle and General Insurance Company Limited, Tribunal, 1971–2).

Management Frauds and the Secondary Banks

It is notorious that, in 1974, a number of secondary banks which had lent unwisely in an increasingly unstable property market crashed and had to be rescued by a consortium led by the Bank of England. Among the ill-fated losers were the Crown Agents who ought never to have lent on their 'own account' at all, and whose choice of investment partners certainly reflected misjudgement. Warnings uttered in the financial press seem wholly to have been disregarded (Crown Agents, 1977–8, p. 41). Not the least interesting aspect of the affair is that some evidence asserted that loans made to Mr. John Stonehouse's London Capital Group Limited were made not for commercial but for political reasons; to obtain support for the Crown Agents in the House of Commons (*ibid.*, p. 113). Whatever the truth of this may be, secondary banks crashed. Thereafter the

Bank of England was given extensive regulatory powers and it is doubtful whether quite the same types of frauds as those perpetrated by the fringe banks will re-emerge. Nevertheless, some of the practices engaged in by such companies could appear in the affairs of other companies, and it is therefore worth sketching at least the outlines of what happened in some of these cases.

One such case is that of London Capital Group Limited which began life as the British Bangladesh Trust Limited (BBT). This was the Stonehouse affair. While the Inspectors concluded that Stonehouse controlled companies saturated with offences, they also concluded that BBT was not conceived in fraud; Stonehouse embarked on serious wrongdoing when stung by bad publicity which attended an offer of shares to the public. However, the Inspectors concluded that he became a sophisticated and skilful confidence trickster whose assistants often were unable to believe in his duplicity. Others became his willing disciples. As not infrequently happens in these cases the controller, Stonehouse, treated the company as if it were 'an additional hip-pocket in his own trousers' (London Capital Group Limited, 1977, p. 18).

BBT was formed to provide a savings and investment medium for the Bangladesh community. It began, unwisely, with a launch of shares to the public unsupported by underwriting. Only major companies with an excellent proven record of performance seek to attract investment from the public without underwriting, and press comment was hostile. Not surprisingly, the issue appeared likely to fail. In an effort to save the venture, Stonehouse procured companies controlled by himself to subscribe for shares, lending, by circuitous means, the purchase price from moneys received by BBT from the public. This is a blatant breach of section 54 of the Companies Act 1948 which prohibits companies, in categorical terms, from advancing moneys for the purchase of their own shares. In the result, BBT received in cash about half the sum which it indicated to the public that it needed to finance its ventures. Whilst the whole sum necessary was shown as subscribed, half of it was represented by Stonehouse company applications supported by loans from proceeds received from the investing public.

Having engaged in wrongdoing Stonehouse was then obliged to conceal it. Nor did wrongdoing stop with the problems associated with initial subscriptions. Loans were made by BBT to Stonehouse-controlled private companies, the ownership of which was not initially appreciated by the auditors. From an early stage Stonehouse drew on these as he wished, engaging, against competent advice, in disastrous share speculations. Loans were frequently made among the three largest Stonehouse private companies, EPACS, Connoisseurs and Global. It became the practice to use the facilities of the other companies to liquidate the overdrafts of any one of the three whose financial year end was approaching. The Inspectors state (p. 46):

> For example, Connoisseurs borrowed from EPACS and Global in December 1972 so that its bank accounts would be in credit at the year end and Connoisseurs returned the compliment at the end of March when it was EPACS' turn to be dressed up. The purpose of these manipulations was to present a year-end picture which did not reflect the typical financial position for the year.

The Inspectors conclude that as the BBT saga developed, the private companies were put to more strenuous use as agents of deceit. An example of the manner in which Stonehouse obtained money for his own use appears from the following exchange between Mr. Michael Sherrard, Q.C., one of the Inspectors, and Mr Stonehouse (p. 47):

> Mr. Sherrard: EPACS drew £10,000 on its account with BBT, payable to Systems. Systems deposited this amount in its account at Lloyds Bank, and then drew a cheque payable to you.

> Mr. Stonehouse: Yes.

> Q: The original amount received from EPACS was shown as a liability to that company, EPACS, and the payment to you was then also charged against EPACS' account, offsetting this liability. So the net result is the same as we have seen before by a slightly different route. EPACS continues to show the amount of £10,000 as being due from Systems; not from you.

Cheques were drawn in odd amounts so that it would not be too easy to marry up the sources. Reduced, for purposes of exposition, to a diagrammatic T set of accounts, the transactions appear as in Table 2.1.

TABLE 2.1   EPACS Accounts (Stonehouse)

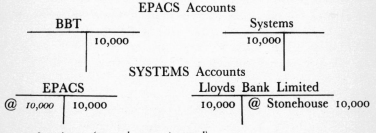

Of course the £10,000 should have been shown as received from EPACS, which should have had an account in Stonehouse's name, but did not.

Stonehouse and his associates took pains to conceal that there had been very substantial loans to BBT directors and their companies during the first seven months of BBT's life. Opposition by the auditors was overcome, despite legal advice to them confirming their view that disclosure in the accounts was required. The directors procured contrary advice that they alone should decide what to disclose, and gave an undertaking that the loan would be cleared. The Inspectors conclude that the auditors should have considered that the undertaking to clear the loans did not affect the obligation to disclose what were irregularities. Unlike the auditors, they were not prepared to countenance the theory that they were made in the ordinary course of business and were thus valid under the Companies Act 1948.[5] In any event, what the auditors who checked to see whether the loans were cleared did not spot was (p. 138):

> that settlement of some of the loan accounts was arranged by means of a deposit of £100,000 by BBT itself with another finance company, Cornhill, which thereupon advanced £100,000 to Global, which in turn lent on to those Stonehouse-related companies in need of funds to settle their debts to BBT.

The circularity of the transactions is plain enough.

When the 1973 accounts were passed, Stonehouse was able to raise money from the public through a Rights issue, and to obtain a moneylender's exemption certificate from the Department of Trade enabling it to lend without regard to the restrictions in the Moneylenders Acts. Blatant window-dressing was engaged in. Money shown in the accounts at call on short notice arose from special arrangements established over the accounting year-end to inflate the balance sheet figures. The accounts were grossly deficient and misleading.

While the basic pattern is not difficult to grasp with the aid of the Inspectors' Report, the actual transactions engaged in were deliberately complicated in order to obscure the true position. BBT and its subsidiaries engaged in an incestuous web of borrowing and lending. BBT shares were parcelled out to nominees who paid for the shares with moneys coming ultimately from BBT funds. Some were unable to pay ultimately. One such was a young woman, selected as being a family friend, who at the time was living on social security. Stonehouse tried to assign the nominees' liabilities to another related company, Dover Street (Nominees) Ltd in order to protect them, but this was ultimately disallowed.

In the result, BBT was terribly vulnerable to the crisis of 1974. Loans secured on BBT shares and loans to two Stonehouse companies accounted for 56 per cent of BBT's total lending, and these loans could not be covered out of profits. The auditors in 1974 uncovered irregularities and pressed for explanations which Stonehouse could not give. Eventually, he faked a suicide, fled to Australia, was returned for trial, and convicted of certain criminal offences. His operations in BBT were summed up by the *Investors' Chronicle* thus:[6]

> The basic ploy in the Stonehouse money-go-round worked as follows. British Bangladesh...made large (though sometimes circuitous) loans to Stonehouse and friends; part of these loans was used to finance the purchase of shares in British Bangladesh; meanwhile the loans increased the volume of the company's lending business in order to support its claim for some sort of banking status. And the more like a bank British Bangladesh could be made to look, the easier it would be to continue to claim that normally irregular loans were all part of its ordinary business.

Stonehouse told the Inspectors apropos statements made to the auditors in respect of window-dressing, that requests for statements and their provision was part of a ritual dance.

London and County Securities Group Ltd. (L. & C.) is another secondary banking case (1976). As with most of these cases, management structures were weak; here, the board and the company's officers were subservient to a dominant controller, Caplan. Among the irregularities allegedly engaged in by L. & C. and its subsidiaries was the use of L. & C. money to enable Caplan and associated companies and nominees to support L. & C. share prices during take-over bids. This would constitute an infraction both of section 54 of the Companies Act 1948, which prohibits a company from giving financial assistance for the purchase of its own shares, and of section 190 of the same Act which then regulated directors' loan transactions.[7] Caplan allegedly engaged in a series of circular repayments of loans with funds borrowed from different subsidiaries in the same group, amounting to some £1,349,546.95 which was used illegally, the Inspectors conclude, to finance share purchases.

Large sums of money were also borrowed from sources within the L. & C. group to protect nominees who had acquired L. & C. shares in order to warehouse them for Caplan and his companies. Warehousing was a device resorted to as a means of supporting the market price of L. & C. shares. Support of this character makes it likely that shareholders in a target company will accept the offerer's shares in exchange for their holdings rather than opting for a cash alternative. The warehousing was done through subsidiary companies which purported to buy and hold shares for customers both of L. & C. subsidiaries and associated companies' directors and staff. Other market-support devices were alleged dealings in L. & C. shares by directors and associated companies, and persuading customers of A. & D., another Caplan company, to buy shares, generally with loans from A. & D. The scale of this can be gauged from the fact that, by 31 March 1973, A. & D. had made advances of approximately £3.5 millions (excluding accrued interest) for the purchase of A. & D. shares. When the loss of confidence occurred in 1973, the share price, which had been artificially supported for a long time, came under pressure from the volume of selling. L. & C. could no longer support the market. The price of shares continued to fall until, on 30 November 1973, the Stock Exchange suspended dealings.

Other questionable practices were freely resorted to. One such was window-dressing. The device used was to inflate the cash figure available at year end by borrowing from another secondary bank on a short-term loan. This was said to be a common City practice at the time. It has been condemned on more than one occasion as intended to present a false picture of liquidity (Crown Agents 1977–8, p. 59). That was certainly how the Inspectors in L. & C. viewed it. The object of window-dressing was to mislead depositors and creditors by inflating the cash balances. This was, in effect, admitted. In respect of one circular transaction, a director, Hillman, said that he did not consider it to be wrong. The following exchange occurred (London and County Securities Group Limited, 1976, p. 173):

> Mr. Leggatt: If you say that you did not regard the effect of the transaction as misleading, what did you think the purpose of it was?
>
> Mr. Hillman: I thought it was that they could show a better cash position at the end of the year.
>
> Q: Than they actually had?
>
> A: Than they actually had. It did not alter their assets and liabilities position; just their cash position.
>
> Q: It showed a million pounds greater liquidity than they in fact enjoyed?
>
> A: I suppose that is right.

The Director of Public Prosecutions and the Department of Trade have not always taken a strong line over the practice which, in some of its manifestations, certainly seems criminal in the light of section 17 of the Theft Act 1968, discussed below. Certain prosecutions were started in the L. & C. case, but these were halted by the trial judge on the basis that window-dressing was sufficiently tolerated in 1973–74 that it would be unsafe to try to assess the degree of criminality involved, if any. No prosecutions were mounted in respect of another report on Ashbourne Investments Limited or as a result of the Crown Agents debacle. Vehement protests in Parliament in the latter case were brushed aside by a government which accepted the findings of the Fay Committee, and of the Director of Public Prosecutions, that no offences had been committed.[8] No one doubts the integrity of either body, nor that the Director acts upon the best advice available, but on the basis of the published documents alone his findings suggest a lack of imagination.

Another questionable practice in L. & C. was to take over a company, Estates Mitchell Limited, by raising a bogus management charge against it, of £239,725, using the income so generated to buy Estates Mitchell shares. It is not only in such instances as this that high management fees are charged to satellite companies. Charles Raw, for example, alleges that Slater Walker drained off the profits of its satellites by charging high banking fees, or high underwriting fees (Raw, 1977, pp. 344–57). Income which should not have been included was shown in L. & C. accounts to inflate apparent liquidity. Merchant banking fees were charged on a 'rolled up' basis, that is, as being repayable at the end of the term of the loan and therefore in fact unpaid at the date of the accounts. Huge sums were involved. The fees were charged to four companies, two of which were associated companies, almost no services were rendered, and the Inspectors concluded that the sums involved were not properly taken to profit and loss. There were other irregularities and indeed illegalities at L. & C. Short-term borrowing designed to mislead the Department of Trade in respect of the Protection of Depositors Act 1963 was engaged in. Offer documents for take-overs were signed by directors who, contrary to assurances, had failed to give them adequate or any consideration. Unrealised capital profits and rolled up charges were shown as income in documents released to the public.

Apart from obvious deficiencies in management, the auditors were also stringently criticised. The auditing work was originally done by a good junior. Caplan, after the 1972 audit, requested his replacement on the ground of inexperience. The audit manager left the auditors to go to L. & C. as chief accountant. The result was that, at a critical time, the audit was in the hands of a new team which had to deal with officials who were determined to conceal as much as they could. While the audit procedures used were imperfect (and the responsibility of auditors is considered later in this work), the case illustrates the problems which can be caused to auditors whose clients would prefer not to disclose dubious transactions. The result of Caplan's alleged machinations was that both the internal and the external safeguards were subverted; the former was subservient, sometimes corrupt, and dazzled by what was thought to be Caplan's financial genius, while the latter was subverted by a seemingly innocent request to have a more experienced man placed in charge.

The weakness which resulted from incestuous lending and from use of the company's funds in a market-support operation for its shares needs little emphasis. Lending to controllers occurred with other banking enterprises of the period, including the Israel-British Bank, apparently the only regular bank to collapse in the 1974 recession. Very large loans were made to a director personally, and to companies controlled by him and his wife, and to other connected companies. £30 million was advanced to four small companies in Liechtenstein which he controlled. One director was gaoled in Israel for fraud and embezzlement; Landy and others who were convicted in England of conspiracy to cheat and defraud saw their convictions overturned on appeal because the trial judge's direction did not put fairly to the jury their defence of honest but careless mistake.[9]

Whatever else may be said of these cases, the policy behind the prohibition against a company lending funds to purchase its own shares as well as that against lending to directors can seldom have been more convincingly demonstrated.

Take-Overs and Looting

The wisdom of the policy embodied in the prohibition against a company lending money for the purchase of its own shares is also demonstrated by the cases in which 'cash' companies were taken over, using their own money for the purpose, and then looted. This sort of fraud is a hardy perennial. Town Centre Properties Limited affords an example of it (1968).

The scheme involved two companies, Town Centre Properties Limited, and Star Explorations Limited. Town Centre, a dormant investment company, was taken over in 1958 by one Rosen, who intended to convert it to a property investment company and offer further shares to the public. Because he was not acceptable to the

Stock Exchange as a director, he procured an independent board of repute to manage the company. By 1964, Rosen was keen to sell. The directors were anxious to ensure that any offer would include an offer for the minority shares as well. In the event, Rosen sold to Robinson and Cradock. Management changed without the minority shareholders being advised. Today, in the case of a quoted company, the rules of the Take-Over Panel would oblige the bidder to make an offer for all shares, and the directors would be forbidden to resign until the offer closed or became unconditional. These rules, which are extra-legal and which are not always obeyed, witness Dowgate, were not in force at the time when these manoeuvres occurred.

At the outset of the meeting when the formalities of sale were completed, the company secretary produced letters of resignation from two existing directors, R and S, whereupon H, as the sole remaining director, appointed a member of the new group, Salmond, to the board. Undertakings were then given concerning compensation for loss of office to the old directors and to make an offer for the minority shares. After this, H resigned and left the meeting. The old directors took no further part in the management of the company. The Inspectors conclude that they acted properly. They could not hold out against a new majority which had the legal power to dismiss them, and they both intended and attempted to safeguard the minority shareholders. Cradock, certainly, had not yet attained notoriety as a fraud.

The purchasers, Robinson and Cradock, lacked the money to buy Rosen's shares. They therefore sought to cause the company to pay for the acquisition by them of the Rosen shares by selling assets to the company and using the cash so obtained for that purpose. How was this done?

A total price of £847,500 was agreed for Rosen's shares. Robinson procured Rosen to make a loan to Town Centre to bridge the gap until an arranged bank loan was forthcoming. Rosen thus lent £647,000 to Trustees for his family interests (Rosen Trustees). Rosen Trustees lent the money to Town Centre. Town Centre paid it to Able Limited for assets (shares in Star Explorations Limited). Able Limited then paid the money to Rosen in part payment for his shares which were held in its name. Able was, of course, a nominee company of Robinson and Cradock. Rosen was well pleased because, although owed £647,000 by Rosen Trustees, the debt was fully secured by a fixed charge to secure the like amount which Town Centre gave to Trustees, thus giving Trustees a secured interest over Town Centre's assets. In this way, Town Centre borrowed large sums of money. Its principal expenditure was £547,000 on Star shares, sold to it by Able. It also gave Able an unsecured loan for £107,000. From Town Centre's point of view the crucial questions were, as the Inspectors note: Were the Star shares worth the price which Town Centre paid; was there any justification for the loan to Able: what prospects had Town Centre for finding moneys to repay the short-term mortgage advances from the Rosen trustees while at the same time meeting pressing demands for working capital?

In brief, the principal asset of Star was a grossly overvalued sports complex, the valuation of which depended entirely upon the validity of estimates which the valuer was given and which he accepted. Star, of course, from Robinson and Cradock's point of view, was put to productive uses. Robinson bought another cash company, Third Mile. Third Mile then bought Star at a gross overvalue, £400,000, which was paid to Star's owners, H. Ltd. Where the cash ultimately went from H. Ltd, the Inspectors were unable to determine. Then Star bought Able, an unquoted public company with only cash assets.

Able then borrowed £200,000 from bankers, which loan was later secured on a large block of Town Centre shares. The main purpose of this loan was to allow Able to bridge the gap between the purchase price from Rosen of £847,500 and the £647,000 which Able was to receive, partly as purchase price for the Star shares and partly as a 'deposit' from Town Centre. Town Centre under an elaborate façade lent money to Able so that Able could pay Rosen Trustees for the Town Centre shares. Town Centre shareholders were not notified of the change of control or the machinations of the new controllers. No offer for minority shareholdings was ever made. Instead, Rosen Trustees, who had a secured interest, eventually sued for their money. Town Centre properties were sold in order to raise money for Town Centre and Able. The former directors of Town Centre threatened to ask for a Board of Trade inquiry, but by this time the affairs of the company had fallen apart and Robinson and Cradock left the country.

It is not only a company's properties which can be looted; it is also possible for rogues, in cases such as this, to obtain large numbers of shares cheaply by selling overvalued assets to the company in exchange for shares. Admittedly, this abuse is struck at in the Companies Act 1980, discussed later in this work, but it would be naive to suppose that the abuse can be entirely eliminated. In Town Centre, this part of the scheme proved abortive. Nevertheless, Robinson and Cradock did cause Town Centre shares to be deposited as security with merchant bankers for a loan taken out by Able for the purchase of Town Centre shares. A small loan was secured by huge quantities of shares. Swiss bankers guaranteed the loan and would, in the event of default, be able to enforce the merchant banker's claim by subrogation. Robinson and Cradock would thus obtain, indirectly, shares in a listed company cheaply. This part of the scheme fell apart and need not be pursued further.

Town Centre is a prime example of a common type of fraud. Similar manoeuvres characterised Dr. Wallersteiner's take-over of Hartley Baird in the 1960s, but there, in addition, Wallersteiner sought to charge a handsome finder's fee to the parent company of Hartley Baird for introducing it to a purchaser—himself (Hartley Baird Limited, 1972, p. 21). Ultimately, in 1975 the Department of Trade moved to wind up Wallersteiner's Anglo-Continental Exchange Bank, not only on the ground that it was used to defraud Hartley Baird, but also on the ground that it had been guilty of exchange control violations.

Conclusions

The preceding pages deal with examples of types of company fraud. They are not exclusive. There are many ways in which a company can be fleeced. It can be charged management fees. It can be milked of money by controllers who cause it to invest in ventures, in England or abroad, which they control, often clandestinely (Ardmore International Film Studios Limited, 1975). Those enterprises must needs pay directors' fees and other emoluments. They can be sold assets by the rogues and those assets are often found to be of little value. Thus the original company's investments result in a draining of capital to no advantage to the company. In the Fire, Auto and Marine Insurance fraud, F.A.M. funds were syphoned through a foreign company, under the guise of being remitted abroad for investment purposes, to the benefit of Savundra, the principal rogue (Connell and Sutherland, 1978). Naturally, internal management controls should prevent this, but too often they have been imperfect. Other directors have been deceived by false valuers' reports, by transactions with other companies, seemingly reputable, and by other accompaniments of lavish schemes of fraud.

References and Notes

1. Companies Act 1980 sections 3–13 and 85; as to insurance companies see pp. 158 *post*.
2. On this case see pp. 219 *post*.
3. Wilson Committee, Second Stage Evidence, vol. 5, *Department of Trade*, at p. 29 (1979).

4. For example, sess. 1976–77, 911 H.C. Deb. (Vth Ser.), col. 1014 (Mr. Ridley), col. 1026 (Mr. P. Rees).
5. Companies Act 1948, s. 190. See now, Companies Act 1980, ss. 49–53.
6. *Investors' Chronicle*, 16 December 1977, p. 845.
7. See now Companies Act 1980, ss. 49–53.
8. Sess. 1977–8, 940 H.C. Deb. (Vth Ser.), cols. 1026–80. Eventually the government agreed to a Tribunal of Inquiry which prevented further proceedings. *Ibid.*, col. 1646.
9. *Reg.* v. *Landy et al., The Times L. Rep.* January 12, 1981; and see Barbara Conway, 'The Israel–British Bank collapse: coming to the end of a two-year trail', *Investors' Chronicle*, 17 December 1976, p. 81, and *Daily Telegraph*, 21 July 1979.

3 Investment Fraud

Investment frauds are of various types, but most take the form of fraudulent schemes concerning shares and debentures or tangible physical assets. It is fashionable to remark that these frauds batten on human greed and gullibility. A more charitable explanation would note that, in an era of rampant inflation in which savings invested in traditional outlets are eroded by constant price rises and by taxation, many normally prudent people look for a hedge or protection from the ravages of circumstance. Speculative investments appear to offer an opportunity to enter the promised land of rapid capital growth. Physical assets, such as pigs, silver and gold, appear to many to avoid the risks inherent in investing in equity securities. In these latter schemes, while particular frauds flourish and vanish, the psychology involved and the methods employed vary little over time.

Investments in Things

I commence with a discussion of the agricultural frauds which characterised the 1950s and 60s. These are dealt with by legislation dating from that era and are now commonly engaged in by Britons and others in foreign jurisdictions. Nonetheless their characteristics linger on, and some schemes do involve the performing of administrative acts here, such as making transfers or depositing funds.

Livestock Marketing Company Limited and its associates illustrate the mechanics involved (Livestock Marketing Company Limited, 1968). These were schemes in which the public was to own sows and receive dividends on the income arising from them, or to own store pigs and to receive dividends from the value of the pigs when fattened. The public subscribed £1,398,000, of which all but £224,000 was lost when the companies went into liquidation in 1962.

The first scheme basically promised the investor that the company would supply him with sows and care for them, and buy piglets from the investor at a profit to him. Glossy brochures were sent to persons who answered press advertisements, and door-to-door

high-pressure selling was engaged in by salesmen who were
paid by commission only and who had a powerful incentive to
increase the sales of contracts. The second scheme, to store and
fatten pigs, was launched when the companies were insolvent as the
result of the first scheme. The group's records were chaotic. From
the outset it had problems in arranging accommodation for the
number of pigs required, as Mascall, the managing director well
knew. In many cases pigs were never bought and the promised
system of identifying pigs to the investor broke down. The sales
literature was deceptive and the companies continued to issue it
after Mascall must have known that the group was insolvent.
Indeed, he was made aware of insolvency from other directors and
an accountant.

Taxed by another director, Bruce, with the argument that there
was undue stress on sales, Mascall replied that increased sales were
required to provide working capital. In fact one failing scheme was
used to support another. Funds from one scheme were run into
another. Money which should have been invested in assets was used
to enable the companies to continue in operation. The Inspectors
conclude that Mascall caused the companies to continue to do
business when he knew that they were insolvent and that their
contracts with investors could not be fulfilled. They were satisfied
that (p. 17):

> ... [Mascall's] main purpose in starting the Store Pig scheme was
> to obtain money with which to finance the Sow scheme and thus
> to enable the Producing Companies to continue in business and to
> continue to afford him the not inconsiderable income which he
> derived from them.

The use of income from one venture in order to support another,
whether in breach of clear undertakings to the investing public or in
breach of a duty to disclose, has not been uncommon. Pinnock
Finance, an investment bubble built upon the unsound foundation
of an Australian sewing machine business, is another example
(Pinnock Finance Company (Great Britain) Limited, 1971). Suffice
it to say that the rogues involved raised huge sums of money from
the public by advertising for deposits, and spent the funds so
obtained, without making disclosure to investors, on a series of
spectacularly unsuccessful trading ventures operated for the interests of Wright, their controller. Cadco, as we shall see, is another
example, and some of the insurance cases exhibit a similar pattern.
The particular type of fraud in Pinnock is struck at today by the
Banking Act 1979 and is unlikely to recur in Britain in anything like
its original form. It does, however, illustrate the pattern of a

company having to generate ever more income to meet trade liabilities and the depredations of fraudulent directors.

Bogus investment schemes flourish despite protective legislation. For example, a recent scheme has just come to light in which a shipping container firm persuaded investors of the advantages of purchasing steel containers.[1] The basic idea was to sell them steel containers at high prices, offering them the prospect of a return of over 25 per cent plus tax avoidance by leasing the containers out and enjoying the proceeds. Investors were offered, according to the *Sunday Times*, 300 sets of North Sea container boxes at a price per set of £5,000. The boxes cost the promoter much less, £2,685 per set, a factor which he naturally did not disclose. Optimistic sales literature was issued, but leasing did not prove to be sufficiently profitable. The supplier of boxes was not paid and, of 900 North Sea boxes sold to investors, only 337 were apparently ever manufactured. The profit earned by the rogue is estimated at £1.75 million. He has since returned to the United States.

Questionable dealings in silver are also current. Former commodity dealers went into 'banking' and offered customers (in this instance expatriate Portuguese) interest-bearing current accounts backed by silver warrants. The *Investors' Chronicle* sums the scheme up thus:[2]

> ...the real gimmick has been the use of silver as security for deposits. The value of the deposit does not fluctuate because the silver is deemed to be held within the company, but the guaranteed repurchase price of the silver credited goes up by 0.2 per cent a week, equal to an annual rate of 10.38 per cent. The brochures do not go into detail about how the company finances the constantly rising repurchase price.

The company, Kendal and Dent Limited, was compulsorily wound up on the petition of the Department of Trade, but a successor company, allegedly controlled by one of Kendal and Dent Limited's principals, has allegedly been incorporated offshore, and functions here.

Another example of a fraud which relied upon obtaining increasing sums of money from the public to sustain itself is Cadco Developments Limited, in which investors and government bodies were milked of huge sums. Loraine, a rogue, exploited a recipe for sausages, allegedly favoured by King Edward VII, through a company which the Board of Trade allowed him to call Royal Victoria Sausages Limited. Everything about it was calculated to mislead (Cadco Developments Limited, 1966, p. 3). In contravention of the Prevention of Fraud (Investments) Act 1958, against which its solicitors failed to warn it, R.V.S. advertised in the press for investments from the public, offering directorships in return.

Whether Loraine, who had a criminal record as a confidence man, ever thought that he could manage the business successfully, is unclear. One early investor with experience in the trade concluded that the scheme was fraudulent from the start:... moneys went into the shop and he [Loraine] just took it out of the till and put it into his pocket. What is clear is that in order to bolster the sausage factory, Loraine needed increasing amounts of money which he obtained from individuals and from public funds made available as incentive schemes. He was able, thanks to the complicity of Roe, an English lawyer based in Switzerland, to tap Roe's clients' accounts. He also deceived individuals and banks concerning his investment plans. Aided by the late George Sanders, the actor, he persuaded government-backed bodies to invest in development schemes in Scotland, none of which were pursued in good faith by Loraine and his associates. The Marquis of Linlithgow, who joined the projects in good faith, rapidly discovered that development funds were being syphoned off through R.V.S. and sought to have matters investigated, but without success. He withdrew, having lost heavily in the venture. Despite a clear recommendation, none of the principals were ever prosecuted, and the report gives no indication why.

The essential point of many of these schemes is that they rely either on successful speculation, or upon obtaining fresh funds from the public, in order to pay the original investors' claims. When speculation fails, increasing sums are needed in order to meet the expectations of early investors. Admittedly, the Bank of England and the Department of Trade have powers to curb such activities, but it sometimes takes time to halt fraudulent schemes, clothed, as they often are, in a semblance of legality.

Investments in Securities

Share promotion schemes are of various types. Dealings may occur face-to-face between the rogue and the victim, as a result of which the victim is induced to part with money against securities in a company or another interest in it. The rogue may seek to sell shares through a dealer in shares who canvasses his clients for the purpose. He may seek to rig the Stock Exchange, selling shares at a profit as a result. He may simply engage in insider dealing.

Dealings in Privity

This is the situation in which the rogue and the victim come into personal contact with each other, the victim buying or selling securities as a result of the rogue's blandishments. An example is afforded by the Canadian case of *Reg.* v. *Littler*[3] in which the accused, chief executive of a large chocolate manufacturer in which he held the majority of shares, became aware that an American firm was to make a take-over bid for the firm. He persuaded minority shareholders to sell shares to him on the false representation that he wanted to consolidate family holdings, and then sold to the bidder. He was convicted of fraud and imprisoned.

The machinations of Sir Denys Lowson, a former Lord Mayor of London, who died before he could be prosecuted, also involve the use of deception, in those instances to companies of which he was a director (First Re-Investment Trust Limited, 1974; The Australian Estates Company, 1975). The essence of the scheme was to induce Lowson companies to sell small shareholdings in other companies to purchasers who, unknown to the vendors, were Lowson nominees. The share values were set in some instances by Lowson, who knew that the market had no material available on which to make a fair judgement, or set below the Stock Exchange price where the shares were dealt with only on foreign exchanges, again without disclosure, or on the basis of valuations which were suspect because they failed to take account of the value to be attributed to control.

The latter point arises thus. In some instances each selling company had a minority holding of shares in those companies which were being sold to Lowson nominees. When, however, the shares were looked at in the aggregate, they amounted to a controlling block. But the value of control was not reflected in the valuation and the (Lowson) purchasers did not therefore pay a control premium to the vendors, nor were the boards of the vendor (Lowson) companies informed of the point. When questions were asked, Lowson replied evasively both to his fellow directors and to the auditors. In some instances where Stock Exchange prices were used, the price indicated was again deceptive. A procedure known as put-through was used. This requires that the jobber who sells, and the broker, need only be satisfied that the price is fair to both principals. But Lowson and a confederate set the price, disarming the jobber, although Lowson told his fellow directors of the vendor company that the shares were being sold at the Stock Exchange price. Eventually the boards, after taking counsel's advice, caused Lowson to disgorge profits. There can be little doubt that some of these machinations were criminal, either as obtaining by deception contrary to section 15 of the Theft Act 1968, or as involving false statements made criminal under that Act, or as a conspiracy to cheat and defraud.

Dealings through Share Dealers

Dealing in shares is not the exclusive prerogative of members of the Stock Exchange. There are a number of dealers off the Exchange. These include members of associations recognised by the Department of Trade as dealers in securities, persons licensed as dealers, and minor classes of exempt dealers. Administrative regulation of them is dealt with later. Most of these dealers are thoroughly honest, but not all. Licensed dealers deal both in shares quoted on the exchange and in those which are not. If dealings on the Exchange are to take place, they must be conducted through a member of the Stock Exchange. Indeed, members of the Stock Exchange may themselves deal, under Rule 163 of the Exchange, in unlisted securities on a *caveat emptor–caveat vendor* basis.

Licensed dealers are regulated by the Prevention of Fraud (Investments) Act 1958. This measure, the successor to an Act of the same name of 1939, was passed as a result of the recommendations of a committee set up before the Second World War to inquire into irregular high-pressure selling of securities, and of those of another committee set up at about the same time to inquire into the regulation of unit trusts.[4] One of the principal vices struck at was high-pressure selling of securities, frequently on a door-to-door basis, using misleading representations and forecasts concerning the companies whose securities were offered. The legislation gave to the Board of Trade, now the Department of Trade, regulatory jurisdiction over such dealings and prohibited the use of misleading forecasts and door-to-door selling, a prohibition which also extends, as will be seen, to unsolicited telephone contacts.

Regulation by the Department of Trade has been fairly effective. Indeed, the City institutions in respect of Stock Exchange dealings are also satisfied with the system. The Stock Exchange notes that there are few cases of litigation involving securities.[5] This may be too complacent; it is hard to get firm information. There is reason, however, to think that some dishonest dealing by stock and share dealers takes place. *Private Eye*, an invaluable source in these matters, notes the presence of one or two such dealers in London but considers that most of these firms are run by Americans or Canadians from Switzerland, France, or even the Cayman Islands, utilising the International Offshore Stock Exchange which emanates from the Caymans and which, by the use of Reuters Monitor Securities Service, gives information to closed circuit television screens in Europe or North America.

Hints of a pointed character sometimes appear in the financial press. Sometimes, the press notes that markets are being made in dubious securities or that individuals are engaged in picking up shares cheaply in near-dormant companies with a view to making a market in them. There have been statements also that 'tip sheets' published abroad are being circulated to persons resident in Britain, inviting them to invest in particular securities. Offshore investment fund swindles have been practised by United Kingdom citizens operating from abroad and selling into foreign countries. Unless there is a suitable nexus with Britain, British courts lack territorial jurisdiction over such schemes. The leading example is Agrifunds; the most celebrated modern example is Investors Overseas Syndicate (Raw, Page and Hodgson, 1971).

These frauds involved mutual funds, which are similar to unit trusts. They offer a spread of risks together with redeemability of investments. Often, a single area for investment is selected, one in which the promoters purport to have expertise, as for example food producing companies. Salesmen are paid on commission; high pressure tactics are employed; the funds received from the public are syphoned off through different foreign banks and trusts, and, as with other frauds which we have noted, the funds rely on incoming capital almost exclusively to meet demands for redemptions. Continuation of the fraud thus depends on a considerable, and increasing, volume of current subscriptions. Provided that a fund operates offshore and sells into third countries there is little that the British authorities can do to stop them, despite the British nationality of their controllers. As will be seen, British courts have in fact extended the territorial basis of criminal jurisdiction very considerably, some would say artificially, in the interests of control.

Dealings through the Stock Exchange

There have been cases also in which dishonest dealings in shares have taken place with the connivance of members of the Stock Exchange, but the Metropolitan and City Police Fraud Squad are satisfied that these occurrences are extremely rare. One such involved a broker, now dead, Russell Colin-Jones. The allegation against him was that he acquired large blocks of shares at a price below the market price for a firm of dealers in securities, using the 'put-through' mechanism, that is, machinery which facilitates a deal between a willing buyer and seller at an agreed price.[6] Rigging the Stock Exchange is an historic mode of fraud, but in its grosser manifestations it is uncommon today. The fact that an Exchange has been rigged does not, of course, mean that a member of the Stock Exchange has acted criminally; in such cases he may well be a dupe.

There are some classic forms of rigging, which is essentially the making of a fictitious market. One form involves the use of false representations and rumour spreading to influence purchasers and sellers. A financial journalist, for example, may be fed a tip and give it currency in all good faith. He may, if he is unscrupulous, buy shares, tip them in his column, and then sell them on the rising market produced by his tip. This is considered to be a gross breach of journalistic ethics (C. Raw, 1977). Directors may wrongly say or do things calculated to produce public confidence in the securities of a company. In his account of Slater Walker, Charles Raw alleges that there was a design to generate activity in securities of satellite companies so that these might be sold to a Slater Walker Unit Trust at a market price higher than their true value would warrant. The units would then be sold to the public. The scheme was unsuccessful (p. 360).

A rise in prices may be produced by sudden active trading. The jobber system in London means that a continuous ticker tape is not available for surveillance purposes. However, in an age of close monitoring, and given the increasing acceptance by the Stock Exchange of a general regulatory function, it is unwise to move too precipitately lest the watchdog be alerted. But, as will be seen, there are genuine constraints against hasty action by the Stock Exchange. Dealings in shares can be suspended, but this is apt to harm investors who cannot freely sell their shares during the period of suspension.

A classic mode of rigging, known in North America as wash trading, is only occasionally heard of today. The Stock Exchange states that the last real instance of it was in connection with Third Mile Investments Limited in 1967. It involves the buying and selling of substantially equal blocks of shares between confederates at increasing prices in order to draw others into the market. The mode is—or, when such practices were current, was—to instruct certain brokers to sell and certain others to buy at gradually increasing prices. Rumours were also used to enhance the price, and market-support buying was resorted to in order that shares coming back into the market would not remain there unsold to depress the price (Croft, 1975; Schwabe and Branson, 1914). Yet another classical fraud is 'cornering', that is, purchasing securities from persons who, when the time comes for delivery, will be unable to obtain them and will have to buy them from the very persons to whom they have to deliver, at a price dictated by those persons. If there are no false representations this will not be criminal unless persons combine together to produce such a result, in which case there may well be a conspiracy to cheat and defraud.

Aggressive dealing which forces share prices up is not unheard of, today, nor is the use of rumour.[7] We have noted the use by London and Counties Securities Group Limited of market-support buying to sustain share prices for the purposes of a take-over bid. Allegations that companies' funds were used to support share prices while directors unloaded their own holdings have been made in other connections. Lord Dilhorne, in *Tarling (No. 1)* v. *Government of Singapore*[8] described such dealings as a classic case of market rigging. Whether market support amounts to market rigging is complicated, because while market rigging, the making of a false market, is universally regarded as wrong, stabilisation is regarded as permissible. The Bank of England, for example, intervenes regularly to stabilise a pound which, left to the blind influence of market forces, might exhibit either an undue rise or a precipitate fall. Manipulation and stabilisation are really the same phenomenon; it is the intent of the actors and the integrity of the operation which enables a distinction to be drawn between them for legal purposes, as we shall see.

Central to a successful fraud, whether through outside dealers or the Stock Exchange, is the ability to acquire large quantities of shares cheaply and to sell them at a sufficiently enhanced price. While it is not necessary to have shares with a stock exchange listing, it is certainly helpful to have such a listing, either on the London Stock Exchange or on a foreign stock exchange. The relevance of such a facility is, firstly, that it gives a price which may be quoted to investors, especially if they are to be offered a 'bargain', and, secondly, that it allows an appearance of activity to be kept up. For these reasons, securities of a listed, relatively inactive, company are desired. Admittedly, if the company is a cash company the quotation of whose shares has been suspended, the promoters will have to satisfy the Stock Exchange that the company has sound trading plans. The Stock Exchange can be, and has been, imposed upon.

Shares may be acquired by taking over a company and selling it over-valued assets for large blocks of shares. This method of operation appears to have been indulged in by two individuals, Leon Davies and Josiah Binstock, both of whom failed to give evidence to the Inspectors, in respect of a company originally known as New Brighton Tower Company Limited (Ardmore International Film Studios Limited, 1975). The story of this company is complicated but, according to Inspectors, Binstock and Davies, having gained control of it, used its facilities to take over the Victoria Sporting Club Limited. In order to do so, they allegedly caused NBT's capital to be increased and granted an option to Brancona, which was their creature and exercised the option on favourable terms. They caused NBT to sell its Victoria shares to two other persons without informing the NBT shareholders of the manoeuvre, even though those shareholders had been informed that the increase in NBT's capital was to buy Victoria. Binstock allegedly retained certain shareholdings in Victoria which he later put into Norwich Enterprises, his creature, for shares in Victoria and the assignment from Norwich to Binstock and Davies of three debts owing from Victoria to Norwich. Norwich increased its capital. Binstock and his associates are said to have obtained 125,000 Norwich shares which they then sold at a large profit that the Inspectors could not compute accurately. Of these transactions the Inspectors state (p. 71):

> There is some doubt regarding the true interests of the purchasers, Messrs Auday and Seidler, and the fact remains that Mr Binstock was deeply concerned in the ultimate sale of all the shareholdings during 1969 to Norwich Enterprises Limited. The sale of the shares to Messrs Auday and Seidler was at a handsome profit to the company of £210,942 of which the preference and ordinary shareholders were to receive by way of dividends and capital payments £20,954 only.

Much company money was allegedly syphoned off by way of loans and purchases of assets into other Binstock promotions.

Another example is E. J. Austin International Limited, some of whose mining ventures were castigated by a consultant mining engineer as a transparent promotion (E. J. Austin International Limited, 1972). One was a venture for the recovery of metal, which depended upon claims that a particular extractive process was of a superior character. The promoters knew this to be untrue. Circulars were issued to shareholders describing ventures in California and Cyprus in glowing terms. Land in California owned by one C was sold to Chambers, who was interested in Austin's, for $100,000 and then sold by him to Austin for $265,000. The purpose of the agreement was to extract money and shares from Austin's. False invoices for the supply of material where raised to cover defalcations. Activities in Cyprus were vastly overblown by the assertion that the company had a contract with Hellenic Mining Company for ore processing. The fact that the total ore contracted for was very small and only for test purposes was not disclosed.

Most revealing was a proposal that Austin's acquire El Sobrante mines for an issue of 6,000,000 2s. shares. The Inspectors conclude that El Sobrante's financial statements were false and known to be so by the two directors of Austin's who were implicated, Chambers and Howarth. They were acting dishonestly in attempting to acquire shares of Austin's then valued at a middle market price of 18s. 3d each. Chambers and Howarth might well have secured a fraudulent valuation of El Sobrante's undertaking. The Inspectors thus conclude (p. 38):

> The fraud was not, therefore, so obvious that it would be doomed to failure and before the fraud was discovered Howarth and Chambers could reasonably be expected to sell substantial numbers of their shares, perhaps at prices inflated by the mining fever which they spread and of salting the money away or transferring it out of the U.K.

The company certainly suffered substantial detriment as a result of Chambers' and Howarth's activities. Fortunately, merchant banking facilities were denied to them because the valuer whom they employed was found to be suspect, and press comment led to remedial action by other directors. The scheme was, nevertheless, a classic mining fraud in which both assets and shares were to be extracted from the company and the latter sold to investors on a market fed by untrue statements and unsound rumours. Thus rogues obtain securities necessary for a share promotion.[9]

Insider Trading

We have noted that insider trading is trading on the basis of price-sensitive information which is known to a person by reason of his association with a company or group or some person associated with a company or group, and which is not known to the public at large. Such information may arise from a decision to make a take-over bid which leads the bidder, for example, to start taking a position in shares on the market before making a formal bid. Directors of the bidder know of the decision and are in a position, either themselves or through nominees, to buy on their own account. So too are persons whom they tip. If a broker is employed to make purchases for that purpose he could equally purchase for himself, through nominees. If a merchant bank becomes aware of an impending bid, it could do the same thing. So could any of its officers with knowledge of the facts. In the *Littler* case, for example, Littler's bank manager dealt for his private benefit. Littler informed his bank manager that he needed money to purchase shares in Lowneys, a large chocolate manufacturer, in anticipation of a take-over bid. The bank manager arranged the loan. He also purchased Lowneys' shares for his own account (Croft, 1975, p. 186).

A merchant bank, indeed, faces a dilemma in some situations, for if it holds securities for clients in a company about which it obtains price-sensitive information, it may become apparent that the interests of that client require purchase or sale, hence the importance of maintaining a strict separation between the different capacities of the merchant bank, the so-called Chinese wall.[10] This, of course, assumes that the merchant bank does not act freely as an insider trader, in which case it is unlikely to worry about such niceties. Naturally, insider trading does not come about solely as a result of leaks by directors. The Stock Exchange states, as does the *Investors' Chronicle*,[11] that the knowledge that there is a big line of shares on offer or a big buyer in the market can be price-sensitive, in the same way as a leak of information about profits. Furthermore, it is the job of brokers and their analysts, investment managers and financial journalists to obtain information upon which investment advice can be based. No doubt companies sometimes unwittingly say more than they should.

Insider trading occurs in various forms. It may, as we have seen, occur when individuals deal in privity or when they deal across the impersonal market. Insider trading may or may not, in the former case, involve affirmative misrepresentation. In the absence of affirmative misrepresentation, there will be no liability in England. There certainly is in America (Yontef, 1979, p. 697). A classic example of the misuse of insider information leading to purchases in the market by an insider is Intereuropean Property Holdings Limited (IPH).[12] Marsh, the chairman and chief executive of IPH, having set on foot a likely take-over bid for IPH by another company, ACC, bought IPH shares in the market. He then sought to obtain ACC shares for them at a much enhanced price. This manoeuvre was successful. The Panel was, however, successful in requiring Marsh to pay his profits to charity.

The Dowgate inquiry affords further examples of insider dealing and related unethical conduct, only some of which would be caught under the new legislation. An example is afforded by the Inspectors' account of the acquisition by Selmes's interests of G. Ltd. Two directors, P. and W., allegedly tried to sell just under 30 per cent of the share capital to R. Ltd. This was supported by some directors and opposed by others. R. Ltd., which acquired 15 per cent of the shares was, the Inspectors state, trying to acquire control without making a take-over bid. The deal fell through because certain directors opposed it, and because a firm of merchant bankers went to the City Panel on Take-Overs and Mergers. Allegedly, Selmes then, as a result of a tip from P., went to a merchant bank for finance, bought the shares held by R. Ltd. and, by warehousing shares with nominees and further purchasing in the market, acquired a 35 per cent shareholding which was not disclosed, as is required by section 33 of the Companies Act 1967.[13] The acquisition set the stage for a take-over.

Another example is of individuals who, acting for a take-over bidder, purchase shares in the market at a price somewhat above that of the bid price, selling them to the bidder at cost, without disclosing that the bidder is the true dealer. This enables the bidder to avoid the obligation, imposed by the City Code, to pay the higher price to all offerees including those who have accepted at the lower price.

Charles Raw concluded that insider dealing had also been rife at Slater Walker Securities (Raw, 1977). After the Heath Government came out strongly in favour of the integrity of the market in shares, a pledge which the present Conservative government has redeemed in some measure, buccaneering can no longer be engaged in with the same confidence in impunity. It would at the same time be naive to think that the enactment of a few penal clauses, whose defects are considered later in this book, can solve the problem. There will continue to be insider dealings, and some of these may emanate from abroad.

References and Notes

1. *Sunday Times*, 9 December 1979; *Investors' Chronicle*, 29 June 1979, p. 150.
2. *Investors' Chronicle*, 22 December 1978, p. 946.
3. (1974) 65 D.L.R. (3d) 443; for further details, see R. Croft, (1975), pp. 183–91.
4. Report of the Departmental Committee, Cmnd. 5539 (1937); Report of the Unit Trust Committee, Cmnd. 5259 (1936).
5. *Committee to Review the Functioning of Financial Institutions*, Second Stage Evidence, vol. 4, The Stock Exchange, p. 17 (1979).
6. See *The Times*, 10 June 1978, col. 19c; *Sunday Times*, 8 October 1978.
7. See, for example *Private Eye*, 8 February 1974; *ibid.*, 11 July 1975.
8. *Tarling (No. 1)* v. *Government of Singapore* (1980), 70 Cr. App. R. 77.
9. The notorious Canadian Aquablast, Inc. promotion also relied on technology, a well-publicised automobile pollution device. For a short account, see *The Financial Post*, 18 April 1975, p. 2, col. 3.
10. The need for separation is implicit in Justice, *Insider Trading* (1972), p. 7. For the leading American case see *Shapiro* v. *Merrill Lynch, Pierce, Fenner and Smith Inc.*, 495 F. 2d. 228 (1974).
11. *Investors' Chronicle*, 10 November 1978, p. 432.
12. City Panel on Take-Overs and Mergers, 12 September 1979.
13. Shareholdings to the value of 5 per cent must now be disclosed, Companies Act 1976, s. 26.

4 Other Commercial Frauds

In this chapter we deal with a heterogeneous collection of commercial frauds, most of which can seriously affect the orderly conduct of trade and commerce or prejudice institutional arrangements in that behalf. All, according to the police and other law enforcement authorities, are common in Britain at the moment.

Cheques, Credit Cards, and Letters of Credit

The misuse of cheques, cheque cards and credit cards is commonplace, but is not a major commercial fraud as we have defined that term. The common pattern is one in which cheques and a cheque card, or a credit card, are stolen and used to obtain goods. Quite large amounts of money can be obtained in this way. Credit cards are difficult, if not impossible, to counterfeit, and provided that their loss is reported promptly, effective counter-measures can be taken.[1]

The misuse of letters of credit poses greater problems. These are documents delivered to account holders for presentation to foreign banks. In recent proceedings involving an international gang of swindlers led by one Henry Oberlander, a sentence of 14 years' imprisonment was imposed for a series of frauds on banks involving the presentation of forged letters of credit. Counsel for the prosecution, who was presumably not indulging in hyperbole, said that, had the fraud gone undetected, it would have undermined the banking system of the western world.[2]

Allied to such frauds as these is the growth of fraudulent banks which inundate certain countries, in particular the United States, but also Britain, with drafts, cheques and credit orders. In some jurisdictions it is possible to form or buy a corporate shell which glories in the name 'Bank', or 'Trust'. Liberal legislation and lax enforcement in their country of origin conduce to their fraudulent use abroad. In Britain, apart from the problem of forged and false documents, there have been well-publicised incidents in which rogues have used such entities to solicit funds from the public. The police consider that these particular frauds have been brought under control, and it is to be hoped that the stringent provisions of the Banking Act 1979 will further help to contain them.

Frauds committed upon banks and other credit institutions may well involve the deposit of shares and other securities as collateral. These may be forged. In other cases they are share certificates, made out in 'street' form to bearer, which were stolen, with the help of bank employees, from North American banking institutions where they were deposited for safety. This particular fraud has been most marked in the German Federal Republic and Austria. These are important frauds. Police sources state that over half of the complex fraud cases investigated by the City and Metropolitan Fraud Squad involve international fraud, that is, fraud committed through offshore banks by the use of forged instruments some of which emanate from abroad, and by other mercantile frauds.

Marine Fraud

Police sources indicate that large-scale shipping frauds are increasing in number and extent. One ancient practice is that of loading worthless cargoes on old vessels and sinking them for the grossly inflated insurance taken out on them. Even where the cargo is valuable, losses may still be claimed for insurance purposes. At the time of writing it has been alleged that a supertanker cargo of oil was sold clandestinely, the ship scuttled and insurance claims raised for loss of both the ship and the cargo. A partial loss may be claimed as total for insurance purposes. Where the loss arises abroad, it may be very difficult to get at the truth. In such cases, one is dependent to a large extent upon the co-operation of a foreign police force which may or may not be familiar with the type of fraud concerned.[3] Of course, the presentation of bogus claims upon London underwriters is not a phenomenon restricted to shipping; it can and does arise with other losses, for example in relation to real property.[4]

Other marine frauds depend for their success upon the practice of payments being made for cargoes against documents such as bills of lading, rather than upon inspection of the cargo. Money can be extracted from banks by presenting forged bills of lading just before the true ones are presented. Alternatively, banks have been induced to part with moneys against cargoes which did not exist, on presentation of wholly bogus documents. Dr. Savundra perpetrated just such a fraud on a Belgian bank early in his career, obtaining large sums of money on the strength of documents showing that a large shipment of rice to Goa, on behalf of a Portuguese bank, had been made by a company which he purported to represent. He was in fact extradited from Britain to Belgium and tried and sentenced there, but that episode did not impede his subsequent career as an insurance fraud (Connell and Sutherland, 1978). Another such fraud is practised by bogus shipping agencies. These often prey on the immigrant communities in Britain. The agent receives payment in advance for undertaking to ship property abroad and then fails to do so. In some instances he arranges for the property to be stolen, thereby setting up a fraud on insurers.

Cube-Cutting

Cube-cutting is a fraud perpetrated by forwarding agents and underwriters on their customers and on shipping firms. Its rewards are magnified by the existence of shipping tariffs used by all the major carriers and computed by reference to the type of cargo shipped and its cubic dimensions.

The Department of Trade report into Kuehne and Nagel Limited illustrates not only the methods adopted, but also the rationalisations employed by those who use such methods (Kuehne and Nagel Limited, 1978). K and N was the British subsidiary of a large and respected firm of shipping brokers. A Department of Trade investigation was commenced as a result of a complaint by a customer who suspected overcharging. The report found that there were very large discrepancies between the freight payments made to the shipping company and the amount paid by the shipper to Kuehne and Nagel Limited as freight charges. What the firm did was to use its knowledge of the tariff to the disadvantage of its customer. It misdescribed the goods to the carrier, obtaining a low rate, and informed the shipper that the goods fell within a higher rate category in the tariff. In this fashion, it earned a secret profit. Another technique employed was to understate the cubic capacity of cargoes to the carrier, thus reducing the shipping charge, but to charge the shipper, their customer, the tariff based on the correct cubic measurement.

These actions are criminal. The report noted that they represented policy decided upon at a relatively senior level. Furthermore, they led to the corruption of staff employed at a more junior level. Consider the implications of the following exchange:

> Miss Heilbron Q.C.: The short answer is that you see nothing improper in describing the material as structural steel to the shipping company and getting a lower rate, but describing it as furnace material to Bechtel [the customer] and getting a higher rate? You see nothing wrong in that?

> Answer (Mr. von der Nuell): For as long as structural steel is structural steel and machinery is machinery, no.

It is fair to add that the witness later said that the practice was one which, though common in the trade, he would not condone. Consider also, the effect on junior staff. One employee stated quite bluntly that the practices described above were dishonest, that she engaged in them, and was tacitly instructed to do so. No doubt the directors of the company were remote enough not to know what was happening, but junior managers plainly did and the atmosphere which they created was corrupting. The Inspectors conclude that employees cut cubes extensively knowing the practice to be dishonest, that they learned the techniques from company files or managers, and that the directors, although unaware of the situation, should have made greater efforts to instal proper accounting controls by which the existence of fraud might have been discovered and ended.

Discounting or Factoring Frauds

The essence of factoring (a perfectly lawful activity) is that a company which needs ready funds assigns its receivables to a finance house which supplies cash against them, less a discount to protect it against the commercial risk involved (Croft, 1975, p. 11).

Factoring frauds are engaged in both by firms which were formed for dishonest purposes and by firms which, though originally honest, encountered liquidity problems and searched for a way out. The company seeks financial assistance from a merchant bank. The agreement provides either: that sales are made on the invoices of the finance company to which payment is made direct by creditors, the object of this being to enable the finance company to control sales while it is advancing capital to the trading company; or that sales continue to be made on the trading company's invoices which are presented to the finance house for a percentage discount.

The fraud involves the presentation of false invoices for discount, or the fraudulent representation of sales in order to induce the finance house to continue to lend moneys.

Advance Fee Frauds

There are several varieties of such frauds. One is described thus by *Private Eye*.[5] A company or businessman needing a loan contacts a money-broker who has placed a newspaper advertisement. The money-broker gives an assurance that a source will be found to lend the money for the term required, at a moderate interest rate. He represents that he acts for another and stipulates for a commission from the client, a portion of which is paid in advance. The broker ultimately informs his client that the lender will not, after all, lend the money, and points to the terms of the agreement which stipulate that no pre-payment of commission is returnable. Police sources describe another variant thus:[6]

> The victim is often a foreign company or foreign resident (usually American) seeking large loan funds for foreign projects. The brokers pretend to have negotiated these loans, but demand an 'advance fee' of c. 5 per cent before revealing the source of the borrowing. Since the borrowings contemplated are for many millions of dollars the advance fee represents a substantial amount. Bogus banks are often utilised as the source of the necessary capital and worthless bonds and letters of credit are given by the broker, who, of course, pretends that he is dealing with the 'bank' at arm's length. Not infrequently the borrower is induced to give some genuine collateral security against the loan. Once the fraudster has got his hands on this, it is, of course, sold and the victim is left without his loan having lost his 'advance fee' and his collateral security.

Apparently, rogues sometimes represent that they act for a rich Arab lender, and may even introduce the victim to an impostor playing that part. Once a commission is collected, both vanish.

Similar to this type of fraud, but affecting ordinary individuals for the most part, is the property mortgage fraud which involves taking large advance fees from persons who cannot obtain mortgages in return for false promises to find mortgages for them. These either never materialise, or are offered on such onerous terms that the prospective borrower cannot take them up. Another mortgage fraud involves the creation of documents evidencing the sale of low-priced property at inflated sums in order to obtain massive bridging loans from banks. Police sources state that these loans are sometimes guaranteed by dishonest or negligent solicitors, or by persons purporting to act as solicitors.

Bankruptcy Frauds

There are various frauds connected with insolvency. The procedure is known as bankruptcy in the case of natural persons, and winding-up in relation to companies. The structure of offences in bankruptcy and winding-up is discussed later in the book. The most common fraud offence is that of an undischarged bankrupt obtaining credit. The principal disability attaching to bankruptcy is that an undischarged bankrupt may not borrow more than £50 without disclosing his status. Not infrequently such a bankrupt will borrow without disclosing, either for personal expenditures or in the course of starting up again in business. The credit obtained in such cases is often relatively small, but it is large in the aggregate.

Other cases are those in which a debtor abstracts property which should be distributed to his creditors. There are a number of cases in which persons finding themselves under business pressures sell vehicles on hire-purchase without notifying the hire-purchase company. In such a case, the crime of theft is committed. In another common class of case, a person under severe business pressure borrows money, mis-stating to the lending institution the purpose for which the loan is required, thereby committing the offence of criminal deception. These are as a rule cases in which the business was honest in its inception and where the debtor, increasingly pressed for cash in order to carry on the business, engages in transactions in the expectation, usually ill-founded, that he will be able to save his business (Leigh, 1980b).

In respect of companies, the most common offence is a failure to keep adequate books and records. More serious is continuing to trade in insolvency, a phenomenon which we have already noticed. Again, it sometimes happens that an undischarged bankrupt takes part in the management of a company, a course which company law forbids. There are few prosecutions annually for offences in winding-up.

It has already been said that bankruptcy and winding-up both provide powerful motives for fraud, and that many bankrupts fall into insolvency through dishonest conduct (Campbell, 1979). This is not altogether true. Naturally, offences of theft and deception of the sort we have noted do occur, but often these, although criminal, reflect incompetence rather than wickedness. A recent study of bankruptcy crimes indicates that, despite the existence of some fraud, bankruptcy is commonly the product of incompetence (Leigh, 1980b). Long-firm frauds which result in insolvency are, of course, a major exception to this pattern, being carefully organised activities engaged in by professional criminals.

Bribery and Corruption

The use of bribery and other corrupt means to secure commercial advantage is a recurrent problem. In recent years, it has been most prominent in respect of public sector contracting. There is, however, no doubt that it affects private sector contracting and contracting with overseas customers. Indeed, when the bribery legislation of 1906 was passed, it was said that solicitors, bankers, architects, insurance agents and accountants were all involved in conduct ranging from direct bribery to more venal, but unjustifiable, gifts and discounts. An army of commission agents made bribery a matter of common resort (Crew, 1913).

Bribery is engaged in to secure a corrupt advantage over

competitors.[7] It has rightly been stigmatised as the corrupting gift which bars the way to freedom (Eliasberg, 1951; Rhodes, 1949). The ties which it creates are not merely emotional; a person who accepts a bribe is thereafter susceptible to blackmail. The same authors note an interesting aspect of the phenomenon, that bribery and corruption often come surprisingly cheap; luxuries flatter, and so does the ability to have them without paying for them. This, in turn, makes it imperative that persons act carefully in accepting even small Christmas gifts. They are potentially dangerous, as recent events— especially those surrounding Crown Agents where officials were insidiously corrupted—have shown, and should in general be eschewed (Salmon Committee, Cmnd. 6524, paras. 214, 217; Crown Agents 1977–8, p. 168). Yet in both the Poulson and Crown Agents affairs they were freely accepted. In the latter case, their value ranged from £50 to £400, as a result of which the donor, William Stern, came to occupy a most-favoured borrower status. It would be hard to accept either that he did not seek to influence the judgement of officials, or that officials could have supposed him to have acted from an altruistic desire to improve their penurious lot.

Corruption in public sector contracting became prominent as a result of the Poulson affair, but it was not confined to Poulson's activities. Its existence had long been suspected, but proof was difficult (Regan and Morris, 1969). Town clerks are said to have been adept at concealing dishonest practices. It was only the unexpected insolvency of the prominent architect John Poulson, and the brilliant performance of counsel at the ensuing public hearing in bankruptcy, which brought matters to light.

The Poulson affair has been examined in detail elsewhere (Borrell and Cashinella, 1975). The fraudulent means used were not particularly unusual or sophisticated, but the fraud was very widespread and extremely complicated in its details. Poulson dealt corruptly with T. Dan Smith, a key figure in municipal development in the North East, to further Poulson's interests with local authorities under the control of the Labour party. T. Dan Smith created public relations companies, appointing councillors on various local authorities as paid consultants to one or other company. Such councillors would then be expected to use their influence on Poulson's behalf without declaring their private interest. Poulson succeeded in corruptly penetrating high levels of the Civil Service, the National Health Service, two nationalised industries, and a number of local authorities including a police authority.

Poulson's activities did not stand alone. In other cases awards were made on a corrupt basis to building firms without proper tenders having been requested. Officials of local authorities suggested sites for redevelopment to property dealers in exchange for corrupt payment of commissions. The extent to which these practices were accepted, and indeed institutionalised, may be gauged first from the fact that in the Peachey case notations of improper commissions in the accounts were in fact used to cover Sir Eric Miller's defalcations, and, secondly, that, according to *The Times*, bribes described as 'commissions' were treated as tax deductible.[8] Indeed, the previous Labour Government stated clearly that it did not propose to alter the rule of confidentiality in tax matters, even where it was plain that there was substantial evidence of corruption or other crimes.[9]

As to the nature of the bribes, these consisted very often in giving gifts, extending hospitality, making cars available, and providing holidays and other forms of financial assistance, as, for example, with mortgage repayments. Some did receive large sums. Pottinger, a senior civil servant, received large amounts for work on his home and an expensive family holiday in Greece. Others were less lavishly treated. Persons who were corrupted often received surprisingly small amounts.

Corruption does not relate to government contracting alone. It affects private firms also, and, indeed, on the other side of a government contract there usually stands a private firm. If private sector corruption seems less prominent, it is perhaps because it conceals matters better. Bribes are often paid to cause an employee to accept lower standards for work and goods than those specified in an invitation to tender, to accept higher prices, 'on cost' adjustments, or overruns, or to accept tender revisions after award of the contract (Comer, 1977).

The Racal case, which is the best known recent example of corrupt dealings, fell outside this pattern. Charges were brought against employees of giving or accepting corrupt payments to help to secure a contract for military equipment sold to Iran. Gifts and commissions were paid by company executives, acting against company policy, to a senior Army officer concerned with procurement to obtain the contract. All were convicted.[10]

There is a rich literature concerning the payment of bribes abroad by multi-national corporations (Conklin, 1977; Delmas-Marty and Tiedemann, 1979; Sampson, 1977). Among United States companies, Lockheed Aircraft and United Brands are particularly notorious examples. The payment of 'commissions' abroad is often justified as necessary if British firms are to do business on a basis of equality with foreign firms which make such payments. British companies are said to pay commissions to local agents who may have to pay commissions to others in cash or entertainments. It is very often not perceived as wrongful to pay such bribes; the morality of the practice is judged by what are thought to be the dictates of morality in the other country concerned, and its business practices. Thus, the Hon. A. Ogilvy, replying to the Inspectors in the Lonrho investigation, stated (Lonrho Limited, 1976, p. 638):

> Can I be quite frank? I was not against the principle of bribery because I think it has probably got to be done in certain countries; it is part of doing business like paying a merchant bank an underwriting fee.

Mr. John Stonehouse also alleged that his companies paid such bribes, but, as in the case of Sir Eric Miller, the Inspectors conclude that this was a cloak for his own defalcations (London Capital Group Limited, 1977, pp. 340–1). The same conclusion was reached in Cadco concerning bribes allegedly paid in Italy (Cadco Developments Limited, 1966, p. 53). When an American company forbade its French subsidiary to pay bribes in order to secure business, the French apparently treated the order as the product of a mind unacquainted with reality (Braithwaite, 1979). It is noteworthy that when, after the Americans had begun to put their house in order by passing legislation directed against the payment of bribes abroad, the Confederation of British Industries still could see no purpose in such legislation which would, in any event, put British companies at a disadvantage when dealing in markets where less scrupulous competitors operate.[11]

There is an extensive literature on the affairs of multi-nationals, much of which strikes a note of hysteria. But it is hardly surprising that states within which such companies trade can, and do, legitimately object to the corruption of their officials by foreign enterprises. The United Nations is certainly aware of the problem; it has under active consideration a draft international agreement to prevent and eliminate such payments.[12] There can be no reason for surprise if, from the known examples of lawlessness which occur, Third World nations, in particular, take the view that foreign enterprises endeavour to secure economic domination by corrupt means. A sweeping puritanical reaction abroad to western companies is not surprising; it is inevitable (Stevenson, 1977). This creates serious contingent risks for firms doing business abroad.

Computer Fraud

Computer fraud has become a fashionable topic. It has been said that business executives and auditors often repose too much faith in computers, the workings of which they do not really understand (Whiteside, 1979). Thus, the mystique surrounding computers helps to make possible a significant increase in illegal manipulations of the computer. The dangers of large-scale frauds facilitated by computer operations have been adverted to in the literature for some years. The police, too, have begun to take an increasing interest in the matter. A recent Interpol conference was told of a large number of computer fraud cases of which the English police were largely unaware.[13] Auditors, or some at any rate, appear to have grasped the dangers early on.

Computer frauds are not unique in character; rather, computers are used to facilitate frauds which might well have been committed by traditional means. Whether the quantitative change posed by the advent of computers has resulted in a qualitative change to new forms of fraud is a barren question. There can be no doubt that they have changed the magnitude of the risks. The reasons why are outlined here (Comer, 1977, p. 182). They are: the introduction of new data forms which sometimes appear difficult to understand and control; the centralisation of data in one easily identifiable place increases the risk and critical character of loss; the introduction of new types of people into critical operations, and it is clear that the integrity of computer systems depends in large measure upon the integrity of personnel who operate them; the absence of a clearly identifiable audit trail in computer operations. It is obviously important that the dangers be grasped and appropriate counter-measures taken.

Apart from the dishonest use of computer time, three types of fraud appear likely to be facilitated by the use of computers: theft by converting an enterprise's assets by insiders, essentially the variants of theft which once were known as embezzlement and fraudulent conversion; pirating the use of programmes, since some programmes are standard-form programmes and can fit more than one enterprise (Gotleib and Borodin, 1973; Seipel, 1973; Davis, 1975); and abstraction of information from corporate records by tapping the computer bank. It is possible to enter a false terminal into a system and use it to abstract information (Comer, 1977). Computer-based information can include such matters as lists of customers, their credit ratings, amounts of credit outstanding, types and quantities of goods sold to them and their discounts, production methods and formulas, costing data for outstanding contracts, and company results prior to public announcement (Waller, 1978). These manifestations are, as will be seen, insufficiently dealt with by the criminal law.

Most frauds have occurred through manipulation of computer systems by employees. It is, however, possible to manipulate actual systems, a process which requires collusion between the programming and systems staff (Comer, 1977; Roddam, 1977). There are of course other dangers than those noted above, but they do not relate to fraud. There are obvious fears for privacy and individual liberty, both from the maintenance and misuse of computer programmes (Younger Committee, Cmnd. 5012). There are dangers from the criminal destruction of a firm's computer records. Fire poses a considerable danger. Most losses result from simple human error in operating systems (Mair, Wood and Davis, 1976).

It is difficult to obtain any clear picture of the amount of criminal misuse of computers; indeed, it may be that the advent of computers has in fact reduced the opportunities for fraud (Comer, 1977). A number of hardy perennial stories circulate such as the one, retailed to the Interpol conference, of an American bank computer operator who added, it was said, 10c to every bank service charge less than $10.00 and $1.00 to those above $10.00, crediting the difference to himself in an account which he opened for himself in the same bank under an assumed name. Other examples include the case in which the address of an approved but unused supplier was changed to that of the embezzler and the computer programmed to print fake invoices for that supplier. A bank programmer opened bogus accounts and caused the computer to pay over-the-counter sundry deposits into it. Another closed dormant accounts, gambling that the owners would not draw on them, and kept the proceeds. The most entertaining account is the following (Marting, 1973, pp. 16–17).

> When a major British chemical company centralised the accounts for its three major divisions, the chief programmer spotted that one division was selling chemicals to another without the 40 per cent intra-company discount that it should have used. In collusion with the chief buyer he started a bogus subsidiary. By doing this, they could offer their customers not only a 40 per cent discount but also extended credit. After operating their 'subsidiary' for some months they were selling chemicals to outside companies, undercutting their own company.

They were eventually caught and dismissed. Most such stories thus concern corporate insiders who steal from their employer by utilising the computer facility. A standard text notes that despite the possibilities of industrial espionage, and the dishonest sale of data and secrets, most cases involve simple theft by embezzlement, of which only one-thirtieth of the losses (in the United States) are actually uncovered.

Even the most celebrated horror story of all, that of the Equity Funding Corporation of America and its insurance subsidiary, Equity Funding Life Insurance Corporation (EFLIC), is curiously disappointing (Loeffler, 1974). In brief, Equity Funding was a stock market manipulation which depended on high stock values. Eventually, when Equity Funding's stock values began to decline, its directors decided to issue their own policies and acquired a company (later changed to EFLIC) for the purpose. One ploy which they adopted in order to obtain ready cash was to create, and then reinsure, bogus policies, thereby giving the impression of both prosperity and solvency. They also created new policies from existing policies by changing the policy numbers and inflating the face amount of premiums. They killed off some bogus policies in order to obtain the death benefits from the reinsurers.

This sort of fraud was necessarily of brief duration. It required the company itself to pay the premiums to the reinsurers lest the scheme be detected. This meant that, in order to continue to give the impression of solvency, more and more fictitious business was necessary. Moreover, the fraud could not rely on computer paper alone; it was eventually found necessary to create bogus policy-holder files to generate fraudulent detail for the bogus business. The bubble finally burst when the State of Illinois, acting on a tip, began a comprehensive audit of the insurance business. Insurance was only a subsidiary part of the fraud and it alone involved the use of computers. But the Official Trustee in Bankruptcy concluded of that (Loeffler, 1974):

> Least of all was this a modern 'computer' fraud. The computer did not even contain complete records for EFCA's legitimate business—let alone the fraud. For example, the critical records for the Company's legitimate funding business were kept on micro-fiche, and were dealt with entirely by hand. The only record for funding business kept on the computer was an inventory of funding accounts. Entries to book fictitious income were made by manual additions to the books and records in total disregard of the Company's computer print-outs. And in insurance, although reams of print-outs were created to support the fraud, there was little or no underlying detail for these print-outs. Hence, while the computer may have generated a paper 'screen' for some aspects of the fraud, in fact the role played in it was no bigger or more complicated than that played by the company's adding machines.

This is not to argue that computers pose no danger either of embezzlement or fraud by, for example, pirating programmes or data. It does, however, suggest that there are advantages to a cool approach to the problem. The dangers involved can in some measure be prevented by proper security techniques. Furthermore, auditors are not powerless. Equity Funding escaped the auditors for some time, but that was thought to be attributable to the shortcomings of the particular audit, and not to any inherent impossibility of conducting an audit. The fraud would not have gone on for so long had the reinsurers taken proper care. With or without computers, cases of embezzlement are often difficult to detect and are not always made the subject of official complaint when they are detected. The dangers suggest, however, that a company should consider whether it needs a computer facility and, if so, that it should be prepared to take sensible precautions against criminal misuse of it.

Revenue and Customs Frauds

In Britain, successive governments have adopted a policy of legislating with some particularity against practices which deprive the Inland Revenue of money. As already noted, we have rejected as an organising principle the notion that one cannot protect against liability by adopting schemes which offend against the spirit of taxing legislation. Thus, United Kingdom legislation is characterised by the use of particular provisions to deal with tax avoidance and evasion rather than by the invocation of a general declaratory principle concerning evasion by which particular practices might be judged.[14]

There is no duty upon a taxpayer to refrain from tax avoidance.[15] The law distinguishes between tax avoidance and tax evasion, and the essence of the difference has been summed up thus:[16]

> [Evasion] . . . denotes all those activities which are responsible for a person not paying the tax that the existing law charges upon his income. *Ex hypothesi* he is in the wrong, though his wrongdoing may range from the making of a deliberately fraudulent return to a mere failure to make his return or pay his tax at the proper time. By tax avoidance . . . is understood some act by which a person so arranges his affairs that he is liable to pay less tax than he would have paid but for the arrangement. Thus the situation which he brings about is one in which he is legally in the right, except so far as some special rule may be introduced that puts him in the wrong.

This distinction, and the basic principle from which it derives, would not be universally accepted as desirable. From the point of view of international action against tax offences, it has been said to be of no use, for what is legal in one country is illegal in another. Therefore, a new, supervening definition is needed, and that, predictably, stresses the artificial character of the avoidance scheme (Huiskamp, 1980). It is, however, well entrenched in English law.

Views no doubt differ also on the morality of tax avoidance. Thurman Arnold remarked that citizens are allowed to take steps to avoid tax which would never be permitted if the obligation were a debt between private persons (1937). There is, however, no doubt that tax avoidance is legal, and that the particularity of taxing legislation renders the British system complicated to the point of unintelligibility. The standard frauds appear, however, to be of a relatively straightforward character, though often complicated in their details. The simplest category of trading frauds, for example, simply consists in the proprietor of a business suppressing cash sales and removing cash from the business. Trading frauds also often involve false invoicing, both in respect of purchases and sales. Sales are understated and purchases overstated. In at least one recent instance, it was alleged that a British company fraudulently sold goods to its foreign subsidiary at a gross undervalue so that profit might be minimised in a lower tax jurisdiction.

It is often stated that large, multi-national companies make a practice of such conduct (Delmas-Marty and Tiedemann, 1979). There is little evidence of such practices in Britain. The Inland Revenue, which monitors such matters, considers that there is little abuse. It seems probable that a rough comparability in tax rates among Western European countries, together with the development of machinery for the discovery and exchange of information, makes such devices unattractive to companies (*Multinational Corporations, United States Senate*, 1973, pp. 105, 713). It is obviously difficult for an outside observer to obtain empirical data.

Other frauds concern the attribution of invoices to the company for expenses which were allegedly incurred on the company's business, but which actually relate to the personal expenditure of the officer. Profits may be syphoned off by other forms of false invoicing as well. This may involve a conspiracy of the following sort: A and B agree that A will cause the business to pay B for supplies allegedly furnished to the business. B raises an invoice accordingly. When money is received from the business, B keeps a percentage and pays the rest to A in cash. Internal frauds are also resorted to. A company's officers may cause it to overstate its reserves or understate its stocks. This is not really a case of directors obtaining money from the company, but rather one in which they endeavour to show the company as earning a lower taxable income than it has in fact earned. Curiously, the exigencies of take-over bids, or of a need for credit, have led companies to overstate their profits in order to present a false picture of prosperity. This, of course, increases the company's liability to tax.

A troublesome category of trading frauds is that which involves international sales and dispositions of goods where invoices may be concealed. While there is provision in double taxation treaties for the exchange of information, the process can be rather cumbersome. Other instances of fraud involve building sub-contractors who avoid the P.A.Y.E. machinery by purporting to deal with workmen as independent sub-contractors. The Inland Revenue has taken steps to correct these abuses.[17] In recent years there has been a sharp rise in the figures for cases prosecuted involving the misuse of sub-contractor exemption certificates.[18] As an example, we may note the conviction of the J. Murphy Company Ltd, and its subsidiary, J. M. Piling, which were fined £575,000 in connection with labour only sub-contractors. The executives concerned were gaoled. The Inland Revenue is disinclined to look favourably on pleas by contractors that their men do not like paying tax. Other common frauds, for example false claims for allowances, really fall outside the scope of this book and need not be pursued further. There is, as we have noted, a delicate dividing line between avoidance and evasion. Even quite large trading frauds are unsophisticated in this sense. Where the legality of avoidance schemes is in issue, as in the *Rossminster* case, the legal issues are horrendous.[19]

V.A.T. falls within the purview of the Customs and Excise and little detail is available concerning its enforcement. Typically, V.A.T. inquiries involve cases where, through neglect, the taxpayer has failed to keep the appropriate documents or to account properly for tax. In some few cases, traders have found it very difficult to adapt to the V.A.T. system, and to the extensive records which this demands. There are cases in which non-payment is wilful, and these, as will be seen, are likely candidates for prosecution. In a surprising number of cases involving traders and haulage contractors, almost no financial records are available at all. Many small traders simply do not keep books. We have noted elsewhere this pattern in the insolvencies of small businesses (Leigh, 1980b). The Customs and Excise also enforces taxes on gambling. Again, little information is available. Under exchange control, it had a major function in preventing the smuggling of currency, but the exchange control system is now suspended (Leigh, 1980a).

Frauds on the Common Market

Frauds on the Common Market come within the purview of United Kingdom enforcement agencies. It is at present impossible to estimate their value and extent.[20] Little information is available about them in Britain although there is a well developed literature on the Continent (Cosson, 1971; Cosson, 1979). In general, frauds on the Common Market involve, first, import-export frauds, that is, frauds concerning subsidies, refunds and levies, and, secondly, internal market schemes relating to United Kingdom producers and users. Two different services of control are involved, the Customs and Excise which administers Customs legislation and the Ministry of Agriculture which regulates the internal market.

The first type of fraud consists in avoiding a levy or customs duty, while the second consists in obtaining a subsidy or grant. The under-declaration of goods is frequently involved, especially where there is a levy on weight. There may be an over-declaration of weight where this results in a refund. In import-export transactions there may be a misdescription of goods; for example, where there is a levy on beef it may be described as offal, or the fat content may be mis-stated. Misdescription as to quality also occurs, in order to take advantage of a different tariff heading. Meat imported from outside the EEC and described as offal would avoid the EEC levy on meat. One such case involved a company which may have been formed for the purpose of acting as a vehicle for fraud and which, over a long period, misdescribed meat as offal for the purpose of exporting to EEC countries and escaped the EEC monetary compensation levy of over £100,000. In another case, involving an import refund claim for £15,000, forged documents including forged veterinary certificates were used.

A figure of £7.5 million has been suggested as the amount illegally obtained by fraud from EEC import-export frauds (Comer, 1977). We do not as yet appear to have experienced the large, circuitous frauds seen on the Continent. Take, for instance, this Danish example: cake dough was made in Denmark, despatched to Switzerland or Austria with export aid, sent on to Romania, re-exported back to Denmark (where it qualified for lower import duties because of its cocoa content), and 're-sold' to the original export firm. The circle then re-commenced. There are similar examples from Germany and France.[21] Persons who commit import-export frauds are often content to make relatively modest illicit profits over a long period; they are thus unlike long-firm frauds which rely on making a large killing. A typical fraud would be to send a lorry load of beef overseas, mis-describing the contents as forequarters rather than hindquarters, taking advantage of a difference in the levy applicable.

Internal frauds have involved butter. In the United Kingdom, for example, the price of butter was kept down by a subsidy on butter intended for retail sale. It is an offence to use subsidised butter for manufacture or export without reimbursing the Treasury. There have been cases of the use of subsidised butter in manufacture. The problem was greatest in the north where a subsidy was paid not on packed, but on bulk, butter, that being the form in which it is commonly sold locally. The butter could then readily be used in illicit manufacture.[22]

Frauds concerning storage aids have not, it seems, occurred. Independent contractors store goods in commercial warehouses under the authority and control of the Ministry of Agriculture if the Intervention Board has bought the produce.[23] If the subsidy is simply given for storage, then the butter or commodity will be stored for an agreed period and then sold. The Board checks storage records. Because large numbers of persons are involved, fraud is thought to be difficult to perpetrate. There have, however, been thefts from warehouses.

There does not seem to be a problem involving fraudulent invoices of goods which are in fact never imported or exported. Physical checks at ports and the documentation required in respect of export shipments are said to make such frauds difficult to perform. The authorities thus consider that the problem in Britain is one of misdescription. If this is so, it indicates that Britain has been fortunate. In Europe, apart from misdescription, and false declarations that goods from outside the EEC originate within the EEC (Delmas-Marty, 1980), there have also been frauds in which all that moved was paper, the invoices relating to the movement of phantom goods being later presented for refunds or subventions (Cosson, 1971, pp. 160–8).

References and Notes

1. It is difficult to obtain information from the clearing banks about such matters. Some snippets were gleaned from Interpol, *2nd Symposium on International Fraud*, St. Cloud, 9–12 September 1974 (unpublished report).

2. *The Times*, 20 January 1978; *The Observer*, '...as Oberlander goes down in style', 23 December 1979.

3. *Investors' Chronicle*, 26 May 1975, p. 725, discussing *The Savonita*.
4. *Investors' Chronicle*, 20 October 1978, p. 182, 'Lloyds calls in the Fraud Squad'.
5. *Private Eye*, 22 August 1975.
6. The quotation is from a memorandum prepared by the police for a law reform committeee (unpublished).
7. *American Distilling Co.* v. *Wisconsin Liquor Co.*, 104 F 2d. 582 (1939) at p. 585.
8. *The Times*, 'Diary', 20 January 1978.
9. Sess. 1975–6, 906 H.C. Deb. (Vth Ser.) cols. 391–92. It is interesting that in the United States, the Inland Revenue Service in the wake of foreign bribery scandals, accelerated its programme to ensure that bribes were not allowed as deductions; see M. Leigh, 'The Challenge of Transnational Corporate Wrongdoing to the Rule of Law', *Dept. of State Bulletin*, vol. 74, no. 1926, pp. 642–8 (1977).
10. *The Times*, 18, 19 and 20 January 1978; for the appeal see *Reg.* v. *Wellburn* (1979) 69 Cr. App. R. 254.
11. *The Times*, 3 April 1978, p. 17, col. e.
12. *Draft International Agreement to Prevent and Eliminate Illicit Payments in International Commercial Transactions*, United Nations Economic and Social Council, Document No. E/1978/115.
13. A. Terry, 'Interpol grapples with the computer criminals', *Sunday Times*, 23 December 1979.
14. *Royal Commission on the Taxation of Profits and Income*, Cmnd. 9474 (1955) (Chairman, Lord Radcliffe), para. 1025.
15. *Duke of Westminster* v. *C.I.R.* (1935) 19 T.C. 490, at p. 520 *per* Lord Tomlin.
16. Cmnd. 9474, para. 1016.
17. *Report of the Commissioners of Her Majesty's Inland Revenue for the year ended 31 March 1976*; see also 1975–6 H.C. Deb. (Vth Ser.), vol. 903, col. 1631–8, and for a recent account of such a fraud, *The Times*, 18 January 1980.
18. 1976–7, 931 H.C. Deb. (Vth Ser.) col. 1626. The whole debate on the Finance Bill 1977 is instructive.
19. [1980] 2 W.L.R. 1.
20. 1974–5, H.C. Deb. (Vth Ser.) cols. 131 and 432.
21. 'Keeping up with Eurocrooks', *Globe and Mail* (Toronto), 13 November 1975; for France and Germany, see J. Cosson, *Les Industriels de la Fraude Fiscale* (1971).
22. At the time of writing the subsidy is £240 per ton, disbursed by the E.E.C. to the United Kingdom as a special concession.
23. The intervention system in agriculture is complicated; for a basic account, see P. Mathijsen (1975).

PART II

THE CRIMINAL LAW

5 Theft and Related Offences

In the next three chapters, we consider the controls which derive from the criminal law, and to some extent, from related doctrines of civil law as well. English substantive law is, as we have noted, reasonably comprehensive in its coverage, but it is undeniably messy, and the relationship of its individual parts to a dimly perceived whole gives rise to avoidable lacunae and to unnecessarily vexing problems of interpretation. In England, unlike some continental jurisdictions, frauds are dealt with under the general criminal law. In Germany special legislation deals with subvention frauds and tax frauds; here, the general criminal law is invoked. Special provisions which relate to particular schemes are thus not of great importance in relation to fraudulent conduct.

No attempt is made to cover the law relating to property offences in a comprehensive way. The Theft Acts 1968–78 are discussed in standard works (Smith, J.C., 1979a; Smith, J.C. and Hogan, 1978). Only an outline of the principal offences is given here, sufficient to acquaint the reader with the extent of the law and of its limitations. Fortunately, many of the problems which afflict this area of the law are of marginal importance only. There are, however, certain offences which need to be dealt with in greater detail since their importance to control is considerable, and the discussion given to them in standard works is sometimes quite cursory. These lesser known offences are considered in rather greater detail. We commence with a discussion of theft and related offences.

The Theft Acts 1968–78

In its evidence to the Wilson Committee, the Department of Trade roundly declared that the great majority of infractions committed against companies were offences of theft.[1] The preceding discussion of modes of fraud illustrates the truth of that dictum; offences involving theft and deception predominate, that is, either offences against the company or offences in which the company is used as a vehicle for fraud, or both. In addition, offences arising under insolvency administration may, as we have noted, involve theft as well.

Theft

The principal general statute is the Theft Act 1968. This Act provides that a person is guilty of theft if he dishonestly appropriates property belonging to another with the intention of permanently depriving the other of it.[2] It is immaterial whether the appropriation is made with a view to gain or for the thief's own benefit.[3] Appropriation does not necessarily connote physical removal of the thing or property interest involved; an unlawful sale by A to B of C's goods could constitute theft, even though A does not physically hand anything over to B. The Act simply states that any assumption by a person of the rights of an owner amounts to an appropriation.[4] There must, however, be an assumption of a right as distinct from a mere invasion of a right; in civil law terms, there must be a conversion rather than a mere trespass.[5]

Property is widely defined to include money and all other property, real or personal, including things in action and other intangible property.[6] Thus a debt represented by a bank account can be the subject of theft, and a director or officer who draws cheques on his company's account for his own purposes, when it is in credit or within agreed overdraft limits, can be charged with theft of the debt.[7] A simpler solution would be to charge theft of the cheque. Land can only be the subject of theft in exceptional cases, a point discussed later.

Theft requires that the thief appropriate property belonging to another. Section 5 of the Act extends the attribution of property. The term includes possession or control as well as ownership. Where a person receives property from, or on account, of another and is under an obligation to that other to retain and deal with that property or its proceeds in a particular way, the property or proceeds shall be regarded (as against him) as belonging to that other.[8] Where a person gets property by mistake and is under a legal obligation to restore the property or its proceeds or value, the property, proceeds or value are regarded as belonging to the person entitled to restoration.

Some general aspects of theft should be noted. First, the thief must have acted dishonestly. That concept is dealt with in part by statute which, for example, provides that a taking is not dishonest where the taker believes, however mistakenly, that he had a proprietary right to the thing.[9] Similarly, he does not act dishonestly where he believes that he had or would have had the owner's consent to the taking, or that the owner cannot be discovered by taking reasonable steps.[10] His appropriation may, however, be dishonest even where he is willing to pay for the goods.

Outside the ambit of these essentially negative rules, there is confusion. The absence of these excusing factors does not mean that the accused must be held to be dishonest as a strict matter of law. His mental state is obviously important; the question is the exent to which it is decisive. What is not clear in the current state of the case law is whether the jury's characterisation of the accused's state of mind as dishonest or whether the accused's characterisation of his intention as honest or dishonest, is decisive. In favour of the former view is the statement of Lawton, L.J. in *Reg.* v. *Feeley* that jurors, in deciding whether an accused acted dishonestly, must apply the current standards of ordinary decent people; in favour of the latter are decisions which seem to hold that the question is purely subjective: how did the accused see himself?[11] The former allows different juries to set standards intuitively; the latter represents the abandonment of standards, and even of common sense.

The problem of dishonesty can be particularly vexing in commercial and company frauds as *Tarling's* case shows.[12] There, the question arose whether a clandestine transfer of shares owned (perhaps) by their company to directors in pursuance of a concealed share incentive scheme amounted to dishonesty sufficient to found either theft or a conspiracy to defraud. Viscount Dilhorne and Lord Edmund-Davies thought that it did. To Lord Salmon, the directors' conduct was uncandid, discreditable and a breach of fiduciary duty, but not theft or fraud. Lord Keith seems to have been of the same opinion, and Lord Wilberforce's opinion could be read in that sense.

The problem of dishonesty does not arise in touting for shares since the applicable legislation excludes dishonesty as a necessary element. But in relation to theft and other frauds the elastic consciences of persons who figure in Department of Trade Reports will be recalled, as will their ability to rationalise their conduct. To what extent are their mores shared by jurors? Where are the lines to be drawn? Would jurors agree with the rather light-hearted approach sometimes taken to tax fraud for example by company directors (Roadships Limited, 1976, p. 128)?

A director can commit theft against his company even though he is the sole beneficial shareholder of it.[13] He cannot of course be the sole shareholder, at least on formation of it, for the Companies Acts require a minimum of two shareholders even for a private company, though one may be a mere nominee.[14] But the rule imposing liability for theft is sound in policy. However small a company may be, in a commercial sense there are important interests other than those of its controller to be protected, for example the interests of creditors and employees. Directors and officers will also be liable for thefts of funds entrusted to the company for specific purposes. These are earmarked and considered to be the property of the person or institution from which they emanate. Thus in a Cadco situation, the dishonest misappropriation of government grants made for specific purposes, and of bank loans advanced on a similar basis, would be theft.[15]

Most cases of looting are uncomplicated. Others, more troublesome, require further analysis. If a controller, who may be a director or may hold no office in the company at all, dishonestly sells property belonging to him or under his control to the company at a gross overvalue, there should be little difficulty in treating this as theft. If he has misrepresented the truth to other directors, a charge of obtaining property by deception ought also to lie. A director must exercise his powers for the benefit of the company as a whole.[16] The company cannot be treated as knowing the dishonest elements of a transaction by which its director seeks to defraud it, and must be regarded as a nonconsenting victim.[17] The fact that the rogue as director consents to the transaction should not preclude guilt, for the vendor director is under a fiduciary duty to act in the best interests of his company, and is under a statutory duty to disclose his interest in any contract with the company.[18] Consent obtained by a failure to disclose in such circumstances, or by misrepresentation, must deprive the company's consent of efficacy. The director has appropriated assets belonging to another.[19]

Unfortunately, this seemingly obvious solution to the problem appears to conflict with passages in the judgement of Lord Wilberforce in *Tarling's* case. According to one school of thought, a transaction dishonestly undertaken can only amount to theft if title to the property does not pass as a result. Lord Wilberforce may have meant to hold that as directors acting improperly may have power to pass a title, albeit avoidable title, a transaction which they or the managing director approve cannot be theft. If this is right, it certainly presents a paradox: there could be no theft, neither could there be a deception, because no deception was used. Nor is the property trust property, because the director while a fiduciary, is not a trustee. A director who caused the company to enter into a transaction for value, however inadequate, could not commit theft, although one who simply skimmed cash from the till or drew on the company's account could. Curiously, that antique document the Indian Penal Code, with its crime of wrongful dealing with property held on trust, a wide term as there used, would appear better able to protect company property than modern English legislation (Malik,

1978, pp. 139–41). The point obviously needs early attention.

Dishonest allotments of shares by public companies otherwise than for cash will necessarily entail a deception because the transaction will involve the submission of a dishonest valuer's report. The Companies Act 1980 now requires that all allotments of shares in public companies for a non-cash consideration must be supported by a valuer's report prepared in accordance with the statute.[20] This should go part of the way to discouraging the fraudulent sales of assets which were a feature of looting schemes such as that in Town Centre Properties Limited.

At the same time, it would be naive to think that the valuation provisions will wholly cure the problem. Valuation techniques have been vigorously attacked as producing inflated figures (Wheatcroft, 1979). It may be difficult, in many instances, to show that a report was so blatantly false that the vendor knew of it, at least in the absence of direct evidence that he procured a dishonest report. The problem is one of proving fraud rather than incompetence. The provisions apply only to public companies, not to private ones. Furthermore, the proposal may be to sell assets of the company either for non-cash consideration other than shares, or for a grossly insufficient cash consideration. Even in these cases, where deceptive documents are likely in order to give the transaction an appearance of regularity, nothing will happen if there is not an independent board or alert body of shareholders ready to question the transaction.

A particularly difficult problem with theft is the requirement that the thief take with intent to deprive the owner permanently of his property in the thing taken. There is a rather obscure exception to this in section 6 of the Theft Act 1968, the purpose of which is to render criminal the permanent deprivation of a temporary interest. Taking a season ticket and retaining it until its value expires is an obvious example, but we are not concerned with this here. The difficulty is that certain invasions of property rights can be accomplished to the great detriment of the victim without permanently depriving him of a thing. For example, copyright material can be removed temporarily and copied. That is not theft. Neither is the interception of computer-based data. To obtain information thus, or simply to obtain confidential information and trade secrets by suborning employees or planting electronic equipment, is not theft, nor would deception necessarily be involved.[21] At present, the crime of conspiracy to cheat and defraud probably gives a measure of protection, but it is to be abolished, and there is, even now, a lacuna to be filled.

The law, whether of theft or of property offences generally, will necessarily have to deal with such invasions of rights which are not characterised in terms of taking things or material objects, or concepts reified for the purpose. Legislation will be required. One may hope that, as American jurisdictions do, our legislation will be specific to the evils complained of, and will avoid the problems caused by a desire to formulate broad concepts upon which to extend property crimes. In 1979, for example, Illinois legislated specifically against the use of a computer system without the consent of the owner, against the alteration or destruction of programmes and against the unlawful use of a computer system as part of a scheme to obtain money, property or services by deception.[22] Similar proposals have been advanced federally (Whiteside, 1979, pp. 129–39). But difficult problems will have to be resolved, both in connection with the misuse of computers and otherwise in the temporary user of property. Should all, or some cases only of temporary user be criminal? What are the principles governing the reach of the law to be? Should we require some form of economic loss in the sense of deprivation of profit? These and similar questions inevitably arise.

Criminal Deception

Much commercial fraud is charged as criminal deception, an offence created by section 15 of the Theft Act 1968. Once again, in order to be criminal, property must be obtained. The definition of deception which applies generally throughout the Theft Acts takes deception to mean:

> ... any deception (whether deliberate or reckless) by words or conduct as to fact or as to law including a deception as to the present intentions of the person using the deception or any other person.

The definition does not include dishonest future forecasts. Such deceptions, however, are caught by special legislation where they relate to dealings in securities (including take-over bids), commodities, and advertising for deposits.[23] Section 15 makes it an offence for a person dishonestly to obtain property belonging to another with the intention of permanently depriving the other of it. It does not matter what interest the rogue obtains, for he is treated as obtaining property if he obtains ownership, possession or control of the thing, and he may commit the crime by obtaining for another.

The crime is, as we have noted, directed towards obtaining property. It is not necessary that the victim suffer loss from the transaction; it is enough that he be induced to enter into it by a dishonest representation.[24] Clearly, the crime may be committed even though the accused intended that no one suffer loss.[25] Indeed, in some of these cases it is difficult to see how, in the light of decided cases, the accused could be said to have acted dishonestly at all. Obtaining property by deception is the charge commonly used when property is obtained by the use of a bad cheque. The person taking a cheque can protect himself by insisting that the person with whom he deals uses a cheque card. This situation is most likely to be met with in consumer transactions since cheque cards only validate cheques to a £50 maximum.[26]

Section 7(3) of the Agriculture Act 1957, read with section 6 of the European Communities Act 1972, empowers the Ministry of Agriculture to make orders by Statutory Instrument providing for the protection of guaranteed prices or assured markets for agricultural producers, and containing special provisions for the importation of livestock. Section 7(3) makes it an offence to make certain false statements, knowingly or recklessly, relating to sums payable under the Act, or making false records required to be produced in connection with agricultural schemes. This offence is used, together with criminal deception, to prosecute frauds on the Common Agricultural Policy. It is thus another useful deception offence.

The law concerning obtaining things by deception is reasonably straightforward and satisfactory. The same cannot be said in relation to obtaining services and intangibles such as financial accommodations. These are dealt with in section 16 of the Theft Act 1968, and by the Theft Act 1978. The latter Act distinguishes, indefensibly it is submitted, between deceptions which induce a transaction and those relating to its discharge. Section 16 of the Theft Act 1968 protects certain banking and insurance operations. It is made an offence by deception to obtain permission to borrow by overdraft or to take out any policy of insurance or annuity contract or to obtain an improvement in the terms on which the actor is allowed to do so. It also makes criminal, deceptions which give the actor the opportunity to earn remuneration or greater remuneration in an office or employment, which may be of a private or public character. The section also deals with deceptions relating to betting, a topic with which it is unnecessary to deal here.

As noted, the Theft Act 1978 deals further with fraudulent conduct relating to intangibles. It is the product of a particularly tortured history into which it is, happily, not necessary to venture (Griew, 1975; Leigh and Temkin, 1975). Suffice it to say, perhaps, that the task of formulating provisions apt to protect intangibles which are at the same time expressed with reasonable particularity, has proven to be difficult, partly because the task of drafting is difficult in itself, but primarily because the policy issues concerning what interests should be legally protected and on what terms, proved difficult to resolve (Smith, J.C., 1979a, p. 113). In the result, the Theft Act 1978 deals with obtaining services by deception, the evasion of liability by deception, and making off without payment. Section 1 of the Act provides that a person who, by any deception, dishonestly obtains from another services for which payment would ordinarily be expected, commits an offence. The section does not deal with a simple diversion of services by a person who has control over the service of another. Thus, it would not cover the case of a director who diverts company workmen to work on his private property, a not uncommon occurrence.

The statute creates three offences of evasion of liability by deception. All relate to legally enforceable liabilities, the extent of which has been determined. The first case is that in which a person by deception dishonestly secures the remission of the whole or any part of any existing liability to make a payment. By remission is meant a legally effective and permanent remission of an existing debt (Smith, J.C., 1979a, pp. 210–22). The second case deals with intent to default in payment. Liability depends expressly on intent to default permanently. Unlike remission, the bundle of legal rights and duties is unaffected by the deception. The limitation to situations where the debtor intends never to pay was adopted because it was thought that, otherwise, there would be an unduly great danger of convicting persons who meant to pay but, finding themselves in temporary financial difficulties, employed a temporising deception only.

One must doubt how workable this distinction is. Whether a guilty mind can be proven will probably depend on the length of time which has elapsed between the initial demand for payment and the complaint, and upon the frequency with which payment is demanded, unless the debtor admits that he intended never to pay. A good deal of blackmail might be employed by debt collection agencies, notwithstanding legislation prohibiting the use of strong-arm methods of debt collecting.[27] However, although temporary default could harm a creditor who might for example fail thereby to seize a depreciating asset, major cases of obtaining goods where there was never an intent to pay will involve deception at the outset. Obtaining goods and intending not to pay will be chargeable as theft or deception, the classic long-firm fraud situation. The third case is that in which, by deception, the actor dishonestly obtains any exemption from or abatement of liability to make a payment. This is intended to deal with such matters as rent rebates. Neither it, nor the offence of restaurant bilking need detain us further.

The effect of limiting liability to the case where a debtor intends to avoid liability permanently by deception creates a lacuna in respect of the coverage of offences committed by the use of invalid cheques. Under section 2(3) of the Theft Act 1978, it is made clear that, for the purposes of that provision, the use of an invalid cheque is an inducement to wait for payment. There is no autonomous offence in English law of passing an invalid cheque; it is simply a mode by which a fraud may be committed. Neither is there anything in the nature of a rebuttable presumption that a person who gives an invalid cheque intended to act dishonestly (Smith, A.T.H., 1978; Anyangwe, 1978). Protection against transactions involving invalid cheques therefore requires that the giving of such a cheque relate to conduct which is itself criminal. By removing certain categories of conduct from the criminal law, it has become possible to circulate invalid cheques, dishonestly, without infringing the criminal law. How great a lacuna has thus been created will depend partly on the readiness of merchants to negotiate cheques, and partly on the readiness of juries to find dishonesty. In some country areas cheques are negotiated through shops. In commercial frauds, it is unlikely that this will happen. In the United Kingdom, the primary protection against the entry of invalid cheques into the stream of commerce comes from the banking system itself. The problems are obviously greater in countries where the issue and acceptance of cheques is less strictly regulated.

Although the coverage achieved by deception offences is wide, it is obviously narrower than the regime in other systems, in particular under Scots law. There, as Sheriff Gordon points out, the essence of the offence goes beyond obtaining goods and services. It extends to inducing the person who is defrauded either to take some article which he would not otherwise have taken, or to do some act he would not otherwise have done, or to become the medium of some unlawful act.[28] Legally significant prejudice is required, but not economic loss. The residual properties of this offence are summarised thus (Gordon, 1978, p. 603):

It may well be that fraudulent conduct is criminal, or at any rate would be prosecuted, only where there is some potential pecuniary or personal injury, unless in very exceptional circumstances when it might be used to punish some significant piece of dishonesty which obviously merited being treated as criminal but did not fall within the normal scope of any common law crime.

The latitude thus given to the courts is breathtaking. Certainly the Scots offence could sweep in most of the problematic cases in relation both to the statutory offence of obtaining by deception, and the residual offence of conspiracy to cheat and defraud.

False Accounting and Related Offences

Other sections of the Theft Act 1968 are used extensively in commercial fraud cases. One such is section 17 which creates the offence of false accounting—essentially the destruction, defacement, concealment or alteration of a document made for an accounting purpose, or using a false account for the purpose of furnishing information. The offence is punishable on indictment with a maximum term of seven years' imprisonment. This provision is not restricted to directors and officers of companies; it applies to all persons. It is confined to documents and records, and was once thought to apply only to documents which related to accounting in the financial sense, whatever that obscure phrase might mean. That was certainly the prevailing view when most of the frauds mentioned in this book arose. That view was abandoned in *Reg.* v. *Mallett.*[29] The court there held that while the document had to be made for an accounting purpose, the false statement in it did not have to be so related; in other words it is the status of the document, rather than the purpose of the particular misrepresentation, which is material.

Gain or loss are to be construed as extending to any gain or loss in money or other property.[30] Such gain may be purely temporary, including a deferment of the time at which a deficiency must be made good.[31] Section 17, because it applies to the use of accounts and records in furnishing information for an accounting purpose, applies to such documents prepared to induce persons to become creditors of a company by presenting a dishonest picture of its affairs, and also to documents which were prepared to persuade shareholders to remain as such, at any rate in cases where the maker seeks pecuniary benefit to himself while recognising that the person deceived may ultimately suffer a loss by his dishonesty. If, for example, directors wished to stabilise dealings in their company's shares in order to facilitate an orderly disposal of their own holdings at a price which the true situation of the company would not warrant, and falsified records and accounts to do so, the 'dishonesty' and 'gain' limbs would be made out.

It is not necessary to show that any detriment actually ensued from acts done contrary to the section. No one need actually be induced to do anything. The section could thus be charged even where attempted deception could not be, for the act of falsification

might be a mere preparatory act to deception or an attempt to emit a false prospectus. Furthermore, a company director who appreciates that falsifying the accounts will cause loss to persons to whose fortunes they are inextricably linked, must surely be taken to have intended that result.[32] It is, however, true that the full potentialities of this section have not been explored in fraud cases.

The provisions of section 17 are not alone. Section 19 of the Theft Act 1968 provides:

> 19(1). Where an officer of a body corporate or unincorporated association (or person purporting to act as such), with intent to deceive members or creditors of the body corporate or association about its affairs, publishes or concurs in publishing a written statement or account which to his knowledge is or may be misleading, false or deceptive in a material particular, he shall on conviction on indictment be liable to imprisonment for a term not exceeding seven years.

Again, the section is restricted to written statements made in relation to members and creditors, and not to persons not associated with the company. It does not apply to exuberant oral statements by directors to the press, even though those may substantially affect public views of the company, as allegedly happened in respect of Pergamon Press Ltd (*Pergamon Press Limited, Further Interim Report,* 1972, p. 344). It is not necessary that any actual harm be caused. While the section does not require an intent to defraud, but only an intent to deceive (a distinction which will further be explored in connection with conspiracy), there seems little doubt that in many such cases the person making the statement will either intend to defraud or at least be indifferent to whether someone is defrauded or not. This provision is, in effect, extended by section 44 of the Companies Act 1948, discussed later in this work.

There is an interesting contemporary example of the use of this section in Australia.[33] A document containing profit figures, which the prosecution alleged were false, was sent to shareholders. The allegation, essentially, was that the transaction which engendered the profit was bogus. The profit allegedly arose because the company sold a certain number of shares in another company to brokers on the understanding that these would be transferred back at the same price to a subsidiary. The transfer was made, and because the price at which the company had sold to the brokers was considerably higher than the price which it paid for the shares, it was able to claim a profit on the sale to the brokers.

The court held that the prosecution could present a case to the jury on the basis that the transactions underlying the documents were shams.[34] Whether they were so was a matter of fact for the jury. If the same reasoning were applied in England, and there is no reason why it should not be, such commercial manoeuvres as emitting profit and loss statements and accounts based upon essentially spurious intra-group transactions, could readily be dealt with. So too, could window-dressing, where, as in the Ashbourne affair, directors knew that shareholders, depositors and lenders would rely on the audited accounts as furnishing a true and fair view of the state of the enterprise (Ashbourne Investments Limited, 1979). Intent to deceive is, as we will see, a less exacting standard than intent to defraud. In fact, section 19 is a wide provision which could, it is submitted, be used far more vigorously than it apparently has been, to safeguard the integrity of accounts. It would seemingly apply against auditors, if they were thought to have participated in presenting false accounts. It also strikes at directors who are primarily liable for the presentation of accounts and reports concerning the enterprise.

The foregoing provisions of the Theft Acts are buttressed by a narrowly drafted directors' liability clause, section 18. It renders a director or officer liable where an offence has been committed by a body corporate, and where it can be proven that the offence was committed with the consent or connivance of a director, manager, secretary or other similar officer of a corporation, or any person who was purporting to act in that capacity.

Another offence which is occasionally used against directors and officers of companies is that of dishonestly procuring the execution of a valuable security.[35] The definition of valuable security is very wide, and would include the making of a share certificate, or a document authorising the delivery of property to a director or officer of a company. There is no need to prove that gain or loss occurred in fact, although the accused must have intended to cause such gain or loss. It is not necessary, unlike the crime of obtaining property by deception, or theft, to prove any intent to deprive any person or company of property permanently. It is enough that the execution of a valuable security, as defined in the section, be dishonestly procured by deception. Thus some documents whose execution is procured by misrepresentation, in order to cloak a transaction with the semblance of legality, can form the basis of a criminal charge. The section thus has considerable potential in cases where assets of a company are diverted, under cover of documents of transfer, where it is doubtful whether the situation comes within theft or deception, and where the authorities are not anxious to probe the construction of the provisions applicable to such offences. The Lowson cases could, for example, have attracted such a charge.

The principal limitation to the section is that which the definition of deception imposes. In effect, representations which consist of affirmative statements made false by material non-disclosure will be caught, because the statements are rendered deceptive thereby; but, where the execution of a valuable security takes place because the person benefiting dishonestly failed to disclose a relevant fact, no crime will have been committed, and this is so even though the person was under a fiduciary duty to disclose in civil law.

Forgery

Offences relating to forgery are also frequently invoked in commercial fraud cases. Once again, it is unecessary to deal with all aspects of forgery offences; an outline will suffice. Forgery is defined as the making of a false document with intent that it may be used as genuine.[36] The offence also extends to the counterfeiting of seals and dies. The legislation distinguishes between the forgery of public documents, which requires an intent to defraud or deceive, and other documents which require an intent to defraud.

In this section, we are primarily concerned with the forgery of documents. Simple forgery is not an offence unless accompanied by the requisite intent. For the purposes of the Forgery Act 1913, fraud requires that there be a person as its object. The important factor is not the gain which the offender expects to obtain, but the effect on the person who is the object of the fraud. To defraud is not, it has been said, restricted to the idea of depriving a man of economic advantage; the issue is, rather, whether another may be prejudiced by it.[37] The notion of intent to deceive is wider, albeit imperfectly defined (Smith, J.C. and Hogan, 1978, pp. 637–41).

It is not clear whether the statement of the mental element needs to be revised in the light of House of Lords decisions on conspiracy to cheat and defraud which hold that, in relation to private persons and bodies, such conspiracies do require an intent to cause economic loss. While the cases are in conflict, it seems to be accepted that conspiracy to defraud does require an intent to cause economic loss to the victim, and it would be curious if the word bore a different connotation in forgery.[38] Happily, in almost all cases of commercial fraud, actual or potential economic prejudice is present. A major exception, the forging of official documents, requires the lesser intent to deceive, and this, it seems, is not restricted to cases of economic prejudice.[39]

Forgery relates to the falsification of documents. There is already much case law on the meaning of 'document', but the problematic cases are of marginal importance and need not be discussed here. A document must be false, and it must be made in order that it may be used as genuine. A document may be wholly false, or it may become so because it has been altered. Section 1(2) of the Forgery Act 1913 deals with the common cases of unauthorised making, or alteration, obliteration, and removal, or making by a fictitious or deceased person. The single most difficult legal problem is to know when a document is itself false, rather than containing a lie within it. In forgery, a document must tell a lie about itself.[40] The better view appears to be that a document to which material alterations have been made becomes a forgery where these cause the document to purport to be other than what it is.[41] In many cases, where there is doubt about the status of a document, the matter can be dealt with by charging another offence, such as false accounting, the making of a false statement by a company director, obtaining by deception or attempting to do so. The falsity must be material. Again, there are peripheral difficulties into which it is unnecessary to venture. It would seem that whether an alteration is material depends upon its character in the circumstances in which it is made. As a New Zealand court stated:[42]

> ... if the surrounding circumstances are not merely indicative of a collateral dishonesty or deception but make the document appear to be the document of a person who is in fact different from the person actually signing it, then, providing the necessary intent to mislead is present, the door is in our view open to a conviction for forgery.

There are other pertinent offences under the Forgery Act 1913 as well. The most prominent is uttering a forged document knowing it to be forged, and with intent to defraud or deceive. Uttering involves no more than making use of the document. In general, conduct which falls under this offence could be charged otherwise, as obtaining or attempting to obtain property by deception, for example, but the fact that there is overlap in the law does not deprive it of utility. Another relevant offence is that of demanding property on forged instruments contrary to section 7 of the Forgery Act 1913. Property must be obtained under, upon or by virtue of the forged instrument. It has been held that the words 'by virtue of' are very wide and that the person who actually hands over the property need not therefore have done so in reliance on the forged instrument, provided that the transaction was one in which the accused's use of the forgery culminated in his obtaining the property.[43] In the case referred to, motor dealers parted with a car because finance had been obtained from a finance house to which a forged document had been submitted.

Perjury

Section 5 of the Perjury Act 1911 contains pertinent provisions. It is an offence if any person knowingly and wilfully makes (otherwise than on oath) a statement false in a material particular and the statement is made in, *inter alia,* a statutory declaration, or in an abstract, account, balance sheet, book, certificate, return or other document which he is authorised or required to make, attest or verify by any subsisting public general Act of Parliament.[44] There seems, for example, no reason why tax returns, or certifications that accounts of companies disclose a true and fair view of the enterprise, should not fall within the provision.

Cheating

In addition to the statutory offences of theft, deception, false accounting, forgery and offences akin to perjury, there is also the common law offence of cheating which was specifically continued in force by the Theft Act 1968, so far as it relates to offences against the Revenue.[45] Its operation was explained in *Reg.* v. *Hudson.*[46] The accused submitted accounts to the Inspector showing the profits of his business to be substantially less than they were and delivered to the Inspector a certificate of disclosure of facts relating to his tax liability which was false to his knowledge. This was held to be an indictable cheat at common law.

It was necessary to use the charge because, as Lord Goddard C.J. noted, sometimes a trader instead of making a return of his profits by inserting a figure in his income tax return sent in accounts, leaving the income figure to be inserted by the Inspector. To send in a specific wrong figure for income would, of course, be an offence under the Perjury Act 1911, as under revenue legislation. The particular conduct would now be caught under section 2(1)(c) of the Theft Act 1978.

References and Notes

1. Wilson Committee, Second Stage Evidence, vol. 5, *Department of Trade*, p. 29. (1979).
2. Theft Act 1968, s. 1(1).
3. *Ibid.*, s. 1(2).
4. *Ibid.*, s. 3(1).
5. *Stein* v. *Henshall* [1976] V.R. 612; [1977] A.S.C.L. 160.
6. Theft Act 1968, ss. 4(1) and (2).

7. *Reg.* v. *Kohn* (1979) 69 Cr. App. R. 395.

8. Theft Act 1968, s. 5(3) and 5(4).

9. Theft Act 1968, s. 2.

10. *Ibid.*, s. 2(1)(c).

11. *Reg.* v. *Feeley* [1973] 1 All E.R. 341; cf. *Boggeln* v. *Williams* [1978] 1 W.L.R. 873 (which may, however, be meant to reproduce *Feeley*); *Reg.* v. *Lewis* (1976) 62 Cr. App. R. 206.

12. *Tarling (No. 1)* v. *Government of Singapore* (1980) 70 Cr. App. R. 77.

13. *Reg.* v. *Sinclair* [1968] 3 All E.R. 241.

14. Companies Act 1948, s. 176.

15. Theft Act 1968, s. 5(3); on the creation of trust, see *Barclays Bank Limited* v. *Quistclose Investments Limited* [1970] A.C. 567; *Re Kayford Ltd.* [1975] 1 W.L.R. 279.

16. *Re Smith and Fawcett* [1942] Ch. 304, and see further J. Northey and L. Leigh (1980), chapter 10.

17. *Reg.* v. *Sinclair, supra,* and *Belmont Finance Corporation Ltd.* v. *Williams* [1979] Ch. 250.

18. Companies Act 1948 s. 199; Companies Act 1980, ss. 49–61.

19. *Lawrence* v. *Metropolitan Police Commissioner* [1972] A.C. 626.

20. Companies Act 1980, ss. 24–30.

21. *Oxford* v. *Moss* [1979] Crim. L.R. 119 and comment in (1980) 1 *The Company Lawyer,* 44.

22. Illinois, Public Act 81–0548, of 11 September 1979.

23. See the Prevention of Fraud (Investments) Act 1958, and The Banking Act 1979.

24. *Reg.* v. *Potger* (1970) 55 Cr. App. R. 42.

25. *Reg.* v. *Greenstein* [1976] 1 All E.R. 1.

26. For the representations on giving a cheque, see *Metropolitan Police Commissioner* v. *Charles* [1977] A.C. 177.

27. Administration of Justice Act 1970, s. 40.

28. *Adcock* v. *Archibald*, 1925 J.C. 58 at p. 61 *per* Lord Hunter.

29. (1978) 66 Cr. App. R. 239.

30. Theft Act 1968, s. 34(2) (a).

31. *Reg.* v. *Eden* (1971) 55 Cr. App. R. 193.

32. J.C. Smith and B. Hogan (1978), pp. 47–51, and see *Reg.* v. *Belfon* (1976) 63 Cr. App. R. 59.

33. *Rex* v. *Lord Kylsant* [1932] 1 K.B. 442 appears to be the most recent example in Britain.

34. *Reg.* v. *M.* [1979] A.C.L.D. 488 (N.S.W., C.A.).

35. Theft Act 1968, s. 20(2).

36. Forgery Act 1913, s. 1(1).

37. *Welham* v. *D.P.P.* [1961] A.C. 103.

38. *Reg.* v. *Allsopp* (1977) 64 Cr. App. R. 29, and see in particular the speech of Lord Diplock in *Scott* v. *Metropolitan Police Commissioner*, [1975] A.C. 819.

39. The Law Commission, Working Paper no. 55, *Report on Forgery and Counterfeit Currency* (1973) suggests that the mental element simply be an intent to induce another to accept the false statement as genuine, and by reason of that, to act to his prejudice.

40. For example, *Reg.* v. *Hassard and Devereux* [1970] 1 W.L.R. 1109, a

difficult case concerning the use of an assumed name by which one accused was known to the bank on which it was drawn.

41. *Reg.* v. *Dodge and Harris* [1972] 1 Q.B. 416; *Gaysek* v. *The Queen* (1971) 18 D.L.R. (3d) 306, *per* Laskin J.
42. *Reg.* v. *Haskett* [1975] N.Z.L.R. 30 at p. 32.
43. *Reg.* v. *Hurford and Williams* [1963] 2 All E.R. 254.
44. Perjury Act 1911, s. 5.
45. Theft Act 1968, s. 32(1); anciently the offence was very wide, see *Rex* v. *Bembridge* (1783) 3 Dougl. 327.
46. [1956] 2 Q.B. 252.

6 Corruption

Corruption is dealt with by statutes creating criminal offences, by wide doctrines of the civil law relating to the conduct of agents, and by extra-legal codes and practices. Our primary concern is with the criminal law, but the other categories cannot simply be ignored. Because offences relating to corruption are seldom fully dealt with in the standard texts, a fairly full account is given here.

Criminal Law

Criminal legislation relating to corruption is fairly extensive. The three principal statutes, the Public Bodies Corrupt Practices Act 1889, the Prevention of Corruption Act 1906, and the Prevention of Corruption Act 1916, strike at corruption both in relation to public bodies and private firms. For these purposes, nationalised industries come within the latter category.

The 1889 Act provides that every person who by himself or in conjunction with another corruptly solicits or receives or agrees to solicit or receive for himself or for any other person, any gift, loan, fee, reward, or advantage whatsoever, as an inducement to, or reward for, or otherwise on account of any member, officer or servant of a public body doing or forbearing to do anything in respect of any matter or transaction whatsoever, actual or proposed, in which the public body is concerned, shall be guilty of an offence.[1] An identically worded provision deals with giving or promising or offering gifts.[2] The 1889 Act applies only to certain dealings with government. The definition section, section 7, defines 'public body' widely, in terms of local governmental authorities and local and public authorities of all descriptions.[3] The list of public authorities has been further extended piecemeal by later statutes.[4] Public bodies are those which carry out public or statutory duties for the public rather than for private profit.[5]

The 1906 Act is considerably broader. It is an offence for an agent corruptly to accept, or obtain or agree to accept or obtain (so that actual obtaining is not necessary) any gift or consideration as an inducement or reward for doing or forbearing to do or for having done or forborne to do any act in relation to his principal's affairs or business. Thus a payment made after such an act has been done or after showing or forbearance to show favour or disfavour, is an offence. Again, there is a parallel provision concerning giving. Both the giving and receiving of gifts are, therefore, dealt with.[6]

In addition, there is a provision relating to deceptive accounts, documents and receipts. It makes it an offence for a third person knowingly to give, or an agent knowingly to use, a document, false in a material particular, which it is known is intended to deceive the principal.[7] This latter provision goes beyond transactions entered into by an agent for the purposes of gain by him; it also comprehends transactions entered into purely with a view to injure the agent's principal. It is not, however, necessary to show that the principal suffered any economic loss, or indeed, any loss at all. Prosecutions under both the 1889 and 1906 Acts require the consent of the Attorney-General or the Solicitor-General.

Similar provisions apply to the Customs and Excise. It is an offence for Customs officers to take or ask for any reward in connection with their duty, or to enter into any agreement to do anything by which Her Majesty may be defrauded. There is also a provision against corrupt giving.[8] Some features of the provisions discussed are noteworthy. The first is the onus of proof, which is reversed where a gift or consideration has been paid in respect of dealings with government. This provision applies not only to matters dealt with under the 1889 Act, but also to certain dealings caught by the 1906 Act. The 1889 Act, as we have seen, applies only to dealings with government. The 1906 Act deals with conduct both in the public and private sectors, and with the nationalised industries. The onus of proof is reversed in respect of dealings with government under either statute.[9]

The term 'corruptly' underlies both statutes. The courts have held that this term means that the accused intentionally did that which the Acts forbid him to do. His motivation is thus treated as not significant. In *Reg.* v. *Smith*,[10] where the accused made a payment to a mayor, intending that the mayor should take the payment and be exposed as corrupt, the court held that he had brought himself within the section and could properly be convicted. The point is that the accused knew that the payment was forbidden and intended that the mayor should take it corruptly. His motive, that of acting as a local government vigilante, could not be set against the intention to make the payment and his knowledge that the mayor, if he accepted it, would do so on account of conduct forbidden by statute. There are other cases to the same effect, and courts have rejected the notion that 'corruptly' is sufficiently akin to dishonesty to enable courts to enquire whether the accused's actions were dictated by such wider motives (Shyllon, 1969).[11]

The Acts catch all manner of consideration. The 1889 Act specifically speaks of obtaining a loan; the 1906 Act speaks merely of 'consideration'. In a Canadian case under legislation corresponding to the 1906 Act, it is said—rightly, it is submitted—that the distinction between a gift and a loan is not decisive: a gift may be cloaked with the appearance of a loan, and, even were it not, the making of a loan might, itself, be an inducement or reward.[12] The legislation does not seem apt to catch a general *douceur*, or sweetener. It appears to be directed both towards specific transactions and to the showing of favour to persons in classes of transactions or, more broadly, in relation to the principal's business. Gifts of a general character which predispose an agent to look with favour upon another, or which tend to compromise the agent's judgement, do not seem of themselves to fall within the Acts.[13] This sort of conduct, of which the report into the Crown Agents affords striking examples, is left to codes of conduct.

There is a problem in relation to past actions. Under the 1906 Act, it has been held that an agent who obtains money on a pretence that he will do certain acts for the payer, the acts having already been performed, cannot be convicted.[14] The point is that the act, when done, was not done to show favour. The offence may be committed, however, even though the agent does not in fact show favour. The fact that the agent double-crosses the giver does not absolve either from liability. If, when the agent accepts money, he does not intend to show favour and immediately reports the matter to his principal, it may be held that he did not accept the favour corruptly.[15] Thus the law is more accommodating to the recipient than to one who gives in order to expose bribery. The agent must take dishonestly. He cannot be convicted merely for showing favour, for that can be done innocently.[16] We have noted that in relation to transactions with government departments, or public bodies, involving persons holding or seeking to obtain a contract, there is a presumption that the gift was made and received corruptly. The burden of proof may be discharged by showing that, on a balance of probabilities, the transaction was innocent.[17]

The provision in the 1906 Act dealing with the giving of false documents is not limited to the case where it is desired to corrupt an agent. It applies whether the person tendering the document intends to mislead the principal through an innocent agent, or intends that an agent, knowing the giver's intention, hand it on.[18] 'Agent' is widely defined. What matters is the status of the person receiving.

He must be an agent and receive; it does not matter if he receives the bribe in connection with a matter with which he normally does not deal as agent.[19] We have seen that 'public body' is similarly widely defined under the legislation.[20]

There can be little doubt that the legislation is sufficiently widely expressed to catch most of the instances of corruption to which we have drawn attention. The Royal Commission on Standards of Conduct in Public Life was generally satisfied with its coverage. It did suggest certain rationalisations and extensions, principally that the increased penalties and reverse onus of proof which apply to the public sector be extended to private sector corruption (Cmnd. 6524, p. 16). The maximum penalty under the 1906 Act is two years' imprisonment, whereas under the 1916 Act a maximum of seven years' imprisonment is provided. The Royal Commission suggested that the legislation be consolidated and its language simplified. It further suggested that gifts to third parties and intermediaries, dealt with under the 1889 Act, should apply generally. Under the 1906 Act an intermediary is caught only to the extent that he actually gives or offers a corrupt gift or consideration to an agent.

Certainly the reach of legislation so consolidated would be as wide as that in most jurisdictions (James, 1962; Anon., 1960). The American Law Institute *Model Penal Code* appears broader, but the only extension of substance is that which renders criminally liable a person who holds himself out to the public as being engaged in the business of making disinterested selection, appraisal or criticism of commodities, and who allows his judgement to be affected by a benefit solicited or received for the purpose (American Law Institute, 1961, s. 224.8). This is conduct which at present is imperfectly covered in relation to advisers in securities transactions, and in respect of which reform has already been suggested.

A principal omission from the catalogue, as we have noted, is any provision to deal with British individuals and companies who offer bribes overseas in relation to contracts. Whether the United Kingdom should so legislate as to enable British courts to take jurisdiction in such circumstances should be considered with some urgency. The United States, where recent revelations, such as Lockheed Aircraft or United Brands, appear to have shocked the conscience of the nation, and where there is a lively realisation of the political and commercial dangers of foreign bribery, has passed the Foreign Corrupt Practices Act of 1977 to deal with the problem. This requires disclosure of certain payments. It also creates offences of bribing foreign officials, and giving money and gifts to influence political parties, officials, or candidates for office in respect of

business dealings with foreign governments (Hermann, 1977).[21] As
we have seen, suggestions that Britain should legislate have been
resisted, and activities of British companies abroad are restrained by
common prudence and morality. However, in the light of forthright
condemnation of bribery by the United Nations, and moves to
secure international action to deal with the problem, it is questionable whether Britain ought to maintain so negative an attitude to the
problem (Committee on Federal Regulation of Securities, 1977).

Civil Law

No attempt is made to deal with the rules of civil law in any detail.[22]
They are, however, very broad, An agent must not, without the
knowledge of his principal, acquire any profit or benefit from his
agency other than that contemplated by the principal at the time the
contract of agency is created. Receipt of a bribe, or a secret benefit,
is a breach of duty. Civilly, the motive of the donor is irrelevant since
there is an irrebuttable presumption that the gift was made with the
intention that the agent should be influenced by it; in other words,
the court will not inquire whether the agent was in fact influenced by
the bribe in a way prejudicial to the principal's interest.

An agent who acts in contravention of his duty is liable to
dismissal. The principal may recover from the agent either the
amount of the bribe or compensation for any actual loss sustained by
him through entry into the transaction in respect of which the bribe
was given, but he cannot recover both.[23] The law relating to
remedies is throughly complicated; its further elaboration can be
pursued elsewhere (Needham, 1979).

Disclosure of Interests, Codes of Conduct, etc.

Here, as elsewhere, sunlight is no doubt the best disinfectant. In
relation to dealings with government, both statutory and conventional rules concerning disclosure exist. Indeed, some rules go
beyond disclosure, such as the conventional rule that Ministers of
the Crown should, on appointment, divest themselves of directorships and shareholdings which would be likely to, or which might
appear to be likely to, conflict with their official duties. For a
Minister of the Crown to accept payments, rewards or compensation
in connection with his official duty, even in circumstances, if there
be such, where no crime is committed, is a grave dereliction of
official duty and must lead to resignation (Lynskey Tribunal,
Cmnd. 7617; Robinton, 1953).

The House of Commons requires that members register their
interests and disclose their interests, where relevant, in proceedings

in Parliament which include debates before the House and in its committees. Parliament can punish by contempt procedure a failure to conform to its rules. The Royal Commission on Standards of Conduct in Public Life has recommended that Parliament consider bringing the matter within the criminal law (Cmnd. 6524, para. 304).

Under the Local Government Act 1972, a member of a local authority who has a direct pecuniary interest in a contract or proposed contract must disclose it and refrain from taking part in consideration of the matter.[24] The Secretary of State has power to lift any disability.[25] A member must also disclose his interest in proposed dealings. A general notification of his interest in a specified company or body is sufficient for this purpose. These provisions have been stringently criticised as failing adequately to protect the public (Hare, 1974). Such a notification may be thought insufficient to give adequate warning. The rules might be justified as similar to those which regulate the directors of commercial companies in dealings with their companies, but those rules have recently been tightened up in respect of substantial property transactions between directors and their companies. Not only is disclosure in advance required, but directors must also disclose in the accounts of the company substantial contracts with the company in which they are interested.[26] Furthermore, the Redcliffe-Maud Committee advocated a much wider measure of disclosure by members and officers of local authorities, and the abolition of disclosure by a general written notice (Cmnd. 5636, pp. ix–x).

References and Notes

1. Public Bodies Corrupt Practices Act 1889, s. 1(1).
2. *Ibid.*, s. 1(2).
3. As amended by the Prevention of Corruption Act 1916, s. 4(2).
4. Civil Aviation Act, 1971 (c. 75), s. 62(2) making the Civil Aviation Authority a public body; Housing Act 1974 (c. 44), s. 1(1) and Sched. 1, para. 4 *re* the Housing Authority.
5. *D.P.P.* v. *Holly and Manners* [1978] A.C. 43.
6. Prevention of Corruption Act 1906, s. 1(1).
7. *Ibid.*, s. 1(2).
8. Customs and Excise Management Act 1979, s. 15.
9. Prevention of Corruption Act 1916.
10. [1960] 2 Q.B. 423; see also *Reg.* v. *Mills* (1978) 68 Cr. App. R. 154.
11. *Reg.* v. *Wellburn* (1979) 69 Cr. App. R. 254 (C.A.); *Cooper* v. *Slade* (1858) 6 H.L. Cas. 746, 773.
12. *Rex* v. *Gross* [1946] O.R. 1; *Dore* v. *The Queen* (1974) 44 D.L.R. (3d) 370 (Can. S.C.).
13. *Rex* v. *Gross, supra*; *Reg.* v. *Cooper* (1977) 74 D.L.R. (3d) 370 (Can. S.C.).
14. *Morgan* v. *D.P.P.* [1970] 3 All E.R. 1053.

15. *Reg.* v. *Carr* [1957] 1 W.L.R. 165; *Reg.* v. *Mills* (1978) 68 Cr. App. R. 154.
16. *Reg.* v. *Millray Window Cleaning Ltd.* [1962] Crim. L.R. 99.
17. *Rex* v. *Carr-Briant* [1943] K.B. 607.
18. *Sage* v. *Eicholz* [1919] 2 K.B. 171.
19. *Rex* v. *Dickinson* (1948) 33 Cr. App. R. 5; *Morgan* v. *D.P.P., supra.*
20. *D.P.P.* v. *Holly and Manners, supra; Campbell* v. *H.M. Advocate,* 1941 J.C. 68; *Graham* v. *Hart,* 1908 J.C. 26 which asserts, uniquely in the case law, that for the purposes of the 1889 Act a constable is the employee of the Chief Constable.
21. Foreign Corrupt Practices Act of 1977, P.L. 95–213.
22. See 1 Halsbury's *Laws of England* (4th ed. 1973), paras. 789 ff.
23. *T. Mahesan S/O Thambiah* v. *Malaysian Government Officers' Co-operative Housing Society Ltd.* [1978] 2 W.L.R. 444.
24. Local Government Act 1972, ss. 94 and 96.
25. *Ibid.,* s. 97.
26. Companies Act 1948, s. 199; Companies Act 1967, s. 16(*c*); Companies Act 1980, ss. 49 and 54.

7 Conspiracy to Cheat and Defraud

Conspiracy to cheat and defraud is a common law offence of uncertain extent. It is also an extremely important one. As we have seen, there are instances where valuable interests can be dishonestly infringed without the perpetrators contravening the specific statutory provisions concerning theft and deception. These lacunae are covered in the criminal law, if at all, by conspiracy to cheat and defraud. It is, for example, one of the primary legal bulwarks against rigging the Stock Exchange and the commodities markets. Conspiracy is the source from which a number of modern statutory crimes derive. The proliferation of statutory offences and the restrictive provisions of the Criminal Law Act 1977 ensure that it has lost some of its former importance. Its significance as a residual provision is, nevertheless, considerable.

It is accepted that conspiracy to cheat and defraud applies both to private persons and to public servants and bodies.[1] Where the intended victim of a conspiracy to defraud is a private individual, the object of the conspirators must be to cause him economic loss by depriving him of some property or right, corporeal or incorporeal, to which he would or might become entitled. The means must be dishonest, but they need not involve deception. Where the intended victim of a conspiracy is a person performing public duties, it is sufficient if the purpose is to cause him to act contrary to his public duty, and the intended means are dishonest. Despite the doubts of Lord Simon of Glaisdale concerning the propriety of forcing this head of conspiracy onto the Procrustean bed of cheats and frauds, it is an accepted category of the conspiracy and has thus been saved by the Criminal Law Act 1977.[2] We now turn to the elements of the offence. Much of the general law of conspiracy is alluded to here, only briefly, since general accounts of it can readily be found (Smith J.C. and Hogan, 1978; Griew, 1978).

Conspiracy to cheat and defraud does not necessarily require deception, although, historically, that was the common mode by which the offence was committed. In *Scott* v. *Metropolitan Police Commissioner*[3] the essence of the conspiracy was an agreement with certain cinema employees to abstract and copy films without the knowledge of the cinema owners or the holders of copyright. The ultimate object of the accused was to make copies and sell them on a commercial basis, thus infringing copyright. The House of Lords held that fraud could be perpetrated by deceit without secrecy and that an intent to defraud does not necessarily involve an intent to deceive. In *Scott*, the means employed was clandestine bribery.

In the case of such conspiracies, an intent to cause economic loss to the victim is required. Deprivation of property falls within this formula, but it is no more than an instance of it. In *Scott* v. *Metropolitan Police Commissioner* the indictment alleged a conspiracy to defraud such persons and companies as might be caused loss by the unlawful copying and distribution of films the copyright in which and distribution rights to which belonged to companies and persons other than the alleged conspirators. This was held to be sufficient. Yet the conspiracy did not involve a loss of property to the victims, but rather an infringement of economic value deriving from exclusiveness, and the ultimate financial rewards which derive from this.

Similarly, in *Reg.* v. *Allsopp*[4] a wide conception of economic loss was used. Where a person intends by deceit to induce another to pursue a course of conduct which puts that other's economic interests in jeopardy, he is guilty of fraud (assuming the presence of other co-conspirators), even though he does not desire that actual loss should be suffered by that other. It is sufficient that the accused was willing to place the victim in danger of suffering an economic loss. Such a loss may, the court states, be ephemeral and not lasting, or potential and not actual, but even a threat of financial prejudice, while it exists, may be measured in terms of money.[5] Similarly, it should not be necessary, in a case where a person as a result of another's fraudulent manoeuvre exchanges an asset purportedly for value, to show an entire want of value in the thing or interest obtained. It should be enough to show a substantial disparity in value, coupled with circumstances which show that the rogue concealed the fact from his victim.[6]

The boundaries of economic loss are thus problematic. They are problematic also in the sense that the word economic has no closely defined limits. The examples given above, and those discussed elsewhere in this work (of the wrongful exploitation of computer-based data, for instance), are all examples of cases in which the loss or gain can be, and is, conventionally expressed in money terms. This will, of course, comprehend the vast majority of cases dealt with in a work such as this. But apart from the question of whether the concept extends to any detriment which a court can be brought to quantify, for any purpose, in money terms—for example, damages (a suggestion which is, no doubt, too broad)—there is also the problem which arises when the victim, although suffering no loss in money terms, notwithstanding parts with property when, had he known the true facts, he would not have done so. Most of the common examples, for instance, presenting a false prescription to a pharmacist, are already covered. The general point, however, remains. It would seem that deprivation of property is covered in such circumstances; at least there is nothing in the leading cases to exclude it.

Economic loss is something of a catch-phrase, and it could prove difficult to interpret. A similar concept apparently underlies the German law of fraud. As Professor Fletcher points out, the crime of fraud is rendered broad because a wide range of interests other than title are protected against fraudulently induced transfer; it is narrower in that there must be harm to the victim's net wealth, which requires that value be not given (Fletcher, 1978, pp. 51–7). In English law a property interest is protected from fraudulent imposition as an end in itself. It would seem that economic loss must be postulated in respect of the particular person or entity upon whom the fraud is practised. In *Tarling's* case, the House of Lords considered that fraud should be charged in respect of a Hong Kong company whose property was allegedly abstracted, and not in respect of the consequential loss to its Singapore parent.[7]

Whatever the meaning of the concept, it is clear that economic loss is a necessary condition to a charge of conspiracy to cheat and defraud in the private sector. In respect of a conspiracy to cause a person performing a public duty to act contrary to his duty, no element of economic loss need be shown. It must, however, be shown that the actor acted in a public capacity and did so in a manner contrary to his official duty.[8] The principal difficulty lies in determining who is a public servant for the purpose. Clearly, a servant of a body considered for the purposes of corruption legislation to be a public body would qualify. The broad question would appear to be whether the individual carries out public duties and would include carrying out duties in the sense of those carried out by central or local government. Indeed, the phrase is broader and would include police, for example. This form of words, however, is apt to exclude officers, agents and servants of nationalised industries since they, although owned by the Crown, are expressed not to function as servants or agents of the Crown. In effect, they are treated in legal theory as autonomous bodies answerable to the Crown as owner (Friedmann and Garner, 1970; Wade, 1978).

The ambit of conspiracy to cheat and defraud depends largely on the construction of the Criminal Law Act 1977, one of the purposes of which was to abolish common law conspiracy. That Act, however, saved conspiracy to cheat and defraud and certain conspiracies to corrupt public morals and public decency. It has now been settled that section 5, which saves conspiracy to cheat and defraud and provides that conspiracies which amount to cheats and frauds at common law shall continue to be charged as such, only preserves the crime to the extent that it is necessary to fill lacunae which would otherwise appear in the law. Where, therefore, conduct can be charged as theft, or obtaining by deception, or as a conspiracy to commit either of those offences, it must be so charged.[9]

Although conspiracy to cheat and defraud can only be charged where there is no substantive offence applicable, it should not be assumed that, simply because there is such a lacuna, a charge of conspiracy may be brought to fill it; in other words, the fact that conduct is not covered by a substantive offence should not mean (whether economic loss is present or not), necessarily, that a charge of conspiracy to cheat and defraud may be brought in respect of it. There may also be a doubt as to whether the conspiracy can be charged where the conduct falls under a specific crime in some aspect but that crime does not adequately reflect the gravity of the conduct, a point discussed later in this chapter. What, therefore, is the coverage of conspiracy to cheat and defraud? It is necessary first to specify an interest which substantive offences do not protect, and then to inquire whether it can be said, essentially as matters of statutory interpretation and judicial value judgement, that conspiracy is available to protect the interest in question. A clear example of an interest which can be so protected is that of the integrity of the Stock Exchange.

In its working paper on conspiracy to defraud, the Law Commission identified interests which are otherwise ill-protected by the criminal law. The relevant instances are dealt with below. The Law Commission undertook its exercise with a view to law reform (Working Paper No. 56, 1974). Some of its assumptions have been criticised elsewhere (Leigh, 1975a). At this point, one would contend that whether a gap can be filled by the use of a conspiracy charge cannot be determined simply by looking to the historical coverage of conspiracy to cheat and defraud and by asking whether the matter is now dealt with by statute, for there is the further question of whether coverage, formerly achieved by the law of conspiracy, should now be regarded as implicitly excluded as a result of a determination not to include it within the ambit of specific legislation. Of the gaps suggested by the Law Commission the most striking is that of temporary deprivation, which, save in the obscure circumstances to which section 6 of the Theft Act 1968 applies, is not theft (Williams, G. L. 1978).

It has been suggested, rather cryptically, that the effect of *Scott* v. *Metropolitan Police Commissioner* is to bring temporary taking within the ambit of conspiracy to cheat and defraud (Smith J. C. and Hogan, 1978, p. 233). This, the author submits, would state the effect of that case both too widely and too narrowly. The gravamen of *Scott* lies not in the temporary abstraction of the thing, but in the infringement of copyright and the loss of profit to the copyright holder which follows from that. The reasons neither decide, nor indicate, what result would be reached either in the case of straightforward temporary taking, or where an employee simply uses his employer's asset in order to make a personal profit.

The Law Commission thought that such cases should be treated as conspiracies to cheat and defraud. The argument, in part, founds on common law cases, but these are unhelpful. The ambiguous case of *Reg.* v. *Button*[10] might have raised the issue, but it was decided on the obscure doctrine of merger of felony, and on the assumption that the crime was theft. Later cases raise but do not decide the issue.[11] One could hardly build an argument from decisions of this character. One could argue, even if these cases are authority for the proposition for which the Law Commission cites them, that theft legislation, by requiring an intent permanently to deprive the owner of a thing, reflects a deliberate policy decision against making simple temporary deprivation criminal.[12] Only section 6 of the Theft Act 1968 stands to the contrary, and its character is clearly exceptional.

No court has yet held that user of goods in circumstances where the owner would be entitled to assert an interest in the nature of a trust in respect of the profits, is criminal. The weight of case law is against such a contention.[13] It has been argued that an employee or agent receives property on terms requiring him to account, since such property is impressed with a trust which arises by operation of law (Smith, A. T. H. 1977). Conversion of it would thus amount to theft. The problem is a difficult one and cannot be pursued here, but, it is submitted, the section of the Theft Act 1968 in question, section 5(3), applies only to cases where receipt is on conditions agreed between the parties, or stipulated by the transferor.[14] If, of course, the theft argument were correct, it would not be necessary to invoke conspiracy to cheat and defraud.

On the other hand, where there is something more than simple temporary abstraction, as for example the use of an interest the exclusivity of which is protected, as in copyright, or the economic advantage of which would be substantially reduced by its being copied or used, as is the case with computer software, or where unfair advantage is taken by obtaining access to confidential files or materials, it seems likely that the reasoning in *Scott* would allow a conspiracy to be charged. So too, it might be possible to charge conspiracy where, under pretence of a job interview, persons worm confidential information from employees of rival firms (Oughton, 1971, p. 93). It is obviously desirable that the law relating to the protection of such interests be developed in a suitable form. The situation is not akin to the temporary borrowing of a cricket bat, and it is absurd to pretend that it is. In the meantime, conspiracy to cheat and defraud is likely to be used to protect intangibles not otherwise adequately covered. But it is not the temporary character of the taking which is crucial.

In respect of transactions involving companies, there may be cases in which directors divert or appropriate assets without committing either theft or deception. In some such cases a charge of conspiracy to cheat and defraud may not be open. Much depends upon whether the court regards the case as one which lay within the power of directors, and which could openly have been undertaken, or regards it as dishonest (and not a mere breach of fiduciary duty) and therefore a criminal abuse of powers. At least this appears to be the line taken in *Tarling's* case to which reference has already been made. The formulae employed by their Lordships are question-begging at best, since, in the law of directors' powers, the issue is not whether the act was formally within directors' powers but whether it was an abusive use of powers. *Tarling* may turn on an absence of evidence of guilty intent.

Certainly, asset-stripping operations ought to come within the offence. We have already had occasion to look at Town Centre Properties Ltd, a classic example of this. The Canadian case of *Reg.* v. *Olan* where the company was looted of blue-chip securities in favour of an asset, a demand loan, upon the rogue's valueless company, is another example.[15] Directors who deprive their company of property in exchange for an asset of greatly inferior value in order to take a benefit, plainly act dishonestly. Because of an absence of misrepresentation, the case cannot be deception. But, given evidence of dishonest intent—an intent to take a benefit which they could not have procured honestly, a charge of theft would seem applicable, *Tarling* notwithstanding. There is, however, doubt concerning the matter.

Suppose, however, that the asset were land. In England, land cannot, in general, be the subject matter of theft. The exclusion is not absolute: land can, for example, be stolen by a trustee or personal representative, or a person authorised by a power of attorney, or the liquidator of a company who appropriates land dishonestly in breach of his obligations.[16] None of these fits a company director who is a fiduciary but not a trustee. But there is no public policy which militates against the protection of interests in land through the medium of a conspiracy charge. There is a need for a substantive offence, drafted perhaps along the lines of s. 1737 of the proposed United States Draft Federal Criminal Code (1971), which creates an offence of dishonest alienation of property by a person to whom it has been entrusted in a fiduciary capacity. Sections 405 and 406 of the Indian Penal Code produce a similar result. One suggested lacuna no longer exists; the Theft Act 1968, it is clear, covers obtaining overdraft facilities by deception.[17]

Conspiracy to cheat and defraud has long been available, in some cases, at least, where the rogue created a false general appearance of solvency. Such cases do, of course, arise; businesses do sometimes trade on a false appearance of solvency. Where particular false representations are made, charges of deception may be laid under the Theft Acts 1968–78. If a limited company trades while insolvent, and goes into winding-up, a charge of fraudulent trading may lie. But where an unincorporated business trades simply on a false appearance of solvency, or a company so trades and does not go into winding-up, only a charge of conspiracy to cheat and defraud lies, assuming that there is a conspiracy. The conspiracy offence is certainly vague: it is not clear that criminal liability for trading under a false appearance of solvency extends beyond credit institutions and banks.[18] In the the case of ordinary businesses, an affirmative representation of solvency may be required, in which case the conspiracy charge is unnecessary. This sort of limitation robs conspiracy of much of its importance in this area. But the law is defective where a trader continues to do business while insolvent. Only if the business is incorporated and goes into winding-up is a substantive offence available.

Certain residual gaps may be suggested. Most are, however, covered. It is doubtful whether there is now scope for a conspiracy offence the essence of which is a combination to avoid payment for goods supplied in circumstances not covered by the Theft Act 1978. That Act, which reflects a marked change from the previous law, which did permit prosecutions for deceptions that merely delayed the creditor, deliberately reserves the criminal sanction for cases where the debtor delays the creditor, and has no intention of paying.

The same argument made above in relation to permanent deprivation applies.

Gambling offences are not the concern of this work. Of other situations once dealt with by conspiracy, most fall within the ambit of specific offences, such as, for example, the making of a false prospectus,[19] falsification of accounts[20] and the publication of false accounts.[21] We are not here concerned with deceiving machines (Smith, J.C., 1979a, para. 159). However, although most heads of commercial dishonesty are covered, in fact, some, dealing with the temporary use of property or the infringement of confidentiality, are not. These, as we have suggested in connection with computer crimes, require to be considered as a matter of some urgency and will best be dealt with by the formulation of new offences directed specifically at the kinds of harm aimed at.

We have referred to problems of gist and gravamen. The point is wholly theoretical at present. It may be asked whether the effect of *Reg.* v. *Duncalf* is that, conspiracy to cheat and defraud can only be charged in the absence of a substantive offence apt to cover any part of the transaction. *Reg.* v. *Olan* suggests the problem: would it be necessary to charge an offence under section 54 of the Companies Act 1948 (company assisting financially the purchase of its own shares) where the object of the conspiracy is to defraud the company of an asset which cannot be charged as theft? It would not seem commensurate with the extent of the ultimate loss to charge a conspiracy to contravene section 54 only, because the maximum penalty is only two years' imprisonment.[22] There may be room for an implied limitation to the general principle against charging conspiracy in *Reg.* v. *Duncalf*. The point is, perhaps, unlikely to arise frequently. The example is one in which the object of the conspirators is fraud, which is not really met by the preferment of a relatively technical charge, the office of which is to deter persons from engaging in manoeuvres which may conduce to fraud.

The *Duncalf* doctrine is not restricted to conspiracies to cheat and defraud private individuals or to cause economic loss. Here, too, substantive offences appear to cover the ground. Forgery is an obvious example.[23] Imposing on a public department to grant a licence or permission may be covered by common law conspiracy, but most such powers are protected from abuse by substantive criminal provisions. Conspiracy thus has, at best, a vestigial residual significance.

References and Notes

1. *D.P.P.* v. *Withers* [1975] A.C. 842.
2. *Ibid.*, at p. 873.
3. (1974) 60 Cr. App. R. 124 (H.L.).
4. (1977) 64 Cr. App. R. 29; see also *Reg.* v. *Olan* (1978) 21 N.R. 504 (Can. S.C.).
5. See further [1977] A.S.C.L. 153.
6. *Reg.* v. *Olan, supra.*
7. *Tarling (No. 1)* v. *Government of Singapore* (1980) 70 Cr. App. R. 77.
8. If, of course, the public servant conspires with others to act contrary to his official duty, it would be necessary in the light of the Criminal Law Act 1977 to charge that offence; see *Reg.* v. *Dytham* [1979] 2 Q.B. 722, and 1 *Russell on Crime* (12 ed. 1964), chapter 24.
9. *Reg.* v. *Duncalf* [1979] 1 W.L.R. 918, disapp. *Reg.* v. *Walters* [1979] R.T.R. 220.
10. (1848) 3 Cox C.C. 229.
11. *Reg.* v. *Radley* (1973) 58 Cr. App. R. 394.
12. See 289 H.L. Deb., cols. 1298–1326, especially per Viscount Dilhorne and Lord Wilberforce.
13. *Reg.* v. *Cullum* (1873) L.R. 2 C.C.R. 28; *Reg.* v. *Rashid* [1977] 2 All E.R. 237, disapproved on another point, *Reg.* v. *Doukas* [1978] 1 All E.R 1060.
14. See further, *Police* v. *Leaming* [1975] 1 N.Z.L.R. 471.
15. (1978) 21 N.R. 504.
16. Theft Act 1968, s. 4(2).
17. *Reg.* v. *Watkins* [1976] 1 All E.R. 578.
18. *Rex.* v. *Parker and Bulteel* (1916) 25 Cox C.C. 145.
19. Companies Act 1948, s. 44; Theft Act 1968, s. 19.
20. Theft Act 1968, s. 17.
21. Companies Act 1967, s. 12; Companies Act 1948, s. 147.
22. Companies Act 1980, s. 80 and Sched. 2; it follows, by Criminal Law Act 1977, s. 3(3), that the maximumn penalty for the conspiracy is two years.
23. For example, *Welham* v. *D.P.P.* [1961] A.C. 103.

8 Offences Relating to Securities

This chapter deals with the protection of transactions on the Stock Exchange, controls over off-exchange dealings, insider trading, and dealings in other related areas, such as controls over equity-linked insurance policies. The emphasis is upon controls through the criminal law. Institutional controls are dealt with later. As the Stock Exchange notes, the courts have had little opportunity to deal with such matters, and in some respects English law remains in a curiously undeveloped state.[1] However little used the criminal law may be, there is a need for a body of legal rules, first, to catch the more blatant forms of fraud and, second, to serve as a framework within which non-statutory regulation can operate.

Protection of Stock Exchange Transactions

English law has not developed any very extensive body of doctrine concerning the prevention of manipulation. Those few cases which have arisen have been prosecuted as cases of criminal conspiracy to cheat and defraud. Indeed, so little known is the topic that the Law Commission treatment of it was quite inadequate (Working Paper No. 56, 1974). Yet share manipulations, as we have seen, do occur. It will be recalled that current examples of making a false market include obtaining securities of a listed company cheaply, establishing a somewhat higher price by influencing movements on the Stock Exchange and then selling them off the Exchange at the listed price, which is treated as though it were a price of integrity.

The earliest reported decision on manipulation is *Rex* v. *de Berenger*.[2] Nine persons, including Lord Cochrane, the most dashing frigate captain of his day and subsequently the founder of the Chilean Navy, were indicted and subsequently convicted on a charge of conspiracy dishonestly to raise the price of government funds and securities. Moving in arrest of judgement, they argued that a conspiracy to raise the price of government funds was not a crime in the absence of some collateral object giving it a criminal character:

> . . . as if it had been shown that on that day the defendants were possessed of certain shares in the funds, and intended to sell them,

and thereby, by raising the price, to cheat the particular persons who should become the purchasers; or if the indictment had alleged that it was the day on which the commissioners for reducing the national debt were wont to purchase, and that the defendants did it with intent to enhance the price of such purchases.

A unanimous court overruled these objections, holding that it was not necessary to show either that the government as such had been injured, or that the defendants had benefited. Both the means used and the end sought were illegal. In the words of Lord Ellenborough:[3]

> ...the conspiracy is by false rumours to raise the price of the public funds and securities; and the crime lies in the act of conspiracy and combination to effect that purpose... The purpose itself is mischievous, it strikes at the price of a vendible commodity in the market, and if it gives it a fictitious price, by means of false rumours, it is a fraud levelled against all the public, for it is against all such as may possibly have anything to do with the funds on that particular day...

Similarly, in *Burns* v. *Pennell*, a civil case in which directors published misleading promotional material and paid dividends out of capital to sustain a market in the company's shares, Lord Campbell declared that:[4]

> There can be no doubt... that a conspiracy by falsehood (or by a fictitious dividend) to raise fictitiously the market value of shares of a railway company, or any other joint-stock company, that the Queen's subjects may be deceived and injured, and that at their expense a profit may be made by the conspirators, would be an indictable offence.

Neither in this nor the earlier case did the courts limit the conspiracy to any particular mode of deception; their remarks are general. Neither did they venture upon a definition of a fictitious market. No doubt the means employed would sufficiently have indicated whether the result was fictitious or not.

In *de Berenger* the court did not discuss the question whether a combination to buy or sell in large amounts for the sole purpose of raising or depressing the market price would be indictable, although there were dicta that such a combination would be criminal. These were fortified by *Scott* v. *Brown*,[5] a rescission action against a broker who had agreed to buy certain shares on the exchange for the plaintiff with the sole purpose, as the court found, of creating trading on the exchange at a premium in order to mislead the public as to the market and to induce public buying. Rescission was denied, some of the judges stating that the agreement amounted to a criminal conspiracy to defraud the public and hence should not be enforced as a matter of public policy. The effect of this decision was mitigated, however, by a subsequent decision which indicated that, where a syndicate was formed for the purpose of 'pegging' the price of a security to facilitate a secondary distribution, and the pegged price was fair, the syndicate did not constitute an illegal conspiracy so as to render unenforceable contracts entered into between the parties.[6]

English law thus came to recognise, to some extent, a public right to a free and open market which would be protected by law against improper tampering. This concept was expanded in *Reg.* v. *Aspinall*,[7] in which a prosecution was successfully brought for obtaining registration of a security on the London Stock Exchange through false representations for the purpose of inducing traders to believe that the rules of the exchange had been complied with. There was no allegation that the object was to injure traders by inducing them to buy shares that were inferior in value to what they appeared to be. Indeed, the defendants were found not guilty upon a further count which averred an intent to defraud the public of money. The case thus stands for the proposition that the false listing is a criminal tampering with a public market, the inevitable tendency of which is to harm third persons; it is therefore criminal, notwithstanding that there is, apparently, no intent to defraud individual members of the public.

Scott v. *Brown* contains a further dictum to the effect that a third person induced to buy from the manipulators at an unfair price may sue any or all of them for damages. In fact, in most cases where third persons sought damages from a market manipulator, the courts either refused to hurdle the barrier of remote injury, or refused to expand the traditional limitations of a civil action based on conspiracy, or became enmeshed in the traps of reliance and privity that bound the common law action of deceit. In criminal law, *Reg.* v. *Gurney*[8] holds that such a conspiracy must be charged generally as a conspiracy to rig the market and not, where the purchase takes place in the impersonal market of the Stock Exchange, as a conspiracy to obtain by false pretences. Again, lack of privity is the key. Thus, both in the criminal law of false pretences and in the civil law of deceit, liability founds on the basis that the victim placed direct reliance on representations made expressly to him.[9] The courts refused to adopt the idea of a tainted market as an independent ground for civil liability. Such liability remained grounded on traditional concepts of fraud and privity, and, in consequence, damages were awarded only where the plaintiff could establish a relationship with the defendant in the nature of contract or trust.[10] Nor could he sue on a false prospectus where he purchased in the market because he was not in privity with the issuer.[11] Conspiracy was held not to create any new civil rights in the plaintiff.

English courts, bounded by notions of privity and remoteness of damages, never thought to hold that a plaintiff might have a civilly enforceable right that a defendant should not tamper with the integrity of a securities market. That protection was left to the criminal law. From this, two consequences flowed. First, because of the difficulties in proving criminal conspiracy, the principal regulatory agency became the Stock Exchange itself, acting through its rules upon its members. Secondly, in marked contrast to the United States, civil actions could not be, and were not, relied upon as vehicles of public redress. There was, and is, a possible charge of conspiracy to rig the market. It does not follow, however, that a combination to affect the market price in shares will give rise to criminal liability. Such combinations are lawful where they are entered into for the purpose of stabilising the market. Here, we deal with secondary distributions, for example sales of large blocks of shares by institutional holders. Primary distributions, that is, allotments of shares on the basis of a prospectus issued by a company or on its behalf, are not affected, because in any event a company may not issue shares at a discount.[12]

It is of the essence of both manipulation and stabilisation that the market in securities be prevented from reaching the levels which it would reach if the promoters were not actively trading in the securities in question. Hence, in both cases, there is an intent to affect the market price in securities. The courts must distinguish between those instances which are manipulation, and therefore unlawful, and those which are stabilisation and thus permitted. In a criminal prosecution, the issue will be one of dishonesty for a jury.

In *Sanderson and Levi* v. *The British Westralian Mine and Share Corporation Limited*[13] jobbers who entered into an agreement with promoters and certain companies to pool shares, regulating the number to be placed upon the market at any one time and regulating the price at which they would be offered, found themselves, at the conclusion of the agreement, with excess shares on their hands. They then called on the other parties concerned, under the agreements, to take the excess shares off their hands. The companies and individuals refused, alleging that the contract was an illegal contract to rig the market, and thus unenforceable. The court upheld the agreement. It found that the companies were well-managed, that the shares were of substantial value and that the price asked was fair in the state of the Australian market. There was no intent to defraud. Thus, the pool, created to stabilise the market, was not illegal. Many years later, an American federal court, discussing the case, concluded that this was a rare instance in which a pool lacked any fraudulent connotations.[14]

This particular mechanism would not be used today; brokers would be asked to purchase shares from jobbers, and told that the parties involved would clear up their position at a given price at the end of the day. The manoeuvre is treated as lawful by the Stock Exchange, provided that there is a real market in the shares. Where, therefore, persons desire to sell large quantities of shares and to stabilise the market while doing so, market-support buying is treated as legitimate. Indeed, in the case of Eurobonds, the managers reserve the right to make market purchases in order to stabilise prices during the first weeks of the market. The Stock Exchange also treats as legitimate market-support action in a share-for-share take-over where the bidder's friends buy shares in the bidder in order to sustain the momentum of the transaction. Again, this would seem to be legal stabilisation within narrow limits. (*Maxwell Scientific International (Distribution Services) Limited*, 1973, pp. 433–7, 491–527). But even where market manipulation cannot be shown, such share purchase transactions can involve breaches both of the prohibition against a company providing financial assistance for the purchase of its own shares, and of the directors' loan prohibitions (*London and County Securities Group Limited*, 1976, p. 35; *Vehicle and General Insurance Company Limited*, 1976, p. 39).

All this is not to suggest that the view taken by the Stock Exchange of stabilising manoeuvres necessarily represents the view which a court or jury would take. But the Stock Exchange appears to operate the same criteria as the courts, and its view of the regularity of transactions engaged in, in the light of the workings of the market, is bound to have a profound influence upon the thinking of prosecutors, judges and jurors if such a matter were to be considered for prosecution or come before the courts. The question arises whether reforms might be suggested. It is clear that a criminal provision is needed, however effective self-regulation by the Stock Exchange, or commodities exchanges, may be. One cannot punish other frauds by the criminal law and leave frauds on the Stock Exchange to internal discipline, even assuming that guilty persons were always members of the Stock Exchange. It is also evident that liability should not be made to depend solely on the presence or absence of an element of conspiracy. Nor can reliance be placed solely on administrative law measures. Some criminal provision is necessary in cases of fraudulent rigging.

Extensive provision is made in the criminal law of some English-speaking countries to deal with the problem. In Canada and in New South Wales in Australia, there are very similar provisions to which we might look with advantage. The principal provision in New South Wales is section 109 of the Securities Industry Act 1976. It provides:

> 109(1). A person shall not create, or cause to be created, or do anything that is calculated to create, a false or misleading appearance of active trading in any securities on a stock market in the State, or a false or misleading appearance with respect to the market for, or the price of, any such securities.

The Canadian provision, section 338 of the Criminal Code 1970, is similar, save that it refers to the public market price of stocks, shares, merchandise or anything that is offered for sale to the public. It thus comprehends dealings in unlisted securities and commodities as well. Both provisions obviously derive from conspiracy to cheat and defraud, *sans* conspiracy, which is not a necessary element. We need not venture upon an extensive discussion of the case law interpreting the Canadian provision in particular. It is perhaps enough to say that both provisions are broad and functional in character, the essence of them, apart from guilty intent, being manipulation of the market. These provisions are not limited to any particular method of manipulation.[15]

The leading Canadian case considers the relationship between manipulation and stabilisation (in effect, as we have seen, share dealing carried on with the intention of preventing precipitous variations in price) and concludes that the hallmark of manipulation is inducing share movements completely unrelated to the intrinsic value of the securities.[16] This formulation is consistent with the English cases noted earlier and, as will be seen, with the applicable rule of the Stock Exchange as well. It is, admittedly, an imprecise standard and, given the strictness with which criminal offences must be proved, really confines the operation of the section to blatant cases. There will, therefore, always be a need for more refined controls by government, industry or both but, within its limits, it is a worthwhile provision.

The second provision which might be considered is exemplified by section 340 of the Canadian Criminal Code, to which section 109(2) of the New South Wales Act corresponds. This derives not from English law but from section 9a of the United States Securities Exchange Act 1934. It provides:

340. Everyone who, through the facility of a stock exchange, curb market, or other market, with intent to create a false or misleading appearance of active public trading in a security or with intent to create a false or misleading appearance with respect to the market price of a security:

(a) effects a transaction in the security that involves no change in the beneficial ownership thereof;

(b) enters an order for the purchase of the security, knowing that an order of substantially the same size at substantially the same price for the sale of the security has been or will be entered for the same or different persons, or

(c) enters an order for the sale of the security, knowing that an order of substantially the same size at substantially the same time and substantially the same price for the purchase of the security has been or will be entered by or for the same or different persons,

is guilty of an indictable offence and is liable to imprisonment for five years.

This section has never been wholly successful in practice because it has always been difficult to prove that orders for purchases and sales matched.[17] It is not necessary to show an intent to defraud particular individuals; the section protects the integrity of the market itself.[18] It is, therefore, a fraud provision particularised by reference to the method employed, a method which we have identified as wash trading. In my submission, it is unwise to rely on a provision so closely tied to a particular method of fraud. Nevertheless, despite the fact that neither the Canadian nor the American provisions have been totally successful, the American Law Institute in its *Federal Securities Code* proposes to retain it (American Law Institute, 1972, s. 1308, revised).

Both the Model Securities Code and section 110 of the New South Wales Act contain provisions against touting. To the extent that touting is intended to create a false market in shares on the Stock Exchange, it is not adequately covered at present in English law, and adoption of anti-touting provisions would seem to be necessary. Dealings in privity where such statements are made are now regulated.

Insider Trading

We have seen that attitudes towards insider trading gradually changed from toleration to strong disapproval. The Stock Exchange, and many companies, adopted codes of conduct to regulate directors in the purchase and sale of securities in their companies.[19] These rules, and in particular the Stock Exchange Model Code, sought to preserve reasonable freedom for directors to purchase and sell securities of their company, subject to notifying the chairman or other directors nominated for the purpose, save when the director wishing to sell was in possession of price-sensitive information which had not been made public. In any event, directors were precluded from dealing in their companies' securities on considerations of a short-term nature. Unlike the legislation which has just been introduced, the Stock Exchange Model Code has the virtues of simplicity and clarity.

The City institutions and others sought, however, to have insider trading made criminal, not in the expectation that many convictions would be registered, but rather in the hope that the moral message of the criminal law would reinforce the inhibitions against insider dealing.[20] The reasons for disapproval of insider trading are various. It is thought to be unfair in itself to persons who buy securities in the market: the trader is an unequal party to any bargain since he alone is in possession of full information. In most cases it involves the misuse of a position of trust and confidence. It can cause conflicts of duty and interest in the timing of announcements, and even in the timing of underlying events. Furthermore, it damages the reputation of securities markets if investors come to think that favourable deals are reserved for a privileged few (Schotland, 1967; City Company Law Committee, 1976). The government was influenced by these considerations.

The insider trading legislation was framed on the assumption, surely a brave assumption given the fact that most complaints about securities matters involve insider trading, that it is a relatively rare phenomenon (Financial Institutions Committee, 1980, p. 310). The government considered that the need was to clear up the market in quoted securities where the big insiders have operated. It was not thought necessary to legislate for face-to-face dealings, because it was assumed that persons engaged in such transactions could protect themselves.[21] The ensuing legislation is undeniably complex. One must hope that it will help to create a moral tone, because it is unlikely that anyone will be convicted under its provisions unless, indeed, he is subject to expiative impulses of a peculiarly intense and durable character.

The legislation applies to anyone who, within the six months preceding the trading, has been knowingly connected with a company. This requires both that he be connected and that he be knowingly connected. A person is connected if he is a director of the company concerned or a related company, or if he occupies a position as an officer, other than director, or as an employee of that company or a related company, or a position involving a professional or business relationship between himself, or his employer, or a company of which he is a director, and the first company or a related company, which may reasonably be expected to give him access to price-sensitive information and which it would be reasonable to expect a person in his position not to disclose except for the proper performance of his functions. This then is the formal nexus.[22]

Unpublished price-sensitive information is defined in terms of specific matters relating to the company, not general matters, so that financial analysts and journalists who trade on the basis of intelligent deduction will not be caught. It must not be generally known to persons who are accustomed or would be likely to deal in the securities in question, and it must be of a character which, if it were known to them, would be likely materially to affect the price of the securities.[23]

The first significant prohibition applies to insider dealing in listed securities on the Stock Exchange. It covers, first, persons who are or were connected with a company within the preceding six months, and prohibits them from dealing on a recognised stock exchange in the securities of that company on the basis of unpublished price-sensitive information.[24] The conditions for liability are threefold: the person must hold the information by virtue of being connected with the company; it would be reasonable to expect a person so connected, and in the position by virtue of which he is so connected, not to disclose the information save for the proper performance of the functions attaching to that position; and the person must know that the information is unpublished price-sensitive information in relation to those securities.

Similar conditions of imputation apply to the succeeding category of persons, knowingly connected persons who by virtue of their connection with one company acquire price-sensitive information concerning another company with which their own company engages in actual or contemplated transactions. Such a transaction may no longer be contemplated, but that does not prevent the information from being price-sensitive, for it may well be so.[25] While this provision could clearly relate to information arising from a take-over or negotiations to that effect, it has a wider connotation. It could, for example, relate to information concerning a joint venture.

The legislation then deals with persons who obtain information from an insider (in American, a 'tippee'). Such a person is precluded from dealing either in the shares of the company of which his informant is an insider, or in shares of the company in respect of which the informant obtained information by virtue of his position as an insider of another company with which the former company was dealing.[26] Here again, there are considerable hurdles to be overcome. The 'tippee' must know that the information is price-sensitive in nature and unpublished. If the information refers to a company with which the insider's company has, or has had dealings, it must relate specifically to the transaction in right of which the informant obtained his information. Information otherwise obtained by the informant, for example other price-sensitive information incautiously disclosed by a director of the other company at a business lunch or social occasion, would not fall within the section and the 'tippee' could deal in reliance on it. Furthermore, the 'tippee' must know that he obtains the information from a connected person, and must know or believe that this person, the insider, held the information by virtue of his insider status, and he must know or have reasonable cause to believe that it would be reasonable to expect the insider not to disclose the information except for the proper performance of his duties in the company.

In an endeavour to ensure that a merchant bank, for example, which acts in several capacities shall not deal in one capacity in inside information which it obtained in another capacity, the statute prohibits it, or an informant who knowingly obtains information from it, from dealing in those securities.[27] These categories of prohibited persons are also prohibited from counselling or procuring another person from dealing in such securities, knowing or having reasonable cause to believe that that person would deal with them on a recognised stock exchange.[28] Counselling or procuring dealings face-to-face is not covered. Equally, an insider is prohibited from disclosing information to any person who he knows or believes may make use of it for the purposes of dealing on a recognised stock exchange.[29]

There are extensive exceptions to this carefully circumscribed liability. Trading is not prohibited where its object is not the making of a profit or the avoidance of loss.[30] This curious wording is apparently intended to permit trustees or legal personal representatives to sell securities pursuant to their legal duties without incurring criminal penalties for doing so.[31] But, plainly, the timing of such transactions may be dictated by a desire to get the best terms available on disposal. Profit or loss is thus in contemplation. It simply is not adequate to remark, as the government did, that a trustee owes his beneficiary no duty to exploit information when to do so would be a criminal offence. Must a trustee then postpone realisation, whatever the state of the estate, or resign without giving reasons for doing so? There is a need to work out proper rules for such situations. The legislation could, however, be widely construed, so that dealings by such persons would only be instances of the exemption. It could then extend to share purchases made to block a take-over bid, and not for private profit (City Company Law Committee, 1976).

There is a cumbersome provision the effect of which seems to be that trustees and personal representatives may act on the advice of a financial adviser unless he, she or it appears to be tainted by inside information. Liquidators, receivers, trustees and jobbers are similarly protected.[32] Similar provisions apply to Crown servants and to those who obtain information from them. This marks a recognition of increased governmental involvement in the affairs of companies, especially in respect of planning agreements, which were a feature of Labour Government policy. Insider trading provisions could, for example, incriminate lay members, including trade union members, of a government board, who traded on the basis of confidential information, or who informed others that they might do so.[33] There are provisions concerning off-market dealers,[34] and to catch persons who counsel, procure or inform others who may deal abroad on other than a recognised stock exchange.[35] The intention is to catch domestic and international dealings both on stock exchanges and on the kerb market. There is a saving provision in respect of acts done in good faith in respect of an international bond issue.[36]

Insider trading is punishable either on summary conviction or on indictment, in which case a maximum term of two years' imprisonment applies.[37] Prosecution requires the consent of the Secretary of State or the Director of Public Prosecutions.[38] As to the civil consequences of an infraction, the legislation provides—no doubt inevitably, given the practical problems of any other solution—that no transaction shall be voidable simply because it is entered into in violation of the provisions.[39] The insider trading legislation could do more harm than good. It could certainly, as will be seen, impair the working of self-regulatory agencies.

Its defects are obvious. Face-to-face dealings should have been included. The notion that one can protect oneself in such situations is not always true; no doubt those who dealt with Sir Denys Lowson or Littler thought that they knew them well. The vice of trading on a basis of inequality where one person has inside information is the same. Even where insider traders come under a duty to disclose in virtue of a fiduciary position which they occupy, one cannot be certain that the law contains adequate controls.[40] Even the City Company Law Committee, which proposed the exclusion of private dealings, envisaged remedial changes to the law of contract to ameliorate inequalities. In Australia, the insider in face-to-face dealings is liable, subject to a defence if he satisfies the court that the other party knew or ought to have known the facts beforehand.[41]

The conditions for the imputation of liability are absurdly complicated. A person must both objectively meet the conditions for a connected person, and know of this. No problem arises where a director is concerned, but it could be difficult to prove that a man knew that his relationship to a company was such as might reasonably be supposed to give him access to confidential information. Suppose that at any given time he is, unusually, charged with the performance of functions which result in his obtaining price-sensitive information. Seemingly, he is neither connected nor knowingly connected. He may, of course, be liable as 'tippee', provided that he knowingly obtained information from an insider. But what of 'tippees' from him? It is not at all clear why a corporate employee who knows that he has price-sensitive information should not be directly precluded from trading on the basis of it, whatever his precise status with the company. Nor, as we have noted, is it desirable that persons dealing in confidence with another company should only be precluded from dealing on inside information relating to the particular transaction. A breach of confidence is involved in either case, and the appearance of unfairness to third parties is also present. The Australian legislation in this regard is simpler and more comprehensive.[42]

The so-called Chinese wall exemption from liability is also better expressed in Australia; in the English legislation, it applies only to take-overs. For example, in Australia, trading by a financial adviser for clients other than those involved in the transactions by virtue of which the information is obtained is permitted, provided that the firm's decision to trade was taken by another person in its employ, that the firm had arrangements to ensure that the information was not communicated to that person, and that information and advice was not in fact communicated.[43] This provision, akin to that proposed by the Conservative Government of 1973, would have provided a better solution to the problem.

What of persons who obtain information at second hand? A recipient of information is only liable where he obtains information from a connected person, an insider. One who receives information from a connected person cannot himself lawfully inform another of it, but if he does so, that other seems not to be criminally liable. In some circumstances, even a connected person, for example a director who is not an officer, might be able to deal. Suppose, for instance, that X, a non-executive director or financial adviser of Y Ltd, obtains information that Y Ltd and Z Ltd are contemplating a joint venture and that the matter has been broached between the managing directors. X obtains his information from, say, Q, Z Ltd's director's wife with whom he is having an affair. May X deal with impunity? The answer would seem to be that he can. He does not receive the information from a connected person and, although himself a connected person, he does not hold information in virtue of that capacity. It may be possible to invoke the civil law of constructive trust to deal with this case; one would have either to treat the information as confidential information misuse of which would carry with it a consequent obligation to restore any profit, or, more broadly, if a court could be brought so far, treat the misuse of the information as carrying a possible threat to the integrity of the company and impose liability for the hypothetical injury which it suffers thereby.[44]

American courts impose liability on the footing that an insider who deals on the basis of confidential information is in breach of his fiduciary duty, and impose a liability on him to account for his profits.[45] Even if this lead were followed, it would be difficult to impose such liability on an unconnected recipient of information from an initial recipient because the former person is unconnected with, and *prima facie* owes no duties to, the company. The topic is a difficult one, and the possible solution, through constructive trust, cannot be pursued here. It is, however, unlikely that such a remedy would be implied. There is no equitable duty on directors, independent of statute, to refrain from insider dealing, and English courts have been reluctant to imply novel civil actions from the provisions of new criminal statutes (Leigh, 1979). It is curious that such a lacuna was left. The City Company Law Committee (1976) saw the problem with directors and recommended that the prohibition should extend to all dealings by directors whether they acquired information as outsiders or not. But the law requires that the director hold information by virtue of his connection with the company.

The greatest defects in the Act stem from an absence of investigative machinery, and a failure to address the problem of civil recovery. The powers which apply to inspections under the Companies Acts do not necessarily apply to insider trading, though they may have some incidental use where a director, as in the Lowson affair, abuses his powers in dealing with his company. Otherwise, even if insider dealing is fraudulent, it is not necessarily fraud in connection with the management of the company. Furthermore, although a court must consider insider trading both criminal and disreputable, it would not necessarily consider it to be fraudulent. There is no intent to deprive another of an opportunity which is regarded as belonging in law to that other, nor, in general, is there a legal rule that one who sells, even face-to-face, must disclose everything which he knows to the other side. These considerations could weigh against a finding of fraud.

Without proper investigative machinery, the task of enforcement will probably be impossible. There is no way otherwise of tracing transactions. Even where foreign institutions are not involved, there is no general power to compel disclosure of financial records to the authorities, nor may the police obtain a warrant to search for them. The government proceeded from the erroneous premise that such powers were not needed elsewhere in the criminal law and therefore were not needed to cope with insider trading.[46] The Act, reflecting a wrong premise followed by a *non sequitur*, gives no such power. Even in a jurisdiction like France, where wide powers of investigation and surveillance are given to the authorities, detection is difficult. It becomes yet more so when dealings take place through foreign sources (Delmas-Marty, 1977; Puech, 1974). Also, a point discussed later, it must be doubtful whether, for the future, the City institutions can expect full co-operation from institutions which may, thereby, incriminate themselves or their customers.

The failure to provide civil remedies, again, must militate against effective enforcement. In the United States there are arbitrary provisions to enable the insider's corporation to recover short-swing profits, an evil identified here in the Stock Exchange Model Code, for example (American Law Institute, 1972, s.1413). The American provisions are complicated and need not be dealt with here but, by arbitrarily designating the insider's company as the recipient of the profit which the insider must disgorge, they create an additional pressure point in the system. In the light of these considerations, it seems improbable that the insider trading provisions will prove to be of value.

Other Transactions in Securities

Criminal law controls over dealings in securities generally are contained in the Prevention of Fraud (Investments) Act 1958, and in regulations thereunder.[47] These apply to most forms of securities, including shares, debentures and unit trusts. Advertising for short-term money deposits is dealt with by the Banking Act 1979. Insurance contracts are dealt with by the Insurance Companies Act 1974. The Prevention of Fraud (Investments) Act 1958 derives from a report of a Departmental Committee in 1937, the Bodkin report (Cmd. 5539). Its primary emphasis was upon the control of individuals and bodies engaged in the sale of shares, and the principal vice with which Britain was then beset was high-pressure selling. The administrative controls instituted by the Act and its forerunner,[48] which have dealt effectively with the particular problem, are dealt with below.

The principal criminal provision of the 1958 Act is that of fraudulently inducing persons to invest money. The mental element required is that of recklessly making a representation which, in context, describes conduct objectively; that is, as a representation made by a person in the absence of circumstances tending to support its truth.[49] *Tarling's* case establishes that there must be a direct representation. Market rigging which causes share values to rise is not of itself an inducement within the section.[50] The representations involved may be statements, promises or forecasts. Very broadly, they relate to inducements to persons to deal in securities, or to enter into agreements the purpose of which is to secure a profit from the yield of securities or by reference to fluctuations in the value of securities (which could refer to gambling on the marginal rise or fall in value of securities), or to take part in arrangements with respect to property other than securities, for example commodities, or to participate in profits or income from dealing in or managing or holding such property. Because the section applies not only to securities, but also to commodities and other forms of property, it strikes at the livestock marketing schemes discussed in chapter 3, and the more modern abuses deriving from schemes advertising investments in precious metals.

Can certain manifestations of insider trading come within this section (Rider, 1978b)? The question must turn upon whether concealment of the trader's status is dishonest, assuming the parties to be in privity and the inducement is to enter into an arrangement for the acquisition or disposal of securities. There are situations to which neither *caveat emptor* nor *caveat vendor* applies. A director who, as in the Lowson cases, persuades his company to sell its securities to a person who, unknown to the company, acts as his nominee, must be in breach of his fiduciary duty to the company. Does he conceal dishonestly? Common sense would answer affirmatively; *Tarling's* case may return a negative answer.[51] Breach of fiduciary duty is not dishonesty as such. When does it become so? Neither in *Tarling's* case nor in the facts postulated here would a director be absolutely barred from taking a benefit, though in this case he would be obliged to declare his contractual interest, on pain of enabling the company to avoid the contract. Perhaps the answer is, simply, that breach of fiduciary duty alone, even though the director obtains a private benefit thereby, is not *prima facie* evidence of dishonesty, but certainly does not exclude it and is a factor to be taken into consideration.

Where, of course, a method of valuation is used which is known to the director (as in the Lowson cases) to be inappropriate and to understate the value of the securities, there can be no doubt that the offence under section 13 is made out, since a statement may be false as much by reason of what it omits as by what it contains.[52] Indeed, a reckless statement about value would be enough, that is, one known to be untrue or unfounded in fact. This provision is buttressed by section 14 which (with exceptions for authorised dealers) makes it an offence to distribute circulars inviting the public to enter into agreements of the sort struck at by section 13, or having such documents in possession for the purpose of distribution. Wide powers to issue search warrants are provided for. Prosecutions require the consent of the Department of Trade or the Director of Public Prosecutions. The offence is punishable, on indictment, by a maximum period of two years imprisonment or a fine of £500 or both, or, on summary conviction, by a maximum of six months imprisonment or a fine of £100 or both. It is clearly regarded seriously.

The Licensed Dealers (Conduct of Business) Rules 1960 contain in rule 6 an important provision intended to curb high-pressure selling. It bans unsolicited house calls, including telephone calls, and provides that a salesman, before entering into a contract, must give the customer a written statement of its terms. In particular, the ban upon such selling by telephone is apt to inhibit substantially the operation known in North America as a 'boiler house' of numbers of salesmen making unsolicited telephone calls offering bargains which must be snapped up quickly or not at all. As we shall see, Investors Overseas Syndicate was forced in Britain to offer equity-linked insurance policies rather than simply securities, in order to circumvent the Act.

The Department of Trade has recently published a consultative document which considers possible reforms to the Act (1977, Cmnd. 6893). Most of these are dealt with below in connection with the Department's regulatory functions. Among the proposals noted at this juncture are those which suggest that restrictions on invitations to the public to invest, whether in the form of circulars, or investments, or in other ways, should be strengthened, that the activities of agents of overseas companies should be brought within the Act, that financial penalties should be increased, and that 'agreements' and 'arrangements' should be defined in order to clarify the meaning of section 13, the most important fraud provision. It is not clear, for example, whether both terms imply a contractual arrangement, though they probably do, nor how wide the concept of an arrangement is, though it clearly comprehends investment schemes of the classic sort relating to securities and to commodities which promise a share in the property managed and of the profits resulting from disposition.

Controls under Banking Legislation

The Banking Act 1979 contains a structure of offences relating to advertising for deposits which is similar to that found in the Prevention of Fraud (Investments) Act 1958 relating to securities. It is a serious offence fraudulently to induce persons to invest on deposit or to enter into or offer to enter into any agreement for the purpose.[53] The penalty on conviction on indictment is a term not exceeding seven years' imprisonment, or a fine, or both. Deposit does not include a loan made to an institution upon terms involving the issue of debentures and other securities, nor does it include a loan made by the Bank of England, a recognised bank, or a licensed institution.

The Act also controls advertisements for deposits. After consultation with the Bank of England, the Treasury may, by statutory instrument, regulate the issue, form and content of advertisements inviting the making of deposits. Advertisement is widely defined to include notices, signs, labels, showcards, circulars, lists, catalogues, photographs, cinematographic films, pictures or models, sound broadcasting, or television.[54] Statutory instruments to be issued will presumably deal with disclosure of minimum amounts to be invested, periods of investment, and notices of interest, assets, liabilities, and the cover for guaranteed assets. Plainly, however, such criminal provisions as these are ancillary to the main scheme of control through the licensing and supervision of institutions by the Bank of England.[55]

Insurance

Similar provisions now regulate the business of insurance. Certain classes of insurance constitute an investment medium for many people as well as a protection against death or loss of earnings. Generally speaking, policies offer a guaranteed return and, frequently, an opportunity to share in the profits. However, in the 1950s a new type of insurance began to emerge, the equity-linked policy (Raw, 1977). The value of the investment was determined by the value of securities to which the policy was linked. The Scott report defined it thus (1973, Cmnd. 5281):

... linked life insurance consists of all life assurance and annuity contracts, the benefits of which are calculated in whole or in part by reference to the value of, or the income from, specified assets or groups of assets or by reference to movements in a share price or other index, whether or not subject to deductions in respect of fees or expenses.

At first linked to units in an authorised unit trust, policies were later linked to internal funds, that is, funds internal to the company, to property, and even to the *Financial Times Actuaries Share Index.* Indeed, it was not necessary that units or securities actually be bought. The essence of some schemes is that benefits be calculated according to a formula keyed to the performance of units or securities or to the increase in the value of assets. This also makes it possible for insurance companies to offer a guaranteed minimum. Equity-linked policies proved popular both with insurance companies and with the investing public. By 1971, they accounted for 21 per cent of ordinary long-term business. To investors they purported to offer a hedge against inflation; to issuers they offered the possibility of selling securities with the income tax advantages deriving from the insurance medium and doing so door-to-door, thus circumventing the Prevention of Fraud (Investments) Act 1958. As investments, equity-linked policies were and are subject to the vicissitudes of the economy, in particular the unstable state of the securities market and, especially in the 1970s, the property market. There were other problems as well. While the business attracted the well-established insurance companies, it also attracted participants whose essence was that of a speculator rather than an insurer. In the case of Dover plan, an Investors Overseas Syndicate venture, the following problems emerged: high service charges on both the first and second year premiums, and high-pressure selling coupled with misleading performance forecasts (Raw, Page and Hodgson, 1971). Widespread investor complaint occurred.

The Scott Report which appeared before the secondary banking and insurance crash of 1974 is a characteristically bland document. It did, however, identify certain problems. Among these are the difficulty of valuing properties upon which schemes are based, the need to ensure that securities and assets have a ready market, the problem of service charges, and the problem of high-pressure selling. It concluded that equity-linked policies should continue to be regulated as insurance, thus enabling policies to be sold door-to-door. The basic prohibition against misleading forecasts should remain. The types of assets and indices employed should be regulated. Matters such as the spread of investments were thought not to be a proper subject of governmental regulation.

The rule with respect to unit trusts is, of course, the exact opposite: the Department of Trade will not authorise a unit trust unless it has an adequate spread of assets. But in insurance *laissez-faire*, for weal or woe, is the dominant philosophy, mitigated by controls over solvency, the status of directors and officers, the integrity of valuations so far as this can be assured by rules, and above all, by disclosure. A draft code of conduct drawn up by the industry was warmly commended. Proposals to license insurance salesmen were disapproved on the singular ground that, 'We doubt whether it is practical to enforce standards of integrity and ethical selling through a licensing system' (1973, Cmnd. 5281, para. 214). It hardly seems necessary to insist that such a licensing system is part of the machinery of control in relation to securities and that in North America, for example, such schemes of control are universally considered to be necessary.

The law reflects the influence of these views. Section 63 of the Insurance Companies Act 1974 contains a provision like that of section 13 of the Prevention of Fraud (Investments) Act 1958 prohibiting the use of misleading, false or deceptive promises or forecasts to induce another to enter into contracts of insurance. Regulations for giving information and regulating contracts are provided for. Breach of the regulations, especially advertising insurance in contravention, and the use of false representations, are offences punishable either on indictment or summary conviction.[56] Provision is made for the making of regulations relating to equity-linked policies.[57] Breach of such regulations is made an offence.

The basic matters subject to regulation concern the valuation of properties to which such policies are linked. They specify the descriptions of property by reference to which benefits may be determined.[58] At present, these comprise quoted securities, land in certain specified jurisdictions, loans secured by mortgages on such lands, units in an authorised unit trust scheme, and certain loans accepted by the Bank of England and other specified bodies. The indices by reference to which benefits may be determined are also specified. The Act and the regulations do not apply to contracts with policy-holders who are not ordinarily resident within the United Kingdom. The Department of Trade has indicated that regulations will be made concerning the valuation of such assets and who may value them. There is a need to ensure that policies will not be offered for sale unless benefits are linked to assets for which there is a market that is not unduly narrow and specialised and which permits sound and objective valuation.[59]

References and Notes

1. Wilson Committee, Second Stage Evidence, vol. 4, *The Stock Exchange*, para. 73 (1979).
2. (1814) 3 M. & S. 67.
3. *Ibid.*, at pp. 72–3.
4. (1849) 2 H.L.C. 497 at p. 525.
5. *Scott* v. *Brown, Doering, McNab & Co.* [1892] 2 Q.B. 724.
6. *Sanderson & Levi* v. *The British Westralian Mine and Share Corporation* (1898) 43 Sol. J. 45.
7. (1876) 1 Q.B.D. 730, aff'd.(1876) 2 Q.B.D. 48.
8. (1869) 14 Cox C.C. 414.
9. *Peek* v. *Gurney* (1873) L.R. 6 H.L. 377, overruling *Bedford* v. *Bagshaw* (1859) 4 H. & N. 538.
10. *Barry* v. *Croskey* (1861) 2 J. & H. 1.
11. *Salaman* v. *Warner* (1891) 64 L.T. (N.S.) 598, aff'd. (1891) 7 T.L.R. 484.
12. Companies Act 1980, s. 21.
13. (1898) 43 Sol. J. 45. Both trial and appeal judgements are also reproduced as appendices to *United States* v. *Brown*, 5 F. Supp. 81 (1935) p. 90.
14. *United States* v. *Brown*, 79 F. 2d 321 (CA2, 1935), aff'g 5 F. Supp. 81.
15. *Reg.* v. *Violi* (1974) 43 C.C.C. (2d) 567.
16. *McNaughton* v. *The Queen* (1975) 33 C.R.N.S. 279.
17. *Reg.* v. *Lampard* [1969] S.C.R. 373.
18. *Reg.* v. *MacMillan* [1969] 2 C.C.C. 289, and for the background, see R. Croft (1975), chapter 3.
19. Wilson Committee, Second Stage Evidence, vol. 4, *The Stock Exchange*, Appx. E (1979).
20. *Ibid.*, pp. 27–8.
21. House of Commons, Standing Committee A, Companies Bill [Lords], col. 616, 6 December 1979.
22. Companies Act 1980, s. 73(1).
23. *Ibid.*, s. 73(2).
24. *Ibid.*, s. 69(1).
25. *Ibid.*, s. 69(2).
26. *Ibid.*, s. 68(3).
27. *Ibid.*, s. 68(4), (5).
28. *Ibid.*, s. 68(6).
29. *Ibid.*, s. 69(7).
30. *Ibid.*, s. 69(8)(*a*).
31. *Ibid.*, s. 69(8)(*a*) read with s. 69(11).
32. *Ibid.*, s. 69(8)(*c*).
33. *Ibid.*, s. 69.
34. *Ibid.*, ss. 70(1) and (2).
35. *Ibid.*
36. *Ibid.*, s. 71.
37. *Ibid.*, s. 71(1)(*a*) and (*b*).
38. *Ibid.*, s. 71(2).
39. *Ibid.*, s. 72(3).
40. *Tarling (No. 1)* v. *Government of Singapore* (1980) 70 Cr. App. R. 77.
41. New South Wales, Security Industry Act, no. 3, 1976, s. 112(10).

42. *Ibid.*, s. 112(1)-(3).

43. *Ibid.*, s. 112(10).

44. *Diamond* v. *Oreamuno*, 24 N.Y.S. (2d) 494 (1969).

45. *Thomas* v. *Roblin Industries Inc.*, 520 F. 2d. 1393 (1975).

46. House of Commons, Sess. 1979–80, Standing Committee A, Companies Bill [Lords], cols. 558–9.

47. See Licensed Dealers (Conduct of Business) Regulations 1960, S.I. 1216.

48. The Prevention of Fraud (Investments) Act 1939.

49. Prevention of Fraud (Investments) Act 1958, s. 13, as amended by The Banking Act 1979, s. 51(1) and Sched. 6, para. 5.

50. *Tarling (No. 1)* v. *Government of Singapore* (1980) 70 Cr. App. R. 77.

51. *Ibid.*, 70 Cr. App. R. 77.

52. *Rex* v. *Kylsant (Lord)* [1932] 1 K.B. 442.

53. The Banking Act 1979, s. 39(1).

54. *Ibid.*, s. 34(2) and (3); note that an advertisement offering a deposit with a person named in it is presumed to be issued by him.

55. *Ibid.*, s. 34(1).

56. Insurance Companies Act 1974, s. 71(1).

57. *Ibid.*, s. 71(2).

58. Insurance Companies (Linked Properties and Indices) Regulations 1975, S.I. no. 929.

59. Wilson Committee, Second Stage Evidence, vol. 5 *Department of Trade* (1979) p. 5.

9 Offences Relating to Companies and Insolvency

The Companies Acts 1948–80 and insolvency legislation contain diverse offences, most of which are regulatory in character. The majority are dealt with in this chapter, but fraudulent trading requires separate treatment. The fact that many such offences are regulatory in nature does not mean that they are unimportant. All too often, reporting requirements imposed under regulatory legislation are not complied with because management chooses to conceal questionable manoeuvres from both the public and its own shareholders. Where intent to defraud cannot be proven, control is often only possible through charging a regulatory offence, a course of action which occasionally is attacked as charging conduct only technically illegal. This forensic tactic naturally underplays the real importance of the legislation, and, as we will see, courts imbued with notions of moral fault opt for leniency in treatment as a result.

Prospectus Requirements
The primary duty to ensure that a prospectus which invites the public to take shares from the company, or more commonly from an issuing house, lies upon the directors and is enforceable under civil and criminal law. The principal criminal offence is contained in section 44 of the Companies Act 1948, which provides that, where a prospectus includes any untrue statement, any person who authorised the issue of the prospectus shall be liable on conviction on indictment for a term not exceeding two years, or to a fine not exceeding £500 or both. On summary conviction the section provides a maximum term of three months' imprisonment or a fine not exceeding £100 or both. An accused person has a defence if he proves either that the statement was not material, or that he had reasonable ground to believe and did believe, up to the time of issue of the prospectus, that the statement was true. In effect, therefore, the accused must prove, affirmatively, that he was not negligent. The Act also provides for the rescission of contracts for subscription for shares where these are procured by misrepresentation.[1] Unlike criminal legislation, the prosecution need not prove dishonesty.

There are few, if any, modern instances of these provisions being invoked. In general, criticism of new issues has, as Dr Hadden notes, been of other aspects of the flotation, of the failure of issuing houses to ensure that the board of directors was strengthened in Roadships Ltd., of directors and insiders in Blanes Ltd. unloading their shareholdings immediately after flotation despite stating publicly that they proposed to retain them, and of British Bangladesh Trust for floating an unsound scheme (Hadden, 1980). But the basic veracity of offer documents will be carefully scrutinised by management and its advisers in the light of the liabilities, civil and criminal, which the law imposes.

The Accounts

The integrity of the accounts is safeguarded by offences relating both to failure to keep proper accounts, and by penal provisions intended to safeguard auditors. The latter are considered in connection with the position of directors and auditors; the former are outlined here.

Section 12(1) of the Companies Act 1976 imposes a basic obligation on the company to keep accounting records. Such records shall be such as to disclose with reasonable accuracy the financial position of the company and to enable the directors to ensure that any profit and loss statement or balance sheet shall be such as will give a true and fair view of the company's state of affairs. The contents of such records are specified in the section which, finally, contains a penal provision. Section 12(10) renders every officer of a company which fails to comply with the section guilty of an offence unless he shows that he acted honestly and that, in the circumstances in which the business of the company was carried on, the default was excusable. Any person convicted of the offence is liable on conviction on indictment to imprisonment for a term not exceeding two years, or to a fine, or both, or on summary conviction to imprisonment for a term not exceeding six months, or to a fine not exceeding £100, or both.

While prosecutions for this offence are increasing in frequency, it is seldom punished with more than a fine. The SUITS case is only the most celebrated instance of this.[2] This was an investment trust which made a loan to another company, Amcal, for £4.2 millions, which it then classified in its accounts as 'cash in bankers and on hand'. Ultimately, the loan proved to be irrecoverable. Charged with an offence under the Companies Act, Sir Hugh Fraser was fined £100, it being accepted that he did not wilfully suppress the loan. The auditors resigned. The sentence reflects the habitual leniency of sentencing courts when no fraud is found. At that time, however, the legislation did not provide for trial by indictment.

Company Assisting Purchase of Own Shares

English company law has always forbidden a company to deal in its own shares, a rule which is justified as necessary to protect the capital of the company.[3] Since the 1929 Companies Act, it has been an offence for a company, whether directly or indirectly, to assist another person financially to purchase its shares. The abuse thus struck at was one which we have seen in respect of Town Centre Properties Ltd. It enables deals to be made which benefit the outgoing directors who sell shares at a premium, and which, by allowing control to pass without the knowledge or concurrence of shareholders, can set the stage for fraud (1926, Cmd. 2657).

The practice is not restricted to cases in which a transfer of control, essentially a take-over, is in contemplation. In several of the cases discussed in chapter 2, notably that of British Bangladesh Trust, loans were made to enable directors, other insiders and anyone else who could be persuaded to act as a nominee, to take shares in the company. In Slater Walker, loans were also made by Slater Walker companies to enable insiders to deal in their shares. In the result, Mr James Slater was convicted by magistrates in this country of the offence.[4] In British Bangladesh Trust, the effect of such lending was to conceal from investors, and from the Department of Trade, the parlous financial state of the company. The same comment may be made of Vehicle and General Insurance Company Limited. In Slater Walker, it would seem that such dealings did nothing to preserve the integrity of the company's capital or resources, and was resorted to in order to enable insider trading by executives to take place. It is right to note, again, the justification suggested for the practice: that it gives executives an incentive by giving them a proprietary interest in the company. It is for the reader to assess the cogency of this justification.

It is clear, however, that although scandalous malpractices have concerned the milking of cash companies, they extend beyond that particular phenomenon. Section 54 is a particularly wide provision, which is essentially preventive in character. Fraud is not an essential element of it. An act done in contravention of the section renders the company liable to a fine, and every officer implicated in the offence to a maximum penalty on indictment of two years' imprisonment.[5]

There are three exceptions to the rule that a company may not give financial assistance for the purchase of its shares. A company which normally engages in money-lending may make a loan to facilitate the purchase of its shares, provided that the lending is part of its ordinary business and is made in an ordinary business manner. Secondly, a company may provide money to facilitate employee share schemes. Thirdly, a company may make loans to employees other than directors to enable them to purchase or subscribe for shares.[6] It is not proposed to discuss the construction of the section in detail; adequate accounts exist elsewhere (Gower, 1979, Northey and Leigh, 1980). But some of its leading features should be noticed.

Section 54 is wide enough to catch a loan made by a company to the purchaser of its shares. Because it prohibits the indirect giving of financial assistance it also catches a case such as Town Centre in which the company puts a person or company in funds by a loan, the borrower, then, to the lender's knowledge, lending the money to the person desiring to acquire control. Its width is also shown by a recent case in which fraud was not involved, *Arthur Hick Northern Ltd.* v. *Whitehouse.*[7] Hick Partners owed Armour Trust £93,000. Hick Northern, a subsidiary of Hick Partners, discharged Hick Partners' debt to Armour, as a result of which W and H were able to purchase shares in Hick Partners at par from Armour. For the purposes of the case it was assumed that Armour would only have sold the shares to W and H if the debt from Hick Partners were repaid. The court held that the transaction could amount to a provision by Hick Northern, of financial assistance for the purchase of shares in Hick Partners, its holding company. The section applies whether the giving of assistance be direct or indirect.[8] What is required is a causal connection between the sale or allotment of shares and the transaction which allegedly breached the section (Prentice, 1976).

Although the section makes criminal the giving of financial assistance by the company, it is the company which the section is intended to protect. Therefore, the company is really a statutory protégé. From this, it follows that the company is not made liable for breaches of the law committed by its controllers, nor is it saddled with their guilty knowledge.[9] Thus, a security which is given by the company in respect of a transaction which contravenes the section is invalid, even though the lender to whom it was given was unaware of the illegality. It is not only directors who may be liable for breach of the section. In civil law the doctrine of constructive trust applies. Where a fiduciary acts in breach of his obligations to his principal, so that the principal's assets are wrongly disposed of, the fiduciary and any person who assists him in the transaction is liable to make good the loss. A company director is a fiduciary of his company. In recent cases, financial institutions which have given assistance in an illegal transaction have been held liable for loss occasioned to the company by reason of transactions contravening the section.[10]

Financial institutions are not, however, held liable simply because they have given financial assistance. It must be shown that they acted with knowledge. The mental element required for liability varies according to whether the defendant received funds, or assisted a fiduciary in the misapplication of funds. In the former case he (she, or it) is liable if he knew or ought to have known of the breach of trust.[11] In the latter, he must have been fraudulent or at least have shut his eyes to the obvious.[12] Cases which suggested a stricter rule of liability for failure to take care appear to have been disapproved.

Whether the rule concerning the mental element required for liability should have been relaxed in this fashion is debatable. The strict rule could certainly bear harshly on an innocent lender. In one such case the transaction was put through a branch of the bank. The branch did not commonly deal with such transactions. The bank bore the loss.[13] Even close students of the section can fail to spot the incriminating features of a transaction. On the other hand, in cases of corporate looting, the provision of outside finance is often crucial to the success of a scheme. Banks and lending institutions are aware of this. Their officers should have the training and experience necessary to enable them to avoid the risks. The stricter rule makes it unwise for them to take chances. There was a period when the co-operation of a bank was apparently easily secured (Finer, 1966). There is some reason to fear that if the less stringent rule prevails, certain lending institutions, fairly confident that the courts would not uncover the nuances of their controllers' states of mind, might fail to make those inquiries which the law requires. At least while the penalty for breach was a mere £100 fine, merchant banks were sometimes said to pay too little attention to it, and even to connive at breaches (Dowgate, 1979).

One's doubts about relaxing the rigour of the section also derive from its relative failure. In part, this has been attributable to the derisory penalty for breach. No doubt the development of the constructive trust gave lenders an incentive to think seriously about it (and also made available a source of financial redress to shareholders). The exempting provisos to the section have also engendered difficulties, in particular, that which permits a company which normally lends money to make a loan for the purchase of shares provided that the loan is made in the ordinary course of business. This has been invoked in an attempt to justify transactions which appear to be indefensible.

In British Bangladesh Trust the Inspectors concluded that the exception, which was being relied on in order to give a spurious picture of the state of the company's share subscriptions, was a cloak for fraud. In that case, of course, loans which were made before the bank formally opened for business, and immediately after funds were received from the public, were thought to be anything but ordinary. Nor did the Inspectors believe that the section was ever intended to allow the security for such loans to be the shares themselves (London Capital Group Limited, 1977, p. 98). Reproached with breaches of the section, John Stonehouse insisted, doubtless rightly, that such breaches were commonplace in the City. Certainly, other investigations such as those into Pinnock and Dowgate evidence a similar, cavalier attitude towards the section. Again, in the London and Counties case, loans allegedly made in the ordinary course of business could not, in the Inspectors' opinion, be so justified, because of the total amount involved, the methods by which the money was obtained and the fact that most of it was used to purchase L. & C. shares in order to support the market price. The Inspectors state (London and County Securities Group, 1976, p. 357):

> In our opinion, Mr. Caplan's activities through Capebourne constitute a prime example of the mischief against which that section is aimed and his contemptuous disregard of it shows how derisory is the penalty which it provides.

They recommended a complete prohibition of the practice.

If there is real ambiguity about the meaning of the proviso, it ought to be clarified, if not abolished. The courts have concluded that whether a loan is, or is not, in the ordinary course of business depends upon whether the loan is at the free disposition of the borrower and in the course of normal lending business and whether it was truly for the benefit of the borrower.[14] Critics note that today many loans are made for special purposes, and that a consequent restriction cannot be taken as an indicium of abnormality. It has also been urged that the notion of 'normal course of business' relates to the normal course of the banking or lending business of the particular company or companies to which the proceedings relate (Hopkins, 1979). That cannot be right; the phrase must relate to the incidents of a lending business as those are generally and objectively understood. One could hardly contend that an otherwise unlawful transaction became lawful simply because the company in question habitually engaged in it. Nor, *pace* certain critics, should it matter whether the loan might in fact benefit the lender as well as the borrower (cf. Hopkins, 1979). The section is general, directed towards certain classes of transactions. In any event, even if the effect of such a loan were to raise the price of the lender's shares, the danger remains that in such circumstances the enhanced price might not correspond to anything like the value which the shares ought to command. In short, there is an obvious danger of rigging, with consequential prejudice to the public.

The very breadth of the section has led to calls for its repeal and replacement. Considering that it was so wide that wholly innocent transactions were caught, the Company Law Committee of 1962 suggested that it should be replaced by a new provision which would declare it unlawful for a company to give assistance for the purchase of its shares unless the transaction were approved by the company by special resolution and the directors filed a declaration that the company was solvent (1962, Cmnd. 1749, paras. 178–9). That might serve, at least in respect of the evils against which the section was originally aimed. It would not be appropriate to cases like British Bangladesh Trust, for there the vice occurred on flotation, before there was an independent body of shareholders. Furthermore, in that situation, the result would be an impairment of capital which could hardly be permitted.

In take-overs, the section is said to inhibit transactions by which a company, at the urging of its financial advisers, procures support for the price of its shares.[15] This has been said by Inspectors at least to infringe the spirit of the section (Ozalid Group Holdings Limited, 1980). The practice does not necessarily involve harm to anyone, but the Committee's recommendation is not an appropriate solution to it and will have to be re-assessed. In America, the solution is to attach civil, trust liability, against directors and others who cause loss to the company as a result of such manoeuvres.[16] This, however, would hardly suffice in a situation where the lender may act innocently (unless liability were based on negligence or failure to exercise due diligence, adopting the model afforded by prospectus provisions) and the rogues have vanished by the time that the harm is discovered.

In sum, the prohibition against a company giving financial assistance for the purchase of its own shares is necessary for the protection of shareholders and investors. It is not an unimportant provision, nor will it, one may trust, be seen in the future as an insignificant obstacle to manipulations. It needs perhaps to be clarified, and the loan provision simplified. At present there are examples in Department of Trade reports where, as a forensic tactic, qualifications to the section were suggested for which, as the Inspectors noted, there was little basis in its terms (Pergamon Press Limited, Final Report, 1973, p. 67). If there is doubt and ambiguity, these should be cleared up, and any other doubts upon its legitimacy dispelled as soon as possible.

Loans to Directors

Section 190 of the Companies Act 1948 prohibited the making of loans to directors subject to certain exceptions, the most troublesome of which permitted loans made in the ordinary course of business by a money-lending company. The secondary banking cases disclosed widespread abuses of the section. Directors obtained loans, on favourable terms, for directors' personal expenditures and, sometimes, to provide funds to bolster an artificial market price in shares. It became clear that the exemption would have to be either reformulated or abolished. Like its predecessor, the government sought to permit directors' loan transactions within reasonable limits. The resulting legislation is, necessarily, complicated. It controls public companies more strictly than private companies, on the assumption that abuses occur more frequently in the former category.

Subject to certain exceptions, all companies are prohibited from making loans to their directors or the directors of their holding company, if any, or their family or associates. This ban applies also to shadow directors who hold no formal office but control the directors. A similar provision deals with guaranteeing or providing security for such a loan.[17] Further prohibitions affect public companies or companies forming part of a group which contains a public company.[18] These may not enter into certain further categories of financial arrangements denoted by the graceless term 'quasi-loan'.[19] The government had in mind arrangements like those which operated at Peachey, where companies in the group spent money on their own account for goods and services for the chairman's personal use, on the basis that he would later make reimbursement.[20]

The legislation also provides machinery for blocking evasion devices such as the assignment of rights or the assumption of liabilities.[21] An example of the first is where a third party makes a loan to a director and, subsequently, the director's company purchases the third party's rights to the repayment of the principal and the interest on it. The company becomes a creditor of the director just as though it had made the loan in the first place. An example of the second would be the case of a third party who guarantees a loan made by a fourth party to a director. If the company enters into an arrangement with the third and fourth parties whereby the third party is released from his liability on the company assuming it, the company again commits resources to a contingent liability. Back-to-back deals are covered also. This situation occurs according to an example given in standing committee, where a company agrees to make loans to a director of another company in return for loans made to its own directors, or where a director persuades a bank to make loans on favourable terms in return for his company placing lucrative business with the bank. The statute operates where there is an arrangement whereby the benefit conferred is a recompense for the facilities obtained by directors.

In respect of permitted loans, a three-tier system operates for public companies. Those which do not lend money in the course of their business may not make loans or quasi-loans for their directors. Money-lending companies may make loans to their directors on normal commercial terms, but subject to a limit of £50,000 to each director taken with his connected persons. Such loans will have to be disclosed in the accounts, and failure to do so will be subject to comment by the auditors.[22] Recognised banks will be allowed to lend to directors on normal commercial terms. Only in respect of house loans will an upper limit, £50,000, apply.[23] Again, there is provision for disclosure. All companies may make small (under £1,000) quasi-loans to directors, provided that they are reimbursable within two months.[24]

The legislation is enforceable civilly and criminally, and quasi-loans are subject to disclosure in the accounts. Civilly, transactions are voidable at the instance of the company unless third-party rights have intervened, and a director who knew that the circumstances placed the company in contravention of the provisions is liable to account to the company for any profit which he made, or any loss which the company sustained thereby.[25] Criminally, a director who knowing or having reasonable cause to believe that the company was contravening the provisions is guilty of an offence triable summarily or on indictment. So, too, is a company unless it acted in ignorance of the circumstances of contravention.[26]

Obviously, some of these restrictions will be hard to regulate. Directors could take an expensive view of their housing needs. They could face conflicts of duty and interest in judging the claims of their peers, difficulties which might not arise in determining the claims of other borrowers. There does not seem to be an incentive for directors to apply the rules stringently against their fellows. Some prohibitions can readily be circumvented. The suggestion was made in Parliament that a person wanting to buy his house on a loan from the company might resign, take a loan, and then procure reappointment to the board.

Although £50,000 does not represent a large amount, it could rapidly mount up if several directors of money-lending companies were to take loans. Nevertheless, the provision of a ceiling ought to go some way towards limiting abuses which have occurred, and, of course, such companies are subject to regulation by the Bank of England. The new legislation ought to strengthen the hand of auditors. By placing them under a positive obligation to comment, it plainly gives them an additional weapon against an unscrupulous management.

Miscellaneous

There are other, regulatory offences, under company legislation. Section 71 of the Companies Act 1948 is intended to protect creditors. This relates to motions for the reduction of the company's capital and provides that if any officer of the company wilfully conceals the name of any creditor entitled to object to the reduction, or wilfully misrepresents the nature or amount of the debt or claim of any creditor, or is guilty of complicity to do so, he shall be guilty of an offence. Section 85 of the Companies Act 1948 contains a very serious offence, applicable only to Scotland, dealing with the forgery or alteration of share warrants. Such coverage is nearly universal and in England the like offence would be charged under the Forgery Act 1913. Section 113 of the Companies Act 1967 prohibits the mutilation or destruction of company documents. It is further noted in connection with inspections and investigations.

Insolvency Offences

Bankruptcy legislation pertaining to natural persons, and the winding-up provisions of the Companies Acts, contain offences intended to punish certain classes of acts which contributed to insolvency, as well as acts which tend to undermine the integrity of insolvency administration. The basic structure of insolvency offences derives from the Bankruptcy Acts and comprises: offences which relate to conduct of the bankrupt's affairs up to the time of the bankruptcy; offences which relate to his failure to perform his duties after bankruptcy; and offences which consist in a disregard of disabilities imposed by law upon an undischarged bankrupt (Leigh, 1980b). Offences in winding-up generally relate to the second category, with the marked exception of fraudulent trading.

Those bankruptcy offences which concern the bankrupt's management of his affairs before bankruptcy include the offences of materially contributing to his insolvency by gambling (a term which does not include taking trade risks),[27] of failure to keep proper books of account,[28] or of falsifying, mutilating or destroying books if done within twelve months before presentation of a bankruptcy petition.

A similar structure of offences applies in winding-up, the Companies Act 1948 containing offences of concealing, mutilating or destroying books of account, making false entries in them, or fraudulently tampering with, altering or making any omission in any document relating to the affairs of the company, an offence which applies to acts done within twelve months of the winding-up.[29]

Offences relating to the failure by a bankrupt to perform his duties after bankruptcy include a failure to disclose all his affairs to the Official Receiver, and to disclose property and effects.[30] In winding-up, there are similar offences concerning failure to disclose the company's property, failing to deliver it up, and concealment of property.[31] In both cases, fraudulent removal of property is an offence.[32] Under the Companies Act 1948, it is an offence, within twelve months of the winding-up, or thereafter, to pledge or dispose of any goods of the company which have been acquired on credit.[33] It is also an offence to make a false representation, or other fraud, for the purpose of obtaining the consent of the creditors of the company, or of any of them, to an agreement with reference to the affairs of the company or the winding-up.[34]

The principal offences in the third group apply to bankrupts. It is an offence for an undischarged bankrupt to operate a bank account without consent.[35] He may not obtain credit in a sum greater than £50 without disclosing his status.[36] He may not, without the leave of the court, take part in the management of a company.[37] Until recently, the legislature did not impose disabilities upon directors of insolvent companies. Now, however, persons who have been successively directors of companies which went into insolvency may be disqualified by the court from acting as a director for a period up to five years in duration.[38]

There are certain general comments which must be made concerning these sections. In the main, they are sufficiently widely drafted to catch dishonest conduct engaged in insolvency, and under the Companies Act 1948 the offences relating to failure to account for property, its fraudulent removal, making material false statements to the liquidator, preventing the production of books, concealing or mutilating them, or making false entries in them, bear a reverse onus of proof by which the officer of the company in default must prove either that he had no intent to defraud or, in respect of some items in the list, that he had no intent to conceal the state of affairs of the company or to defeat the law.[39]

Some limitations to the offences contained in insolvency legislation represent a deliberate value judgement. For example, the gambling offence excludes risks undertaken in connection with the enterprise, a limitation evidently intended to preserve scope for entrepreneurial initiatives involving risk. Similarly, the mere fact that an insolvent lived extravagantly is not an offence, though it is a circumstance which may delay his discharge from bankruptcy. In this, English law contrasts with that of France (Del Marmol, 1936; Kellens, 1974). As a matter of policy, our law was directed towards specific wrongful acts (Leigh, 1980b).

Other limitations result from the operation of legal doctrines, the significance of which may well not have been appreciated when the legislation was drafted. For example, the notion of credit means that a person who obtains a thing, for example a car, under a classical hire-purchase contract under which title does not pass to him until the final instalment is paid, does not obtain credit and cannot therefore be held guilty of doing so as an undischarged bankrupt.[40] There are sundry other peculiarities of this character as well. They are not of great moment. There is also overlap between certain offences under the Theft Acts 1968–78 and the Bankruptcy Acts, the Companies Acts and the Insolvency Act 1976. Again, the fact of overlap is not of great moment. It is in any event only partial. The offence of false accounting, for example, applies whether the company is in liquidation or not; the like offence under the winding-up provisions applies to insolvency only.

References and Notes

1. Companies Act 1948, s. 43(1).
2. For accounts, see *The Economist*, 11 September 1976, p. 100; *ibid.*, 4 December 1976, p. 145 for an account of a report by the Stock Exchange; and for the trial in Glasgow Sheriff Court, see *The Times*, May 20, 23, 24 and June 15, 1978.
3. Companies Act 1980, s. 35(1); *Trevor* v. *Whitworth* (1887) 12 App. Cas. 409.
4. *Fowlie* v. *Slater* (1979) 129 N.L.J. 465.
5. Companies Act 1980, s. 80 and Schedule 2; formerly the penalty was only a fine of £100.
6. Note that the exemptions are subject to capital maintenance provisions; Companies Act 1980, s. 80 and Sched. 2, para. 10.
7. *The Times*, Law Report, 26 February 1980.
8. *Wallersteiner* v. *Moir* [1974] 1 W.L.R. 991.
9. *Belmont Finance Corporation Ltd.* v. *Williams Furniture Ltd.* [1979] Ch. 250.
10. For example, *Selangor United Rubber Estates Ltd.* v. *Cradock (no. 3)* [1968] 1 W.L.R. 1555.
11. *Belmont Finance Corporation Ltd.* v. *Williams Furniture Ltd. (no. 2)* [1980] 1 All E.R. 393 at p. 405 *per* Buckley J.
12. *Ibid.*, at p. 413 *per* Goff L.J.
13. *Selangor United Rubber Estates Ltd.* v. *Cradock (no. 3)* [1968] 1 W.L.R. 1555.

14. *Fowlie* v. *Slater* (1979) 129 N.L.J. 465; *Steen* v. *Law* [1964] A.C. 287.
15. *Accountancy*, December 1973, p. 19.
16. *Insuranshares Corporation of Delaware* v. *Northern Fiscal Corporation* 35 F. Supp. 22 (1940); *Gerdes* v. *Reynolds*, 30 N.Y. Supp. 2d 755 (1941).
17. Companies Act 1980, s. 49(1), 63 and 64.
18. *Ibid.*, s. 65(1).
19. *Ibid.*, s. 49(1)(*b*).
20. H.C. Standing Committee A, Sess. 1979–80, Companies Bill [Lords], cols. 432 ff.
21. Companies Act 1980, s. 49(3) and (4).
22. Companies Act 1980, ss. 50 and 59.
23. *Ibid.*, s. 50(7).
24. *Ibid.*, s. 50(2).
25. *Ibid.*, s. 52.
26. *Ibid.*, s. 53.
27. Bankruptcy Act 1914, s. 157.
28. *Ibid.*, s. 158.
29. Companies Act 1948, s. 328(*i*), (*j*) and (*k*); s. 329 (mutilation with intent to defraud).
30. Bankruptcy Act 1914, s. 154.
31. Companies Act 1948, s. 328(*a*), (*b*), (*d*).
32. Bankruptcy Act 1914, s. 154(5); Companies Act, 1948, s. 328(*e*), s. 330.
33. Companies Act, 1948, s. 328(*o*).
34. *Ibid.*, s. 328(*p*).
35. Bankruptcy Act 1914, s. 47(3).
36. *Ibid.*, s. 155.
37. Companies Act 1948, s. 187.
38. Insolvency Act 1976, s. 9.
39. Companies Act 1948, s. 328.
40. *Reg.* v. *Garlick* (1958) 42 Cr. App. R. 141.

10 Fraudulent Trading

Fraudulent trading, prohibited by section 332 of the Companies Act 1948, is an offence in winding-up. It is of sufficient general importance to merit separate treatment. Section 332 contains both civil and criminal provisions. The relevant parts provide:

> 332(1) If in the course of the winding up of a company it appears that any business of the company has been carried on with intent to defraud any creditors of the company or creditors of any other person or for any fraudulent purpose, the court, on the application of the official receiver, or the liquidator or any creditor or contributory of the company, may, if it thinks proper so to do, declare that any persons who were knowingly parties to the carrying on of the business in manner aforesaid shall be personally responsible without any limitation of liability, for all or any of the debts or other liabilities of the company as the court may direct...

> (2) Where any business of the company is carried on with such intent or for any such purpose as is mentioned in subsection (1) of this section, every person who was knowingly a party to the carrying on of the business in manner aforesaid, shall be liable to conviction on indictment for a term not exceeding two years or to a fine not exceeding five hundred pounds or to both.

The fraudulent trading section is narrow in scope and obscurely drafted. This has tended to limit its practical importance and mask its general significance. Civilly, it represents a clear departure from the separate legal entity principle, that is, the legal principle which holds that the debts of a limited liability company are its debts and not to be imputed to its controllers.[1] It is just such an imputation which the section permits.

Criminally, the offence of fraudulent trading affords a model for a necessary extension to the criminal law. Unlike classical theft offences, it is not directed towards obtaining a thing and, unlike deception, it concentrates on representing a state of affairs in general terms rather than upon a specific misrepresentation. We have seen that, historically, this would not found a charge of obtaining by false representation.[2] In relation to theft, it is notorious that where a firm takes in money in the course of trade, against a contractual obligation to supply goods and services, the fact that the firm was practically insolvent at the time will not support a charge of theft of the moneys received.[3] Only where both sides, the firm and the customer or person dealing with it, hand over money on an express understanding that it will be earmarked for a particular use will a fiduciary obligation arise capable of impressing the money with a trust and rendering misappropriation of it theft.[4] From the point of view of the customer who suffers the loss, this result is apt to look artificial. Hence, the prospect of a rule which would render criminal at least a knowingly false representation of solvency by continuing to do business while insolvent would be welcome.

Fraudulent trading is, however, narrow in scope. This reflects the fact that it was introduced on the recommendation of the Company Law Committee of 1926 to meet a specific situation which had been discovered in winding-up. The vice struck at was the case, met with principally in private companies, where the person in control of the company held a floating charge and, aware that the company was on the verge of liquidation, 'filled up' his security by means of goods obtained on credit and then appointed a receiver.[5] The result was, of course, that the loss fell upon trade suppliers and other creditors, while the controller, who held goods covered by a security, was able to insulate himself against loss, the receiver enforcing the security against the company on his behalf. Even today, a similar fraud occurs in which a controller grants a debenture to his friend who then puts in a 'tame' receiver to enforce it against the company. If the receiver does not report the circumstances to the Department of Trade, and in such circumstances he will not do so, there can be no readily effective mode of redress. The facts will simply not become known in most cases.

In the result, the Committee, proceeding from this narrow perspective which reflected its preoccupation with company law matters alone, proposed that a director found to be guilty of fraudulent trading should be subject to unlimited personal liability, that any security which he took from the company should be charged with his liability, that fraudulent trading should also be a criminal offence, and that it should be a ground for disqualifying a person from acting as a director (1926, Cmd. 2657, para. 61). These provisions were duly enacted.[6]

Elements

Certain elements are common both to the civil and criminal limbs of fraudulent trading. In both, there can be no proceedings unless the company actually is in winding-up.[7] The business must have been carried on with intent to defraud creditors of the company, or creditors of any other person, or for a fraudulent purpose. It is thus important to know what may be said to be a business of the company, and what is meant by 'defraud' and 'fraudulent purpose'.

Liability attaches to any persons who were knowingly parties to the carrying on of business in a fraudulent manner. It thus extends beyond directors and officers, to persons who control in fact. A contemporary problem has been that holding companies or parent companies in groups have put subsidiaries into liquidation owing debts, rather than bailing them out. This has been felt to be unfair. There can be no doubt that the fraudulent trading section is wide enough to comprehend the activities of a holding company, but in order to render it liable, the prosecution would have to show, not that the subsidiary was insolvent, but that the parent company knew of this and permitted it to continue trading. Under existing law, a parent company is not liable for the debts of its subsidiary in the absence of dishonesty.[8] The problem is thus the difficult practical problem of demonstrating dishonesty in the appropriate quarter.

Certain principles relating to carrying on business have been established. Business includes any part of the business of a company.[9] Thus, a single transaction may suffice; it is the activity, rather than the particular act considered in isolation, which is important.[10] The action of a company in collecting and realising its assets with a view to paying a creditor or creditors is also considered to be a carrying on of business. The term is thus a wide one.

The notion of 'fraud' and 'fraudulent purpose' is incapable of close definition, but the courts have clarified it somewhat. Originally, there was an attempt to assimilate the notion of carrying on business with intent to defraud creditors to that of intending to create a fraudulent preference. That argument was rejected, the court pointing out that the creation of a fraudulent preference did not necessarily imply any element of moral fault, but only an intent to prefer certain creditors unjustly at the expense of others. Fraudulent trading requires moral fault.[11] This formula, however, poses two problems: what is capable of being construed as moral fault, and how may this be proven? Not surprisingly, the former question has produced wide and unspecific formulae. In *Re Patrick and Lyon Ltd*, Maugham J. was content to hold that the terms connote actual dishonesty, involving, according to current notions of fair trading among commercial men, real moral fault.[12] For the purposes of criminal law, the conception of moral fault is that of the jury, and the formula espoused is apt to cause the same problems which arise in relation to dishonesty under the Theft Acts, namely, that different juries will view the morality of identical conduct very differently.

The fraudulent intent must, of course, be an intent to do acts which constitute fraudulent conduct. *In re Sarflax*[13] illustrates the point. The company, a subsidiary of F. Ltd, ceased trading and sold its assets to the parent company. The issue was whether its directors contravened the section by causing the assets of the company to be distributed among creditors other than S.A.F.E., a principal trade creditor, which, after trading had ceased, obtained a large judgement against it on a claim in contract. The sale price from Sarflax Ltd to its parent company was, seemingly, at an appropriate price. Oliver J. holds that a debtor who knows or believes that his assets will not be sufficient to pay his creditors in full, and who prefers some at the expense of others, does not act fraudulently. Apart from insolvency legislation, a person may pay his creditors in whatever order he pleases.

There are limits to this principle. Thus, the court suggests that dishonesty may be found where a payment is made in respect of which there is no proper claim, or where assets are improperly realised, or where other special circumstances arise. An example would be where business is carried on to satisfy a security held by the company's controller, but the mere fact of preference does not, so it is said, amount to carrying on business fraudulently.[14] Of course, for a subsidiary to gather in assets with a view to preferring a parent company is not very different, if at all, from the original vice of 'filling up' a security in anticipation of insolvency at which the section was aimed.[15] Proof of actual dishonesty will normally be inferred from the activity of trading while the company was in fact insolvent. But a court may, not must, infer dishonesty from such conduct.[16] It is in this sense that remarks of Maugham J., that a company carries on business with intent to defraud creditors where it continues to carry on business and incur debts at a time when there is, to the knowledge of the directors, no reasonable prospect of the creditors being paid, must be understood.[17]

There are circumstances, both common and unusual, in which it would be difficult to conclude that fraudulent trading occurred. It is common for businesses facing financial problems to continue trading in the hope of turning the corner into prosperity. If fraudulent trading was to be inferred in all cases in which it could not certainly be said that there would be a revival of fortunes sufficient to protect creditors, directors of some well-known companies would find themselves in the dock, not necessarily rightly. The moral dilemma, of directors who wish to save their business and who no one would wish to constrain so rigidly that they could not take any risks in doing so,[18] has been put by the late Mr Justice Finer thus (1966, p. 47):

> The company has small reserves and has suffered a bad season. Next season, if trade revives...all should be well. Meantime, the company needs to purchase materials for next season's products. Thus, there is a real and appreciated risk, not possible to calculate precisely, that the suppliers of such materials will not, in the event, be paid. Does that exposure of creditors to a contingency of this kind involve real moral blame according to current notions of fair trading? Will the conclusion be the same if the chairman of the board happens, some years previously, to have taken a charge over the assets of the company to secure advances by him, so that if the company does become insolvent the value of the materials purchased will be used to pay him off instead of the creditors at large?

As an example of an unusual situation in which creditors sought to preserve the company and therefore allowed it to continue trading without calling in their debts, we may cite Court Line Limited. The Inspectors noted that, although the firm crashed owing many millions of pounds, the co-operation of creditors ensured that it could not be said that collapse was certain until all steps to save the company had failed (Court Line Limited, 1978, p. 2). There are, of course, cases in which dishonesty may properly be inferred from continued trading. They include carrying on business in order to tap accounts receivable of the company,[19] appropriating income of the company as loans and advances to directors and employees,[20] and the common case of misappropriating assets, in particular assets and money entrusted to the company by others for a particular purpose.[21]

The position of a creditor as party to an offence could be a difficult one. The position, apparently, is that a creditor who presses for payment is not a party to a fraud merely because he knows that no money will be available to pay him if the debtor acts honestly and ceases trading. He is, however, a party to carrying on a business with intent to defraud if he accepts money which he knows has, in fact, been procured by carrying on business with intent to defraud creditors for the very purpose of making the payment; '...a man who warms himself with the fire of fraud cannot complain if he is singed'.[22] The problem is whether a creditor who presses hard for his debt from a debtor who is known to be insolvent should be held criminally liable for doing so as a secondary party to the debtor's offence of fraudulent trading. The better view, seemingly, is that he should not be so liable unless he encourages or threatens the debtor to carry on business to the prejudice of other creditors in order to secure repayment of the debt.

Problems of Civil Liability

Civil liability for fraudulent trading is intended to provide compensation to creditors, but the prospect of it also has a possible deterrent effect against officers. There are, however, in respect of civil liability, certain points of obscurity. These concern, first, the extent of liability which the court may impose and, secondly, whether he who moves the court may take the benefit of any recovery to the prejudice of other creditors.

Personal responsibility can only be for the liabilities of the company, and no more. The section is so expressed as to permit imposition of such liability only. In practice, while the court could declare a person liable for all the debts and liabilities of the company, it is unlikely to do so because it is usually not known, until a fairly late stage in the liquidation, what the aggregate of such liabilities is likely to be.[23] In general, the court is likely to make an order for liability in respect of those creditors proven to have been defrauded, but the section is penal and the jurisdiction is not so limited. It does, of course, enable the court to declare that the liability of any such person under the declaration shall be a charge on any debt or obligation owing from the company to him, and enables the interests of assignees from him to be attacked unless they took in good faith, for valuable consideration, and without notice. The question of who may benefit from a claim is difficult and there is conflict in the case law. The section gives power to move for a declaration to the Official Receiver, the liquidator, or any creditor or contributory of the company. The original purpose, it seems clear, was to ensure that a receiver's hand could be forced by another interested party (Cmd. 2657, 1926, para. 60).

The conflict concerns whether a creditor who brings proceedings does so in a personal or representative capacity. If the former analysis is correct, he will obtain the benefit of the recovery exclusively. Courts which take this view treat the section as being penal, and the overriding need that of establishing a regime which will induce creditors to bring proceedings.[24] If the latter analysis is correct, all creditors share in the recovery. Courts which take this view regard the section as part of the machinery of winding-up, and are apt to impose a liability on directors for the company's debts, but not to adjust the rights of creditors *inter se*, or to create new rights for creditors.[25]

It is the latter view which, the author submits, is correct. To give the benefit to any one creditor would prevent an orderly scheme of distribution. No guidance is given to the court concerning how to solve questions of priorities. The debtor's fault is, seemingly, equal—at least as among creditors upon whom fraud has been practised. The court's power is to make a declaration of liability in respect of the company's debts and liabilities, and it cannot, surely, have been assumed that, because officers were at fault, one group of the company's creditors could be subordinated to another, whatever the differing nature of the risks to which each was exposed.[26] Nor would it seem right to benefit one creditor or group because the directors acted towards them with intent to defraud, whereas other creditors were merely victims of the director's recklessness. Hence, it would seem that the insolvency aspects of the fraudulent trading provision, at least in its civil features, must predominate over its penal aspect, indicating that recovery goes into the common fund. General equitable principles may thus blunt the deterrent benefit which might otherwise have been derived from the ability of individual creditors to recover fully, but the predominance of equitable principles seems to be dictated by the scheme of the section.

Reform

Fraudulent trading could, with advantage, be reformed in several respects. There is no reason why the offence should be limited in operation to cases where a winding-up has been ordered. After all, the fraudulent trading precedes the date of insolvency proceedings, and the question whether criminal or civil proceedings may be commenced relates not to fault, but to the accident whether proceedings have been commenced. The section, as drafted, simply reflects the perspective of a committee which was charged with company law matters and not with the general criminal law. There is no good reason why the offence should be restricted to companies. Trading under a false appearance of solvency can occur in all forms of business organisation, and affects creditors adversely in all cases. A wider offence would not only extend coverage beyond that provided for by section 17 of the Theft Act 1968, but would apply generally to all forms of business. In one respect, the need for reform has been met; fraudulent trading is now punishable with a maximum of seven years' imprisonment on indictment, or six months and a fine not exceeding the statutory maximum on summary conviction.[27]

The fraudulent trading provisions could then advantageously be split, with the criminal offence going into the general criminal law and the civil provision placed in companies' legislation. The elements of liability might well differ in either case. There is an argument for retaining a narrow mental element of intent to defraud criminally, even though other jurisdictions have extended liability to recklessness,[28] and even though few prosecutions are now brought for the offence. There is, for example, a substantial question of whether the courts would consider themselves able to pronounce with sufficient expertise upon whether willingness to run a risk was in fact justifiable, for in any finding of recklessness a court must determine both that the accused was aware of the risk and that it was unjustifiable for him to run it. English courts have been disinclined to censure the taking of commercial risks. We have seen, also, that directors and others are apt to take risks with companies on the verge of insolvency, with a view to turning them around. No one wishes to prevent directors from taking steps which might result in the recovery of a company in difficulty. The moral message of the law has already been said to be doubtful, and it has been said that this results in few prosecutions being brought (Finer, 1966).

Would doubts about the criminality of conduct be more acutely felt if the mental element were extended? Criminally this could be more inhibiting than civilly, for the assessment for the justification of risk-taking would lie upon a lay jury, rather than upon a judge with experience in commercial matters. Would juries convict, save where the risks were truly appalling, or disregarded? There is a risk either that overbroad prosecutions would be brought, or that prosecutors would react too timidly, and there is a further practical danger that if an unwise prosecution failed, the prospect of bringing civil proceedings might be compromised. There is thus an argument for leaving the criminal offence with a narrowly drawn mental element. This was the view taken by the Company Law Committee of 1962 (Cmnd. 1749, 1962).

Civilly, liability could well be extended. This would both increase the possibility of recovery for creditors and reinforce whatever deterrent value the section has. Here, one is not dealing with a lay jury. A court should be able to determine whether a risk was of a character and gravity such that it should not have been run, and whether directors were, or should have been aware, of the point. Matters of business judgement are no doubt difficult, but they are not impossible for a court, particularly a commercial court, to evaluate, and in case of doubt, civilly as well as criminally, the controllers' view will prevail. Already, in general company law, civil actions by shareholders are permitted where directors, by negligence, have come into possession of the company's property, and a statutory extension of the sort advocated here would be but an extension of a developing and wholesome trend.[29] Directors can, in many cases, protect themselves and their company by taking specialist advice. Equally, there should, for example, be no inhibition to their personal liability where, for reasons which are plainly inadequate, they disregard it and the company becomes insolvent as a result.

References and Notes

1. *Salomon* v. *Salomon and Co. Ltd.* [1897] A.C. 22.
2. *Reg.* v. *Gurney* (1869) 14 Cox C.C. 414 at p. 438 *per* Cockburn L.C.J.
3. *Reg.* v. *Hall* [1973] Q.B. 126; *Reg.* v. *Hayes* (1977) 64 Cr. App. R. 82.
4. On the tests see *Barclays Bank Ltd.* v. *Quistclose Investments Ltd.* [1970] A.C. 567 at p. 581; *Re Kayford Ltd.* [1975] 1 All E.R. 604; *Reg.* v. *Prast* [1975] 2 N.Z.L.R. 248.
5. A floating charge is a device by which a creditor can take a secured interest over property and, in particular, stock-in-trade. The company can continue trading under such circumstances and can give good title to goods which it sells since, as long as all goes well, the security does not vest possession in the creditor. If the company becomes insolvent, the floating charge 'crystallises' (a notorious mixed metaphor), the holder of the floating charge takes possession of such assets as the company then has, and does so in priority to other, unsecured, creditors. In the example posed in the text, the controller gains because he holds the goods as a secured creditor, whereas the defrauded supplier ranks as a general creditor, behind him, unless the supplier can prove that the transaction was fraudulent. (Northey and Leigh, 1980; Gower, 1979).
6. Companies Act 1928, s. 75; Companies Act 1929, s. 274.
7. *Reg.* v. *Schildkamp* [1971] A.C. 1.
8. See discussion in Sess. 1979–80, H.C., Standing Committee A, Companies Bill [Lords], cols. 715–16.
9. *In re Cyona Distributors Ltd.* [1967] 1 Ch. 889.
10. *In re Cooper Chemicals Ltd.* [1978] 2 W.L.R. 866.
11. *Re Patrick and Lyon Ltd.* [1933] 1 Ch. 787.
12. *Ibid.*
13. [1979] 2 W.L.R. 202.
14. *In re William C. Leitch Brothers, Limited* [1932] 2 Ch. 71.
15. Note that whether or not the security can be avoided is not decisive, for one of the purposes of the section is to impose liability on directors and others where it cannot be; also, see *Re Patrick and Lyon Ltd.* [1933] 1 Ch. 787.
16. Criminal Justice Act 1967, s. 8, and, in addition to cases above, *Hardie* v. *Hanson* [1960] A.L.R. 209; *Re Day-Nite Carriers Ltd. (In Liquidation)* [1975] 1 N.Z.L.R. 172.
17. *Re William C. Leitch Brothers, Limited* [1932] 2 Ch. 71.
18. This certainly influenced government thinking; see Companies Act 1929, *Minutes of Evidence Taken Before the Company Law Amendment Committee*, 1943–4, p. 119.

19. *Re William C. Leitch Brothers, Limited* [1932] 2 Ch. 71.
20. *Reg.* v. *Wax*, 1957 (4) S.A. 399.
21. *Reg.* v. *Lavender* (1971) 56 Cr. App. R. 355; the *Cadco* and *Pinnock* Reports are also good examples of the genre.
22. *In re Cooper Chemicals Ltd.* [1978] 2 W.L.R. 866 at p. 871.
23. *Per* Maugham J. in *Re William C. Leitch Brothers Limited, supra.*
24. *In re Cyona Distributors Ltd.* [1967] 1 Ch. 889.
25. *In re William C. Leitch Brothers, Limited (no. 2)* [1932] 1 Ch. 261.
26. See *dicta* of Russell L.J. in *In re Cyona Distributors Ltd., supra.*
27. Companies Act 1980, s. 80 and Sched. 2.
28. See *McPherson* v. *Carrigan, ex p. Carrigan* [1978] A.C.L.R. 514. Section 374c. (2) of the New South Wales Companies Act 1961 as amended by s. 9(*i*) of Act no. 61 of 1971 is to this effect as is s. 424(1) of the Companies Act 1973 (South Africa).
29. *Daniels* v. *Daniels* [1978] Ch. 406.

PART III

THE INSTITUTIONS OF CONTROL

We now turn to consider the functions and powers of the institutions of control within Britain. The control of commercial fraud is the responsibility both of governmental and of self-regulatory bodies. Of these, the body which, historically, has been most intimately connected with the regulation of commercial and financial institutions is the Department of Trade. It has, of course, a general oversight over company administration and company law. It exercises control over insurance companies. This control is closer in character than that which it exercises in respect of ordinary trading companies, because insurance is a primary investment medium for many people. It also exercises control over certain sectors of dealings in securities and other investment media. Together with the Bank of England, it forms part of the Joint Review Body, charged with surveying the markets and reviewing arrangements for their supervision and for the delimitation of the respective competences of governmental and self-regulatory bodies (Financial Institutions Committee 1980, pp. 308–10).

For the purposes of this work, we concentrate upon the following aspects of the Department's responsibilities: the control of investment frauds, and of dealings in securities (but not of deposit-taking, which now falls under the Bank of England); frauds by those operating insurance companies; frauds by those running companies generally; frauds revealed by the compulsory liquidation of companies and reported by Official Receivers to the Department; frauds revealed by bankruptcy proceedings, or by complaints to Official Receivers about bankrupts.

We thus do not concentrate upon the routine work of administration conducted by the Department, but its importance to the control of fraud should not be underestimated. By reducing the number of dormant companies on the register, it inhibits their purchase and use for improper purposes. By prosecuting for failure to submit returns, it strikes at inactivity which can cloak fraud, and it can, as will be seen, set the stage for an application for an order to disqualify a person from acting as a director. By law reform, it can increase disclosure to shareholders, reduce the possibility of unredressed abuses of power and improve standards of disclosure. But these are matters which must be left, for the most part, to general works on company law and practice.

Control over Dealings in Securities and Unit Trusts

Control over securities and unit trusts is secured by the Prevention of Fraud (Investments) Act 1958, the derivation of which has already been noted. The Bodkin report, which found that the principal vice in connection with dealings in securities was high-pressure selling of speculative shares, often in foreign companies, suggested, as a basic approach, regulation of dealers in securities rather than close regulation of the terms of such dealing. This emphasis has altered to some extent, to comprehend obligations to furnish certain information to customers and, until recently, to impose limits on servicing charges on unit trusts.

The primary thrust of the legislation was, however, to regulate entry into the securities industry and to prohibit certain activities, engaging in which could subject the individual to prosecution and to the possible loss of any facility which he had to engage in the securities market. The right to deal in securities was thus restricted to persons licensed by the Department of Trade, to members of a recognised stock exchange or association of dealers in securities (in practice the Association of Stock and Share Dealers), to the Bank of England, certain financial institutions and exempted dealers, and to the manager or trustee of an authorised unit trust scheme.

The Department of Trade grants licences upon receipt of a proper application (Cmnd. 6893, 1977; Financial Institutions Committee 1980, p. 302). Licences are issued to principals or their representatives, and require a deposit of £500 or a guarantee. The Department has power to revoke licences for a number of reasons. A licence may be revoked if the licence holder (or applicant) fails to provide information about himself and the way in which he is likely to carry on business.[1] Revocation is also provided for under the following heads: that the applicant, or the holder of a licence or any person employed with or associated with him for the purpose of his business,[2] was convicted within the British Dominions of any offence involving a finding of fraud or dishonesty; was convicted of an offence under the 1958 Act or its predecessor; committed a breach of the rules regulating the affairs or conduct of business of licensed dealers; has ceased to carry on business as a licensed dealer in securities in the United Kingdom. The omnibus provisions of section 5(2)(b) of the Prevention of Fraud (Investments) Act 1958 provide for revocation where circumstances suggest that business is likely to be conducted improperly, or discreditably, by the applicant or holder of a licence or his associates.

Before revoking a licence, the licence holder must be given a hearing before a tribunal. The applicant or licence holder may appeal to a tribunal of inquiry. There have only been five refusals or revocations in the past ten years, generally relating to cases where there has been fraud or a breach of the Licensed Dealers rules (Financial Institutions Committee 1980, p. 301). Moreover, there have only been seven appeals since the Act came into force.

The Department of Trade recognises associations of dealers in securities, of which there are five. In practice they adopt rules similar to those which govern licensed dealers. Uniformity of rule thus results. Orders for recognition may be revoked, but this has only been done for technical reasons, following mergers of such associations. Exempt dealers are bodies such as banks, discount houses, and the like, which deal in securities only incidental to their main activities. Authorised unit trusts are those which satisfy departmental criteria concerning the status and independence of trustees and managers, the requisite spread of investments and their liquidity.

Terms of trading are not in general regulated. We have already noted the protective provisions of the applicable rules and, in particular, the prohibition against door-to-door selling.[3] Once a dealer has established business relations with his customer, however, he is free, within the limits of the civil and criminal law relating to misrepresentation, to circulate literature recommending and offering shares or other securities which he wishes to promote. It is generally agreed that the present system needs to be reformed. The structure of the 1958 Act is in some ways antiquated and its terms are often ambiguous (Cmnd. 6893, 1977). Thus, the Department of Trade considers that the range of occupations covered by the Act needs to be reviewed. In fact, control has been fairly successfully accomplished by controlling entry into the industry, although there are more exempt dealers than was originally contemplated. But the scope of the present system does not, for example, embrace a number of investment advisers and consultants whose activities may include making investments for clients. This is not to say that all activities of investment advisers fall outside the control of the Act. The Department considers, for example, that an investment adviser may not charge a performance fee to investment clients without obtaining a departmental licence, and would not, in any event, be prepared to grant a licence in respect of activities so speculative in nature (Raw, 1977).

The number of investment advisers has increased greatly in recent years, and the distinction between those who do and those who do not require to be licensed has become blurred. The Department proposes that persons offering an advisory service for the management or investment of securities in return for a fee (whether related to the value of the securities or not) should be licensed, either under the same system as dealers in securities or under some other system. At present, the criterion would appear to be whether the fee is related to performance so as to appear to be an agreement whereby a profit is secured from the yield, or performance, of securities. Licensed investment consultants would be permitted to distribute investment circulars to their clients without contravening the Act.

Currently, certain persons are allowed to distribute circulars by special permission. There is a problem concerning the offer of securities in smaller companies, particularly in relation to take-overs. The Department has been unwilling to force bidders to consult licensed dealers and it has therefore granted permission on an *ad hoc* basis, provided that adequate safeguards are maintained. Where public companies are concerned, it has stipulated that the offers comply with the City Code on Take-Overs and Mergers.[4] The mechanism is to be reviewed.

Originally, it was thought that the exempt dealer category would apply only to a few banks or discount houses whose dealings in securities formed but a small part of their total dealings or took the form of 'wholesale' dealings in which the public was not involved. This has become distorted with the rise of new types of financial institutions. Furthermore, exemption has been sought as a mere status symbol. The Department proposes to exercise discretion over bodies like banks and insurance companies which are presently regulated statutorily over their main field of activity, and to employ the licensing system to cater for other types of financial institution (Cmnd. 6893, 1977, p. 9).

The Department needs a more flexible structure of powers respecting the granting and revocation of licences. At present, it can only grant or refuse a licence; it feels the need for a power which will enable it to defer a decision on a licence or to suspend a decision rather than to refuse a licence outright. Powers both to revoke and to suspend should be provided for. In determining fitness the Tribunal should have access to material uncovered in an inspection under section 109 of the Companies Act 1967. At present such information cannot be disclosed.[5] Further suggested changes are: to require an applicant to disclose court-martial convictions; to provide for the revocation of a representatives' licence when the holder ceases to

deal in securities; to require a valid representatives' licence to be
held by an eligible person where the principal licence holder is a
corporation; to grant power to the Department to inspect the books
and papers of non-corporate licence holders;[6] and to grant five-year
licences after an initial probationary period.

None of these are particularly sweeping suggestions. North
American agencies would, for example, require an applicant to
disclose criminal convictions in any part of the world, and would
take these into account in reaching a decision (Leigh, 1979).
Continental legal systems permit their authorities to do likewise.[7]
Powers to defer and to suspend are common elsewhere. One striking
omission from the catalogue of actual and proposed controls is any
requirement that the applicant or licence holder demonstrate
competence in his profession. In North America, there are well
developed examination systems, designed to ensure that salesmen
will have a basic minimum knowledge of the securities industry.
Neither in securities nor, as will be seen, in insurance does the
Department lay down standards of competence for salesmen.

Similarly, unit trusts, as we have indicated, are regulated in
certain important respects. Restrictions on the mode of sale are
those which apply to securities under the Prevention of Fraud
(Investments) Act 1958. Changes in the structure which regulates
unit trusts will come through the European Economic Communities.
The Department, in anticipation of a directive on the matter, has
not formulated a consultative document (Financial Institutions
Committee 1980, pp. 444–5). Finally, we may mention the
investment trust company. This is an ordinary company which
invests in securities and property and sells shares in itself to the
public. It comes under the general regime of companies legislation,
but is entitled to certain tax concessions which are also enjoyed by
unit trusts.

Insurance[8]

The Department of Trade enjoys extensive regulatory powers over
insurance. Its broad philosophy is that companies shall be free to do
business as they wish, subject however to certain constraints on their
investment policies that result from the solvency requirements of
insurance company legislation, to controls on entry into the industry
and on who may manage, and to the provision of information
sufficient to enable the Department to perform its monitoring
function. Thus, the Department does not regulate the terms of
policies, or premium rates or, with the exception of equity-linked
policies permitted forms of investment, policy conditions or methods

of sale (*Equity-Linked Life Insurance,* Cmnd. 5281, 1973). Departmental control may be summed up under three heads: control over entry into the industry; continued monitoring of a company's affairs, and intervention in order to ensure continued solvency.

Insurance companies are subject to a minimum capital requirement. After the financial difficulties of 1974 in which twelve motor insurance companies and one life insurance company collapsed, control by the Department of Trade was strengthened (Financial Institutions Committee 1980, pp. 289–94). A recurrence of the troubles of those years is unlikely. Indeed, flotation of a new insurance company has become very difficult. In brief, controls over entry are devoted to ensuring that a company will have sufficient financial resources and reinsurance arrangements. Its controllers must be fit and proper persons. The Department has powers to ensure that insurance companies will not commence or carry on business where it does not consider controllers to be fit and proper.[9] The company must give information about the company's business plan, that is, its proposed capital structure, types of policy to be offered, marketing methods, estimated premium income in respect of the initial years of operation, and likely capital expenditure.

The Department is also concerned with monitoring continuing requirements. The question of controllers is important here, as it is in relation to initial approval. Where the Department considers that a controller is unfit, it can restrict new business, require that certain classes of investments be not made or be liquidated, require it to maintain a portion of its assets in the United Kingdom, vest custody of assets in a trustee, limit premium income and order investigations. The prior consent of the Department is necessary for the appointment of new controllers, managing directors and chief executives of authorised insurance companies. Consent may be withheld if it is thought that a person is unfit. He has, of course, the right to make representations.[10]

The Department has encountered difficulties on civil liberties' grounds in exercising this jurisdiction. One case has apparently gone to the European Commission on Human Rights, while the Ombudsman has said that objections to fitness must be put with particularity to the individual concerned (Financial Institutions Committee 1980, p. 292). Individuals must, of course, be protected. On the other hand, the industry and the Department accept that controllers must be fit and proper persons morally and commercially.

The Department also regulates solvency requirements, the valuation and spread of assets, the deposit of accounts and, where solvency is in issue, the classes of business in which the company may engage. It has wide powers of investigation. In right of its powers over insurance, the Department regulates equity-linked insurance. We have noted that, as the legislation stresses the insurance aspects of such instruments, they are regulated as such and not as securities.

Insolvency

Under this head, we deal with insolvency administration, both in relation to ordinary persons and to companies. This is one of the earliest heads of power developed in the Board of Trade (the predecessor of the present Department). Certain offences, as we have seen, grew up in order to eradicate abuses found to exist as a result of insolvency administration; fraudulent trading is an obvious example. Furthermore, it is to stresses and strains in enforcement, and an unwillingness on the part of liquidators to procure the commencement of criminal proceedings for fraud, that we owe our present arrangements, which include reliance on judicial supervision and the competence to prosecute of the Director of Public Prosecutions.[11]

The general structure of bankruptcy administration has been considered elsewhere (Leigh, 1980b). The principal actors in bankruptcy proceedings are the Official Receiver and the trustee. In the case of companies the officer corresponding to the trustee is the liquidator. The Official Receiver is an officer of the court appointed by the Department of Trade. In the exercise of his functions and in taking decisions concerning enforcement procedure he is obliged to act judicially and therefore independently of Departmental pressure.[12] His duties include that of investigating the bankrupt's conduct. The trustee, normally appointed by the creditors, is obliged to realise the property of the bankrupt for distribution among the creditors. Among the duties of the Official Receiver is that of conducting a public examination of the debtor, unless the court orders otherwise. He may, when applying for an order that the debtor be adjudged bankrupt, ask that the debtor be arrested, and his books, papers and property in his possession be seized.

The function of a public examination is to ensure that a thorough inquiry into the debtor's conduct will be made. The debtor must answer questions put to him and these may be given in evidence at his subsequent prosecution, but this does not apply in the case of theft.[13] It is the duty of the Official Receiver to report to the court on the bankrupt's affairs, including whether he has misconducted himself. If he has done so, his discharge may be delayed and the

Official Receiver will, if there is evidence of criminal conduct, report the matter to the Department of Trade with a view to prosecution. The gambling and books of account offences require the consent to prosecution of a court of bankruptcy jurisdiction. Furthermore, if the court acting under these provisions orders prosecutions, the Director of Public Prosecutions must take the case. By a proviso to the section, where the order of the court is based on the application and report of the Official Receiver the Department may prosecute the matter itself unless circumstances arise which in the opinion of the court or the Department require the Director of Public Prosecutions to be brought in. In effect, he must be brought in where the accused elects for trial on indictment.[14] This procedure is unnecessary and antiquated.

The structure of bankruptcy administration thus involves the oversight of the Official Receiver in every case. In most cases, the bulk of work is done by the trustee, the bankruptcy does not involve an offence and there is no need for the Official Receiver to intervene. Company winding-up presents a more complicated structure. Essentially, there are three modes of winding-up, namely, voluntary winding-up, winding-up under supervision of the court and compulsory winding-up by the court. There is thus a progression, from minimum interference in a procedure dominated by the creditors, to a procedure the major aspects of which are controlled by the court through the medium of the Official Receiver. Furthermore, one type of winding-up may be converted to another in order that the matter may not fall outside the ambit of judicial control where there are suspicious elements in the case. That is not to say that provisions concerning theft and fraud do not apply to voluntary liquidation. By law, a liquidator is bound to report offences to the Director of Public Prosecutions, and a court may give directions to that effect.[15] It is, however, doubtful if the machinery works well in the absence of control by the Official Receiver, which is a feature of compulsory winding-up.

We do not pretend to give a full account of winding-up. There are useful standard treatments of the topic (Pennington, 1979). Our concern is to elucidate the structure of control and so much of the doctrine as bears upon the discovery and prosecution of fraud. For our purposes, the most important mode is compulsory winding-up by the court, since voluntary winding-up is essentially a voluntary liquidation with some, but not extensive safeguards for those concerned, such as the requirement of quarterly reports to the court, protection against actions against the company (which could be unmeritorious but colluded in by other creditors and the liquidator) and the opportunity to make applications to the court.[16]

The Companies Acts set out the grounds upon which a winding-up petition may be presented to the court. Among these are failure to comply with the reporting requirements of the Companies Acts.[17] The most prominent provision is, however, section 222(*f*) of the Companies Act 1948, which permits the court to order a winding-up where it is of opinion that it would be just and equitable to do so. This latter ground is of cardinal importance. It includes cases of fraud and illegality in the conduct of the company's business, but it is not restricted to those grounds. It also extends to cases where the company is run in a manner oppressive to any part of its members.[18] It is a ground the importance of which is stressed by the Department, which, in fraud cases, does not see its functions as that of a prosecuting agency, solely, but also considers that it has a duty to salvage assets of the company as well as to prevent fraud. Its actions in the Kendal and Dent silver investment matter, for example, have largely been directed towards ensuring that moneys received from the public as deposits will not be spirited away.

In addition to the Department of Trade, a petition may be brought by a receiver, contributory or creditor. But the power of the Department of Trade to petition in cases of fraud is important because a shareholder can only bring proceedings if he can show that there would be assets available for distribution in a winding-up, or that he would be personally liable for the company's debts.[19] Thus, if matters were left to shareholder action, an insolvent company whose affairs were tainted with fraud might escape judicial scrutiny. Shareholders could not act, and creditors, fearing that nothing would be available for distribution, might not consider it in their interests to do so.

In order that cases which merit inspection will not escape it through adoption of a voluntary liquidation, the legislation provides that a creditor or contributory, or the Official Receiver or the Department of Trade, may petition for a compulsory winding-up, even though the company is in voluntary liquidation. The views of the members are given weight, but are not treated as decisive. Also considered are those of creditors.[20] Where the Department petitions, the court gives its views considerable weight since it acts in the public interest, and not in that of any particular class or group. Where there is evidence of fraud, it is particularly important that a compulsory winding-up be ordered, for this involves the Official Receiver in the process.[21]

Apart from fraud, the court will intervene where the liquidator is incompetent in performing his statutory duties and the creditors are

unwilling to replace him or seek his replacement by the court.[22]
Equally, the court will act where a contributory can show that the
liquidator refuses to investigate a *prima facie* case of misfeasance by
directors or promoters where there appear to be serious irregularities in the management of the company which call for an
investigation.[23] Old cases suggest that a court will not order a
compulsory winding-up where the petitioner can take proceedings
against the director in a voluntary winding-up.[24] It is debatable
what weight a modern court would give to this consideration. The
structure of the law reflects the extent to which the state has become
more interventionist since 1900. It is doubtful whether a member
would be forced back on his own resources in a case where the
conduct of directors appeared seriously to have injured the company
(cf. Pennington, 1979, pp. 714–15). Nor, one may hope, would a
court refuse a compulsory winding-up simply because an investigation would be unlikely to turn up assets for the benefit of creditors
and contributories. Parliament, by empowering the Department to
petition, surely signalled sufficiently its intention to depart from a
theory which premised judicial control simply upon the possibility
of minimising pecuniary loss to creditors and members. Recent
legislation emphasises wider public interests, including detection and
punishment of dishonesty by controllers of companies.

Even so, it is questionable how effective the present structures are.
Many cases are not brought within the compulsory procedure, nor
are creditors astute enough to ensure that liquidators report
instances of criminal conduct to the authorities. There is no sanction
upon a liquidator for failure to report. The Department of Trade at
present can issue guidelines to liquidators in voluntary liquidation,
but it cannot give directions to them. The consequence is that frauds
in medium-sized companies are sometimes not reported. Liquidators may in any event not wish to pursue matters which will not
result in a dividend for creditors (from which their fees are payable).
Furthermore, lacking training as investigators or prosecutors, they
are said sometimes to misplace documents and rarely to record their
origin. The consequence is that the task of the police is made
difficult when they come to deal with the matter. The problems
which arise in voluntary liquidation no doubt account for the
provision in the Companies Act 1980 which permits inspections
even where voluntary winding-up has commenced.[25]

Official Receivers probably cannot be expected to oversee all
corporate insolvencies, but liquidators could surely be better
instructed. In cases where a criminal investigation appears
appropriate, they should be encouraged to apply to the Official

Receiver for help, and their fees should be paid from public funds. The Official Receiver oversees compulsory windings-up. It is he who investigates. Because he has wide powers to compel statements of witnesses and the production of documents, the Department of Trade does not order investigations and inspections in such cases. A statement of the company's affairs must be submitted to the Official Receiver.[26] This is an accounting document which sets out the assets of the company and their expected realisable value, and its liabilities and the estimated deficiency or surplus. It is intended to show what assets are available to meet the liabilities of the company, and the reasons for any deficiency. Such a statement may be used in civil or criminal proceedings as evidence against the person making it.[27]

The Official Receiver must report to the court whether there has been fraud by any person in relation to the promotion or formation of the company or by any officer of the company since its formation.[28] He also reports instances of offences under companies legislation and other legislation to the Department of Trade, which can then make inquiries itself or ask the police to do so. Departmental annual reports show that about 75 to 100 reports are made in any given year, and prosecutions for offences under insolvency legislation, theft and forgery brought by the police or the Department.

It has been asserted that the Official Receiver's obligation to report only applies where the fraud relates to promotion or formation, and not where it is a trading or financial fraud practised upon the world at large (Magnus and Estrin, 1978, p. 279). This, if true, would leave a gap in the structure of control. It would not necessarily be critical, because, while in many cases there would be no obligation to report matters to the court, the Official Receiver could, and indeed often does, report matters to the Department. But the case cited for the proposition, one of some antiquity though upon an identically worded statutory provision, is not directly on point.[29]

If the Official Receiver reports that further investigation is necessary, the court may make an order for the public examination of an officer or member of the company.[30] This power is, indeed, not restricted to the Official Receiver or to compulsory winding-up. A liquidator, creditor or contributory may apply to the court for such an examination in a voluntary winding-up, and it is not necessary that there be a report by the Official Receiver.[31] The Company Law Committee recommended that this provision be extended to empower the court to order the public examination of all or any of the directors or other officers of an insolvent company where there is some *prima facie* evidence of culpability, impropriety, recklessness or incompetence (Cmnd. 1749, 1962, para. 503(a)). This proposal was linked to another, to extend the grounds upon which persons could be disqualified from acting as directors, which will be considered later in this work.

All liquidators also have power to order the private examination of an officer.[32] In addition, the liquidator may examine evidence given to a Department of Trade Inspector under the general inspection provisions.[33] But courts have been reluctant to grant to liquidators facilities for the discovery of evidence, and the incrimination of officers, which they would deny to ordinary litigants in civil proceedings. It is the model of the civil trial which dominates judicial thinking, and not a conception of the wider public purposes of liquidation procedure, although those considerations play an important subsidiary role. Thus courts are chary of ordering an examination of an officer who is, or who is about to be, a defendant in a civil action to be brought by the company. Such a circumstance is not an absolute bar, however, provided that the liquidator can show that he needs information in order to enable him to proceed successfully with the winding-up.[34] The rule thus reflects a judicial desire to act fairly towards the director or officer involved as well as an unwillingness to concede to the liquidator as litigant powers to obtain discovery of information which an ordinary litigant would not have through interrogatories.[35] It is the duty of officers of companies to assist the liquidator in any winding-up by producing books and papers and delivering up property, and by providing full and accurate information concerning the affairs of the company.

There are other aspects of control by the court and by the Official Receiver in compulsory winding-up, for example, over the liquidator and his powers, the auditing of his accounts, the appointment of special managers, and the like. It seems unnecessary to dwell upon such details here. The fact is, as we have seen, that substantial powers in relation to fraud are to be found in both bankruptcy and winding-up procedure, even though there are few prosecutions in any given year (Dpt of Trade 1979, *Companies in 1978*, Table 12). Reasons are various. The Department does not have a large corps of lawyers and investigators. In the prosecution of bankruptcy offences for example, it has seven legally trained persons, supported by twenty case clerks and up to thirty investigators, but these individuals have other work to do as well. The establishment is thus a small one. Then too, some prosecutions do not result from this machinery because they are dealt with throughout by the police. This is certainly true of offences in bankruptcy such as that of obtaining credit by an undischarged bankrupt. Winding-up procedures are important in the control of fraud. But it could hardly be denied that powers of investigation and examination are not well integrated across the field of fraud.

Company Investigations and Inspections

The extensive provisions of English law for the investigation and inspection of companies are intended to assist the Department of Trade in pressing for remedial orders for companies, in obtaining information to enable prosecutions to be mounted, and in indicating areas where law reform is needed. Such investigations also, in the words of a Departmental official, hold up a mirror to the City, enabling the City and the public to obtain some idea, at least, of the current state of practices in commerce and finance.

These provisions originally stemmed from a narrower root. The Company Law Committee of 1943–4 was concerned because the system of prosecutions for fraud was relatively inefficient. Wide powers of examination existed in winding-up, but where winding-up procedures were not invoked the power was narrow, exercisable only on the petition of shareholders, and intended to obtain information for the use of shareholders in controlling management (Instone, 1978).[36] Few inspections were ordered in any given year (Cmd. 6659, 1945, paras. 154–6). There seems to have been a general view among members of the Committee, Sir Tindal Atkinson, the Director of Public Prosecutions dissenting, that wider inspection provisions and procedures would provide a useful mode of obtaining information and a stimulus to more vigorous prosecutions.

In the result, the Companies Act 1948 gave power to the Board of Trade (now the Department of Trade) to order an investigation on its own initiative, as well as on the initiative of shareholders. The Act contained the important principle that the costs of such investigations could fall on public funds. In effect, there was a shift in emphasis, from the inspection as a vehicle of private redress for the shareholders to that of a vehicle for obtaining information in the general public interest. This shift, indeed transformation, was not at once perceived. For some time after the passing of the 1948 Act, even departmental officials took the view that the reason for inspections remained that of eliciting facts for information purposes only (Rider and Hew, 1977). The Companies Act model was applied, in turn, with some alterations, to insurance companies, deposit-taking institutions, and building and provident societies.

Structure of Powers under the Companies Acts

The Companies Acts contain provisions both for preliminary

inspections and full investigations. Section 109(1) of the Companies Act 1967 gives power to the Department of Trade to conduct a preliminary inspection in unqualified terms; it may order an inspection at any time if it thinks that there is good reason to do so.[37] There is no requirement of suspected oppression or dishonesty, though that may well be implied. The Department may require the production of books and papers specified by it, either in the order or upon the request of an authorised officer. It has power also to order the production of such documents from any other person having possession of them. The Department may also require the person from whom production is demanded, or any other person who is a present or past officer of, or was at any time employed by, the company, to provide an explanation of them. Copies and extracts may be taken. If the papers are not produced, the person required to produce them must state, to the best of his knowledge and belief, where they are.[38] Failure to comply is made a criminal offence.[39] Answers so made, under compulsion of statute, are admissible in civil and criminal proceedings against the person making them.[40] The courts have held that the inspection is a policing measure; departmental officers are expected to act fairly, but a company or individual cannot decline to produce documents on the ground that the Inspector is biased against it or him.[41]

A justice may grant a warrant for search and seizure of documents which have not been produced after a demand for production has been made. Such documents may be retained for three months or until the conclusion of criminal proceedings commenced under sundry statutes.[42] Information so obtained is treated as confidential,[43] except so far as it is needed for criminal prosecutions arising under the statutes specified or, broadly, for the purpose of enabling the Department to exercise powers under companies and insurance legislation, or for the purpose of complying with powers relating to full investigations, or in aid of civil proceedings brought by the Department under section 37 of the Companies Act 1967, or with a view to winding-up the company, or to enable the Bank of England better to perform its statutory fuctions under the Banking Act 1979. It is not clear why information obtained by the use of such powers is protected so rigidly. There must, of course, be some limitations upon disclosure but, as admissions made in full investigations may be given in evidence in civil and criminal proceedings generally, it is curious that the use of information garnered in preliminary investigations should not be so available. The Department of Trade itself wishes the restrictions to be eased so that such material may be used in connection with either appeals from a refusal to license a person as a dealer in securities, or a decision to revoke such a licence.[44]

The inspection provisions are enforced by criminal penalties of some severity, in particular relating to the destruction or mutilation of documents[45] or the disclosure of confidential information.[46] Full powers of investigation are contained in sections 164, 165 and 172 of the Companies Act 1948, as amended by later legislation, and section 32 of the Companies Act 1967. The first two powers relate to the affairs of the company in general and overlap to some extent. The latter two relate to interests in securities. Under section 164 of the Companies Act 1948 the Department of Trade has a discretionary power to appoint Inspectors provided that the application is supported by a sufficient proportion of the membership. The applicants must show good cause for requiring an investigation, and the Department may require them to provide security for costs.

Section 165 contains broader powers. If the company by special resolution, or the court by order, declares that a company should be investigated by an Inspector appointed by the Department, the Department must appoint Inspectors and this duty can be enforced by *mandamus*.[47] In practice, most investigations are conducted under powers contained in section 165(*b*). This enables the Department to appoint Inspectors on the grounds that the business of the company is being carried on with intent to defraud creditors, or otherwise for a fraudulent or unlawful purpose, or in a manner unfairly prejudicial to its members, or that it was formed for a fraudulent purpose, or that its promoters or managers have been guilty of fraud, misfeasance or other misconduct towards it or its members, or—a ground which has become prominent in recent cases—that its members have not been given all the information with respect to its affairs which they might reasonably expect. These provisions are thus not limited to fraud. The jurisdiction of the Department is much wider.

Inspectors appointed under either of the preceding sections have power to investigate associated companies of the company primarily under investigation, that is, its subsidiary or holding company, if any, or a subsidiary of its holding company, or a holding company of its subsidiary. This power has long been thought to be too narrow. It is not possible, for example, to investigate the affairs of companies which are controlled by the same shareholder but in respect of which there is no nexus of shareholding (Cmnd. 1749, 1962, para. 217). This seems to have caused difficulty in the Pergamon investigation where the Inspectors, desirous of investigating the integrity of sales to associated companies, found distinctly inhibiting the fact that certain companies were separately controlled by Maxwell family trusts while others were incorporated abroad (*Pergamon Press Limited, Final Report*, 1973, pp. 457–66 and 483–91).

Officers and agents and former officers and agents of the company and other companies which are being investigated under these provisions must produce books and papers which are in their power. They must attend before the Inspectors when required to do so, and they must generally give to the Inspectors all assistance in respect of the investigation which they are reasonably able to give. Failure to comply may be brought before the High Court and there treated as a contempt of court.[48] This does not apply to directors' private bank accounts, an omission strongly criticised in the Ozalid investigation (1980). If an Inspector thinks it necessary to examine a person on oath whom he has no statutory power to examine, he may apply to the court for an order that the person be examined before the court. Admissions made before the court, like those made before Inspectors, may be used in evidence against the witness in later proceedings, whether civil or criminal, and whether brought by the Department, the company, or a liquidator.[49] The witness may be legally represented before the court.

Inspectors must make a final report.[50] They may make interim reports to the Department and may be directed to do so. Where there is reason to suspect the commission of criminal offences, Inspectors may so inform the Department without making a formal report.[51] The Department has power to print and publish reports. Apart from the *Rolls Razor* case, where some directors were acquitted, it does so in respect of all reports made by outside Inspectors. Internal reports, often into private companies, are not published unless they contain material of general public interest. Reports are admissible in legal proceedings as evidence of the opinion of the Inspectors in relation to any matter contained in the report. They are not evidence of findings of fact. Thus, in this respect, they are of limited utility in subsequent litigation. They do, no doubt, afford valuable assistance in organising litigation against the controllers, and of course the fact that admissions may be used is valuable also.

In addition to the foregoing provisions, there are also powers to investigate ownership of the company[52] and any share dealings which may have contravened provisions relating to dealings in directors' and family share interests.[53] In the former case, the investigation is to determine the true persons who are or have been financially interested in the success or failure of the company, or are able to control or materially to influence its policies. The same general regime of powers applies to these as to other inspections. In respect of inquiries into share ownership, the Department may require information from persons by request, and such information must be produced but the procedure is not that of a formal inquiry. The procedure applies to licensed and exempt dealers in securities in respect of directors' share interests.

In respect of investigations into ownership, the Department has power to impose restrictions on shares and debentures. If it encounters difficulty in obtaining information because of the attitude of the person under investigation, it may subject the shares to restrictions, concerning the alienation or voting of those shares, upon the payment of dividends on them and upon rights issues deriving from them. Once again, contravention is made a criminal offence.[54] There is, as we have seen, no general investigative power in respect of insider trading. Some, but not all of its manifestations will fall under the foregoing powers. The resulting deficiencies might be mitigated were the Department's suggestion that inspection powers be extended to non-incorporated dealers in securities to be adopted, but there is no indication that this is at all likely (Cmnd. 6893, 1977). Similar powers exist under legislation relating to building societies and credit unions. We do not consider their details here.[55]

The powers which relate to insurance companies reflect, as we have noted, a closer system of control than that which obtains in the case of ordinary trading companies. The structure of powers of investigation reflects these predilections, in particular the need for speed and for wide powers in view of the huge amounts of money invested in the industry (*Equity-Linked Life Assurance*, Cmnd. 5281, 1973, paras. 119–27). The Insurance Companies Act 1974 provides an elaborate structure. This includes the power to require a company which carries on long-term business to cause its actuary to make an investigation into its financial situation.[56] There is also a power to obtain information about matters which the Secretary of State specifies.[57] The most significant power is no doubt that which enables the Secretary of State to require production of books and papers. As with section 109 of the Companies Act 1967, the person producing the books or papers and any person who is a past or present director of the company may be required to provide an explanation of any of them. These powers are wider than their counterparts under the Companies Acts: information may be required from the company's controllers and from its auditors.[58] Under ordinary company legislation, there would seem to be no actual power to do this short of a full investigation. In practice, auditors would no doubt co-operate.

The interesting aspects of these powers are the wide grounds upon which they may be exercised and the uses to which they may be put. Under section 109 of the Companies Act 1967, the powers are used to obtain information for use in specified sorts of proceedings, in particular in determining whether to order a full investigation or to take certain classes of criminal and civil proceedings.[59] Under the Insurance Companies Act 1974, the powers may be exercised on the broad grounds of doubtful solvency, of failure to satisfy reporting obligations or to arrange adequate reinsurance, and of unfit management.[60] And whilst the Secretary of State must give the company one month's notice of intent to exercise the powers, within which period the company may make representations that such powers should not be used, no such period of notice is prescribed where the fitness of managerial personnel is in question, unless the person in question is a non-executive director. The requirements of speed and effectiveness have clearly been taken seriously. In addition to these broad powers, the normal structure of formal investigation powers under the Companies Act 1948 applies.

Historically, powers of investigation were only used sparingly. Practice, too, was conservative, both in ordering and conducting investigations. The Company Law Committee of 1945 found that during the period 1930–44, only 70 applications were received because persons holding at least 10 per cent of the issued equity shares had to apply and had to show that they did not act from any malicious motive (Cmd. 6659, 1945, para. 154). Powers were extended in 1948, but the Department was not given power to conduct a quiet preliminary investigation until 1967. Because of the danger of damaging a company through adverse publicity, the Department insisted upon a very high standard of proof before it would act. The Company Law Committee of 1962 found that a practice akin to Morton's fork was being exercised; that is, without considerable evidence to substantiate allegations, complainants were turned away on the ground that their applications were premature, whereas if a great deal were shown, the applicants were left to their remedies before the courts. Furthermore, it was the practice to send an indication of the complaint to the company concerned, which forewarned the directors (Cmnd. 1749, 1962, paras. 213–15).

Cadco shows the effect which this practice had upon complainants and their advisers. When the Marquis of Linlithgow bearded Loraine, charging him with misappropriating £30,000 for 'this rotten little factory of yours in London', he received scant satisfaction. When, having personally lost £20,000 in the venture, he considered the possibility of a Board of Trade investigation, his solicitors told him that he lacked the evidence to do so, and it was not until much further damage was done that Inspectors were appointed (*Cadco Developments Limited* 1966, p. 46). It is unlikely that the Department would be so reticent today. Nevertheless, a disabling attitude persisted for some time after the introduction of wider powers. In the Vehicle and General Insurance case, one reason why the Department failed to intervene at an earlier stage was that a policy persisted under which inspection powers were not used unless the insurance company was *prima facie* insolvent (*Vehicle and General Insurance Company Limited*, Tribunal, 1971–2, H.C. 133, paras. 162–6). Even today, problems of financial embarrassment sometimes govern action. Apparently, a full inspection was not conducted into Slater Walker (although a section 109 investigation was) because the Bank of England persuaded the Department of Trade that such an investigation would produce a disastrous loss of confidence. The circumstances of the secondary bank crash were of course exceptional, and the new management under Sir James Goldsmith did undertake to commission an investigation by independent accountants (Raw, 1977).

Inquiries were conducted on conservative lines also. The discretionary powers of the Board of Trade were, as we have seen, new in the 1948 Act. Hitherto, inquiries had been conducted with a view to informing shareholders. Furthermore, early inquiries under the 1948 Act were brought as a result of shareholder resolutions. As a result, some early reports tended to find facts, but not to evaluate nor to venture constructions on disputed points of law, a function which Inspectors, conscious that their opinion could not be binding, left to the courts. Thus, in Hide & Co. Ltd., the Inspectors stated: 'consideration of any extension of an auditor's rights and duties is obviously outside the scope of this report' (Report 1958, p. 54). In Town Centre Properties, the Inspectors declined to express an opinion on the proper construction of section 54 of the Companies Act 1948, again on the basis that their proper task was that of fact-finding. They did, however, cast considerable doubt on the propriety of one class of transaction in the light of that section (Report 1968, p. 57). In Gordon Hotels Limited, perhaps the least valuable of a long line of such reports, Mr. (later Mr. Justice) Melford Stevenson determined, in the light of allegations of fraud, to exclude from consideration all matters which would not be admissible in a court of law, and that notwithstanding that, as was admitted, the strict rules of evidence did not apply before him. As a result, one barely knows even the broad outlines of the matter (Report 1957, p. 4).

Today, in both the ordering and conduct of investigations, practice has changed considerably. Powers of investigation are more widely used and Inspectors regard their functions more expansively. The relative confidentiality of section 109 procedure, under which most investigations start, enables the Department to intervene without fearing detriment to the company under investigation to the same extent. Furthermore, Inspectors are prepared to express opinions on such matters as business and accounting practices and standards, and the law and its shortcomings. Most inspections are ordered under the Department's own powers in section 165(*b*) of the Companies Act 1948. The Department considers that its powers are aimed principally at fraud, misfeasance or other misconduct, and are not used solely to investigate insolvency or as a substitute for civil remedies available through the courts (Dpt of Trade 1979, *Companies in 1978*, p. 1).

Evidently, powers of inspection are not restricted to fraud. Oppression, misconduct, and conduct unfairly prejudicial to members are not necessarily indicative of a scheme to defraud. Nor is a failure to keep members informed, an important ground invoked in the Lowson and Pergamon cases, indicative necessarily of fraud, and indeed, there was no finding of fraud in the latter case. But the provision, plainly, is not used as a recourse in cases of simple bad management, although simple mismanagement is often the vice uncovered by reports. Situations which appeared fraudulent were revealed as examples of incompetence (*Electerminations Ltd.*, Report, 1978). One is not surprised to find mismanagement in the case of private, and even locally-based small public, companies in some aspects of their affairs. The revelation that the amateur directors of the North Devon Railway Company Limited were not conversant with the flotation procedures for public companies is not surprising. The Inspectors conclude, somewhat optimistically perhaps, of the scheme to purchase and operate the Barnstaple to Ilfracombe railway line, that 'It must be rare that an operation of such magnitude has been undertaken, when virtually everyone involved with it has been so manifestly unfitted for the task' (Report 1979, p. 49).

It is rather more discouraging to find that a company as large as Court Line Limited suffered from woeful mismanagement. Yet the Inspectors attributed the failure of that enterprise to large borrowing, over-optimism, an expensive and disastrous incursion into the Caribbean, inadequate overall management and a share of ill-luck. A lack of management systems may sound arcane. Many irregularities occurred. But even the common reader (if such there be, of departmental reports) would appreciate that it takes a mind of some buoyancy to venture into Caribbean hotel developments in entire ignorance of the costs likely to be incurred, the rate of hotel occupancy to be expected, the probable availability of staff, and even the possibility of mooring leisure boats at the sites selected for the purpose (Final Report, 1978). If, therefore, mismanagement is not a ground for appointment, it is a phenomenon often uncovered, and draws attention to management weaknesses which occur both within and outside fraud situations.

It has long been the tradition to appoint as Inspectors of major public companies an eminent Queen's Counsel, chosen after consultation with the Attorney-General, and an eminent accountant, who may be chosen after consultation with the appropriate professional body.[61] The smaller investigations are conducted by departmental personnel. The practice of using outsiders to conduct major inquiries has been criticised, but it should conduce to judgements of an authoritative character on the matters under review.

There is no even pattern of investigations. The numbers vary from year to year, and there was a notable bulge at the time of the secondary bank crashes of 1974. Most matters do not go beyond the preliminary stage, since the appointment of an investigator under section 109 is often enough to cause the company to put its affairs in order. But, today, in about one-quarter of the cases in which a full investigation is requested, action under section 109 is at least taken (Dpt of Trade 1979, *Companies in 1978*). The necessity for something akin to moral turpitude as the foundation of an investigation governs the approach of Inspectors and courts to procedures which are, frankly, inquisitorial. Their nature was put thus in the Peachey case (*Peachey Property Corporation Limited* 1979, p. 4):

> The powers and procedures of company inspectors are exceptional in English jurisprudence. They sit in private. As the case develops they must devise and frame their own provisional charges and accusations and then proceed to test them. Everyone may become a 'defendant' to a possible criticism but he is not able to cross-examine his accusers. Even mild criticisms of professional men can be extremely damaging. Unless inspectors are very careful a witness may not be aware of the strength of the evidence against him in time to make his answers.

The legislation does not prescribe any procedure for investigations and does not, therefore, specify any safeguards for witnesses who may in turn become the object of civil or criminal proceedings. It is true that investigations do not determine rights. The possibility of eventual legal proceedings together with the undoubted prejudice which adverse publicity causes and the threat of exposure, however justified, led to accusations of Star Chamber procedures.

The extent to which Inspectors are prepared to express strongly worded criticism should not be underestimated. For example, in Lonrho, the former chairman and joint managing director, Ball, was said to have acted improperly and to merit severe criticism in respect of certain option dealings. The same criticism was made of another director, the Hon. A. Ogilvy who, in addition, was said to have acted negligently in respect of Lonrho transactions concerning Rhodesian sanctions to an extent that merited severe criticism. Mr. Rowland, the chief executive, was himself criticised in respect of several transactions concerning option dealings (*Lonrho Limited*, Report, 1976, pp. 622, 632, 636, 643).

Gerald Caplan, the moving spirit in the London and County Securities Group Limited, was said to have less regard for the truth and a lower standard of integrity than is reasonably to be demanded of the chairman and managing director of a public company. His example was said to have had the effect of corrupting junior members of the staff who 'could only suppose that if they were told what to do by a person of the wealth and power of Mr. Caplan, it must be unexceptionable' (Report, 1976, pp. 24 and 252). The wounding fluency of the Inspectors in London Capital Group Limited led them to conclude that '[in] relation to the subject of our investigation we concluded that for Mr. Stonehouse truth was a moving target' (Report, 1977, p. 2). In E.J. Austin International Limited, the Inspectors stigmatised certain of the individuals concerned as parties to a conspiracy to defraud (Report, 1972, p. 52). It would be possible, but unprofitable, to multiply examples. There can be no doubt that reports must be frank if they are to be useful. But the need for frankness carries with it an obligation to act fairly. Persons under investigation are naturally concerned to ensure that proper procedures are adopted.

Issues concerning the conduct of investigations came to a head in the Pergamon investigation. Mr. Robert Maxwell, who the Inspectors were to conclude was unfit to manage a public company (*Pergamon Press Limited*, Interim Report, 1971, p. 207), objected most strongly to the conduct of the investigation. Ever resourceful, he took a series of counter-measures. These delayed the investigation considerably, but led the courts to lay down some of the ground rules for the conduct of such procedures. The procedures in question were parliamentary, administrative and judicial, and they were based on heads of Board of Trade practice, in particular as it evolved to the time of the Report of the Company

Law Committee in 1962. For example, when the Inspectors sought to investigate the affairs of Robert Maxwell & Co. Ltd., a private Maxwell company, Mr. Maxwell sent a complaint to the Ombudsman via his M.P. that the Board of Trade had been guilty of maladministration in appointing the Inspectors without giving Mr. Maxwell an opportunity to comment on that decision in advance (*Pergamon Press Limited*, Final Report, 1973, p. 371). Parliamentary questions were asked concerning the obligations of Inspectors to allow witnesses to see draft sections of reports relating to them (*Pergamon Press Limited*, Further Interim Report, 1972, pp. 349–50). Judicial redress was sought.

In the first Pergamon case, Mr. Maxwell declined to give evidence unless the witnesses were allowed to read transcripts of evidence adverse to them, to examine documents used against them, and to cross-examine witnesses.[62] The Court of Appeal concluded that Inspectors are obliged to act fairly. They must, before reporting, give the directors a chance to answer criticisms and allegations, and for that purpose an outline of the criticisms will usually suffice. Otherwise, there is no set procedure. In particular, the action of the Inspectors in offering to witnesses transcripts of their own evidence, but not of those of other witnesses, was upheld in the interests of encouraging witnesses to come forward; assurances about confidentiality made to them by Inspectors were necessary and ought to be upheld. While the court was mindful of the need to act fairly, it had to balance against this the need for expeditious procedures if some of the purposes of the investigation system were to be attained, and in particular the need to make speedy interim reports for prosecution purposes.

In the second Pergamon case, these considerations were reiterated.[63] Mr. Maxwell contended that the Inspectors ought first to formulate their provisional conclusions in a draft report and put these to the witnesses before proceeding to submit a final report. This contention was also rejected. The court was anxious to avoid a situation in which witnesses would seek to refute tentative conclusions by calling other witnesses or asking for further investigations, since that would hold up the inquiry indefinitely. It is sufficient if the Inspectors put the points fairly to the witnesses when they come in the first place. The Inspectors need not formulate draft conclusions for comment. In any event, the Inspectors in the Pergamon case had acted fairly. They had put the substance of their criticisms before Mr. Maxwell, and they had given him ample opportunity to explain his conduct. Their obligation is to give the witness a fair opportunity to explain the facts; the inferences to be drawn from the facts is a matter for the Inspectors. Furthermore, the fairness of the inquiry is to be judged not by looking at isolated aspects of it, but on a view of the whole of the procedure. In respect of the particular investigation, the attacks upon the Inspectors did not emerge with much credence. Lord Denning M.R. castigated the harassing attack upon them as unseemly. Lawton L.J. remarked: 'For my own part I can but admire the way he [Mr. Owen Stable Q.C.] dealt with a witness who tended to be verbose and irrelevant.'[64]

A third significant case, *Norwest Holst Ltd.* v. *Department of Trade*,[65] settles the principle that the Department need not warn a company to be investigated under section 165(*b*) of that fact and invite it to make representations before Inspectors are appointed. If there were such a requirement, there would be an obvious danger that books and papers might be destroyed or lost. In deciding whether to order an inquiry or not, the Secretary of State must act fairly. He must weigh the need for an investigation against any possible prejudice to the company, and the court cannot review that decision.[66] Certainly, the Labour Government declined to revert to the former practice of forwarding a statement to the company before appointing Inspectors, on the ground that to do so would risk the destruction or alteration of documents and threats to witnesses.[67]

Inspectors, naturally, tend to work to the guidelines laid down by the courts. These, however, state a minimum. Inspectors may adopt more stringent rules in the interests of fairness. In general, witnesses are supplied with transcripts of their own evidence. They may not only be shown documents upon which they are to be examined, but given copies of them. Witnesses are given full opportunity to develop their version of the case, are informed of any criticisms to be made of their conduct, and invited to make representations upon them. In Larkfold Holdings Limited, the witnesses were informed that their answers might later be used in evidence against them (Report, 1979, p. 2). Legal representation is freely permitted. In some instances, Inspectors went beyond the minimum. In Roadships Limited, Peachey Property Corporation Limited and in Larkfold, they gave the witnesses the opportunity to comment on draft conclusions. Inspectors show, or should show, restraint in important respects. They should be sure before they criticise, and should give witnesses the benefit of any reasonable doubt before doing so. But a criminal standard of proof need not be met. Because Inspectors do not wish to embarrass criminal proceedings, full reports are often withheld until such proceedings (which sometimes derive from interim or informal reports) are concluded.

Inspectors have not been prepared to allow witnesses to examine other witnesses or have transcripts of the evidence of such witnesses. Several grounds have been advanced to support this. If the investigation is to be reasonably thorough, and yet not unreasonably protracted, it must be held in private. It is therefore impossible to allow cross-examination of witnesses by other witnesses. Nor is it possible to supply transcripts to other witnesses without risking the possibility that witnesses will be inhibited from giving the evidence which they would otherwise give *(London and Counties Securities Group Limited,* 1976, p. 5). In Lonrho, the Inspectors refused to have a joint meeting with contradictory witnesses, partly on general procedural grounds and partly because they feared that one would intimidate the other *(Lonrho Limited,* 1976, p. 617).

The procedures which Inspectors have adopted seem fair, given the nature of their function. Indeed, the procedure has become so elaborate that the investigation process can be time-consuming enough to thwart, partially at least, the purposes of such an inquiry. It is, nevertheless, regarded by the Department of Trade as an acceptable compromise.[68] Despite elaborate attempt at fairness, complaints of Star Chamber procedures are still made (Sealey, 1974). It is not surprising that this should be so. A person under investigation may feel that he has a justified grievance, even where he has none. Complaints may be made for more sinister reasons,— to inhibit the investigation, or detract from the authority of the report when it is completed.

It is disconcerting that patently unfounded smears are sometimes given currency by an otherwise astute financial press. Dowgate affords an example of this. Mr. Christopher Selmes, whose activities were under review, sought to denigrate the lawyer Inspector by raising a specious conflict of interest point against him. The Inspector took the advise of the Bar Council which confirmed that no such conflict arose. Yet Selmes used this allegation to explain his unwillingness to return to England to testify, and contrived to convince the *Investors' Chronicle* that he was the victim of unfairness *(Ferguson and General Investments Limited, formerly Dowgate,* Report, 1979).

The credence to be given to the factual conclusions in the report, and its style, are matters for the reader's judgement. But the alleged conflict of interest is hardly convincing. The report notes that Selmes had been a client some years previously on a matrimonial matter. The Bar Council could see no conflict of interest; neither could the Secretary of State. The Inspectors conclude, in effect, that Selmes was afraid to give evidence for fear that his conduct would not stand close scrutiny. Lurid allegations of

Star Chamber tactics are curiously at variance with the procedures detailed in the report as those followed by the Inspectors. On the whole, given the advantages to persons under investigation, of spoiling attacks, a certain scepticism regarding their allegations is warranted.

The Result of Investigations

Investigations may lead to criminal prosecution or civil redress, at the suit of either the company or the Department of Trade. It is not, of course, necessary to have an investigation before a prosecution is commenced. In 1976–7 the House of Commons was informed that of seventeen company cases currently referred to the Director of Public Prosecutions, nine were the subject of investigations under section 165(b), and eight of inspections under section 109.[69] In any event, it is not necessary to wait for a full report since Inspectors can, and do, make informal reports using section 41 procedure, as they did for example in Roadships Limited. This ought to speed matters up, but the police sometimes delay completion of their inquiries until the end of a formal investigation because they are thus able to obtain transcripts of the evidence of witnesses. In addition, the preliminary procedure under section 109 is not as helpful to the police as it should be, since the Department of Trade takes the view that the restrictions on the communication of information contained in the relevant section precludes turning material over to the police simply for use in a criminal investigation.[70] This is certainly a reasonable construction of the section which stipulates that information can only be disclosed for the institution of certain categories of prosecution. But the restriction hardly seems desirable.

Apart from civil proceedings for the recovery of damages and property, which are not restricted by any need to show moral turpitude on the part of directors, the Department of Trade may also petition for a winding-up, or for an order to rectify a situation whereby the members of the company are being unfairly prejudiced by the manner in which its affairs are being conducted.[71] No such order has ever been made (Instone, 1978).

A copy of the final report is sent to the company concerned.[72] In cases where fraud is not shown and neither a prosecution nor civil proceedings are taken, the company is left to reform itself. Naturally the stricter regime which applies to insurance companies may lead to the forced removal of a controller as an unfit person notwithstanding that formal civil and criminal procedures are not taken. But, in the case of an ordinary trading company, matters are in the hands of the shareholders, influenced no doubt by creditors and others. In the result, executives may be retained despite stringent criticism in the report. This happened in the cases of both Lonrho and Pergamon, where contributors to the Pergamon scientific journals displayed great loyalty to Mr. Robert Maxwell. It is not surprising that, on occasion, shareholders prefer the entrepreneurial drive of a man who has created an enterprise to the consolidating methodicalness of more orthodox figures. Even so, the inspection may, by bringing a dominant figure under control, have done much to put the enterprise on a firmer footing.

Evaluation

In what terms, then, is the investigation and inspection system to be judged? It would seem to have four functions: to inform shareholders; to form the basis for criminal prosecutions and civil proceedings; to find the lacunae in systems of legal and administrative control; and to enable the informed public to judge the propriety and the wisdom of current business practices. There is no doubt that the system. suffers from inhibitions which prevent it from fulfilling all its functions as effectively as one would wish. The system, inevitably, embodies compromises. It is both expensive and slow. Dr. Hadden notes that in 1977, payments to external Inspectors totalled £999,000 and in 1978, £919,439 (Hadden, 1980). A single major inspection can cost up to £500,000.

Delays are notorious. The same author notes cases such as Dowgate, which take up to 48 months to publish, while periods of 24–36 months are not uncommon. This means that a prosecution may not be commenced, because the cause is old by the time that it has been prepared. Justice, Coke said, ought to be quick, for delay is a kind of denial.[73] Inspectors can, as we have noted, make interim reports, and some do so very speedily. But the element of delay is gravely troubling. Delay stems from a number of reasons, some of which result directly from the fact that the investigation system serves a number of purposes, only one of which is the prosecution of fraud. Among the causes are: the use of outside Inspectors who cannot give their full time to an inquiry, the need to observe fairness in the conduct of the inquiry, and difficulties encountered, in some cases, in securing the attendance of witnesses.

Because the system embodies compromises, the problems which it presents are not readily resolvable. If the sole end of investigations were to prepare cases for trial, affording to the police a wider measure of discovery than the normal rules of criminal procedure permit, reform might be more usefully directed to such matters. Indeed, a case for this can be made out anyway, although the results are not always popular politically. In an effort to improve the system, without sacrificing its wider purposes, the Conservative Government has announced three reforms to it. It is to require that Inspectors produce reports within twelve months. This may be hard to achieve, given the need to meet criteria both of natural justice and efficiency. It is to publish the guidance notes provided to Inspectors and—more importantly—it is to specify with greater particularity those aspects of the company's affairs into which investigation is primarily desired. This is commonly done in Australia and is regarded as advantageous (Paterson and Ednie, 1972, vol. 2, p. 2299).

The search for total truth which can involve wearisome delays in endeavouring to locate and secure the assistance of witnesses located abroad might, with advantage, be eschewed. The Report is intended to inform and to guide action; it is not, of itself, a criminal investigation, and the desire to close every gap extends the time taken to report, without necessarily further elaborating the essential narrative or benefiting a future prosecution. The company inspection affords a means by which financial records can be investigated. It forces useful disclosures. But it is peripheral to the control of fraud and, in terms of police powers, only of supplementary value.

The need for the elucidation of weighty and complex affairs, and for obtaining authoritative conclusions about them in the public interest, dictates the use of outside inspectors, and there are apparently no reforms envisaged to this aspect of the system. Although the Department of Trade is an investigating agency with, as will be seen, wide powers to prosecute, it does not see its procedures and functions solely, or even primarily, in terms of prosecution. It sees its primary function as helping to co-ordinate activities with a view to combating fraud. In particular cases, where it has taken action through inspections, it sees its functions as not only to prosecute but also to try to salvage assets for shareholders. More broadly, through its powers to apply for orders disqualifying directors, it endeavours to cleanse the market place of fraudulent individuals. Evaluation of its effectiveness must await the concluding chapter.

References and Notes

1. Prevention of Fraud (Investments) Act, 1958, s. 5(1).
2. *Ibid.*, s. 5(2).
3. Licensed Dealers (Conduct of Business) Rules 1960, S.I. no. 1216, Rule 6.
4. Wilson Committee, Second Stage Evidence, vol. 5, *Department of Trade* p. 17(1979).

5. See Companies Act 1967, s. 111.
6. The inspection provisions of the Companies Acts apply only to companies and not to other modes of organisation.
7. See for example, Commission De Révision Du Code Pénal. Projet Définitif de Code Pénal, Livre 1 (1978).
8. Wilson Committee, Second Stage Evidence, vol. 5, *Department of Trade* (1979) is the basis for much of what follows.
9. Insurance Companies Act 1974, s. 7.
10. Insurance Companies Act 1974, ss. 7, 28, 29–37.
11. See, for example, Companies Act 1929, *Minutes of Evidence Taken Before the Company Law Amendment Committee*, 1943–4, p. 37.
12. 'Public Examinations' [1894] W.N. 44 (a practice direction by Vaughan Williams J.).
13. Theft Act 1968, Sched. 2, Pt. III am. s. 166; Bankruptcy Act 1914.
14. Bankruptcy Act 1914, ss. 157, 158 and 161.
15. Companies Act 1948, ss. 334(1) and (2).
16. *Re Manual Work Services (Construction) Ltd.* [1975] 1 All E.R. 426 at p. 428 *per* Megarry J.
17. Companies Act 1948, s. 224(1) as am. by Companies Act 1980, s. 80 and Sched. 3, para. 28.
18. Companies Act 1948, s. 224(1)(d) and Companies Act 1967, s. 35 and on fraud and illegality, see *Re Travel and Holiday Clubs Ltd.* [1967] 2 All E.R. 606; *Re SBA Properties Ltd.* [1967] 2 All E.R. 615; *Re Allied Produce Co. Ltd.* [1967] 3 All E.R. 399.
19. *Bryanston Finance Ltd.* v. *de Vries (No. 2)* [1976] Ch. 63; *Re Gattopardo* [1969] 2 All E.R. 344.
20. *Re Southard & Co. Ltd.* [1979] 1 All E.R. 582.
21. *Re Lubin, Rosen and Associates* [1975] 1 All E.R. 577.
22. *Re Ryder Installations Ltd.* [1966] 1 All E.R. 453.
23. *Re United Service Co.* (1868) L.R. 7 Eq. 76; *Re Gold Co.* (1879) 11 Ch. D. 701; *Re National Distribution of Electricity Co. Ltd.* [1902] 2 Ch. 34; *Re Gutta Percha Corporation* [1900] 2 Ch. 665.
24. *Re National Distribution of Electricity Co. Ltd.*, *supra*; *Re Hadleigh Castle Gold Mines Ltd.* [1900] 2 Ch. 419.
25. Companies Act 1980, s. 80 and Sched 2, para. 21.
26. Companies Act 1948, s. 235.
27. Companies Act 1967, s. 50.
28. Companies Act 1948, s. 236(1).
29. *Re Medical Battery Co.* [1894] 1 Ch. 444.
30. Companies Act 1948, s. 270; the court may issue a warrant for the arrest of a person who does not attend, Rule 66 of the Companies (Winding-up) Rules 1949.
31. *Ibid.*, s. 307(1), and see *Re Campbell Coverings Ltd. (No. 2)* [1954] 1 Ch. 222.
32. Companies Act 1948, ss. 268 and 307.
33. *Ibid.*, s. 307, and see *Re Rolls Razor (No. 2)* [1970] 1 Ch. 576.
34. The principles are elaborated in *Re Bletchley Boat Co. Ltd.* [1974] 1 All E.R. 225; *Re Spiraflite Ltd.* [1979] 1 W.L.R. 1096; *Re Castle New Homes Ltd.* [1979] 1 W.L.R. 1075.
35. Interrogatories are written questions addressed by one party to litigation to another, before trial, and the procedure is administered by a judicial figure, the Master in Chambers.

36. Companies Act 1929, *Minutes of Evidence Taken Before the Company Law Amendment Committee*, 1943–4, pp. 25–38.

37. On the types of companies covered, see Companies Act 1967, ss. 109(a)–(e).

38. Companies Act 1967, s. 109(3)(b).

39. *Ibid.*, sub-s. (4).

40. *Ibid.*, sub-s. (5).

41. *Reg.* v. *Secretary of State for Trade, ex p. Perestrello* [1980] 3 W.L.R. 1.

42. Companies Act 1967, s. 110(3); the criminal proceedings referred to arise under companies, insurance and banking legislation.

43. Companies Act 1967, s. 111.

44. Wilson Committee, Second Stage Evidence, vol. 5. *Department of Trade*, p. 18 (1979).

45. Companies Act 1967, s. 113.

46. *Ibid.*, s. 111 (2).

47. *Reg.* v. *Board of Trade, ex p. St. Martin's Preserving Co. Ltd.* [1965] 1 Q.B. 603. In the result, the inspection found nothing untoward.

48. Companies Act 1948, s. 167(3).

49. Companies Act, 1967, s. 50; *London and County Securities Ltd.* v. *Nicholson*, [1980] 1 W.L.R. 948; *Re Pergamon Press Ltd.* [1970] 2 All E.R. 449.

50. Companies Act 1948, s. 168.

51. Companies Act 1967, s. 41.

52. Companies Act 1948, s. 172.

53. Companies Act 1967, s. 32.

54. Companies Act 1948, s. 174.

55. Building Societies Act, 1962, s. 110; Credit Unions Act, 1979, s. 18; for deficiencies in the powers relating to building societies, see Registry of Friendly Societies, *Grays Building Society*, Report (1979) Cmnd. 7557, pp. 2–3.

56. Insurance Companies Act 1974, s. 34.

57. *Ibid.*, s. 36.

58. *Ibid.*, s. 36(3).

59. Insurance Companies Act 1974, s. 28 read with s. 7.

60. *Ibid.*, s. 39.

61. Sess. 1976–7, H.C. Deb. (Vth Ser.), vol. 931, cols. 216–7.

62. *Re Pergamon Press Ltd.* [1970] 3 All E.R. 535.

63. *Maxwell* v. *Department of Trade* [1974] Q.B. 523.

64. *Ibid.*, at p. 541.

65. [1978] 3 All E.R. 280.

66. *Ibid.*, at p. 295 *per* Ormrod L.J.

67. Sess. 1977–8, 939 H.C. Deb. (Vth Ser.), cols. 380–2.

68. Wilson Committee, Second Stage Evidence, vol. 5 *Department of Trade* at p. 34 (1979).

69. Sess. 1976–7, 935–2 H.C. Deb. (Vth Ser.), col. 259.

70. Companies Act 1967, s. 111.

71. Companies Act 1967, s. 35; Companies Act. 1980, s. 75.

72. Companies Act 1948, s. 168(2)(a).

73. 2 Inst. 56.

12 The Bank of England

The Bank of England has traditional and unquestioned responsibility and authority over the money markets.[1] Although in what follows we shall stress its control over deposit-taking institutions, it has primary responsibility over the exchange control system, now abolished, and it controls the money and foreign exchange markets. While it took a lead in the formation of the Council for the Securities Industry, and traditionally saw itself as a bridge between the government and the City, it did not regulate the domestic securities market directly. Indeed, formerly, control over deposit-taking institutions and their activities fell under the Department of Trade (Cmnd. 6584, 1976). The Bank now has a direct statutory role in regulation, and with the Department of Trade forms part of the Joint Review Body to assess the system of government controls.

The Banking Act 1979 represents a considerable shift from *laissez-faire* to direct regulation. We have already partially sketched the background. A number of institutions which had to be rescued in 1973–4 were deposit-taking institutions, not recognised as banks by the Bank of England, but certified by the Department of Trade under section 123 of the Companies Act 1967, as bona fide carrying on the business of banking. We have noted that this released companies from the onerous provisions of the Moneylenders Act 1927, and that companies such as British Bangladesh Trust manipulated their financial documents in order to obtain the certificate.

A number of the so-called secondary banks adopted, as we have seen, improvident investment policies. The drop in property values left them vulnerable and the Bank of England and the major banks were obliged to step in to save financial markets from disaster. Thereafter the Bank of England accepted that there was need for continuing prudential supervision of deposit-taking institutions and for a strengthening of controls over deposit-taking and advertising for deposits.[2] The Bank began, at first on an extra-statutory basis, to call for quarterly returns from all banks other than clearing banks and British overseas banks, disclosing the main components of their business. The returns required the institutions concerned to provide a wide range of financial information, including details of large deposits and loans together with those made by or to others with whom the institution or its directors had a connection—a clear blow at the incestuous lending patterns which had developed before the crash. Analysis of the returns enabled the Bank to conduct interviews with officers of the institutions concerned.

In turn, the elaborate voluntary system instituted by the Bank was put on a statutory footing. The Bank assumed the jurisdiction over advertising for deposits and financial reporting, which formerly was vested in the Department of Trade. The resulting Banking Act 1979 controls both banks and licensed deposit takers (Ashe, 1979). The Act prohibits a person from taking a deposit in the course of carrying on a business, which is a deposit-taking business for the purposes of the Act unless it falls within certain permitted categories.[3] These include the Bank of England, a recognised bank, a licensed institution, or one of a category of businesses specified in Schedule 1, namely, other EEC central banks, the National Savings Bank, the Post Office, Trustee Savings Bank, building or friendly societies, credit unions, local authorities, and members of the Stock Exchange. Most of these are already regulated.

Recognition is granted by the Bank of England.[4] In respect of domestic corporations, it polices its own criteria. These criteria specify that the body seeking recognition or a licence must enjoy and have enjoyed a high reputation and standing in the financial community. If the institution has not carried on business for sufficiently long to win such a reputation, the criteria may be satisfied by looking to the reputation of its controllers. The criteria also deal with the range and type of services provided and the professional skills required.[5] The criteria are more exacting for a recognised bank than for a licensed deposit-taking institution, which may not describe itself as a bank.[6] The situation which obtained at one time in which evanescent bodies freely described themselves as banks, should not recur.

The Bank of England recognises overseas institutions if it is satisfied by the appropriate authority concerning the management of the business, and its overall financial soundness, and as to the nature and scope of the supervision exercised by those authorities.[7] It is to be hoped that the Bank will be decently sceptical. We have noted that press reports suggest that an overseas successor to Kendal and Dent Ltd. has been operating illicitly here and proposes to seek recognition. There are countries which freely permit the formation of financial institutions within their territory, provided that their business is conducted elsewhere; press reports indicate that Barbados is the latest entrant in the list.

The Bank has power to grant or refuse a licence, and to revoke a licence once granted. A person or institution to which a licence is refused has the right to make representations to the Bank, which must take account of them.[8] The grounds upon which revocation may be ordered are wide. They clearly strike not only at conditions which favour fraud, but also at lack of expertise, insolvency, failure to fulfill reporting requirements, which strikes at the integrity of the scheme of control, and, an omnibus ground, at any other way that the institution has so conducted its affairs as to threaten the interests of its depositors.[9]

In cases of revocation, the Bank has wide powers to act immediately, but subject, ultimately, to a full measure of judicial control. It may revoke recognition of a licence and grant a conditional licence or another conditional licence.[10] A conditional licence can supervene immediately and may prohibit the taking of deposits.[11] There is thus no apparent lacuna in powers which could inhibit effective enforcement. Normally, the Bank gives notice in writing and the institution concerned then has 14 days in which to make representations. A decision is made within 28 days. In cases of urgency, the Bank may act without notice.[12] In such a case, reasons are given and the Bank must confirm or rescind its decision.

Recognition permits a bank to carry on business in the normal way, without restrictions. Licences may, however, be made conditional, and a recognised institution may find itself relegated to the status of a licensed institution. Conditional licences may impose limitations on the acceptance of deposits, granting of credit, or making of investments.[13] They may prohibit the soliciting of deposits.[14] They may require the removal of any director, controller or manager.[15] Indeed, a licensed institution is required to notify to the Bank of England any change in its directors within 21 days of that occurring.

As with insurance, governmental powers to ensure the integrity of management thus go far beyond any which apply in respect of ordinary trading companies. Furthermore, the provisions of the Rehabilitation of Offenders Act, 1974, are excluded, concerning directors, controllers or managers, both with respect to answering questions in applications for recognition or a licence, and to questions administered to a person seeking employment as a director, controller or manager of such an institution. The Bank may refuse to grant a licence to an institution or may revoke it on the ground that, by reason of a past conviction, an individual is not a fit and proper person to take such a part in management, and it may take such a conviction into account in directing that a person be excluded from management, or dismissed, in proceedings concerning the granting or revocation of a licence.[16] The Rehabilitation of Offenders Act 1974 in any event excludes from the category of spent convictions to which no reference is to be made, sentences of imprisonment of 30 months or more. The breadth of the Bank's powers to compel disclosure of quite minor convictions will be appreciated.

When the Bank acts respecting revocation, it may give directions of a wide sort to the institution.[17] These are such as appear to the Bank to be desirable and in the interests of depositors, whether for the purpose of safeguarding the assets of the institution or otherwise. They include power to prohibit the institution from dealing with or disposing of specific assets, to prohibit it from soliciting deposits, and to require it to follow a particular course of action.[18] It is an offence to fail to follow such directions, punishable, against directors and officers, with up to two years' imprisonment.

There is an appeal structure. Appeals from refusal to grant recognition or a licence, or in respect of revocation, go to the Chancellor of the Exchequer who refers them to a tribunal.[19] There is a further appeal to the High Court on matters of law only.[20] If the High Court considers that the tribunal erred in law, it refers the matter back to the Bank of England for final decision. This obviously preserves whatever discretionary jurisdiction the Bank may have in a particular case.[21] The Financial Institutions Committee has suggested that this pattern might also be applied to dealers in securities (1980, p. 293).

In order better to enable it to perform its supervisory functions, the Bank of England has powers both of preliminary inspection and of investigation of licensed institutions. The powers are akin to those of the Department of Trade under the Companies Acts but with certain significant differences which, again, reflect a regime of close control. The Bank may, for example, require information about the nature and conduct of the institution's business, and its plans for future development.[22] It may require an accountant's report on the information so furnished.[23] Orders may be made to produce documents and provide explanations of them.

The formal investigation power may be exercised when it appears to the Bank desirable to do so in the interests of the depositors of a recognised bank or licensed institution, and is an investigation into the conduct and state of its business.[24] Two aspects of the scheme deserve attention. The first is that it perpetuates the restriction of powers, in the same way as the Companies Acts, to holding and subsidiary companies.[25] The second is that a person is only criminally liable for failure to answer, or to produce documents, where he lacks reasonable excuse for failing to do so.[26] This particular facility is not available under the Companies Acts. It might easily cause problems of construction. It does, for example, appear apt to permit a person to decline to answer on the grounds of self-incrimination.[27] Whether it is intended to reflect some wider privilege pertaining to banking transactions is doubtful. One would expect some express provision to that effect, such as is contained in the Companies Act 1948.[28]

These powers are not intended to be exclusive of those contained under the Companies Acts, and if there were a suspicion of fraud the more stringent powers under the latter Acts would certainly be used.[29] It is intended that the powers under the Banking Act will be used where a speedy investigation is required, for example, in aid of rapid action to meet a liquidity crisis. Unlike the Companies Act 1967, the Banking Act 1979 contains wide powers to disclose information obtained as the result of an investigation. Information obtained by the Bank may be disclosed for the following purposes: of any criminal proceedings whatsoever; to enable the Bank to comply with any obligation imposed on it under the Banking Act 1979; to the Treasury (which has a general policy role concerning the money markets) where this is expedient in the interests of depositors or in the public interest, or to the Deposit Protection Board; to the Secretary of State for Trade for the purposes of an investigation under the Companies Act 1948; of disclosure to a foreign regulatory authority where a body wishes to carry on business abroad.[30] The last facility reflects the desire of the Bank to regulate bodies incorporated abroad on a basis of mutual recognition and enforcement. The Department of Trade may disclose information to the Bank from both inspections and investigations so far as this is necessary to enable the Bank better to discharge its functions.[31] The grant of permission is thus a wide one.

The criminal provisions relating to speculative advertisements and to breach of the applicable regulations governing advertising have already been alluded to. Certain other matters may be mentioned briefly. The legislation creates a Deposit Protection Fund to enable payments to be made to depositors of banks and licensed institutions which become insolvent.[32] The depositor may be paid two-thirds of his protected deposit to a maximum of £10,000 unless he profited from the circumstances giving rise to insolvency. There are, as we have noted, wide provisions for institutional criminal liability and for directors' liability under widely drafted provisions to that effect.

References and Notes

1. See Wilson Committee, Second Stage Evidence, vol. 4, *Bank of England* (1979).
2. *Ibid.*, pp. 97–8.
3. Banking Act 1979, s. 1(1) and 2. 'Deposit' is defined in such a way as to exclude inter-group loans, etc. The fact that a deposit is taken in contravention does not affect civil liability of the borrower arising in respect of the deposit, *ibid.*, s. 1(8).
4. The Banking Act 1979, s. 3(1), (3) and Sched. 2. Giving false information in order to obtain a licence is by section 5 punishable on indictment or summary conviction.
5. The Banking Act 1979, Sched. 3, Pts. i and ii.
6. For general controls on the use of the word 'bank' by companies, see The Banking Act 1979, s. 36.
7. *Ibid.*, s. 3(5). The Bank's relations with foreign banks operating in Britain are detailed in Wilson Committee, Second Stage Evidence, vol. 4, *Bank of England*, p. 100. (1979).
8. The Banking Act 1979, s. 5(1).
9. *Ibid.*, s. 6.
10. *Ibid.*, s. 7(1).
11. *Ibid.*, s. 7(1)(*b*).
12. *Ibid.*, s. 7(4) and Sched. 4, Pt. iii.
13. *Ibid.*, s. 10(3)(*a*).
14. *Ibid.*, s. 10(3)(*b*).
15. *Ibid.*, s. 10(3)(*c*).
16. *Ibid.*, s. 43.
17. *Ibid.*, s. 8(1).
18. *Ibid.*, s. 8(2).
19. *Ibid.*, s. 11(1) and (2). Appeal may be taken against the conditions of any conditional licence.
20. *Ibid.*, s. 13. There is a further appeal on law to the Court of Appeal.
21. See The Banking Act 1979 (Appeals) Regulations 1980, S.I. no. 353, and its counterpart, S.I. 1980 no. 348 for Scotland.
22. The Banking Act 1979, s. 16(1)(*a*).
23. *Ibid.*, s. 16(1)(*b*).
24. *Ibid.*, s. 17(1).
25. *Ibid.*, s. 17(2) and (6).
26. *Ibid.*, s. 17(4), (6)(*a*)–(*c*).
27. See further *Re Atherton* [1912] 2 K.B. 251, and G. Borrie and N. Lowe (1973) pp. 28–29 and 333.
28. Companies Act 1948, s. 175.
29. H.C. Standing Committee A, Banking Bill, Fourth Sitting, Tuesday, 16 Jan 1979, col. 203.
30. The Banking Act 1979, s. 19(2).
31. *Ibid.*, s. 20.
32. *Ibid.*, s. 28.

13 The City Institutions

Self-regulation by City institutions plays a crucial part in ensuring the integrity of the British capital market. Other countries, it is true, also employ a mixture of governmental and non-governmental controls, but the emphasis placed on self-regulation in Britain is particularly marked. The strategic position of London, and the extent to which financial life is centred upon the City, make this possible. Wide advantages are claimed for it—speed, flexibility and cheapness, in particular. Both governments and the institutions themselves regard the adoption of a more strongly statutory system as undesirable. The Treasury, for example, considers the existing system comprehensive, authoritative, and efficient in enforcement. Whilst, therefore, prepared to envisage legislative intervention in respect of vexed matters such as insider trading, it does not, generally, support further governmental intervention.[1] The same is true of the Department of Trade.[2] The Financial Institutions Committee also accepted the desirability of the main features of the system (1980, pp. 301–18). Despite dissatisfaction with the system in some quarters, it is likely that change, when it comes, will come not from domestic pressure but from the necessity, as a member of the E.E.C. of adopting a system more firmly based on statute.[3] Such a change is, one suspects, unlikely to alter the fundamental character of the system. It is, after all, a system which has proved to be congenial both to Labour and Conservative governments, which in these matters are pragmatic rather than ideological.

We must first, however, note the governmental Joint Review Body. This is formed of representatives of the Bank of England and the Department of Trade. Its job is to oversee the functioning of the combined statutory and self-regulatory system in order to ensure that the two parts of it operate efficiently together. The Financial Institutions Committee considers that in its present form it is little more than a formalisation of discussions which would have taken place anyway. The outcome of its discussions simply forms part of the background to general policy formulation within the Bank and the Department of Trade. It concludes that a body with wider, general responsibilities for keeping the system under review should be formed (1980, pp. 299, 309).

The self-regulatory body with a general oversight function is the Council for the Securities Industry (C.S.I.). It was created with the encouragement of the Bank of England, which regards itself as a bridge between the City and government. The C.S.I. has important functions (Financial Institutions Committee, 1980, pp. 308–9). These are: to maintain high ethical standards in the industry; to keep the practice of the securities industry and its codes of conduct under review; to maintain arrangements for the investigation of cases of alleged misconduct within the securities industry, and breaches of codes of conduct or best practice, and to keep them under review; to initiate new policies and codes; to resolve differences of principle between constituent parts of the securities industry; to consider the need for changes in legislation and to examine relevant proposals; and to ensure liaison with the E.E.C. on securities industry matters and the implementation of the E.E.C. Capital Markets Code of Conduct. This is an ambitious role; it will require tact in its execution since it is unlikely that regulatory bodies, in particular the Stock Exchange, would readily compromise their independence in disciplinary matters. The C.S.I. has already begun to take certain initiatives; to comment on insider regulation and the conduct of company investigations,[4] and on the duties of Issuing Houses in respect of new issues—the latter a much criticised initiative.[5] It is plainly in the early stages of evolution and it cannot be said as yet how significant it will be. But although important in setting standards for the industry, it is not primarily concerned with fraud.[6]

A number of institutions have regulatory functions. For our purposes, the most important are the City Panel on Take-Overs and Mergers, and the Stock Exchange. The former's position is entirely extra-legal; the latter is recognised for the purpose of exemption from the prospectus requirements of the Companies Act 1948. Both are essentially private bodies performing public functions, a status which their functional relationship with government emphasizes. The government has, for example, indicated to the E.E.C. that these bodies are regulatory authorities for the purposes of directives relating to listed securities, yet they are regarded as sufficiently remote from government not to be endowed with compulsory powers in respect of the examination of witnesses and the production of documents.[7] Their status is thus, like that of Royal peculiars, unique.

The Take-Over Panel

The principal function of the Take-Over Panel is to administer the

City Code on Take-Overs and Mergers (Rider and Hew, 1977). That document is primarily directed towards ensuring fair play; it is not directed expressly at the prevention of fraud, and its orientation limits its effectiveness in that respect. The City Code consists both of general principles and, increasingly, of detailed rules. The institutions which compose the Panel have always insisted that the Code must be obeyed both in the letter and the spirit. The principal functions of the Panel are to interpret the rules, and to give timely advice on bids while they are in progress. Admittedly, the Panel has had to deal with instances of insider trading, but that, hitherto, has not been a crime.

It would be out of place in a work of this character to deal with the substance of the City Code, which is directed towards fair dealing rather than fraud (Hadden, 1980). The Panel does, however, touch on matters which relate to crime. First, there is insider trading which is now criminal and, as we have seen, can arise in a take-over where directors, or persons to whom they give information, or financial advisers, deal in shares of the target company with knowledge that a bid is to be made. This has long been reprobated by the City institutions.[8] Then there is the problem of profit forecasts. The City Code does not require profit forecasts to be supplied, but insists that they shall be reasonable and corroborated by the auditors. Obviously, there have been cases in which the documents have not been properly prepared, and some no doubt to which the epithet 'fraudulent' could properly be applied.

Bodies which obtain securities without notifying the Registrar of Companies when their holding exceeds the prescribed percentage, currently 5 per cent,[9] commit an offence. Bodies may contravene the City Code when they obtain more than 15 per cent of a company's shares for cash within a 12-month period, in which case the Code requires that a bid be made.[10] More broadly, the documents issued in a take-over battle could well contain dishonest statements concerning the bidder's future plans for the company, the soundness of the bidder company, and the like. Thus, in Dowgate, the Inspectors conclude that the shareholders in a target company were not told that the object of the bid was to acquire control of the company and strip it of its assets (1979, p. 106).

There is, thus, no doubt that the Panel operates in a milieu in which the presence of fraud and illegality is to be expected to some extent. The part which the Panel can be expected to play in situations where fraud may be present is limited by its constitution, objectives, functions and procedures. The Panel is a body created by the securities industry to police take-overs. It is not a general law enforcement agency. It is, in effect, an emanation of what may be thought of as a club, that is, the financial institutions of the City of London operating under the benevolent gaze of the Bank of England. Its effectiveness depends both upon the moral force of its rules and the sanctions which it can impose. The latter naturally affect persons who need to use the facilities and institutions of the City. They are less effective against outsiders and, with the abolition of exchange control which enables British companies to maintain funds and enter into obligations abroad freely, financial assistance may be expected to originate more frequently from foreign sources. How troublesome this may be cannot at present be assessed, but the most recent cause célèbre did involve bidding by a South African company for the shares of a British company in defiance of the City Code, though not the law, from abroad.[11]

The Code itself is not a code in the legal sense of an exhaustive capitulation of rules. It contains, as already stated, both general principles and detailed rules, but the latter have steadily expanded as institutions and their clients have sought more detailed advice from the document. When the first version of the City Code was prepared it was determined to avoid a document clogged with minute rules, in favour of broad principles interpreted according to an underlying spirit. This works when bidders and their advisers emanate from the system and are prepared to work within its confines. Where outsiders are concerned, the blunt point is sometimes taken against the Panel that the Code is either a code or it is not, that is, that whatever is not prohibited by it is permissible. This point was, for example, taken in *Dowgate* by Camamile, its chairman (Report 1979, p. 9). Merchant banks and other financial institutions would be unlikely to take the point before the Panel whatever view their underlying actions might evidence.

The Panel has a small executive staff of some fifteen persons. It advises when bids are in progress, and it does some investigating after the fact when cases appear to require it. The staff is composed partly of permanent members and partly of persons expert in various fields and with an intimate acquaintance with City practice. Its small size must, however, militate against its assuming wide enforcement functions. Its remit is essentially narrow: it investigates, but with a view to determining whether the Code has been complied with. It is not a substitute for the Fraud Squad or the Department of Trade. Because the Panel is a self-regulatory body, it has no legal powers of coercion. Thus, while it can investigate, hold hearings and impose punishment within the club rules, it cannot compel the attendance of witnesses either within Britain or from abroad, or the production of documents. A person who could give important evidence can always refuse to attend, alleging bias or some other cause.[12] There are limits therefore to the effectiveness of the Panel against outsiders.

The Panel's procedures are intended to elicit the relevant facts in the context of a self-regulatory agency which is dependant upon the support of the very institutions which it regulates. Its procedures are premised upon the co-operation of City institutions which must, in turn, be prepared to bring pressure on both their own personnel and their clients to abide by the rules or to submit to discipline if they do not. This approach would hardly be possible if the Panel were a statutory administrative agency wielding compulsory powers, or a criminal investigation unit, although in the former case, as the history of some American agencies shows, co-operation remains a desired mode of proceeding (Leigh, 1979).

If breaches of the Code are alleged, and allegations of breaches may come from the other party to a bid or from a financial institution acting on its behalf, the executive investigates the case, interviewing persons and examining documents. It may employ accountants if necessary. If it decides to bring the case before the Panel, it will inform the defendants concerning the nature of the evidence against them. The hearing will be a full oral hearing, but there are no strict rules of evidence. Following the decision of the Panel, there is an appeal to an Appeal Committee presided over by an eminent retired judge. The integrity of the hearing is not, of course, protected by the laws against perjury, but lying to the Panel would be treated as a matter warranting discipline. To someone determined to thwart the proceedings this may not be a real threat. On the other hand, as the Financial Institutions Committee noted, if compulsory powers were given to the Panel, there would be a need to elaborate safeguards for witnesses and this would delay procedures (Report 1980, p. 315).

Whatever is said to the Panel is treated as having been said in confidence, save that a public statement may be made at the conclusion of a hearing. Because the Panel considers that persons would not give information to it if their statements were not treated in confidence, it will not disclose the information without the consent of the person providing it. This latter rule may be necessary in order to operate a system which depends so strongly upon co-operation. It is one in which the police and the Department of Trade apparently acquiesce. If there is evidence of crime, the police are informed at a very early stage. It is, however, rare for the police to ask the Panel for assistance.

The principle of confidentiality has, nevertheless, produced some bitter exchanges between Inspectors appointed by the Department of Trade, and interested to get at the truth, and the Panel, determined to uphold the confidentiality of its proceedings. In *Dowgate*, the Panel refused to make a transcript of the hearing before it available to the Inspectors who, having other sources of information, decided not to press the matter, presumably by seeking the compulsory judicial examination of the executive or Panel members. From the Inspectors' point of view the matter was important because they believed that the Panel had been imposed upon by certain of the actors involved, that its procedures had been defective in not asking for the evidence of certain persons, and that, as a result, it had failed to uncover not only breaches of the Code but also possible corruption (Dowgate, Report 1979, p. 133).

Dowgate illustrates the further point that the Panel depends crucially upon the co-operation of the institutions concerned. As it explained to the Inspectors, it expects absolute honesty and frankness. Lacking a large staff and compulsory powers, it can be misled by a determined rogue. The most stringent hearing can be disarmed and institutions themselves may sail close to the wind. In either case procedures will not work. Viewed thus, and having regard to the fact that the Panel very often engages in policing aspects of a bid in progress without the time at its disposal to make the very thorough and painstaking investigations of departmental investigators or Fraud Squad detectives, one must ask not whether Panel procedures are as such defective, but rather whether the enforcement system is prepared to take suspicious matters further, ensuring that rogues do not reap the benefit of their improper activities without redress or punishment.

In many cases, the investigation and hearing procedure works well. The institutions do co-operate and they are able to require their clients to inform the Panel fully of what took place. The Panel can then dispose of formidable sanctions, both formal and informal in nature. It may have recourse to private reprimand or public censure; it may report to a professional body to which the offender belongs. Thus, for example, if an auditor acted irresponsibly in endorsing a plainly insupportable profit forecast, he could be reported to the appropriate accountancy body. If a licensed dealer misbehaved, he could be reported to the Department of Trade. In a flagrant case, the Panel might take further action designed to deprive the offender, permanently or temporarily, of his ability to enjoy the facilities of the securities markets. In one case an offender was banned, as a result of Panel action, from dealing on the Stock

Exchange for six months (Rider and Hew, 1978); in another, the Panel said that certain persons should not be allowed to deal in securities. The Panel may, thus, refer certain aspects of the case to the Stock Exchange, the Department of Trade, or an appropriate private body. In Pergamon, it was the Panel which requested the appointment of Inspectors.

Public censure is thought to be a sufficiently grave sanction in most cases. To be sure, the Panel has been harshly critical of the conduct of certain take-over bids from the time of the Pergamon Press–Leasco affair to the present (*Pergamon Press Limited*, Interim Report 1971, p. 189). But it has not as yet said that it would not accept forecasts in the future from an auditor or merchant banker. This has led to unfortunate results. In at least one case, that of Edward Wood and Company Limited, an individual who had previously been censured was able to take part in the preparation of a take-over as a result of which grossly misleading documents were issued (Report, 1977, pp. 35–44). But its censure can result in pressure by other directors requiring a director who has engaged in insider trading to resign. It has, as we have noted, succeeded in forcing directors who have engaged in insider trading to give their illicit profits to charity.

Where the matter is seen to involve fraud or other misconduct, the Panel passes it to the Department of Trade or the police. In the former case, it will suggest that an inspection or investigation seems to be appropriate. Referrals of this character are selective. An infraction which appears to be insignificant, or 'not real crime', will not be passed on. The Panel executive considers that it has an accurate impression of which matters the Department of Trade and the Fraud Squad would be interested in pursuing, and this, in general, is probably correct. There is perhaps a danger that, because the Panel and its executive are not oriented towards fraud, it will fail to perceive it. Certainly, in Dowgate the Panel and the Inspectors put very different interpretations on the statement allegedly made by one of the actors: 'I have looked after your chairman' (Report 1979, p. 108).

The fact that the Panel, in outlook, organisation or powers, is not really intended to deal with breaches of the criminal law, leads one to wonder whether making insider trading a criminal offence risks making a moral point to the prejudice of practical regulation. This also arises with respect to the activities of the Stock Exchange. Essentially, the point is that if institutions cannot confide in the Panel without incriminating themselves or their clients, they may be unwilling to speak. No claim to confidentiality would be allowed in a criminal trial. It would be impossible to force institutions into a position in which they could be expected to incriminate themselves or their clients. The matter will have to be dealt with by the police. There is also the problem whether the *sub judice* rule might not be invoked to dissuade the Panel and the Stock Exchange from investigating matters which might become the subject of a criminal charge (Justice, 1974), but that would be appropriate only if a case were pending. But the Panel will, correspondingly, find it more difficult to enforce the provisions of the City Code in that regard. The Panel itself regards the appropriate emphasis as upon prevention by ensuring earlier announcements of bids, and securing the early suspension of share quotations, in order to inhibit speculative dealing. Given the inherent difficulty of policing insider trading, this seems to be the correct emphasis.[13]

The Stock Exchange[14]
The Stock Exchange has long been regarded as a private body performing certain public regulatory functions. It has a commanding position: there is now one unified Stock Exchange in Britain and the securities market is concentrated in London. The Stock Exchange claims that the securities market is regulated by it at virtually no cost to public funds, through a highly sophisticated system which is flexible and responds to developing public opinion. It assists in enforcing the rules and regulations of other self-regulatory bodies, taking disciplinary proceedings where its members infringe the City Code. It has recently intimated that it will suspend the listing of companies which flout accepted accounting standards in such a way as seriously to mislead shareholders.[15] The Exchange will not list cash companies, favourite target for looters in the past.

Because of the possibility of market rigging, which can cause loss both to its members and to the general public, the Stock Exchange has long been alive to the problem of fraud and dishonesty. Its rules prohibit the making of a false market in securities. The police consider that frauds on the stock market are a rare occurrence and that the regulatory machinery of the Stock Exchange works well. The Stock Exchange exercises control at various points. It controls listings, and it enforces disclosure through its listing requirements. Its quotations department vets flotations and appears successfully to prevent fraudulent flotations (Hadden, 1980). Indeed, Department of Trade Inspectors have suggested that its flotation rules should apply even where the Stock Exchange is not used, as in the British

Bangladesh Trust case (*London Capital Group Ltd.*, 1977, p. 62).

The Stock Exchange requires directors of companies which request listing to provide full personal details including their criminal record, if any, but it leaves the question of their basic integrity to the company. It does, however, maintain a list of known offenders. Through its listing agreement it enforces continuing disclosure of relevant information. It has long prohibited insider trading, and it has formulated a model code which informs directors when they may deal in their company's securities. From publicly available sources, it maintains records which enable its members to assess persons and companies for whom they may not wish to act.

Certain improvements have been suggested to the declarations required to be made by directors of companies. In particular, it has been suggested that directors of subsidiaries of public companies should be forced to declare their prior convictions. As the Inspectors in Roadships Limited state, there is a possibility that the main board of a holding company may be a front for the activities of subsidiaries run by disreputable individuals (Report, 1976, p. 112). The primary safeguard against fraud and dishonesty lies in the integrity and perceptiveness of members of the Stock Exchange. In particular, where there is a suspicion of market rigging or insider dealing it is the duty of the member to question the deal. The Stock Exchange rule against market rigging is, indeed, the only text against rigging in Britain today. It affords an admirable functional standard and might well serve as a drafting model for legislation. It provides:

73b. (1) No member shall knowingly or without due care deal in such a manner as shall promote or assist in the promotion of a false market.

(2) A false market is defined as a market in which a movement in the price of a share is brought about or sought to be brought about by contrived factors, such as the operation of buyers and sellers acting in collaboration with each other, calculated to create a movement of prices which is not justified by assets, earnings or prospects.

This sets the standard against which dealings must be assessed.

The Stock Exchange conducts both surveillance and investigations. The latter are into specific occurrences, but they may be conducted under a wide mandate. In the recent Gold Fields case, the committee was asked to examine the facts, to look at company law as it affects disclosure, asking if registration could be expedited and looking to amendments of codes of practice.[16] The purpose of surveillance is to determine whether share price movements were caused by manipulation. The Financial Institutions Committee (Report, 1980, p. 305) gives the following figures:

	1976–7	1977–8	1978–9
Abnormal price movements	1,861	1,336	1,170
Preliminary investigation	31	56	39
Full enquiries	30	11	12

The Committee plainly thought that not much could necessarily be inferred from abnormal price fluctuations. Dr. Hadden, noting that in only one case, SUITS, was there a clear finding of impropriety, concluded that Stock Exchange procedures were ineffective to cope with insider dealing, whence, he apparently assumes, such movements derive (Hadden, 1980). Whatever the truth of the matter, insider dealing now falls within the criminal law, albeit on terms which seem likely to preclude effective enforcement. The Stock Exchange has never denied the reality of the problem. It notes that, increasingly, in bad cases of insider dealing and of affecting Stock Exchange prices by false rumours of take-overs, the manoeuvres involved are carried out professionally, often behind the façade of Swiss and other foreign banks and financial institutions, and are, effectively, untraceable. One cannot proceed against a person on the basis of rumour. The emphasis must be on prevention by concentrating on security within companies.

Investigation and disciplinary procedures are very formal.[17] Where it is considered appropriate to do so, an investigation committee will be appointed which is required to investigate the case and frame charges if necessary. The Committee then reports to the Council, which determines whether to proceed with them. If it decides to do so, it remits the case to a disciplinary committee before which the defendant may call witnesses and adduce evidence on his behalf. Statements made before the Committee are treated in confidence. Like the Take-over Panel, the Stock Exchange regards this as necessary in order to secure necessary evidence.[18] If the person under investigation is found guilty, he may appeal to an appeal committee or plead to the Stock Exchange Council for clemency. In one respect the rules are suitably drastic. It is an offence against the Stock Exchange rules to contravene the City Code, and a person who is found by the Take-over Panel to have done so may not re-open the issue of fact before the Stock Exchange disciplinary committee.

The rules specify what constitutes misconduct or gross misconduct in general terms, including conduct which is detrimental to the interests of the Stock Exchange, and dishonourable or disgraceful conduct. The Stock Exchange is concerned to enforce standards of ethics and best practice. In reality, the sorts of cases which come before it include insider trading, or conduct such as that of Sir Hugh Fraser in SUITS, who dealt actively in the shares of his own company without notifying the Stock Exchange or the Registrar of Companies. Another case of discipline involved Hedderwick's, in which a person in charge of the broker's gilt-edged department dealt for clients, concealing from them that he was not getting the best price because he was taking a one-sixty-fourth turn on dealings to which the clients should have been entitled. Some partners were expelled and others censured. Unethical conduct has included the case in which a broker dealt ahead of his client, that is, dealing by the broker knowing that he has an order to buy from the client which will enhance the price of the shares. The broker is thus able to get in first.

There have also been rare cases of market manipulation. One, involving the firm of Burge and Co. and a broker, Colin-Jones, who later committed suicide, was done by put-throughs to cause an increase in the price of shares in which the market had previously been inactive. Finally, there was the Chapman and Rowe affair, ultimately tried in the criminal courts, where there was pledging of clients' securities without permission as security for bank loans, stealing, and conspiracy to cheat and defraud.[19] Apart from breaches of ethics, the cases thus involve violations of the duties owed by agents to their principals, and market manipulation. These cases are both dealt with internally and referred to the police. They are few in number, and it should not be overlooked that in some frauds the actual Stock Exchange transactions were regular. The Stock Exchange's figures show that, between March 1973 and March 1978, 14 members or firms were reprimanded, 8 were censured, 11 suspended, and 6 expelled.[20]

Where listed companies knowingly contravene its rules or fail to abide by the listing agreement, the Stock Exchange can take effective action. It can, and has, prohibited members from transacting business with specified individuals whose conduct it has stigmatised in strong terms.[21] It can suspend the listing of a company, but this is apt to prejudice the interests of shareholders and is therefore a weapon which is sparingly employed. The effect of a suspension is to lock in shareholders, who cannot then deal through brokers on the Stock Exchange. Individuals and licensed dealers may buy and sell such securities, the latter with permission of the Department of Trade. Such dealers may offer to buy the shares at knock-down prices. The *Investors' Chronicle* concludes that there is a flourishing kerb trade in suspended shares which is not advantageous to shareholders.[22] Stock Exchange publications indicate that such suspensions are few, and that most are short-term in nature, intended to prevent speculative dealings where a take-over bid is in prospect.[23]

There are, however, cases which suggest that the Stock Exchange is sometimes culpably slow to move. The *Investors' Chronicle* draws attention to an instance in which a listing was not suspended even though the company had delayed in submitting accounts, and the shadow of a Department of Trade inquiry hung over it. In the result, the auditors produced four pages of qualifications to the accounts (Rudofsky, 1978). The disadvantages of suspension are such that, inevitably, the Stock Exchange prefers to use other sanctions. In particular, it can be devastating to a highly geared company (Slater, 1977, p. 61). It regards publicity, and the threat of publicity, as a considerable deterrent. The appeal is basically to the standards of the City, of brokers, merchant bankers and accountants, to persuade a company management that a course of action which it wishes to pursue is wrong.

There have been stringent criticisms, both of the self-regulatory system and of particular aspects of it. It is, for example, argued that the inability of the Stock Exchange to control persons who are not members limits the utility of its investigations. Thus, while the investigating committee can obtain lists of transactions from brokers and jobbers, and the names and occupations of clients and clients' spouses and employers, there is no way in which the Stock Exchange can go behind the client's alleged reason for selling (Conway, 1976). The Stock Exchange notes, however, that outsiders do come forward to assist it. It is not deterred by threats of libel action[24] and has become more forthright in recent years in criticising individuals (Financial Institutions Committee, 1980, p. 310).

Orders placed from overseas cause difficulties which would inhibit any regulatory agency. It is difficult to determine what sort of market is being made. Pressure can be exerted through the broker which may flush the bidder out. This happened in the De Beers case where, apparently, no law was broken.[25] There was, however, a sudden flurry of share dealings, and many persons who might have desired to sell shares in the target company at the high price bid were unable to do so, raising broader issues of fairness. The matter is currently under investigation by the Stock Exchange and the Department of Trade. Incidents of this character do not demonstrate that self-regulation will not work, although they may indicate the need for a somewhat greater reliance on statutory controls. But it is clear that where dealing occurs through the opaque medium of foreign financial institutions, any system of control, voluntary or statutory, is bound to encounter insurmountable obstacles in the course of its work.

There is a further point. There are, plainly, cases which cannot be handled through self-regulation alone, if only because there is no suitable sanction within the self-regulatory system for all the participants. Thus, for this reason and for reasons of basic equity of treatment, cases like SUITS, Hedderwicks, Chapman and Rowe and Burge and Co., must be dealt with both internally and by the police and the Department of Trade. But this is true also of participants whom discipline can reach. Institutions and their rules complement and supplement the law, but no one doubts that in cases of theft and fraud the criminal law must be invoked.

Other Institutions

Other institutions and professional bodies have a part to play in the scheme of self-regulation but they are less prominent and their role is less well-defined. There is, for example, the Issuing Houses Association which, as we have noted, may fall under C.S.I. rules in respect of flotations, deriving from disquiet aroused by findings of Department of Trade Inspectors that such bodies failed to ensure that companies for which they acted discharged undertakings which they had given (*Blanes Limited*, 1975, pp. 218*ff*; *Roadships Limited*, 1976, pp. 63*ff*). The professional bodies such as the Law Society and the Institute of Chartered Accountants in England and Wales also have a part to play. Indeed, at the time of writing, the latter body has stringently criticised, admittedly somewhat after the event, auditors implicated in the Stonehouse affair.[26] The Association of Stock and Share Dealers has a disciplinary competence and, like the Stock Exchange, treats Take-over Panel criticisms as a basis for action against members. As with Stock Exchange proceedings, there are problems concerning obtaining information from outsiders and from clients who fear adverse publicity. And of course there is, on the part of the person under investigation, the fear of ultimate criminal prosecution. But the disciplinary function is essential, notwithstanding, and the hearings which are held also serve the useful purpose of drawing lessons of general importance from facts disclosed in Department of Trade Reports.[27]

References and Notes

1. Wilson Committee, Second Stage Evidence, vol. 5, *Treasury*, p. 19. (1979).

2. *Ibid.*, p. 28, evidence of the Department of Trade.
3. For example, E.E.C. Council Directive of 5 March 1979, co-ordinating the conditions for the admission of securities to official stock exchange listing, Official Journal, 16.3.79, no. 66/21.
4. Press release of 17 December 1979.
5. *Investors' Chronicle*, 6 July 1979, p. 14.
6. The C.S.I.'s view of its functions can be gleaned from its first report, summarised at [1979] J.B.L. 370.
7. Wilson Committee, Second Stage Evidence, vol. 4, pp. 78 and 84 (1979) on the E.E.C.'s disagreement with this, and *ibid.*, vol. 1 at p. 56 on the C.S.I.'s position as an E.E.C. reference body. The Financial Institutions Committee's Report 1980, p. 295, does not mention any conflict.
8. Wilson Committee, Second Stage Evidence, vol. 4. *The Stock Exchange*, pp. 57 ff. (1979) for the model code for securities dealings.
9. Companies Act 1967, s. 33 as amended by Companies Act 1976, s. 26.
10. City Code on Take-Overs and Mergers, Rule 33; note that the Code contains an 'acting in concert' rule.
11. This was the bid by De Beers Consolidated Mines for Consolidated Gold Fields in February 1980; both the Stock Exchange and the Department of Trade have commenced investigations.
12. As, for example, happened in the recent proceedings against one Raper and certain companies which allegedly bid in concert for St. Piran. Raper remained abroad, alleging bias. See *The Times*, 2 April 1980, 'Takeover Panel rules on St. Piran'; 'Takeover panel unable to force St. Piran bid', *ibid.*, 12 June 1980.
13. See summary of Panel Report [1979] J.B.L. 368.
14. Most of this discussion derives from oral interview and from Wilson Committee, Second Stage Evidence, vol. 4, *The Stock Exchange* (1979) and Report, 1980, pp. 303–306.
15. *The Times*, Tuesday 29 January 1980, p. 18.
16. 'SE orders inquiry on Gold Field dealings', *The Times*, 15 February 1980.
17. For details, see The Stock Exchange, Council Notice, 11/78.
18. See 'Stock Exchange Sets New Standard', *Investors' Chronicle*, 3 December 1976, in which the writer concludes that Sir Hugh Fraser would not have co-operated freely in compulsory procedures.
19. *The Times*, 17 January 1978.
20. Wilson Committee, Second Stage Evidence, vol. 4, *The Stock Exchange*, at p. 20 (1979)
21. For example, 'Mr. Raper barred from S.E. dealings', *The Times*, 13 June 1980.
22. *Investors' Chronicle*, 6 February 1980.
23. *The Stock Exchange Fact Book*, March 1979, p. 22, Table B2; 30 September 1977, Table 9.
24. Wilson Committee, Second Stage Evidence, vol. 4, *The Stock Exchange*, p. 23 (1979)
25. *The Times*, 13 February 1980, 'Anglo-American Makes Its Move'.
26. *The Times*, 8 April 1980, pp. 15 and 18, 'Censure for Stonehouse company auditor'.
27. *The Accountant*, 26 January 1978, vol. 178, p. 98.

The prevalence of companies in the commercial life of the United Kingdom, and therefore of company fraud in commercial fraud, makes it important that adequate controls against fraud and dishonest dealing be located within the company itself. Obviously, prevention is the ideal. But the need for control within companies is not restricted to the prevention of activities which are plainly fraudulent; it applies also, and no doubt more commonly, to keeping entrepreneurial activities within legal boundaries. It is difficult to prevent outright fraud, but proper controls can minimise its effect, while a propensity to cut corners and to risk incidental crime in doing so can similarly be curbed. This is quite apart from the desirability of proper management controls within companies generally. Few companies, apparently, become insolvent through fraud; many more become so because their management structures were inadequate (Argenti, 1976).

External controls, those wielded by the Department of Trade, the police and the City institutions, are inevitably limited in their effect. There is simply too much work for them to cope with. Enforcement must, therefore, be located within enterprises, as well as imposed by the organs of the state generally. There are three foci of control within a company, namely, the board of directors and the managing director, the shareholders and the auditors. We need not labour points already made concerning the potential for shareholder control. Whatever may be one's views concerning the desirability of shareholder control, it must be admitted that the law can at most provide shareholders with the means of control. What happens thereafter is in their hands. If they wish to condone irregularities, little can be done about the matter unless, indeed, the courts are able to impose a disqualification, or the City institutions with which the company deals are able to enforce the resignation of a director or directors.

The history of company law reform during the last thirty-five years has been one of endeavouring to increase disclosure by companies to their shareholders, rendering directors more democratically accountable to shareholders, and tightening up accounting and auditing requirements. Until the Companies Act 1980, controls were increasingly applied to both public and private companies. Certainly, some striking frauds, for example the deposit-taking frauds in Pinnock, were perpetrated through forms designed to accommodate small family businesses by exempting them from onerous reporting requirements. Now, under the aegis of the E.E.C., controls are being more stringently applied to public than to private companies. The details of this, and indeed its desirability, are matters outside the scope of this book, but the contradictory trends are evident. In this chapter we deal with the position of directors and auditors of companies with reference to the prevention of crime generally. Matters such as the form of accounts, and many of the details relating to directors' duties, must be left to the standard texts.

Directors and Their Duties

English company law does not force companies to adopt a particular managerial pattern. Companies differ in the way in which boards are composed, the proportion of executive to non-executive directors, and the like. Indeed, no legal rule impedes an English company from adopting a continental two-tier board with worker directors, if it so wishes. As a broad generalisation, however, it may be said that the management of a modern company is vested in the board of directors which, during its term of office, exercises plenary powers without reference back to the general meeting of shareholders.[1] Indeed, the general meeting cannot require the directors to use their power in a particular way, nor can an exercise of powers be attacked provided that it is done bona fide and for the benefit of the company, by which, historically, is meant for the general body of shareholders taken as a whole.[2] The constituent documents of a modern company normally give to the managing director powers equal to those of the board.[3] Within the managerial structure of the company there are two figures of great importance. One is the managing director, who functions as the chief executive of the company; the other is the chairman of the board of directors whose function it is to oversee and, if necessary, check the managing director by ensuring that initiatives are, where appropriate, brought to the board's attention (Florence, 1961, pp. 80–2).

Company directors are subject to fiduciary duties and to common law duties of care and skill. Fiduciary duties are owed to the company, and not to individual members of it, unless the director has constituted himself as their agent for some particular purpose, for example by recommending acceptance of a take-over bid.[4]

Because a director is a fiduciary, he may not place himself in a position in which his personal interests could conflict with those of the company for which he acts.[5] He thus may not take for himself opportunities which it is his duty to secure for the company, or make secret profits by the use of its assets, or divert its property for his own use.[6] Nor may he, without first disclosing his intention and obtaining permission, take personal advantage of an opportunity of which he acquires knowledge as a director, even though the board decided not to take it up.[7]

Duties of care and skill are much less exacting, at least so far as the position of a director who has no other position with the company is concerned. Directors are bound to exercise ordinary care and skill, and they must exercise an independent judgement even as directors of subsidiaries.[8] If possessed of special skill, knowledge or experience, a director must use it on behalf of his company.[9] Thus, a director with accounting experience who failed to use it, as by signing cheques in blank, would be liable to the company for loss caused thereby. But in general, directors' duties cannot be expressed with any great degree of particularity. Directors' functions are very broad, and courts are reluctant to intervene in matters which essentially involve business judgement. But directors may not avoid liability by pleading that they were ignorant of matters through failing to attend board meetings.[10] Also directors who hold other offices within the company are held to duties of care and skill appropriate to such offices.[11]

In addition to broad common law duties, directors are placed under a number of specific statutory duties. Some of these, contained in the Companies Acts, extend disclosure both in the general public interest and in the interests of shareholders. They help to mark out the limits of fiduciary obligation. Examples are: the duty of directors to notify the company and the Stock Exchange of acquisitions in their company's shares;[12] the duty to notify shareholders in the context of a take-over bid of compensation which they are being offered for loss of office;[13] the duty to disclose in the accounts details of share option schemes for the benefit of directors;[14] or the duty to disclose, in the accounts of the company or group, substantial contracts with directors and their associates.[15]

Other duties relate to the position of the company generally, as for example: the duty to make an annual report; to obtain and file with the registrar a valuer's certificate where shares are to be allotted for a non-cash consideration;[16] the duty to file annual accounts;[17] and the duty to proceed upon properly audited accounts when paying dividends.[18] In addition to these, directors' liability clauses are found in a wide range of legislation. The effect of such provisions is not only to render directors responsible for aiding and abetting infractions of the law by their companies, but also to render them criminally liable where it can be shown that their failure adequately to perform their duties facilitated commission of the offence.[19] We have dealt elsewhere with problems in the construction of such provisions (Leigh, 1969). However wide their theoretical extent, they are seldom invoked in practice, in part because once enough evidence has been obtained against a particular director to employ them guilt can usually be proven anyway.

Other jurisdictions have sought to make directors' duties generally enforceable by the criminal law. For instance, section 124(1) of the New South Wales Companies Act, which is in this respect identical to other Australian statutes, provides both civil remedies and a criminal fine for failure to perform directors' duties.[20] The section has begun to lead to a wider conception of such duties than obtained at common law. It has, for example, extended liability to directors who trade in their company's securities and who tip others on the strength not only of specific confidential information but also of alternatives which the director, because of his knowledge of the company's affairs, is aware may be forced upon it.[21] Indeed, it is in relation to such information that the section appears to have made its greatest impact. But no such development is anticipated in Britain at present. The insider trading provisions obviously partially fill the gap.

The preceding discussion obviously focuses upon particular breaches of directors' duties of which there are many examples in Department of Trade reports. Directors give gifts with company moneys; they use the company as a private bank; they put shares in their own, or the company's name, depending upon whether the transaction is expected to produce a profit or a loss. One even reads of directors who, it is said, would never prefer the company's interests to their own. These frauds are of course facilitated by other derelictions of duty, and, in particular, as has already been emphasised, a failure by directors to develop proper management structures. Department of Trade reports make clear how often, in cases of fraud or breach of fiduciary duty, the breaches complained of have been facilitated by the lack of such structures. Such neglect may be engendered, as in Roadships Limited, by a failure to recognise that a company has outgrown a primitive management structure. Inspectors concluded that Lonrho Limited had also expanded beyond the capabilities of the existing management. In other companies, control systems were undoubtedly neglected because it suited a dominant figure to do so. His manoeuvres could not be effectually checked in the absence of a strong board, strong officers and proper procedures. This does not imply that autocracy means fraud, necessarily. Autocrats, whether honest or dishonest, are apt to chafe under restraint (Argenti, 1976).

In some of the fraud cases noted in this book, such weaknesses served fraudulent controllers well. Sir Eric Miller is said to have run Peachey Properties Ltd. virtually as his private bank. He left able, but insufficiently assertive executives, to wither on the vine. Segregation of functions and a lack of communications within the enterprise, fostered by the controller, conduced to fraud. Similarly, one supposes that the controllers of London and County Securities Ltd. and British Bangladesh Trust were not displeased that effective management structures, capable of exercising strong control, did not exist. Indeed, in these cases internal accounting systems were pressed in aid of fraud by disguising the nature of improper transactions. No strong board or strong body of executives was so placed as to prevent or inhibit such manoeuvres.

The absence of proper controls, and the subversion of those which exist, produce noxious results, conducing to, for example, a lack of direction in the business. The functions of a proper board are to import a sense of purpose and direction to the affairs of a company or group, to formulate wise policies and to monitor the execution of such policies by the executive. In some of the instances noted in this book, even though the controllers of a company paid lip service to these principles the board was subverted, either by compromising its independence of judgement or by ignoring it until after important decisions had been taken and matters could not be reversed. Where direction is lacking and the business begins to fail, there is, even on the part of otherwise honest managements, a tendency to rely upon creative accounting and other questionable, if not criminal practices, although managers may not recognise them as such.

Furthermore, the insidious example of corruption affects persons lower down in the corporate structure. The corrupting effect of managerial attitudes at Kuehne and Nagel Ltd. has already been noted, as has the example of certain of the controllers at London and County Securities Ltd. Echoing Professor Sutherland, Conklin concludes that business crime is often learned from superiors, and that learning in the social context is probably a more important determinant of business behaviour than the personality of individual businessmen (Conklin, 1977, p. 80). Whether the whole of this generalisation is valid or not, there can be little reason either to doubt that business criminality is learned or that the example of those who set the tenor and tone of the company's operations has an important influence on subordinates.

Accordingly, if fraud is to be prevented, a proper board is needed and the offices of chairman and managing director should be separated. Also, internal accounting systems (a vital factor and one lacking in, for example, Roadships Limited) will need to be created, proper formalities introduced, management information provided, and the board consulted. It hardly seems necessary to stress that proper books of account and minutes are necessary, but there are cases where these were not present (*Edward Wood and Company Limited*, 1977, p. 44; *Dowgate*, 1979, p. 348). Even so, given that outside directorships are effectively in the gift of the controllers and that the dependence of directors upon their chief may well be emotional rather than institutionalised, fraud within the social system can at best be minimised, not eradicated. Furthermore, controls over directors are only one necessary condition for the prevention and detection of fraud within the company. Disclosure, strengthening the accounting and audit requirements, and giving more powers to shareholders and the Department of Trade to seek remedial powers, are also helpful. But at this juncture we turn to the integrity of the accounts and the position of the auditors.

Accounts, Directors and Auditors

The requirements of the Companies Acts concerning accounts are long, and no explantion of them can be given here. But certain leading principles are important. It is the duty of the directors to prepare, lay and deliver accounts of the company for each accounting reference period.[22] The accounts comprise a profit and loss statement and balance sheet, a directors' report and an auditors' report.[23] The accounts must be such as give a 'true and fair view' of the state of the company's affairs and to explain its transactions.[24] Nowhere is the phrase true and fair view defined. It seems clear that the words are meant to be read together (Cooper, 1974), although at least one authority formerly thought that something could be true without being fair, and fair without being true (Gower, 1969). A paper prepared by the English Institute of Chartered Accountants points out that truth and fairness are subjective, not absolute (*Court Line Limited*, 1978, pp. 143–4). The truthfulness of the accounts can be determined by ascertaining whether the components are true; fairness has to be judged on a view of the accounts as a whole. But the phrase has no single meaning and it is important that the way in which it is being used be understood by those who rely on the accounts.

An audit may be defined as, such an examination of the records underlying a financial statement as will enable the auditor to report whether, in his opinion, the accounts show a true and fair view. The responsibility of the auditor is to report on the financial statements as presented by management (Cooper, 1974, Combined Committee of Accounting Bodies, 1980). The auditor owes his duty to the company, and not to the directors.[25] His duty is to report on the state of the accounts. The duty to prevent fraud is primarily a matter for the directors rather than for him. Obviously, the audit is a prime weapon in controlling fraud, and the relationship between the principles which govern the audit and those which govern the responsibilities of directors needs to be elaborated further.

The powers and the position of auditors have been delineated both by common law and statute. Auditors are appointed by the general meeting of the company.[26] If the company fails to appoint auditors, the Secretary of State for Trade may do so.[27] The remuneration of the auditor is fixed by the directors, although there is provision for it to be fixed by the general meeting in cases where the directors do not do so. In reality the position of the auditor is in the director's gift.

An auditor is not immune from dismissal. He may be dismissed by an ordinary resolution of the company.[28] This power is subject to important safeguards. In respect of proposed resolutions to remove an auditor, to reappoint as auditor a person other than the retiring auditor or to fill a casual vacancy in the office, special notice is required to the members. Furthermore, the retiring auditor, or the auditor to be removed, has a right to present his case to the general meeting and to have written representations to that effect circulated to members.[29] And he may attend the meeting at which the matter is to be discussed.[30] The Registrar of Companies is also informed. Similar provisions relate to auditors who resign their office. An auditor may canvass the general body of shareholders with the reason for his resignation in order that directors may not be able to stifle criticism.[31] He may also requisition a general meeting.[32] Where there is default in circulating the auditor's statement, the company and every officer in default is guilty of an offence and liable on indictment to a fine, the upper limit of which is in the discretion of the court.

These provisions, together with those which restrict the appointment of auditors to persons who belong to accountancy bodies recognised by the Department, are intended to ensure, so far as rules can, the competence, integrity and independence of the auditor. There is, obviously, a point beyond which rules alone will not work.

Formal independence is one thing, psychological independence another. There is a danger of a symbiotic relationship between auditors and controllers of the companies which they audit. This can lead to an uncritical approach and even to a tendency to hush up awkward phenomena (Devine, 1976). It is said to be a particular problem in the case of small companies. Auditors are given wide powers of access to books and papers of the company. They are entitled to demand explanations and information from the directors, and it is a criminal offence, punishable either on indictment or summary conviction, for directors knowingly or recklessly to make such a statement to auditors which is false in a material particular.[33]

We may now consider further the roles of directors and auditors in relation to fraud. Where there is fraud, the directors have *prima facie* failed in their duty to prevent it. This may be because they have not created adequate internal machinery, such as internal accounting systems and audits, or because they have not seen that such systems operated efficiently, or because they have turned internal systems into vehicles for fraud, as apparently happened in London Capital Group Ltd., and, allegedly, London and Counties Securities. The integrity and efficiency of internal accounting systems are of course crucial to the prevention of fraud.

Despite disclaimers of wide responsibility by accountants, the audit, while not primarily directed towards fraud, should take that possibility into account (Cooper, 1974). The auditor must use reasonable care and skill in conducting the audit. He is, in the time-honoured words of the courts, a watchdog, but not a bloodhound.[34] He need not approach his task on the assumption that frauds or irregularities have been committed, unless, indeed, there are circumstances apt to put him on inquiry.[35] The accountancy bodies conclude that, while the auditor's duties do not require him to search specifically for fraud, he should recognise the possibility of material irregularities or fraud and plan his audit so that he has a reasonable expectation of detecting material misstatements deriving from it.[36] This is stressed also in a leading Australian case.[37] A similar approach applies also in the United States where the detection of fraud is considered an important part of the auditor's work.

There is general agreement that the auditor's ability to detect fraud is limited; fraud detection cannot usually be achieved as an incidental benefit from conventional auditing. It is a task for which resources must be specially committed (Combined Committee of Accountancy Bodies, 1980; Owles, 1978; Comer, 1977). This is particularly true of management fraud, where often the internal audit mechanism does not cope and directors fail to deal adequately or correctly with accounting matters. In recent years, there have been both frauds and irregularities involving initial wrongdoing or carelessness by management which auditors did not pick up. In SUITS, which, the court accepted, was not a case involving fraud, both directors and auditors concurred in accounts which showed a cash position of £ 10 million, whereas some £ 4.2 million of this had in fact been lent to a property company as an unsecured loan and proved to be irrecoverable.[38] The auditors resigned. The *Investors' Chronicle* has spoken of a rash of mis-classifications.[39] In London Capital Group Limited, the Inspectors castigated the failure of the auditors to discover fraud as 'astonishing', and the accountancy body to which they belonged has since, as we have seen, censured the senior partner responsible for the audit. In several Department of Trade reports, aspects of the audits under consideration were stringently criticised.

We are thus bound to consider the criticisms which have been made of auditors in the light of what can reasonably be expected of them. The first and most obvious point is that in management frauds it is the first care of the rogue or rogues to conceal the truth. Whether the auditor is to be censured for not discovering the truth depends upon the skill and sophistication of the fraud and the integrity and adequacy of the audit procedure. Such a procedure ought to be framed having regard to the possibilities for fraud that exist in the particular type of business which the firm under audit conducts.[40]

In the Grays Building Society case, Jaggard was able to avoid detection not because his fraud was particularly sophisticated but because he was able to take advantage of the routine and unimaginative way in which the audit was carried on for many years. In Roadships Limited, deliberate forgeries were submitted to the auditors, a practice which the Inspectors conclude the auditors could not reasonably have anticipated. In London and County Securities Group Limited, a worthless cheque for £1 million was deposited so that, over the period before it was presented, a false picture of liquidity would be shown. In London Capital Group Limited, loans were concealed by the use of nominees, a web of misleading entries employed and ledger cards altered. In Ashbourne Investments Limited, deliberate lies were told to the auditors. In Ozalid, which like Ashbourne is not classified by Inspectors as a fraud case, directors are alleged to have helped to create non-existent companies or business names, to have made undisclosed overseas remunerations to directors and to have concealed this from the auditors (Ozalid Group Holdings Limited, 1980). Other ploys have also been used. For example, the secondary banks engaged in window dressing in order to deceive everyone, including the auditors, concerning their liquidity. In Dowgate, auditors were changed in order to avoid awkward questions. In London and County Securities Limited, the directors procured a change of audit personnel, partially disarming inquiry as a result.

Window dressing is the obnoxious practice of taking in moneys on short-term loan over the financial year-end in order to show greater liquidity than in fact exists. It has been much criticised. Despite the failure of prosecution agencies to press prosecutions in respect of the matter, primarily because it is thought to engender sharply differing expert views by the accounting profession concerning its propriety, which could result in expensive and abortive proceedings, there seems little doubt that where such lending takes place with intent to deceive the auditors, and thus shareholders and the public, concerning the true financial position of the company, the practice is not only wrong, but criminal. In Ashbourne Investments Ltd, the Inspectors, despite a lack of authoritative pronouncements on the matter, concluded (Report, 1979, p. 384):

> The practice of taking in extra short-term deposits at accounting dates to improve balance sheets may now be less widespread than previously. As a general practice we can see no justification for it, and regard it as improper. It cannot be right for shareholders, prospective depositors, lenders or whoever else relies on an audited balance sheet as a means of assessing the true worth of a bank at a particular date, to be presented with a document which does not disclose its normal level or pattern of business.

It has been argued that the impropriety or illegality of the practice was not recognised until recently. This overlooks the reality which is that auditors did not regard the practice as proper in some of these cases, and the directors, aware of this, took pains to conceal the true nature of the transaction from them. Thus, in London and County Securities Ltd., Caplan had agreed with the auditor that 'there should be no special transaction which created a liquidity more favourable than that which might have existed at some other time during the year' (Report, 1976, p. 134). In Ashbourne itself, certificates were provided to auditors which some officers of the companies concerned knew to be false (Report 1979, p. 363). We are here dealing not with standards the existence or application of which are doubtful, but with deliberate concealment from auditors.

We may, perhaps, sum up this part of the saga with two quotations, one illustrating the regime under which some audits are carried on, the other summarising what, to Department of Trade Inspectors, can reasonably be expected of an audit when the company is permeated with fraud. The first comes from London and County Securities Ltd. (Report 1976, p. 229):

> The auditors had a particularly difficult job... They tried to make notes on the accounts informative with some resistance from their client. The company's officials appeared to have taken the view that it was fair to try to get anything past the auditor's scrutiny. No example has been drawn to our attention where any director of the company or a subsidiary appears to have taken any stand on doubtful points in order to make the accounts show a true and fair view.

The second comes from Peachey Property Corporation Ltd. (Report 1979, p. 63):

> This inquiry has convinced us that a powerful chairman and managing director, with a board of directors which is not able or willing to play an inquisitorial role into his transactions and expenditure, has immense scope for diverting company money to his own use over a long period of time, and that normal audit procedures will not necessarily bring to light, at least at an early stage, the diversion of the money.

While the auditor's task is a difficult one, there are dangers and pitfalls against which he can guard, and standard procedures which he can invoke with some measure of success. He must, first, guard his independence. In Blanes Ltd. the auditor and the company's solicitor compromised their independence by holding shares in the company for which they acted and by accepting the benefit of a share subscription scheme which gave them an advantage the general public did not share. In Roadships Ltd. the Inspectors point out three principal ways in which independence can be destroyed (Report 1976, p. 75): by the auditor having a financial stake in the company; by the auditor being controlled in the broadest sense by the company; by the auditor reviewing work which has previously been done by his firm as accountants. It is generally considered undesirable that auditors should provide routine accounting assistance to the company which they audit. Public companies should put their internal accounting systems on a solid footing. Additional hazards arise for auditors where the internal accounting staff are insufficient in numbers, or inadequate in quality, or lack independence (Holmes, 1976).

The auditor should ensure that the audit is within the capacity of his firm. In Roadships Ltd., Vehicle and General Insurance Co. Ltd. and Pinnock, the auditors were not capable of dealing with an audit of the magnitude involved. Sometimes this arises because a small company audited by a small firm becomes too big and complicated for the existing auditors to handle. In Pinnock, the auditor was chosen on the basis, seemingly, that he was sufficiently inexperienced to be deceived and too subservient to ask awkward questions. The law lays down general standards of qualifications (which did not in fact apply in that case since the business was carried on under the wholly inappropriate guise of an exempt private company) but the questions of experience and competence must be left to individual judgement.

Problems have arisen in connection with joint audits. There is a need for each auditor to know something about the other auditor, his skills, mode of work, and the like. The firms must decide on a programme for the audit and the division of work, and it will normally be convenient for both firms to use the same audit programme and documentation (Elliott, 1975). The obvious danger, which materialised in Bernard Russell Ltd., is that each firm will rely on the other to do some important part of the work, in that case, stock verification. In the result, the task was not done properly by either. Quite apart from fraud, liability arising from deficiencies in the audit will be joint as against both auditors.[41]

Auditors must also consider their position carefully when faced with a dominating chairman or chief executive, particularly where the internal accounting controls are imperfect in either design or functioning. The possibilities for abuse in such instances are great. Unusual circumstances such as, for example, a substantial late claim for expenses or an abrupt change in the accounting conventions employed, especially concerning valuations, ought to put the auditor on inquiry. Property valuation is a particularly difficult area. It is said to be the most common cause for qualifying accounts. Above all, the auditor must be alive to a pattern of irregularities.[42] The Combined Committee of Accountancy Bodies (CCAB) auditing guidelines indicate this clearly. They provide, for example, that the auditor must ascertain the system of recording and processing transactions employed by the enterprise, and assess its adequacy as a basis for the preparation of financial statements. They provide that the auditor must obtain reliable and relevant internal audit evidence. If he wishes to rely upon internal controls, he should ascertain and evaluate those controls, performing compliance tests on their operation. Internal audit controls are particularly important in the case of large companies because auditors cannot be expected to pick up every transaction or even more than a small proportion of them.[43] The auditor must review the financial statements in conjunction with the other audit evidence obtained, in such a way as to give him a reasonable basis for his opinion on the financial statements.

In the major frauds under review, there was fault in the application of some or other of these criteria. Irregular transactions were not properly vetted. Sufficient evidence of stock, of the value of personal guarantees, and of the true parties to loans, was not secured. Reliance was placed on directors in circumstances where the managerial infrastructure was obviously defective. This is not to draw a bill of indictment against the accounting profession, for that profession is fully alive to the problems, as the great attention paid to auditing standards and practices shows. The CCAB guidelines on auditing standards state that, where the auditor cannot report affirmatively that the accounts give a true and fair view of the company's state of affairs, his report should be qualified. The auditor should qualify his report by referring to all material matters about which he has reservations. He is required to give the reasons for his qualification together with a quantification of its effect on the financial statement if that is relevant and practicable. In addition, reference may need to be made to non-compliance with relevant legislation and other requirements.

The CCAB guidelines state that the qualification should leave the reader in no doubt as to its meaning and its implications for an understanding of the financial statements. This point is important. In Peachey Properties, the accountants gave a qualified report but the words used were not strong enough. The City did not suspect the truth and, to the auditors' surprise, failed to react to the qualification. The Inspectors state, in words which might equally be applied to legal, sociological or criminological jargon (*Peachey Property Corporation Limited*, 1979, p. 156):

> It is our impression that the sparse terminology employed by auditors has reached a stage of evolution when it may be described as hieratic...Hieratic language suffers from every possible deficiency, being neither comprehensible as ordinary speech, nor adequately defined to a specialist.

The CCAB guidelines then proceed to set a standard for the types of qualification used. If there is uncertainty about a material but non-fundamental matter, the auditors qualify the accounts as 'subject to' the uncertainty. If the matter is fundamental, for example an unjustified departure from standard accounting practices, he will disclaim an opinion on the accounts. If he is in disagreement with the directors and the matter is not fundamental, he will pass the accounts except for the disagreement. If the matter is fundamental, he will emit an adverse opinion. This certainly gives a clear set of conventions to work to.

The auditor must of course reach a responsible judgement about the materiality of the matter. There must be good reason for qualifying accounts (Renshall, 1978). If the auditor takes a public stand, he may do considerable damage to the company. That, in turn, could damage the interests of the very shareholders whose interests he is bound to protect. He needs to be sure. Thus, as the Inspectors in Peachey Properties point out, it may be easier for an auditor of a subsidiary to take a stand privately than it would be for the auditor of the group to which it belongs to do so publicly. But in a proper case, qualifications can afford a valuable indication of mismanagement and worse. For a qualified report to be fully effective, governmental and self-regulatory agencies must, of course, be prepared to move swiftly. There have been complaints in the press that regulatory agencies are sometimes culpably slow to react.

Auditors can wield other weapons than qualification of the accounts. They can resign and, using the statutory procedures outlined at the beginning of this chapter, draw the relevant matters to the attention of shareholders.[44] Even before these provisions were inserted into the law, the auditors in London and County Securities Ltd. threatened resignation and, suspecting that the matters were being concealed from the board, sent a copy of their reasons to all the board members (Report 1976, p. 233). It would, I suggest, be worth adopting a provision like section 167(8) of the New South Wales Companies Act, under which auditors must report breaches of the statutory provisions concerning accounts to the appropriate government agency.

Suggestions have been made for making the audit function more effective, notably by adoption of the audit committee, the underlying idea being that auditors should refer at various stages of their work to a committee of outside directors, thus strengthening the organs of control against a chief executive who may, for the best or worst of motives, be tempted to ride roughshod over the board of directors (Boyle, 1978). Voluntary adoption of the device has strong support in some accounting and investment circles (Davison, 1978). Sir B. Rhys Williams has, for example, argued that audit committees should be required for companies with balance sheet assets of more than £100 million, or with 10,000 employees or more. This would strengthen the position of outside directors and auditors who work retrospectively, some of whom are remote from senior management, and it would assume a monitoring function which institutional investors cannot assume without becoming insider traders.[45]

Governments have resisted pressures to make such committees compulsory. They have preferred to strengthen the auditors' position directly, leaving other initiatives to companies themselves. There are real problems with the notion of audit committees. Outside directors are not always independent since such directorships are often in the gift of the chairman (Tricker, 1979). It is not always easy to find persons of the right calibre and standing. A recent study indicates that only 25 per cent of companies in *The Times* 1,000 for 1975–6 had more than two non-executive directors, and 25 per cent had none (Davison, 1978). An audit committee formed to control a dominating chief executive could readily fail in its purpose, since such a man will endeavour to ensure that the committee functions only superficially, for cosmetic purposes. No doubt the use of such committees will evolve in Britain, but it seems unlikely that they will be required of companies by legislation, nor are they appropriate for all companies.

We may conclude this discussion with some comments about the auditor's role in general. He needs intellectual curiosity. He needs to work to a suitable plan and according to recognised conventions. Although not a lawyer, the auditor requires a good deal of basic legal knowledge, enough certainly to pick up not only basic, but some quite sophisticated points of company and commercial law. He may well be censured for failing to appreciate the significance of, say, a lack of consideration in a transaction which the company claims as a debt due to or from it (*Electerminations Ltd.*, 1978, p. 62). In doubtful cases, he is bound to obtain and act on legal advice. Not the least surprising aspect of London Capital Group Ltd. was the failure of auditors to act on the correct advice of their own solicitors, preferring instead the unsound advice given by the controller's solicitor.

Auditors are reluctant to claim too much for audit procedures as a weapon against fraud. The prospect of large damage actions, of which there have been some striking recent examples, and even criminal prosecution for aiding and abetting offences concerning the accounts by directors, no doubt helps to engender caution. But modesty is not wholly self-serving; the possible impediments to the discovery of the truth are real enough, and auditors cannot possibly investigate all transactions. Furthermore, auditors should not be viewed as the moral censors of commercial life. That is not a task with which society has invested them. The duty of the auditor is to determine whether matters shown in the books as having occurred were properly recorded. If illegal transactions occur, or transactions which amount to an abuse of power by the directors, or about the accounting treatment of which there are irreconcilable differences of opinion, the auditors are bound to report the matter to directors and shareholders and, where necessary, to qualify the accounts. Where matters do not fall into these categories, the auditor is not regarded, at present at least, as being under a duty to comment upon them.

Institutional arrangements reflect standards. Professional standards are inevitably related to legal requirements, especially in so closely regulated an area as corporate accounting. If a given practice is regarded as wrong, it is the existence of a legal rule which triggers a duty to report. The rule may be specific, or it may be general, admitting different views concerning its interpretation. But the rule is a necessary condition to fix the duty, even though it be mediated through, and refined by, standards adopted by a self-regulatory body. This, no doubt, suggests a narrow approach to the problem, but it is one which prevails today, and the idea that the auditor should act as a moral or ethical censor according to his own conceptions of commercial morality is one which does not prevail, nor should it.

Remedies of Minority Shareholders and the Department of Trade

Space precludes an extended discussion of minority shareholder actions. These afford an opportunity for minority shareholders to prevent or terminate actions by controllers which are illegal or in violation of their fiduciary duties or duties of care and skill. Minority shareholder actions are inhibited by an antique rule known as the rule in *Foss*. v. *Harbottle*.[46] This depends on the view that a company is rather like a partnership in which matters should be dealt with internally by majority vote. It holds that whether a company is to sue its directors should be decided within the company. But large companies do not function as direct democracies, whatever the theory may be.

Boards of directors are often oligarchical in character and can, by means of proxy machinery and the ability to canvass shareholders by using the company's civil service, stultify quite worthy initiatives. Hence, by exception to the rule, minority shareholders have been able to sue on the company's behalf where controllers have filched its assets or diverted from it opportunities which in equity they are regarded as holding on behalf of the company.[47] Recently, courts have gone much farther. They have first held that where directors, by breach not of fiduciary duties but of duties of care and skill, produce a situation in which they derive benefit at the expense of the company, minority shareholders may sue.[48] Secondly, they have recognised that directors can wield control in fact with much less than 50 per cent of the voting power.[49] In the latest case, 26 per cent was regarded as a control block, a result long accepted in America, but novel here. Thirdly, and most importantly, they have permitted the bringing of a class action in a claim for damages.[50]

This latter point, which is of great potential significance, requires a brief explanation. Some actions are brought because shareholders rather than the company are regarded as injured, as, for example, where they have been victims of deceptive documents issued in a take-over bid. Formerly, it was thought that one shareholder could not bring an action on behalf of himself and all other shareholders as a class because each had to prove damages. Now it is established that one shareholder may do so, and may settle in respect of all other claimants such matters as the falsity of documents and responsibility for their emission. Other injured shareholders need not litigate these issues again; they need only prove individual loss. The result, provided that shareholders, perhaps institutional shareholders, are prepared to take a lead, could be revolutionary. It would put directors under a considerable deterrent of personal liability. In the United States, where the class action has always been available in this way, it has been half transformed from a private remedy to a public recourse against wrongdoers (Leigh, 1979).

Action on behalf of the company may also be brought by the Department of Trade, in which case the rule in *Foss* v. *Harbottle* will not apply at all.[51] However, few such actions are brought. In many cases, even of quite large fraud, it is difficult to obtain a judgement which is readily enforceable against the rogue. He may by then be abroad, or insolvent and, as with Dr Savundra, be living on his wife's untouchable property. It may, as will be seen, be possible to make a criminal bankruptcy order against such a person, a recourse dealt with later. In addition, there are statutory provisions which enable a minority shareholder to complain of mismanagement. One such, already noted, the ability to move for a winding-up on a just and equitable ground, can also be invoked by the Department of Trade to freeze the assets of a company which has been used to defraud the public. Another, contained in section 75 of the Companies Act 1980, enables a shareholder and the Department of Trade to petition the court for relief where the affairs of a company are being conducted in a manner unfairly prejudicial to its members. The court has a complete discretion to make such order as it sees fit. Such an order may regulate the affairs of the company for the future, require it to do, or refrain from doing, acts complained of, buy out dissenting interests, or authorise the bringing of civil proceedings on behalf of the company.

It is too early to predict how widely the courts will construe this section which, in any event, is applicable to conduct which is not fraudulent as well as to fraud. In cases of fraud, prosecution is possible, and, in respect of insurance companies, the Department of Trade has ample powers to force a change in management—powers which it may not have under this section in respect of trading companies generally. In respect of fraud and criminal conduct, section 75 ought to be thought of as a useful auxiliary weapon, and not as a substitute for prosecution.

References and Notes

1. *John Shaw & Sons (Salford) Ltd.* v. *Shaw* [1935] 2 K.B. 113.
2. *Greenhalgh* v. *Arderne Cinemas Ltd.* [1951] Ch. 286; by Companies Act 1980, s. 46, directors are also to have regard to the interests of employees.
3. *Lennard's Carrying Company* v. *Asiatic Petroleum Company Ltd.* [1915] A.C. 705.
4. *Briess* v. *Woolley* [1954] A.C. 333; *Gething* v. *Kilner* [1972] 1 W.L.R. 337.
5. *Aberdeen Railway* v. *Blaikie Brothers* (1854) 1 Macq. 461.
6. *Cook* v. *Deeks* [1916] 1 A.C. 554.
7. *Regal (Hastings) Ltd.* v. *Gulliver* [1942] 1 All E.R. 378; *Industrial Development Consultants Ltd.* v. *Cooley* [1972] 1 All E.R. 162.
8. *Selangor United Rubber Estates Ltd.* v. *Cradock (No. 3)* [1968] 1 W.L.R. 1555 at p. 1578 *per* Ungoed Thomas J.; *Lonrho Limited* v. *Shell Petroleum Co. Ltd.* [1980] 2 W.L.R. 367 *per* Lord Denning M.R.
9. *Re Brazilian Rubber Plantations and Estates Ltd.* [1911] 1 Ch. 425.
10. *Dorchester Finance Co. Ltd.* v. *Stebbing*, 22 July 1977, discussed in (1980) 1 *The Company Lawyer* 38.
11. *In re Duomatic Ltd.* [1969] 2 Ch. 365.
12. Companies Act 1967, ss. 24–7
13. Companies Act 1948, s. 193.
14. Companies Act 1967, s. 16.
15. Companies Act 1980, s. 54.
16. *Ibid.*, s. 25(2).
17. Companies Act 1948, s. 147.
18. Companies Act 1980, s. 43(3).
19. For example, Merchant Shipping Act 1979, s. 46; The Banking Act 1979, s. 41; Employment Protection (Consolidation) Act 1978, s. 155.
20. Companies Act 1961 (N.S.W.), s. 124.
21. *Commissioner for Corporate Affairs* v. *Green* [1978] V.R. 505; *Es-Me Pty. Ltd.* v. *Parker* [1972] W.A.R 52.
22. Companies Act 1976, s. 1.
23. *Ibid.*, s. 1(3) and (4).
24. Companies Act 1948, s. 147.
25. *Re London and General Bank (No. 2)* [1895] 2 Ch. 673.
26. Companies Act 1976, s. 14(1).

27. *Ibid.*, s. 14(2).
28. *Ibid.*, s. 14(6).
29. *Ibid.*, s. 15.
30. *Ibid.*, s. 15(6).
31. *Ibid.*, s. 16(2)(*b*).
32. *Ibid.*, s. 17(1). The auditor can require the directors to circulate a statement of his reasons to the members and the auditor is entitled to attend the meeting at which the matter is to be discussed.
33. Companies Act 1976, s. 19.
34. *Re Kingston Cotton Mills (No. 2)* [1896] 2 Ch. 279.
35. *Re Thomas Garrard & Son Ltd.* [1968] Ch. 455.
36. CCAB, *Auditing Standards and Guidelines*, Explanatory Foreword, paras. 9 and 10. (1980).
37. *Pacific Acceptance Corporation Ltd.* v. *Forsyth* (1970) 92 W.N. (N.S.W.) 29.
38. *The Times*, 20 May 1978; *The Economist*, 4 December 1976, p. 145.
39. *Investors' Chronicle*, 17 November 1978, p. 508.
40. *Pacific Acceptance Corporation Ltd.* v. *Forsyth* (1970) 92 W.N. (N.S.W.) 29 at p. 67.
41. *Ibid.*
42. *Ibid.*, pp. 62–64.
43. *Ibid.*, at pp. 40–2 and 87.
44. *Ibid.*
45. B. Rhys Williams, 'Why companies need audit committees', *Investors' Chronicle*, 17 February 1978, and see H.C. Standing Committee A, Sess. 1979–80, Companies Bill [Lords], cols. 21–30.
46. (1843) 2 Hare 461.
47. *Cook* v. *Deeks* [1916] 1 A.C. 554; *Regal (Hastings) Ltd.* v. *Gulliver* [1942] 1 All E.R. 378.
48. *Daniels* v. *Daniels* [1978] 2 All E.R. 89.
49. *Prudential Assurance Co. Ltd.* v. *Newman Industries Ltd. (No. 2)* (1980) 130 N.L.J. 392.
50. *Prudential Assurance Co. Ltd.* v. *Newman Industries Ltd.* [1979] 3 All E.R. 507. These were earlier interlocutory proceedings in the same case.
51. Companies Act 1967, s. 37.

PART IV

PROSECUTION AND TRIAL

15 The Investigation of Crime

In this chapter we consider who investigates commercial fraud, and what provision is made for co-operation among the various agencies involved. We are, necessarily, concerned with the powers which such agencies wield. It is not intended to give a full account of police powers, which can be found elsewhere (Leigh, 1975b), but rather to concentrate upon those aspects which pertain particularly to commercial fraud and which investigative agencies find particularly troublesome. The principal agencies concerned are the police, who handle the bulk of commercial fraud work, the Department of Trade, the Customs and Excise, and the Inland Revenue.

The Police

By far the greatest number of serious commercial frauds occur in the Greater London area, although there are also frauds in other large cities. In order to combat fraud there has, for many years, been a City and Metropolitan Police Fraud Squad, and fraud squads also exist in other large metropolitan areas. These vary in terms of expertise, size and efficiency. The City and Metropolitan Police Fraud Squad consists of about 210 officers, conducting 65 to 75 investigations at any given time. There is a substantial foreign element in these investigations. It is possible for the London fraud squad to send officers to help in provincial investigations, provided that the local force requests assistance. Such a request may arise because the Director of Public Prosecutions suggests to the local force that such assistance would be useful in developing a particular case. In other instances the initiative comes directly from the local force.

Members of the Fraud Squad are in essence generalists. In other countries such as Canada, and in Germany and France where prosecution units are created specially to deal with commercial fraud, officers become specialised and in some instances are even trained as accountants or lawyers. In England, the police service is opposed to long-term postings to any one branch, partly in order that officers may gain a broad experience of the different aspects of policing, partly to avoid elitism, and partly to avoid the dangers of corruption. There is, thus, no career structure in the Fraud Squad, and by the time that a young detective has learned the ropes a substantial part of his time in fraud work will have elapsed. This policy may have to be reconsidered in the interests of efficiency.

Detectives are posted to the Fraud Squad for a maximum period of three years. They have no prior training in accountancy techniques or commercial law, but the Police College at Hendon does conduct short-term training courses conducted by police officers with the help of lawyers and accountants. These are practical courses, intended to acquaint detectives with the working of markets, typical schemes of fraud, book-keeping and accounts, and techniques of investigation. It gives the trainee an indication of what to look for. Most of his knowledge is gained on the job.

There is no desire on the part of the police to train detectives as accountants; the short-term nature of postings to the Fraud Squad would in any event militate against the usefulness of doing so. If specialist help is required, it can usually be obtained from other agencies, in particular the Department of Trade, from firms of accountants one of whose members will have been appointed a departmental inspector where a concurrent company inspection is being undertaken, and even from stockbrokers. In many cases a basic scheme of fraud is in issue which can be unravelled without extensive accounting analysis. There can, however, be no doubt that police and other enforcement agencies are keenly aware of the desirability of developing more sophisticated skills, and that, to this end, techniques of co-operation are increasingly being developed.

Complaints of fraud by defrauded members of the public usually come to the police in the first instance. Information may also come from the City institutions. Complaints are sometimes made to the Director of Public Prosecutions, for example from liquidators or Official Receivers or from foreign agencies. These are passed either to the police or to the Department of Trade. Complaints of company mismanagement are often submitted to the Department of Trade. There are, however, overlapping competences. Some company matters, for example long-firm frauds, may be dealt with wholly by the police without the intervention of the Department of Trade. In some cases the Department may request the police to deal with a matter, in which case the police often prefer to deal with it entirely on their own. On the other hand, where the matter is very technical, the police may refer it to the Department of Trade (*Electerminations Ltd.*, 1978).

Apart from the sheer bulk of work, the police are hampered by two factors. The first is a lack of powers; the gaps in the armoury previously mentioned can prove troublesome and, even when they can be surmounted successfully, are time-consuming. The second is a lack of direction in the preparation of cases for prosecution which, it is said, can lead to over-elaboration of investigations and consequent delay, not only at the police stage, but also at other stages in the prosecution process. Unlike street crime, it is not usually difficult to determine who is the author of a fraud, but it is often very difficult to unravel.

The problem of bulk is notorious. Some examples may serve to put it into perspective. Investigation into the Poulson case began in 1972, with four officers assigned to the task. Within a year, twenty-five officers of the City and Metropolitan Police Fraud Squad were involved, several of these being of the rank of Detective Chief Inspector and above. Officers from other fraud squads were engaged in investigations at the fringes. There was also participation by the investigations branch of the Department of Trade. The paperwork was enormous. A recent large banking fraud involving the passing of forged documents by a ring occupied seven fraud squad officers in investigations around the globe. Over 900 documents were involved and 148 witnesses. Another fraud, involving obtaining money from persons who were dishonestly promised appointments with a travel concern, involved 11,000 police hours, the interviewing of 100 witnesses, and the collation of 550 documentary exhibits. It is not surprising that the police are overworked, nor that in our system of strict proof, fraud cases, however thoroughly investigated, do not always end as successfully as the authorities would wish.

The greatest gap in police powers is their inability to obtain direct access to financial records. But there are others, too. The police have no power of arrest for conspiracy to cheat and defraud. They therefore cannot bring persons under compulsion to a police station and interview them there. To what extent this is a real problem is not known. It is sometimes alluded to by the press, but police officers deny that it is a real impediment. In the first place, many of the persons concerned are intelligent enough to know when to keep silent and are able to afford good legal advice when they need it. They rarely show guilt or remorse and are difficult to interview (Comer, 1977, p. 295). Secondly, many crimes which formerly were charged as conspiracies to cheat and defraud should now be charged as conspiracies to steal, or to obtain by deception, or to falsify accounts, and for such statutory conspiracies the police have a power of arrest.

The police lack the wide access to papers of Department of Trade Inspectors. They can rely on section 441 of the Companies Act 1948, however. Section 441 enables the Director of Public Prosecutions, the Department of Trade, or a chief officer of police in England and Wales, to apply for an order enabling the person named in it to inspect the books and records of a bank, or company, provided that there is reasonable cause to believe that any person who, while serving as an officer of the bank or company, has committed an offence in connection with its affairs and that evidence of the commission of the offence is to be found in its books and papers. The Court of Appeal has recently given the section a liberal interpretation, holding that the general object of the section is to enable the state to get at the books of the company when there has been wrongdoing. Whenever anyone in a superior position in a company encourages, directs or acquiesces in defrauding creditors, customers, shareholders or the like, then there is an offence committed in connection with the company's affairs by its officer. A fraud committed by a rogue for his benefit can still be an offence in connection with the management of the company; it is not restricted to offences in connection with the internal management of the company. The House of Lords on appeal has held that the order can be made without notice to the company involved. A decision to grant or refuse an order cannot be appealed.[1] It did not dissent from the broad construction of the section.

Helpful though this decision is, the section is still narrow in its terms because it does not touch the case where evidence of fraud in relation to another company or firm, or in relation to the officer's private affairs, is concerned. What is needed is a wider provision to enable inspections or searches by the police where either an offence of fraud, or perhaps an indictable offence generally, is reasonably believed to have been committed, and evidence of its commission is reasonably believed to be located in its financial records (in their broadest sense). This would assimilate powers in respect of financial records to powers to search under warrant for stolen goods, for example.[2] A second provision, again less useful than one would wish, is the Banker's Books Evidence Act 1879 which enables any party to legal proceedings to apply to a magistrates' court, or a judge, to inspect and take copies of entries in a banker's book for any purpose in connection with the proceedings.

The definition of 'banker's books' has been extended in recent years, by Schedule 6 of the Banking Act 1979, to include modern systems of data recording. A microfilm record is admissible evidence as a banker's book, which includes any form of permanent record kept by a bank by any means available to modern technology.[3] But the provision is limited in several ways. It does not extend to correspondence between customers and banks, or mandates. An application must indicate with some particularity what entries it is desired to inspect; the machinery must not be used to conduct a fishing expedition, and the period under inspection is limited to that which is strictly relevant to the charges.[4] The application may be made *ex parte,* but in general notice must be given to the persons whose accounts it is desired to inspect.[5] The provision applies to a stage after the commencement of proceedings. But the police need a power at an earlier stage, for the purposes of investigation. The restricted powers conferred by these provisions apply to companies and not to other forms of business organisations. This could be a significant limitation where an unincorporated association was run by persons not thought to be parties to a fraud who refused co-operation. Such cases are, however, likely to be rare.

The need for a power to inspect books and records was emphasised by the *Royal Commission on Standards of Conduct in Public Life* which, viewing the matter from the perspective of corruption, advocated granting a power to a judge, on *ex parte* application, to grant an order to search for financial records in corruption cases, such order to include bank accounts, credit transfer slips, credit slips, microfilm records of cheques, lists of securities and like documents relating to the account. The police should also, on the order of a High Court judge made on application by the Director of Public Prosecutions, be able to search for and photograph files and books of account and other relevant documents in the possession of or kept by any suspect or company of which he is an officer (Cmnd. 6524, 1976, paras. 82–3).

Wider powers are, of course, desirable, in particular where it is desired to search records held by a financial institution which is not thought to be party to the crime. Where the suspect holds such documents, it may be possible to use normal search warrant procedure, provided that a statutory power to issue a warrant exists. It would be impossible to search, however, in cases of conspiracy to steal or to cheat and defraud, for no appropriate statutory provision exists; one would not be searching for stolen goods, but for evidence of a conspiracy to steal, and while such evidence could be seized incidental to a lawful search for stolen goods, a warrant could not be issued simply to search for evidence.[6] There are, thus, real lacunae in the law concerning police powers. There is a general need for powers which would enable police to inspect financial records of persons and institutions where an offence is reasonably suspected to have been committed. The person concerned can, at present, make it difficult, if not impossible, for police to discover evidence of fraud against him. Admittedly, present police powers to enter and search premises generally are rather restricted, but there should be a general power to search premises for evidence of indictable offences (as there is in Canada) and a similar power should exist concerning the inspection of financial records, whether held by the suspect or an innocent institution.[7]

Another gap, though one little spoken of in police circles, is the inability to require prospective witnesses to talk to the police. Much commercial fraud involves the use of nominees and nominee accounts. If, of course, an inspection or investigation is mounted under the Companies Acts 1948–80, it will be possible to obtain statements and admissions on oath. Otherwise, it may be impossible to do so, and thus impossible to predict with certainty what a witness will say, if called, or even to determine whether he ought to be called in the first place. Furthermore, in the case of some investment frauds, gulled investors are reluctant to talk because they fear that by doing so the company will be pushed into further decline, and the remainder of their savings lost. Rogues are adept manipulators of investors' anxieties. In Scots law there is the useful device of precognition, by which a witness may be required to appear before the procurator-fiscal to make a statement on oath. Such a power could be most helpful in complex fraud cases.

The police can overcome some of these problems by co-operation with other agencies. The most obvious avenue for co-operation is with the Department of Trade in connection with investigations and inspections under companies legislation. For the future, another avenue of co-operation will be the Bank of England. It is generally recognised that co-operation among the agencies is necessary in order to avoid delay in prosecution. In cases of bankruptcy fraud, for example, Official Receivers will co-operate with the police. Similarly, the Companies Acts themselves make provision, where crime is apparent, for the submission of interim reports which can be passed on to the police for action.[8] There is no public information concerning how often this happens.

Recently, the last government was asked by Mr. John Stonehouse whether figures could be given of the company investigations in which information was given to the police in advance of the publication of reports. The existence of such a practice was tacitly admitted, but the disclosure of numbers was denied, and said to be contrary to the public interest.[9] The information which can be made available to the police, particularly of preliminary inspections under section 109 of the Companies Act 1967, is limited, as we have seen, to cases where prosecutions have commenced and cannot be made available to the police at the investigation stage. The same inhibition does not apply to full inspections. Apart from information about inquiries, the Department of Trade will assist the police in their investigations, suggest lines of inquiry and supply specialist legal advice where requested. There are limits to this set by the relative smallness of both the Fraud Squad and the enforcement side of the Department of Trade.

There is doubt about the efficacy, from a police point of view, of some Department of Trade procedures. A departmental inspection or investigation may in fact alert officers of companies, giving them the opportunity to conceal evidence. The police may come in at a later stage, needing to interview witnesses who have been alerted and to obtain evidence which will be admissible in a court of law. They thus need to embark on inquiries when the case is fresh. Sometimes, of course, they are asked to conduct inquiries for Inspectors, when their own needs can also be met. It is important, if a departmental investigation is being conducted, that the police obtain a report of suspected crime rapidly. Some investigations are conducted with this in mind; those into London Capital Group Limited, and Roadships Limited, afford examples.

It can be very helpful to the police to have available answers given on departmental inquiries, and these, as we have noted, are admissible in evidence against a person who is later accused of an offence.[10] Similarly, the ability of the police sometimes to obtain accounting advice from the accountant Inspector's firm can give them a fairly direct route into the interstices of complicated frauds. But there are also disadvantages to the system. It is sometimes said that the police delay investigations in order to obtain transcripts of evidence when they ought rather to proceed at once. Inspectors are not obliged to supply the police with transcripts or other assistance, and some consider that a close connection with the police might well inhibit witnesses from speaking as freely as they would otherwise do.

A second set of problems concerns the provision of legal advice to the police, and the shaping of cases. In all fraud investigations, help of this sort becomes necessary from time to time. Where the Department of Trade invites the police to investigate a case, perhaps a bankruptcy or company fraud case, the normal practice is to consider the lines of inquiry and possible charges with the police, and the Official Receiver where appropriate. The Department seeks to give the police such advice and assistance as it can, and as is needful, about the requirements of such offences as fraudulent trading, which from a police point of view are relatively exotic. It will also provide the police with written observations on the available evidence before inquiries begin.

Both provincial forces and the City and Metropolitan Police forces can call on the Director of Public Prosecutions for advice, and do so in complex fraud cases, even though most forces have a prosecuting solicitor's department. The work is of a specialised character; only the Director's staff has the necessary expertise. Such advice is less useful where the Director has not actually taken over the case. Frauds are often complex, and legal advice upon particular points given by someone who is not steeped in the details of the case can be too abstract to be really helpful. The fragmented character of our procedural arrangements is thus unhelpful. If, of course, the Director ultimately takes the case with a view to prosecution, he can ask the police to undertake further inquiries to fill up gaps in the evidence needed for conviction. Inevitably, this makes investigation and preparation for trial a longer, more ragged matter, than it needs to be. This, leads in turn, to futher problems.

If police approach the Director, his staff may be able to suggest ways in which the case might be developed. If not, he will be the recipient of the finished investigation. These police reports are very thorough. It is arguable that sometimes they are too thorough. Very often, it is not clear what course an investigation into a major fraud will take. If the police commence investigations concurrently with departmental Inspectors they may be able to help each other, but the outlines of the case may not be apparent to each until some time has elapsed. It may be difficult to know who, primarily, is to be regarded as a suspect or target and who is likely to be a witness only. There is also likely to be doubt about which matters are central and which are to be regarded as of marginal significance only. The same problems have been observed in the United States (Leigh, 1979, pp. 603–15).

Under these circumstances there is a natural and inevitable tendency to investigate all aspects of the case in detail, which poses the problem of excessive diligence (Will, 1980), and prolongs investigations. It also makes it more difficult for the prosecuting authorities to reduce the fraud to proportions which can be understood by themselves, counsel, the judge and a lay jury. The way ahead must lie in co-operation. In other countries, investigation is supervised either by a specially trained magistrate or prosecutor (Leigh & Hall Williams 1979). In England, we need machinery to monitor the investigation, and to act as a reference point for the police. Furthermore, while police work on fraud cases is admirable, their relative unfamiliarity with some commercial and accounting procedures may lead them to draw the bounds of fraud too narrowly.

One cannot penetrate the opaque screen which surrounds decisions in actual cases. There have been cases involving inter-company sales within groups, or the integrity of balance sheet figures based on asset valuations, or forecasts as to profits, where failure to prosecute seems surprising. In some such cases, one cannot but wonder whether relative unfamiliarity with aspects of accounting and commercial practice leads to phenomena not being recognised as fraud at the investigation stage. This is, however, only speculation. There are other, perfectly plausible explanations for non-prosecution, and these are considered below. One should be mentioned here, namely that investigations are often so drawn out that prosecution is felt to be unjust. In such cases, criminals benefit both from the obscurity with which they contrive to cloak business affairs and from governmental inhibitions which stem in part from the inefficient character of institutional arrangements.

The Department of Trade

The Department of Trade investigates crimes relating to those areas over which it has statutory control, notably companies and bankruptcy. It has an investigation staff which includes members with police, accounting and legal training. Investigations under bankruptcy legislation are relatively straightforward. They are, in fact, ordinary criminal investigations and departmental investigators adopt the procedures which apply to all criminal investigations, including the invocation of the Judges' Rules. Not all investigations in bankruptcy matters are dealt with by the Department; some are dealt with by the police. This occurs not infrequently in cases of theft, deception, and the obtaining of credit by an undischarged bankrupt (Leigh, 1980b). Some such cases are dealt with by complementary investigations, but usually one body or the other conducts the investigation in any particular case.

In company matters inspections and investigations may give rise to criminal prosecutions in which the matter is dealt with throughout by the Department. If it is of sufficient importance, or politically sensitive, the case will go to the Director of Public Prosecutions who may ask the Department or the police to conduct further inquiries. An inspection may be commenced with a view to assisting in the ultimate institution of a prosecution. Not uncommonly, prosecutions are commenced directly as a result of an inspection under section 109 of the Companies Act 1967, without a full investigation being ordered. This is most likely to happen in the

case of private companies. The matter is then concluded by the
police and the Director of Public Prosecutions. More frequently,
however, the bulk of investigations and subsequent prosecutions
found upon normal investigations and not upon the exceptional
powers contained in the Companies Acts.

The Inland Revenue and Customs and Excise[11]

The Inland Revenue conducts its own investigations and prosecutions in England and Wales, as does the Customs and Excise. In the
case of the Inland Revenue the reason is that tax matters are
traditionally kept confidential, even where the taxpayer is suspected
of having committed other offences.[12] The practice of internal
investigations enables the Inland Revenue to define and apply a
coherent policy. Furthermore, taxation is a specialised topic.
Investigators require a knowledge of it, necessitating technical
training and practical experience. Furthermore, most cases are not
in fact prosecuted, but are rather dealt with by pecuniary
settlement. The Inland Revenue considers that in most cases it
would not be practicable or desirable to change the investigation
from the Revenue to the police if it looked as though criminal
proceedings might ensue.

The bulk of investigative work, which leads to pecuniary
settlements, is carried out locally in local tax districts. In 1978 there
were approximately 50,000 investigations into the affairs of Schedule
D taxpayers, or about 2.7 per cent of the total, and approximately
130,000 other investigations, approximately 0.5 per cent of the
total.[13] Serious cases, and all cases where criminal proceedings are
in contemplation, are dealt with centrally in the Enquiry Branch or
the Special Investigation Section. The Enquiry Branch is the main
investigation section of the Board of Inland Revenue, staffed with
some one hundred higher-grade and senior Inspectors of Taxes
and professional accountants. Cases may originate from local tax
offices, or as a result of information from informers, Customs and
Excise, or the police. Some are generated by the Enquiry Branches'
own researches.

The procedure followed on investigation, assuming that the
Enquiry Section is involved, depends upon whether at the outset the
case is thought likely to involve a pecuniary settlement or a
prosecution. The bulk of cases fall within the former category. The
taxpayer is invited to attend before two inquiry officers, and it is
suggested that he obtain professional advice. He is given a copy of
the Hansard leaflet and asked to consider his position. The Hansard
leaflet is a statement of policy in terms given to the House of

Commons in 1943 by Sir John Anderson.[14] The Inland Revenue has powers to settle cases rather than to prosecute. The taxpayer is asked whether his tax affairs are in order or not and whether he is prepared to give the Revenue access to his books and papers. The leaflet informs him that the Inland Revenue may take his co-operation into account in deciding whether or not to prosecute, but also that there can be no guarantee that what he says will not be used in evidence against him in criminal proceedings.[15] The Revenue investigators make their own investigations, applying such checks to the applicant's papers as they consider necessary. Few such cases are prosecuted. The principles which govern prosecution are considered below. From the point of view of the Revenue, which is interested in tax collection, the procedure has advantages. Taxpayer complaints stress the time and the emotional and financial cost to the person under investigation (Coffield, 1967).

The Board of Inland Revenue considers that those cases which are worked by the Enquiry Branch as potential criminal prosecutions can be divided into three categories. The first is where the case is of so grave a kind that public policy may require prosecution even if the offender makes full disclosure. Examples are: where an accountant who is a tax adviser is the taxpayer; where the frauds are highly sophisticated and calculated, involving forgery of documents, for example; and where the taxpayer has been in collusion with others to defraud the Revenue. The second category is where the taxpayer, on challenge by the Enquiry Branch, either denies irregularities or fails to make proper disclosure within a reasonable time. The third category is that in which the taxpayer purports to make full disclosure but does not in fact do so. All these cases are handled as potential criminal prosecutions. Interviews are conducted in accordance with the Judges' Rules, and the suspects duly cautioned. Those involved may make written statements under caution if they wish, but the usual method adopted is that of recording questions and answers. Interview normally takes place by appointment in the presence of the taxpayer's advisers.

The Investigation Section deals with a wide variety of offences against the Revenue where trading accounts are not involved. At present, frauds by sub-contractors are a major problem. Again, investigations are conducted subject to the Judges' Rules. Some few revenue cases are investigated by the police. The circumstances are exceptional, for example where a foreign element is involved requiring their assistance. In such a case the matter is referred by the Board of Inland Revenue to the Director of Public Prosecutions. The police are also brought in to deal with stolen Inland Revenue payable orders, since apart from the source of the document there is nothing about them peculiar to the Inland Revenue. A significant number of offences against the Revenue are discovered by the police when investigating other matters. Construction industry sub-contractors may be found to be in possession of false or forged Inland Revenue documents. In such cases the local police force and prosecuting authority are encouraged to conclude the matter, the Inland Revenue giving information and advice where necessary.

The Inland Revenue has wider powers in respect of books and documents than has the police. These derive from the Finance Act 1976.[16] Both the Board and an Inspector may require a person to deliver up documents which are in his possession or power and are reasonably thought to contain, or may contain, information relevant to any tax liability to which he is or may be subject. A taxpayer's spouse or any son or daughter, or his business present or past, are also so subject in respect of the taxpayer's affairs. There are wide powers requiring a taxpayer who has acted as an accountant and been convicted of a tax offence, or recently had a penalty awarded against him, to deliver up documents relating to the actual or potential tax liability of any of his clients.[17] This provision only operates respecting convictions arising after the passing of the Act.

Another sweeping power, which caused much anxious parliamentary debate at the time of its enactment, is the power to enter under warrant for the purposes of search and seizure.[18] This is section 20c of the Taxes Management Act 1970, as amended. The approval of the Board is required before a warrant can be applied for. If it is forthcoming, application is made by an officer of the Board to a circuit judge. The applicant must show that there is reasonable ground for suspecting that an offence relating to fraud in connection with tax has been committed and that evidence relating to it can be found on specified premises. If the warrant is granted, the officer entering specified premises may take not only matter specified in the warrant, but also other things found therein which he has reasonable cause to believe may be required as evidence in proceedings for tax fraud. In an endeavour to avoid disruption of business affairs, the Act provides that the Revenue shall give to the occupier of the premises, or the person in possession of the papers, a list of them and, where access to seized documents is required for the purpose of a business, shall afford reasonable access to the person conducting the business.[19]

These powers are sweeping, as is illustrated by *Reg.* v. *Inland Revenue Commissioners, ex parte Rossminster Limited.*[20] The Revenue, suspecting that Rossminster's tax schemes fell on the wrong side of the line which separates avoidance from evasion, obtained a warrant and, at 7 a.m. on 13 July, 1979, swooped upon the homes of two of Rossminster's principals and the company itself. If not quite the 'knock in the night' envisaged by opponents of the measure, it came close to it.[21] Files were taken at the rate of one per minute. The applicant, Rossminster, and its directors, alleged that a ransack took place. The Inland Revenue referred to it as a disciplined search.

The principles laid down by the House of Lords demonstrate the breadth of the law. While the circuit judge, in granting the warrant, must be satisfied that, objectively, there is reasonable ground for doing so, the applicant who seeks to attack the warrant bears a heavy, perhaps impossible burden, for he must show that there was no evidence upon which the judge could act. As the taxpayer is not present when the warrant is granted, his chances of doing so are few. Nor can the warrant be challenged where it simply recites that there is reasonable ground for suspecting fraud in connection with tax. While the warrant must specify the place to be searched, it need not condescend to a catalogue of applicable offences. Indeed, it would not help the taxpayer if it did so, since a capitulation of, for example, theft, common law fraud and the like, would be unhelpful. Nor is it necessary that the Inland Revenue indicate who the suspect is at that stage. To do so might alert the actual suspect, an argument no doubt valid generally but rather hollow in this case. The warrant can be executed at any time of the day or night.

The powers of the officer, once on the premises, are also wide, although no wider than the powers which exist under, for example, section 26 of the Theft Act 1968. He may seize and remove any documents which he has reasonable cause to believe may afford evidence of a fraud in connection with, or in relation to, tax. Not only is it not necessary to itemise in the warrant the articles to be seized, but any general description would not serve as a limitation since the officer's statutory power is general; it is not limited to documents of any particular class nor to the affairs of any particular person.

In the Court of Appeal, Lord Denning, the Master of the Rolls, spoke feelingly of ransacking premises, although he himself had markedly extended police powers in relation to theft,[22] evoking, wrongly so their Lordships held, the great general warrant cases of the eighteenth century which held that a warrant must be specific both as to the place to be searched and the articles which might be seized. His Lordship had been markedly expansive where the powers of the ordinary police were concerned. Presumably, his strictness towards the Revenue reflects a view that tax fraud is less heinous than real crime. The House of Lords holds that the warrant must be specific as to the place to be searched. Only articles having evidentiary value in relation to tax may be seized. In almost all cases, however, it will only be possible to challenge the propriety of seizing particular articles; and where, as in *Rossminster*, documents are removed by the van load, it cannot be expected that anything more than a superficial consideration of files will take place. The taxpayer must seek redress at a later stage, save in exceptional cases, when the question whether the Revenue officer reasonably thought that the document had evidentiary value can be fully explored.

It is undeniable that the Revenue authorities have much greater powers to obtain access to and information concerning financial records than have the police. In some respects they are better armed with powers than the Department of Trade. Their powers are also greater than those of the Customs and Excise in relation to Value Added Tax since their powers are specific to business premises, permitting entry at any time.[23] The power of a Customs officer to enter premises under Writ of Assistance is nearly unlimited, but it is only available in relation to things liable to forfeiture.[24]

Customs and Excise have an investigation division and investigation units which are their equivalent to the C.I.D. They are able to consider matters on a basis of centrally determined policy. Investigators report to administrators and then to the legal branch of the Customs and Excise. The matter is, however, not one of mere formal reporting. Investigators can and do ask advice, for example concerning how an investigation ought to be conducted, what records need to be obtained, and how far they are to go. The Customs and Excise has power to administer written questionnaires, the answers to which can be given in evidence. This is certainly a striking power but, because it is a tedious procedure, is seldom done. In addition, Customs and Excise have available the ordinary techniques of questioning. In fact, Customs and Excise and Value Added Tax inquiries tend to turn on documentation, and if documentation can be shown to be false there is little need for extensive interrogation. The unified investigation system has the advantages that because the investigators work closely with the legal branch, it is possible to prepare cases for trial efficiently and economically. The solicitors who prepare the case have a general oversight of the matter at its various stages.

Conclusion

There is a clear need to give wider powers to the police to get at financial records. It is a pity that the Revenue exercised their powers in *Rossminster* in quite the way they did. Seizures at unsocial hours should only be resorted to where it is absolutely necessary to do so. Certain foreign systems have limitations of that character in the general law (Stefani and Levasseur, 1977, para. 479). The problem with an overly exuberant use of powers is that it is likely to poison the atmosphere and thus inhibit reform. That may well have happened; certainly the House of Lords indicated that some aspects of the Revenue's powers should be reviewed. We ought also to consider generally whether we could not minimise the dislocation which results from large-scale searches and seizures by relying, as is done in West Germany, on investigative audits at the firm's premises. (Leigh and Hall Williams, 1979). These questions are further considered in connection with reform of the system, but the present structure of powers must militate against extensive consideration of what items are to be seized when seizure actually occurs.

References and Notes

1. *In re Racal Communications Ltd.*, [1980] 2 All E.R. 634 (H.L.) reversing *Re a Company* [1980] 1 All E.R. 284.
2. Theft Act 1968, s. 26; for a detailed account, L. Leigh, *Police Powers in England and Wales* (1975b), chapter 9.
3. *Barker* v. *Wilson* [1980] 2 All E.R. 81.
4. *Williams* v. *Summerfield* (1972) 56 Cr. Ap. R. 597.
5. *Reg.* v. *Marlborough St. Metropolitan Stipendiary Magistrate, ex parte Simpson* [1980] Crim. L.R. 305.
6. See *Ghani* v. *Jones* [1970] 1 Q.B. 693; *Frank Truman Export Ltd.* v. *Metropolitan Police Commissioner* [1977].Q.B. 592.
7. On search warrant powers in Canada, see Criminal Code, 1970, C-34, s. 433.
8. Companies Act 1967, s. 41.
9. Sess. 1975–6, 906 H.C. Deb. (Vth Ser.), col. 95, on the provision of published reports, see *ibid.*, cols. 542–3.
10. Companies Act 1967, s. 50.
11. Most of the following derives from notes of interview and from Board of Inland Revenue, *Evidence Submitted to the Royal Commission on Criminal Procedure* (1979), available in the Board's library.
12. Sess. 1975–6, 906 H.C. Deb. (Vth Ser.) cols. 391–2.
13. Sess. 1978–9, 963 H.C. Deb. (Vth Ser.) col. 706.
14. See Parliamentary Question and Answer of 5 October 1944 by Sir John Anderson to Major Studholme, 403 H.C. Deb. (Vth Ser.), cols. 1149–50; *Minutes of Evidence* taken before the Select Committee on Public Accounts published with the Third Report from the Committee, Sess. 1974, paras. 237, 240, 248.
15. Under s. 105 of the Taxes Management Act 1970 such statements are admissible in evidence against their maker.
16. Finance Act 1976, section 57 and Sched. 6, substituting 20–20D for section 20 of the Taxes Management Act 1970.

17. *Ibid.*, s. 20A. Board approval is required before such notice can be given. By section 20B, the person concerned must first be given a reasonable opportunity to produce.

18. Sess. 1975–6, 911 H.C. Deb. (Vth Ser.), cols. 981 ff.

19. Taxes Management Act 1970 (as amended), s. 20(C)(4) and (5).

20. [1980] 2 W.L.R. 1 (D.C., C.A. and H.L.).

21. Sess. 1975–6, 911 H.C. Deb. (Vth Ser.) col. 992 (Mr. David Mitchell).

22. *Chic Fashions (West Wales) Ltd.* v. *Jones* [1968] 2 Q.B. 299, and *Ghani* v. *Jones* [1970] 1 Q.B. at p. 698.

23. Finance Act 1972, s. 37(1); they have also a broader search warrant power; *ibid.*, s. 37(3).

24. Customs and Excise Management Act 1979, s. 161(1).

16 Criminal Intelligence and the Exchange of Information

Intelligence gathering and its dissemination is crucial to the fight against fraud and corruption. This is an activity which has both internal and foreign aspects. One would expect police forces, including the Fraud Squad, to maintain indexes of known criminals and of their manner of operation. A Home Office circular to the police deals explicitly with criminal intelligence in matters of company fraud.[1] It exhorts the City and Metropolitan Police Fraud Squad to maintain a comprehensive index of persons and businesses whose dealings have come under suspicion of fraud. There is an index of unsatisfactory businesses at Scotland Yard containing details of: companies and firms suspected or convicted of commercial fraud; individuals suspected or convicted of commercial fraud and bankruptcy offences; individuals so suspected or convicted operating at national or international level; suspicious transactions in stocks, shares and bonds; companies and persons who are, or have been, subject to investigation by the police or, where known, other authorities, for example the Department of Trade or an Official Receiver. Provincial forces, also, are urged to contribute to the index. The index is obviously not fully comprehensive in respect of matters which might be covered. We have noted already that there is no standing machinery for picking up and collating qualifications to company accounts.

Internationally, in respect of the general run of crimes including trading frauds, but not tax or certain economic offences, Interpol acts as an agency to exchange information. It is not an international police force, and its activities are limited to ordinary criminal law offences (Bossard, 1980). However, for ordinary large frauds, it affords a reasonably satisfactory medium for the gathering of intelligence. The greatest problem faced by its users is that Interpol functions through national bureaux, not all of which are efficient (Feraud and Schlanitz, 1975). It has been suggested that police authorities should also exchange directly information concerning suspected fraud offenders and their modes of operation (Anon, 1975). This is of course done already (Nepote, 1978). Police forces will exchange information domestically with other law enforcement agencies. They will, for example, notify the Department of Trade of offences falling within the purview of that body. They will also, on occasion, enforce the law themselves and inform the Inland Revenue of tax offences which they discover in the course of their normal investigations.

The extent to which the police receive information varies according to the other agency concerned. Information flows fairly freely from the Department of Trade, subject to the statutory limitations already noted on divulging information obtained as a result of company inspections. The City institutions will disclose information to the police in a clear case of fraud. We have noted that the Stock Exchange, for example, passes information both to the police and to the Department of Trade. Whether the police would pass information to the City institutions is more problematic. Such matters as individuals' criminal records are treated as confidential. They are used to inform a trial court at the sentence stage and, sometimes, but not often, to determine whether charges should be laid against an individual. Full access by the City institutions to relevant matters such as an individual's criminal record will require legislation to oblige the police to disclose them. One would expect such information to be disclosed to the Department of Trade in respect of the suitability of persons to control insurance companies or to hold licences to deal in securities.

In revenue matters, the law is in a most unsatisfactory state. The Inland Revenue does collect intelligence concerning tax evasion, and has set up special offices in London, Birmingham, Manchester and Edinburgh to deal with difficult cases.[2] The problem is with disclosure. We have noted that the Inland Revenue is obliged to hold tax matters in confidence, and maintains silence even though a taxpayer's affairs indicate that other offences have been committed by him. Historically, the reason assigned for this remarkable state of affairs is that confidentiality would lead taxpayers to disclose their incomes fully. The Royal Commission on the Taxation of Profits and Income of 1955 concluded that there could be no general principle that information available to one of the multifarious organs of government should be available to all its other organs (Cmd. 9474, 1955, para. 1063).

More recently, a majority of the Royal Commission on Standards of Conduct in Public Life concluded that, while the Inland Revenue should not take an initiative in passing information to the Director of Public Prosecutions, it should be required, in corruption cases only, to disclose information on the order of a High Court Judge made at the instance of the Director of Public Prosecutions (Cmnd. 6524,

1976). The overriding value expressed, in rejecting the notion of any affirmative obligation, was that, otherwise, candid disclosure by the taxpayer might be impaired. This would affect the conduct of interviews and would lead to an inhibiting formalism in relationships between the taxpayer and the Revenue.

The Inland Revenue itself expressed doubt as to whether it was in possession of information about corruption sufficiently often to make any real difference to law enforcement. Its evidence did not consider wider issues about the availability to it of information concerning commercial fraud generally. It seems implausible that taxpayers now disclose to the Revenue, in an undisguised form at any rate, evidence of frauds in which they engage, nor does it seem plausible that the Revenue is never in possession at least of indicia of fraud which they could pass on. But despite these considerations, and the undoubted point that bribes are in effect now claimed as tax deductible, the majority report is cautious and the rules have not been changed. Confidentiality is not absolute. There now exist arrangements for the exchange of information between the Inland Revenue and the Customs and Excise.[3] Because of undertakings given during the passage of the legislation concerned, exchanges of information have only been given under head office arrangements, and not directly between local offices. The previous government sanctioned an exchange of information at local office level in the Leeds area as an experimental measure.[4]

Internationally, extensive provision is made for the exchange of information both in respect of income and corporation tax and in respect of customs and excise matters. Liaison among customs authorities is facilitated by the Customs Co-operation Council founded in 1952 which, though not an enforcement body, conduces to international co-operation. In the countries of the E.E.C., there is a Naples Convention of 1967 on mutual assistance. Furthermore, section 5(7) of the European Communities Act 1972 expressly provides that the Commissioners of Customs and Excise are to co-operate with other customs services on matters of mutual concern, and in particular may give effect to any reciprocal arrangements made between member states for securing the due administration of their customs laws and the prevention or detection of fraud or evasion. It is generally recognised that it would be anachronistic to regard the funds of the E.E.C. as those of another sovereign state and therefore not the proper object of enforcement by the Customs authorities of the particular member states. In virtue of this recognition, there is an E.E.C. Draft Treaty proposal for the protection of the financial interests of the European Communities under criminal law, which would also comprehend the free exchange of information among the law enforcement authorities of the member states.[5] As with other E.E.C. initiatives which meet with a mixed response, it has spent a long time as a chrysalis.

In respect of revenue offences, a series of double-taxation conventions provides for the exchange of information in tax matters. Provisions exist for a full exchange of information concerning a taxpayer's affairs and cover the United Kingdom in its relations with its principal trading partners.[6] They do not, however, envisage the institution of an investigation by the tax authorities of the requested state. The information to be exchanged is that which is obtained in the course of normal administration. In addition, by statute implementing an E.E.C. Directive, extensive provision is made for mutual assistance in tax matters.[7] The Nordic countries, most of which are not members, have recently asked to join this scheme. The Directive, reciting the presumed harmful effects on competition and capital movements from tax evasion and avoidance, the need for international measures on a multi-national rather than a bi-national (tax treaty) basis and the need to strengthen collaboration in tax administration and the exchange of information, provides in part for the exchange of information on request, subject to the requesting state having exhausted its usual sources of information in such cases. The question of transfer of profits within groups of enterprises across national frontiers appears to be a particular object of concern.[8]

The Directive is implemented by section 77 of the Finance Act 1978. It enables the Commissioners of the Inland Revenue to disclose information required to be disclosed by virtue of the Directive without regard to any existing obligation of secrecy. Such disclosure can only be made provided that the tax authorities of the requesting state are under an obligation to keep the matters confidential, as is the Inland Revenue, and the information is only to be used for tax purposes. Welcome as this new measure is, it serves once again to emphasise the self-contained nature of revenue enforcement. The regime is one of the general confidentiality of revenue information. In other matters there do not seem to be standing arrangements for the mutual disclosure of information. In this there is a contrast with the Securities Exchange Commission in the United States, which appears to be ready to exchange or simply to provide information concerning persons suspected of crimes in relation to securities (Raw, Page and Hodgson, 1971, p. 272; Leigh, 1979).

The relative isolation of revenue cases is undesirable. Not

infrequently, persons committing revenue offences will be found to have committed other fraud offences as well. In other jurisdictions, connections between revenue offences and such crimes as narcotics and arms smuggling have been found (Rider, 1980). It hardly seems appropriate that the provision of information should occur exclusively in one direction, to the revenue but not from it. One would have thought that such matters as the identity of informants and the information given could be protected otherwise; in normal criminal matters the police do this, and the courts have long recognised and given effect to the need to do so. The identity of informants is protected from disclosure.[9] Furthermore, the unreality of supposing that the confidentiality of tax matters will induce a criminal more freely to declare his income to the Revenue, and the potential centrality of the Revenue to enforcement as a whole, ought to cause current practices to be reassessed.

References and Notes

1. See *Home Office Consolidated Circular to the Police on Crime and Kindred Matters* (1969 ed. as amended) Section 31F.
2. Sess. 1976–77, 931 H.C. Deb. (Vth Ser.), col. 395.
3. Finance Act 1972, s. 127.
4. Sess. 1976–7, 926 H.C. Deb. (Vth Ser.), col. 300.
5. Commission of the European Communities, *Draft for a Treaty to permit the adoption of common rules on the protection under criminal law of the financial interests of the community*, COM (76) 418 final.
6. For example, Canada, Double Taxation Agreement of 12 December 1966, S.I. 1967, no. 482; France, Double Taxation Agreement of 22 May 1968, S.I. 1968 no. 1869.
7. The United Kingdom has reserved its position on Value Added Tax, Sess. 1977–8, 954 H.C. Deb. (Vth Ser.) cols. 503–4.
8. E.E.C. Council Directive of 19th December 1977, Official Journal of the European Communities, no. L/336/15, 27 December 1977.
9. *Reg. v. Inland Revenue Commissioners, ex parte Rossminster Ltd.* [1980] 2 W.L.R. 1.

17 The Prosecution and Trial of Offences

In England and Wales, because of the absence of a fully developed system of public prosecutions, the prosecution of fraud is the responsibility of several different bodies; the police, the Director of Public Prosecutions (D.P.P.), the Bank of England, the Customs and Excise and the Inland Revenue. In Scotland, by contrast, the prosecution of offences is the responsibility of the Lord Advocate, and in practice is dealt with by procurators-fiscal.

Save in those matters enforced by government departments, the primary responsibility to prosecute is that of the police. They investigate and determine whether a charge is to be brought, and what the charge is to be. In this, they are aided by prosecuting solicitors who advise upon legal issues arising, and who prepare the matter for committal proceedings and later for trial (Sigler, 1974; Home Office, 1978). In major fraud cases, however, the matter is often remitted to the Director of Public Prosecutions. Prosecuting major commercial fraud cases is a specialist task and one for which many prosecuting solicitors are not trained. Hence, in practice, the Director of Public Prosecutions enjoys a strategic position.

Responsibility to Prosecute

The Director of Public Prosecutions

There are, as we have seen, some few cases, arising under bankruptcy legislation and under the Companies Act 1948 concerning offences reported by voluntary liquidators, which the D.P.P. is obliged to prosecute. Otherwise, his power to do so is discretionary. There are, in addition, a number of cases in which either his consent, or that of the Attorney-General, is required before a prosecution may be commenced.[1] The discretionary powers of the D.P.P. to commence or take over a prosecution are dealt with by a regulation which provides that it shall be his duty to do so in any case which appears to him to be of importance or difficulty, or which for any other reason requires his intervention.[2] He maintains a Fraud and Bankruptcy Division which deals with major frauds, in particular company frauds, and with his role as Official Petitioner in criminal bankruptcy matters. The Division is small in number, comprising one Assistant Director, four Senior Legal Assistants and one Legal Assistant with a small supporting staff.

The Director states that about 150 cases of company fraud are referred to him each year from the police, the Department of Trade, and by liquidators of companies.[3] In some of the most complex cases, the matter is first referred to him by the Department of Trade, which has initiated the investigation by appointing Inspectors under the Companies Acts. It also refers cases to the Director following a report by an Official Receiver of a criminal offence arising out of a winding-up. Cases referred to him by liquidators are usually comparatively minor, and are passed by the Director to the Department of Trade for investigation and prosecution.

The burden on the D.P.P.'s office is heavy. Because of the pressure of work, the Director and the Department of Trade instruct counsel to advise in the larger cases and, if appropriate, to conduct the prosecutions. In London, Treasury counsel are instructed, whereas in the provinces counsel are nominated by the Attorney-General. Such counsel are few in number and invariably busy. Often, they cannot give priority to fraud cases. Some time may elapse before they can formulate advice, and on occasion they consider that further investigation needs to be done before a prosecution can be mounted. There is, thus, an element of delay at this stage.

The Department of Trade

The Department of Trade also maintains a prosecutions staff. While not obliged to report serious fraud cases to the D.P.P., it tends to do so in practice. The D.P.P., however, frequently leaves the Department to continue with cases arising out of the administration of companies and insolvency legislation, for example fraudulent trading. Conversely, he will take over cases where there is a threat of political pressure against the Department. There are, in addition, cases in which both the Department and the police are involved. If the police have asked the Director to act, the Department will also place the matter in his hands.

At one time, it was assumed that all indictable cases would go to the D.P.P. There is now a tendency to offer only those cases to him that really warrant such a referral. Informal procedures have evolved to regulate referral, and as a result little time is lost in the referral. This procedure sometimes co-ordinates the investigation and prosecution of offences coming to the attention both of the Department, perhaps through the report of an Official Receiver or liquidator, and the police. When the investigations are completed, it will be for the departmental solicitors, or in some cases for counsel, to advise on the charges to be brought. Whether counsel is instructed before committal proceedings and therefore is able to advise on the charges to be brought, or after committal, is a decision taken pragmatically in the light of the case concerned.

Customs and Excise

The Customs and Excise is an important prosecuting agency because it handles not only customs and V.A.T. matters but also, in the right of the former, cases arising under legislation applicable to E.E.C. schemes. In Scotland, cases go to the procurator-fiscal, who himself determines whether cases should be brought to prosecution or not. In England and Wales the D.P.P. may take serious cases, in particular those which involve violations of the general criminal law and not in specialist legislation administered by the Customs and Excise. Otherwise, cases are dealt with internally. There is a unified prosecution procedure, with decisions to prosecute being dealt with centrally by the same personnel, who can thus develop practical guides to prosecution policy. The fact that investigation itself falls within the purview of the Department's legal branch helps to eliminate wasted effort. The system appears to be a smoothly articulated one.

The Inland Revenue

The Inland Revenue also has an elaborate system. Once again, prosecutions, and therefore the exercise of discretion, fall under the procurator-fiscal in Scotland. In England and Wales prosecutions are conducted by the Solicitor of Inland Revenue and counsel instructed on his behalf. There are cases which are notified to the D.P.P. These are:[4] where the tax loss alleged is very large; where a nationally important company is involved; where the question whether any person should be granted immunity from prosecution and called as a Crown witness must be considered; where the case has a political aspect; and where it appears likely to give rise to great public interest. It is not assumed that all such cases will in fact be prosecuted by the D.P.P.

If after obtaining their solicitor's opinion the Board of Inland Revenue considers a case to be appropriate for prosecution, and the decision is taken at Board level, the papers are returned to the Solicitor's Office. The prosecution is mounted by a professional officer supported by executive and clerical officers. At present twenty-one persons are employed on criminal and penalty work of whom nine are lawyers. The Inland Revenue is represented on each circuit by one Standing Counsel on criminal matters appointed by the Attorney-General. In London and the South-Eastern Circuit there are two. Counsel is usually appointed after committal proceedings.

In England and Wales the extent to which proceedings are dealt with internally permits a high degree of unification of procedures. The Inland Revenue makes the point that this degree of unification is much more difficult to achieve in Scotland where the procurator-fiscal could decide to prosecute in cases where the Board would not. Furthermore, investigators may not prepare the case as thoroughly as they would in England and Wales if they assume that the procurator-fiscal will want aspects to be investigated by the police.

Prosecution Policies and the Exercise of Discretion

All prosecuting authorities have a discretion whether or not to prosecute. In general, this discretion founds on the common law. In Inland Revenue and Customs matters its foundation is partly statutory. There are criteria which govern the decision whether or not to prosecute. How evenly these criteria are applied it is difficult to say, but a settled body of principles does seem to have emerged. Since Department of Trade reports give no indication of why a decision whether or not to prosecute is made, it is often difficult, if not impossible, to determine what weight was given to the various principles applicable. In 1977 the Solicitor-General (Mr. Peter Archer Q.C.) raised certain questions and stated the principles.[5] These may be paraphrased thus: Is there evidence on which a jury could be asked to convict? An affirmative answer does not necessarily mean that there will be a prosecution. Is there a reasonable prospect of conviction? How much time has elapsed since the offence was committed? This is an important consideration because witnesses' memories may have faded to the point where they cannot be relied on. This criterion must be weighed against the seriousness of the offence, the importance of the matter generally, and the sentence which is likely to be passed. Also considered important are factors personal to the accused, his state of health, his age, and whether it would be oppressive in all the circumstances to prosecute him.

In an earlier study of bankruptcy cases, the author found that the relevant factors personal to the accused appeared to be the same, save that the sex was important, and so was the question whether the accused had been convicted for another, similar offence, in the interim (Leigh, 1980b). The attitude of the victim is taken into account, for example whether he is prepared to give evidence, but it is not decisive. The police, for example, are reluctant to drop cases simply because restitution is offered, regarding this as coming close to paying for immunity. Nor will they drop a case simply because a prosecution might embarrass persons such as local councillors, or auditors, whose negligence had permitted thefts to continue (Wilcox, 1972). The fact that police may well want to prosecute leads some companies dealing with internal thefts and frauds, and desirous primarily of recovering their loss, not to call them in (Comer, 1977).

The ultimate question is whether it would be in the public interest to bring proceedings. The major factor in all criminal cases must be whether there is sufficient evidence to obtain a conviction. If there is not, it would be unethical for a prosecuting authority to bring proceedings. It is, after all, the duty of the authority not only to enforce the law, but also to stand between the citizen and the State, ensuring that prosecutions are brought only in meritorious cases. The prosecutor must therefore determine what matters must be proven, whether there is evidence to establish these, and how cogent that evidence is. Admittedly, it is for the jury ultimately to rule on what weight should be given to admissible evidence, but it would be a dereliction of duty for a prosecutor to ignore that certain evidence is of so dubious a character that a jury would be extremely unlikely to believe it.

Evidentiary problems do not strike all prosecuting agencies alike. The Department of Trade, for example, considers that it seldom has to make difficult judgements on the adequacy of evidence to support particular charges. It is either satisfied at an early stage that it will not succeed or that it has a good prospect of success on the available evidence. The D.P.P., in the nature of things, handles more complex cases which can be expected to produce difficult questions of judgement. He applies what he refers to, rather inelegantly since the underlying notion is that he must be satisfied that there is a good probability of success, as the fifty-one per cent rule; that is, is there a fifty-one per cent chance that the matter will end in a conviction?[6] This is obviously an impressionistic guide only. The D.P.P. has also stated that he is unwilling to prosecute stale offences, those which were committed three or more years before the trial, unless they were of so serious a character that a custodial sentence is likely to be imposed. This has obvious implications in fraud cases where the delay is the product of the accused's often very successful attempts to obfuscate matters.

We have noted that the Inland Revenue and the Customs and

Excise wield a discretion which is partly founded on statute. Both have full power to settle criminal matters without prosecution.[7] Both treat prosecution as an exceptional recourse, but this tendency is more marked in the case of the Inland Revenue than it is in that of the Customs and Excise. The Inland Revenue proceeds on the assumption that its primary function is to collect taxes. It therefore prosecutes only in exceptional cases which it grades according to its criteria in the various categories involved, for example, trading frauds, frauds by sub-contractors, false claims to personal allowances, and expense claims. Thus, a large fraud in connection with trading profits may not be prosecuted because it is not serious enough within the category, whereas a false claim for personal allowances involving much less money may well be.[8] These distinctions are treated as inevitable if the Board is to continue to prosecute in some examples of all types of case. This is not, incidentally, necessarily lenient to the taxpayer since he, being, as we have noted, under some pressure to admit his sins and settle, is thereafter in peril of extended investigations covering his whole career as a taxpayer, and of a large assessment.

The Customs and Excise also exercise discretion, which was very marked under the former system of exchange control (Leigh 1980a).[9] Many cases were dealt with by forfeiture. Where tax evasion produces a substantial loss, the Customs will prosecute, as it will in cases involving fraudulent agricultural import-export schemes. In revenue cases, apart from the normal criteria, the Customs seek to select clear cases of fraud in which the immoral character of the evasion is manifest. If a settlement is offered and refused, the Customs must prosecute; there is no other recourse. Two significant questions arise concerning discretion to prosecute. The first is whether the criteria enunciated by the D.P.P. are in fact applied. The second is whether they achieve the correct balance.

The first question, that of the application of criteria, attained prominence as a result of the Director's decision not to prosecute in respect of breaches of legislation forbidding the supply of petroleum products to Rhodesia, during the period when it was a colony in rebellion. The Labour Government commissioned an inquiry, the Bingham Inquiry, into breaches of sanctions legislation by British-owned companies, with specific reference to whether there was sufficient evidence to mount a prosecution (Foreign and Commonwealth Office 1978). The matter admittedly does not involve commercial fraud. Some of the statements made to the House of Commons purport to apply generally. The matter was one of some delicacy in any event because ministers appeared at one time to give the impression that they were interested rather in maintaining appearances than in the substance of regulation, and the situation was in any event one in which it was impossible to prevent some supplies getting through.

The criteria applied by the D.P.P., the Attorney-General informed Parliament, were: the grave difficulties in obtaining admissible evidence against the companies and in particular those officers who were guilty agents in the matter; whether the supply had been made in contravention of any alleged understanding with ministers; the impossibility of obtaining documentary evidence from abroad when both South Africa and Rhodesia forbade disclosure under criminal penalties; the difficulty of securing witnesses abroad, since the crimes involved fell outside the scope of any extradition arrangements; and the death and retirement of some of the officers concerned. Trial would inevitably be complex and prolonged and a jury might well be reluctant to convict if it thought that offences were attributable to understandings with government. Having taken the advice of counsel, the Director decided against prosecution.[10] He later amplified his reasons, noting that essential documents could not be obtained, and that there was a slender chance of obtaining convictions.[11]

This decision produced a storm, attributable in part to the fact that many minor offenders had been successfully prosecuted.[12] In those cases, presumably, the evidentiary problems were not so great. Members of Parliament questioned vigorously whether, in the application of criteria, large offenders were favoured in the result whereas smaller ones were disfavoured. The question is one which cannot readily be answered without access to the documents. It is noteworthy that the former Labour Law Officers maintained a discreet silence on the application of principles, neither joining in the hue and cry nor defending the Director.

The difficulties faced in the sanctions case were great, and the context rather unusual. Complexity is found in all fraud cases. In many, it is difficult to obtain documents. Admittedly, the political considerations involved were unusual, but there is a class of cases which, constitutionally, the Law Officers can refrain from prosecuting on political grounds (Edwards, 1964). In the sanctions case, there would be problems of consequent unfairness to the individuals and companies concerned, and not simply that of embarrassment to government. The only remarkable criterion apparently applied by the Director was that certain individuals had retired, and that was explained as signifying that they had left the jurisdiction and could not be brought back for trial. Some were South African or Portuguese citizens.

The question relevant to this book is, 'what result application of the criteria brings in major fraud cases?' Here, one must register disquiet. Certain points must be conceded. Cases are difficult to mount; no one with practical experience of fraud work will underestimate the difficulties. Guilt must be proven beyond a reasonable doubt. Gaps in the evidence may well be difficult to fill convincingly. Persons may be reluctant to give evidence and may, if they have acted as nominee for a suspect, essentially be allied to him in interest. Frauds are characterised by complexity, sometimes deliberately engineered in order to make them difficult to unravel, but sometimes the result of exuberant manoeuvring as distinct from acts done pursuant to a master plan of fraud. Investigations can take years, and legal proceedings can be tortuously slow. Inevitably, a prosecution authority will want to have a good case, both in the sense of one which can be proven satisfactorily, and one in which the court will impose a severe penalty on conviction. Yet, even with the care which is taken in the selection and preparation of cases for prosecution, difficulties of proof and other hazards of the trial process result in a substantial acquittal rate for such crimes tried on indictment.

The structure of fraud also has a marked effect on decisions to prosecute. Where there is a deliberate scheme of fraud, it is likely that a good case will be found, and prosecution will result. But there seems to be a considerable reluctance to bring prosecutions in cases which are less blatantly clear, and this perhaps prevents or inhibits the evolution of standards applicable to fraud, which continues to be thought of and dealt with in traditional terms. Where, for example, investigations disclose that a commercial or financial rogue elephant endowed with entrepreneurial drive committed acts which come within the criminal law, but cannot strictly be shown to have been done with intent to defraud, it may be less apparent that a good case exists. Inevitably, the infractions will appear in the context of a larger mass of business transactions, and any sentence will reflect this.

Admittedly, some offences do not require an intent to defraud; emitting false written statements by directors requires, as we have seen, an intention to deceive only.[13] Others, however, either require that intent or that the director acted dishonestly, a supposedly plain English word that invites the jury to proceed on an impressionistic basis.[14] Where there is no intent to defraud, it cannot be expected that courts will impose very severe penalties. It may be that as a result the very breadth of the provision prevents its invocation save as a make-weight in a case where more serious charges are preferred. Even where directors act wrongly, a jury or a court may be doubtful, either in assessing guilt or penalty, about the essential morality of the matter.

This is, of course, hypothesis. But one must ask whether some view of infractions as merely incidental crime underlies decisions not to prosecute in some cases. One thinks, for example, of the use of inflated profit forecasts in take-over situations, or the manipulation of transactions within groups to give an impression of solvency which will enable take-overs to proceed on a share-for-share basis, or will induce banks and other institutions to lend money. Improper charging of expenses of various sorts may appear essentially as matters to be dealt with by shareholders, but the same consideration would clearly not be persuasive in the context of a revenue prosecution.

There is another, and related, point. Matters falling outside the normal range of those dealt with by police and prosecutors may not bear the appearance of fraud. The matter may appear to be one of disputable accounting or commercial practice. It would not be surprising if the prosecuting authorities were reluctant to use criminal proceedings as the vehicle for establishing the impropriety of current practices, even if the possibilities of fraud were perceived. A conviction may appear doubtful where there is likely to be a clash of accounting evidence. Preparing such a case may require the committal of resources thought to be disproportionate to any likely benefit to be derived from doing so. Yet such caution, however understandable, may result in a substantial measure of immunity to malefactors, except insofar as civil and administrative remedies may be brought to bear upon them.

For the future, the authorities may be even more selective than hitherto. The present government has indicated that it wants only the principal figures in major frauds to be prosecuted. This is again an understandable emphasis, but it could well permit an undesirable demi-monde to continue to flourish. Many fringe figures are dishonest and deserve to be prosecuted. The suggestions above point to reasons why some fraud offenders are not prosecuted, and endeavour to explain why there may appear to be bias in the machinery of enforcement. In the case of ordinary crimes committed on the street, for example, there is no course of business affairs to which activities could be incidental, nor can questions be raised about the legality and honesty of commercial practices. Ordinary criminals are softer targets, although a thief could scarcely complain about that. But blatantly differential justice is obviously intolerable.

The adoption of delay in bringing proceedings as a criterion is also disquieting. Clearly, proceedings should be brought expeditiously, and English law, which allows prosecutors the power to pick and choose aspects of cases for prosecution, conduces to this. It does not, however, eliminate delay. In the Bingham Report, some offences were indicated as ten years old, with several more years needed before proceedings could be mounted, had prosecution been decided upon. As a result of law and practice, we have avoided the unconscionable delays and interminable procedures which disfigured certain continental proceedings (Poncet, 1977).

Delay, however, is often intentionally caused by the rogue. Where the case is a large and blatant fraud, delay does not appear to militate against prosecution; where what is done falls within the category of what might be called incidental crimes, it may have a disproportionate effect. This, if so, would be attributable to the relationship of the gravity of the unlawful act, viewed in the context of the enterprise as a whole, with the view which it is assumed courts will take of the matter. Again, in the absence of reasons by prosecutors for reaching decisions in particular cases, one can only look to published materials and construct hypotheses. But it does not seem unreasonable to assume that cases fall through the net in this way. Other factors which militate against prosecution have been alluded to. Where there is an extra-territorial element, difficulties arise both concerning obtaining documents and witnesses, and securing the accused for trial. While Britain has extradition arrangements with other countries, there are still havens in which offenders come to rest. The procedure is cumbersome and expensive, and used only in serious cases. It is undeniable that a number of likely candidates for prosecution find it convenient to remain abroad.

Preparation for Trial

Preparation for trial is a crucial stage in the proceedings since failure at this stage may not be detected until trial, when it may be impossible to remedy. Successful preparation requires the deployment of sufficient experienced personnel with adequate time to deal carefully with the file in question. Neither condition is easy to achieve at present. Moreover, some duplication of effort is inevitable. If, for example, a matter has originated in the Department of Trade and is offered to and accepted by the D.P.P., the case will have to be considered and developed by the Director's staff and by counsel chosen by him. The same may well be true of files submitted by the police which may, first, have been considered by the local prosecuting solicitor's staff. In any event, counsel and his instructing solicitor will have to master the brief.

The problems of duplication are fewer where prosecution remains in the hands of the same body throughout, for example the Department of Trade, the Inland Revenue or the Customs and Excise, since, while counsel must be briefed in any indictable case, the same solicitor can continue to deal with it. Duplication may be minimised by appointing counsel to advise and then actually to prosecute, in both the magistrates' and the Crown Court. We have noted that, in London, Treasury Counsel are appointed. The D.P.P. stresses both their specialist knowledge and their close working relationships with each other and with the Director's staff, which assists considerably in the efficient conduct of prosecutions.[15] Their workload is, however, very heavy.

Preparation for trial involves the preparation and proof of both oral and documentary evidence, instructing the completion of inquiries if necessary, and selecting the issues upon which it is desired to proceed. English criminal procedure is adversary in character. The accused need not testify and certainly is not obliged to assist the prosecution in the preparation of its case. Whereas in civil procedure there are compulsory interlocutory procedures to narrow issues, to obtain a sight of documents and to obtain information from the other side, criminal procedure proceeds from the premise that such devices would detract impermissibly from the protections rightly accorded to accused persons. Admittedly, a minor inroad into this principle was created in 1967 by requiring an accused to give advance notice of an alibi defence, but that is not significant in major fraud cases.[16] The rigour of English criminal procedure ensured that until recent years the defence could not even concede the admissibility of a document; it had solemnly to be proven even though its existence and contents were not in dispute.[17]

The onerous business of preparation may be assisted by the practice rules adopted at the Central Criminal Court. These provide for the hearing of practice directions on applications by a solicitor acting for any party. There is, however, no compulsion on any party to move for directions. The application is heard before a judge. Counsel at the hearing is expected to be able to inform the court of the pleas to be tendered at trial, of the prosecution witnesses to be called, of further evidence to be brought by the prosecution, of facts which can be and are admitted, and which will thus be admissible at trial, of exhibits and schedules which can be admitted, of points of law relating to evidence which will be argued, and of any other significant matter which might affect the proper and convenient trial of the case.

These rules, while helpful, are thought to work only imperfectly in difficult fraud cases. Counsel cannot be forced to make admissions; the decision is his, and he must have regard to tactical exigencies. Too often, it is said, counsel who attends such a hearing is a junior who does not wish to compromise his leader by making unwise or damaging admissions. The judge may not be the actual trial judge. In the absence of compulsory procedures, natural caution plays the part which one would expect. The procedure limps. The case may, thus, be unaided by admissions which facilitate proof and narrow the issues. Despite procedural reforms, a large fraud case remains a forensic minefield. Furthermore, despite the fact that English practice, in any event, provides for disclosure to the defence of the witnesses to be called, and access to documents, the latter does not always occur until defence counsel is briefed, and the accused's solicitor may not be informed until late. No provision for inspection by solicitors has yet been made.

Counsel experienced in the preparation of such cases puts the problems vividly. He writes:[18]

> Most criminal cases deal with one or two major incidents, proof of which comes from oral evidence as to things seen or heard. In fraud cases, however, one is following out a transaction or series of transactions going on for a long period of time, in which many people will be involved and most stages of which will be evidenced by documents. Since there is no way of telling which documents will be admitted by the defence, care has to be taken that they are all capable of strict proof. This means that there may have to be proofs from innumerable witnesses, most of whom do little but produce one or two documents from proper custody ... Schedules often have to be prepared but since there is no pre-trial means of compelling the defendants to admit the accuracy of schedules or even to specify which parts they say are inaccurate, vast bundles of the original documents from which the schedules were prepared have to be kept in readiness ... If there are documents in foreign languages translations have to be provided. If matters of foreign law have to be proved, expert witnesses have to be retained. There are the usual complications about documents being admissible against some of the defendants but not others ...

He goes on to point out that it is sometimes difficult to be sure what important witnesses will say. I do not think that his account is exaggerated. In the one major fraud prosecution in which I was engaged, in Canada, the prosecution had to call more than sixty witnesses, most of whom were friendly to the accused and would rather not have been in court, and some 2,000 documentary exhibits.[19] It was necessary to show that an extensive series of apparently regular transactions were in fact fraudulent. No admissions were made, as a result of which witnesses from several provinces of Canada and States of the United States had to be called, and some prospective witnesses fled to Europe. It is doubtful whether the case would have been brought to trial had there not been a prior inquiry on oath under the Income Tax Acts which gave the prosecution an accurate idea of what witnesses would say.

Committal Proceedings

In theory, committal proceedings offer a screening process which should ensure that only meritorious cases go forward for trial. Historically, all committal proceedings took place as a hearing before magistrates at which the prosecution was obliged to lead and examine those witnesses whose account, forming part of a connected narrative, was essential to prove the matters in issue.[20] A minimum of documents also had to be adduced. Since 1967, it has been possible to commit an accused for trial on the papers. Today, therefore, it is possible to have a full oral committal, or a hearing in which the defence desires that certain prosecution evidence alone will be led, or a committal on the papers when the accused does not challenge the evidence (Hampton, 1977).

Nowadays, most committal hearings, even in fraud cases, take place on the papers. There can be no doubt that a substantial saving in magisterial time results. Formerly, committal proceedings could take weeks to conclude, and the Rolls Razor case, a *cause célèbre* of the 1960s, which was dealt with under the old procedure, lasted for 117 days, the longest proceedings ever in Britain.[21] But while the new procedure saves the time of magistrates, it also has disadvantages. Statements concerning committal proceedings may not be served upon the accused until very late. This may make it impossible to decide sensibly whether to opt for the full committal or not, so the documentary procedure may be used and the case not fully reviewed before trial. The use of written committal procedures may fail to uncover weaknesses in the prosecution's case. These weaknesses, for example the need to prove additional documents, or the fallibility of witnesses, may persist to trial. Oral committal helps to avoid these dangers. Hence it is said to be the better practice for the prosecution to opt for oral committal proceedings when there is doubt whether its evidence will stand up.

Certainly, there is an increasing body of evidence which suggests that current pre-trial screening devices are not sufficiently effective. It has been discovered that almost one-third of all acquittals in indictable cases are directed verdicts, that is, the judge has not seen fit to allow the charge to go to the jury (Baldwin and McConville, 1979). This rate has increased since the new procedure was adopted.

Even the Home Office notes that the prosecution case is now less thoroughly examined than formerly; the independent checks of the past have been removed (Home Office, 1978). It does not, of course, follow that directed verdicts are attributable only to weaknesses of preparation which oral procedures could have detected; the passage of time since the infraction, leading to lapses of memory, and even the interference with witnesses, play a part. But it seems altogether likely that some cases which now collapse either would not have been brought, or would have been brought in a modified form, had they earlier been subjected to the degree of preparation necessary to survive the rigours of oral committal proceedings. It is, of course, true that few cases were lost at committal even under oral procedure, but that must be attributable substantially to care taken in preparation, and not simply to the allegedly perfunctory character of the proceedings.

Trial

Trial will be a matter for magistrates' courts or for superior courts (Griew, 1978). Serious cases will go to the latter. The bulk of such cases will be tried by a circuit judge attached to a Crown Court. High Court Judges tend to try only those fraud cases which are exceptionally notorious. At the Central Criminal Court a High Court Judge and Circuit Judges, for example the Common Serjeant, sit. Such cases are tried before a jury which is apt to be a lay jury in two senses: it is not knowledgeable about the law, or about the business or commercial matters which form the setting for the fraud.

The difficulties are such that the actual trial is often aborted by plea, or more commonly charge, bargaining which results in a plea of guilty to certain charges and a decision by the prosecution not to proceed on others. The institution and characteristics of plea bargaining have been dealt with elsewhere (Baldwin and McConville, 1979). In effect, a bargain may take two forms. The form known as charge bargaining involves an agreement between the prosecution and the defence that the accused will plead guilty to certain charges if others are not proceeded with. The judge is not involved. He may be asked to direct that certain charges lie on the file not to be proceeded with save by leave of the court, but he is not privy to the bargain, and his freedom to sentence is not impaired. As the prosecution does not in fact recommend any sentence to the court, the accused must take his chances that the manoeuvre will result in the court taking a less grave view of his actions than it would otherwise have done. Just how effective a tactic this is from the accused's point of view, is problematic. The dropping of some charges may not have a particularly marked effect on sentence, and it is unlikely that prosecuting counsel would agree to drop those charges which, if well founded, clearly indicate the essential gravity of the accused's conduct.

The second form, which involves the judge, is much deprecated and may be used only in the most exceptional circumstances. The judge may be asked whether or not, on a given view of the facts, he would in any event be minded to impose a custodial sentence. But the judges dislike the practice, and resort to it has been strongly condemned (Seifman, 1977).[22] It does, however, still occur from time to time. A successful bargain saves time, and a sentencing judge is entitled to take the accused's co-operation in not fighting charges into account when sentencing. It can thus have advantages to both sides, even though serious charges remain before the court.

Fraud cases present difficulties which beset all complicated criminal cases, but they are apt to do so particularly intensively. The rules of evidence are not always well adapted to modern problems. Admittedly, statements made under compulsion of statute, by company directors and others, are admissible in evidence against their makers.[23] The prosecution thus benefits from compulsory self-incrimination by the accused. On the other hand, the rules of evidence relating to the admissibility of records, and in particular of documentary records, is defective. Recently, for example, a print-out from a computer was tendered in evidence to identify certain banknotes allegedly obtained by burglary. It was rejected on the basis that, because the machine did not simply record the totality of the numbers of each note fed into it but also separated and recorded the numbers of defective notes and, secondly, recorded the numbers of notes at the beginning and end of each bundle, it could not be said that the numbers of the rejected notes were ever in anyone's mind.

The relevant statute required that the document be a record relating to a trade or business, a condition which was satisfied, and that it be compiled by persons who have, or reasonably may be supposed to have, personal knowledge of the matters dealt with in the information they supply.[24] The dual function of the computer was held to preclude the operator having such knowledge.[25] The point in issue was indeed, as the court remarked, technical. The President of the Institute of Internal Auditors, in a letter to *The Times*, stated that the existing law of evidence is quite inadequate to deal with computer crime, with the result that many cases of computer-based crime cannot be prosecuted under existing law.[26] Furthermore, where records other than business records are concerned, records other than original records continue to be inadmissible under the rule against hearsay.[27]

Fraud cases are long and complicated. Often, several accused are on trial at the same time, perhaps on conspiracy charges. The jury must determine what evidence is admissible against which accused. A standard textbook states, quite impeccably (Nokes, 1967, p. 302):

> A confession by one accused person is not generally evidence against another, for a person cannot confess to another's actions. But where two prisoners are tried together, the statement of one prisoner may be read even though it implicates the other.

The consequence is that an accused who is tried jointly with another is placed in a disadvantageous position. The jury, even though it is instructed against whom evidence is admissible, may find it difficult to keep the evidence separate (Williams, 1963, pp. 244–52). Yet, an accused who is in fact prejudiced by this will not have an appeal if the judge has correctly instructed the jury.

While the court can lessen prejudice by ordering separate trials, it will be reluctant to do so. There are several reasons for this. Separate trials can lead to inconsistent verdicts where one accused is acquitted and another convicted. The fact that there is an apparent inconsistency will not result in the conviction of one co-conspirator being quashed unless, in all the circumstances of the case, his conviction is inconsistent with the acquittal of the other person or persons in question.[28] A may have made an admission which is evidence against himself, but not against his fellow B, and there may not be evidence sufficient to convict B. Nevertheless, inconsistency is undesirable, and joint trials help to minimise the danger.[29] Moreover, separate trials are even more time-consuming and costly. They may make it difficult for each jury to determine fully what happened. The applicable rules themselves assume that joint trials are desirable where the accused allegedly acted together.[30]

The case is judged by a jury which not only has no personal knowledge of the case, a circumstance which applies to all juries, but is also ignorant of the financial and commercial matters dealt with in it. Juries are supposed to reflect a cross-section of the community. There was once provision for a jury with special knowledge of commercial matters, but this was abolished in 1949.[31] Other suggestions for the use of special juries were not adopted (Cmd. 6659, 1945, para. 163). There is now no property qualification for jury service, the minimum age is 18 years, and it is said to be rare to get a jury even one member of which has specialist knowledge of the type of matter being dealt with. It is also said that, because there are now a large number of persons available for jury service, persons who run their own businesses, or professional men who are likely to prejudice their careers by long absence, are frequently excused by the court. Although the defence now has but three peremptory challenges, it may choose to exercise these to rid the jury of anyone having specialist knowledge.[32] Even if a jury is selected, the case may still go awry if there is reason to suspect that the jury is being tampered with, as occurred in at least one recent case involving a £27 millions fraud.

The jury must attend a lengthy case for weeks, perhaps months. They must master a vast bulk of evidence, not all of which will be admissible against each accused. Furthermore, they have little opportunity to study the evidence. The judge's direction, even after a conscientious effort by him to simplify it, may not be fully understood. Professor Cornish in *The Jury* cites the experience of an accountant who served on a jury in a fraud case, and who discovered, after seeking to explain the facts to his fellows, that nine of them had been unable to follow this information in any adequate fashion (1968, p. 181). Courts have stated that jurors have not understood complicated fraud cases.[33] Suggestions have been made for, trials by judge alone or with assessors (Mannheim, 1937, Canada, Commissioners for Uniformity of Legislation, 1965). A less drastic reform, considered below, would be to allow non-jury trial in all indictable cases at the accused's option. Even if few fraud cases were so tried, the facility, if used generally, would lessen pressure on the jury system.

There is no easy solution within the present system of criminal procedure. The constraints are painfully obvious. The prosecution can, admittedly, select charges arising out of fraudulent conduct. It could fasten on particular instances, given that many frauds are not the product of a master plan but rather are incidents in a ragged encounter battle. But this risks the court, when sentencing, underestimating the full gravity of the accused's conduct. On the other hand, bringing a full range of charges risks baffling the jury, and thus the failure of the whole enterprise. It is clear that many counts in indictments are lost in any event. Courts have rightly stressed the undesirability of charging too many counts, and especially of preferring an omnibus count of conspiracy together with charges of specific offences, lest the jury lose its way and the accused be sunk under the weight of prejudice. On the other hand, where substantive charges do not fully represent the overall gravity of the accused's conduct, it may be appropriate to include a conspiracy count.[34]

Another possiblity is to inform the accused that the court will try the case on the basis of sample counts. If the accused is found guilty, he may be sentenced on the basis that other infractions also took place. But this is only possible in relatively simple cases where repeated infractions of the same sort are alleged and the defence is common to them all.[35] In the end, the prosecution must select and present charges in such a way as to conduce to jury understanding, whilst demonstrating to the court the culpability of those involved. It is thus a system of tactical compromises, and one which seems likely to endure.

References and Notes

1. The relevant offences include those under corruption legislation; Insurance Companies Act 1974, s. 18; Prevention of Fraud (Investments) Act 1958, and the Banking Act 1979. A complete list is appended to Royal Commission on Criminal Procedure, *Evidence of the Director of Public Prosecutions* (1978).
2. Prosecution of Offences Act 1979, s. 2, and Prosecution of Offences Regulations 1978, S.I. no. 1357, Reg. 3.
3. Royal Commission on Criminal Procedure, *Evidence of the Director of Public Prosecutions* (1978) Appx. 8.
4. Royal Commission on Criminal Procedure, *Evidence of the Board of Inland Revenue* (1978), para. 9.2.
5. Sess. 1976–7, 930 H.C. Deb. (Vth Ser.), cols. 1402–13; the statement was given in answer to complaints by Sir Graham Page M.P. arising out of alleged non-prosecution in a fraud case.
6. 'But how does he decide?', *Sunday Times*, 13 January 1980, p. 12.
7. Taxes Management Act 1970, s. 105; Customs and Excise Management Act 1979, s. 152, but note that the power does not extend to settling criminal cases in Scotland, a matter which is competent only to the Lord Advocate.
8. Royal Commission on Criminal Procedure, *Evidence Submitted by the Board of Inland Revenue* (1978), pp. 17–18.
9. In abeyance by the Exchange Control (General Exemption) Order 1979, S.I. no. 1660.
10. Sess. 1979–80, 976 H.C. Deb. (Vth Ser.), cols. 627–9; *The Times*, 20 December 1979 (Parl. Report for 19 December).
11. 'But how does he decide?', *Sunday Times*, 13 January 1980, p. 12.
12. Details are contained in *The Times*, 10 January 1980.
13. For example, Theft Act 1968, s. 19.
14. For example, Theft Act 1968, ss. 1, 15 and 17 (false accounting).
15. Royal Commission on Criminal Procedure, *Evidence of the Director of Public Prosecutions* (1978), paras. 165–7.
16. Criminal Justice Act 1967, s. 11.
17. *Ibid.*, s. 10.
18. W.A.B. Forbes, Q.C., in an unpublished memorandum to the Royal Commission on Criminal Procedure (1979).
19. One accused was ultimately sentenced to five years imprisonment; *Reg.* v. *Ciglen* [1970] S.C.R. 804.
20. *Reg.* v. *Epping and Harlow JJ., ex p. Massaro* [1973] 1 Q.B. 443.
21. *The Times*, 24 January 1969.

22. *Reg.* v. *Turner* (1970) 54 Cr. App. R. 342; *Reg.* v. *Coward* [1980] Crim. L.R. 117.
23. Companies Act 1967, s. 50; *Reg.* v. *Harz* [1967] 1 A.C. 670.
24. Criminal Evidence Act 1965, s. 1(1)(*a*).
25. *Reg.* v. *Pettigrew* [1980] Crim. L.R. 239.
26. G. Ward, *The Times,* 13 February 1980.
27. For criticism, see Editor's comment [1980] Crim. L. R. 240; the Criminal Law Revision Committee, 11th Report, *Evidence (General)* (1972) at pp. 195–7 proposed a clause to deal with the problem, but it has not been enacted.
28. Criminal Law Act 1977, s. 5(8).
29. In Australia, in order to avoid inconsistency, the judge summed up generally, and then directed the jury on each accused, taking verdicts *seriatim* and not discharging the jury until all verdicts were delivered, thereby retaining control in the interests of avoiding inconsistency; *Smith* v. *Reginam* [1971] A. L. R. 193.
30. *Reg.* v. *Flack* [1969] 2 All E.R. 784; *Reg.* v. *Scarron* (1968) 52 Cr. App. R. 591; *Reg.* v. *Assim* (1966) 50 Cr. App. R. 224.
31. Juries Act 1949, ss. 18 and 19.
32. Criminal Law Act 1977, s. 43.
33. *Reg.* v. *Jeffs* (1978) N.Z. (unrep.), discussed in (1980) 1 *The Company Lawyer,* 45.
34. *Reg.* v. *Griffiths* (1965) 49 Cr. App. R. 279; *Reg.* v. *Jones* (1974) 59 Cr. App. R. 120; *Reg.* v. *Doot* [1973] A. C. 807 at p. 827 per Lord Pearson.
35. *Reg.* v. *Mills* (1978) 68 Cr. App. R. 154.

No view is more strongly entrenched in the literature of white-collar crime than that which holds that white-collar offenders benefit from leniency at all stages in the system of criminal justice (Leigh, 1978). From bail through to sentence, evident and unjust disparities of treatment are said to exist between such offenders and ordinary thieves, robbers and persons convicted of minor crimes of violence. Furthermore, it is a commonplace of criminological writing to assert that just such individuals as these are more sensitive to the loss of social status consequent on conviction and imprisonment than persons of lower social status, and therefore more readily susceptible to deterrence. From this rather presumptuous view derives what some see as a central paradox, that those who can most readily be deterred by severity benefit from leniency throughout (Conklin, 1977, p 138).

Certainly, the argument is apt to become a bit muddled and to rely on impression not wholly supported by fact. Surely, one would not advocate denying bail as a punishment. The dominant criterion is whether the accused will appear to stand his trial. In fact, while many fraud offenders are bailed, so are other categories of offender. Such bias as appears to exist in the system concerns burglars and robbers, the very categories of offenders who pose a threat of violence to persons within or outside their homes.[1] Someone once said that history consisted of a hard core of interpretation surrounded by a pulp of disputable facts. The same remark might be applied to our fragmentary knowledge of sentencing patterns. The available sources include the Criminal Statistics, D.A. Thomas's work on sentencing, Dr. Levi's work on long-firm fraud, the author's work on bankruptcy, and impressions derived from press and governmental sources.

Sentencing Fraud

There are, of course, quite striking examples of severity in sentencing. Savundra is one such case. In passing sentence, Judge King-Hamilton advanced three reasons for passing a sentence of eight years imprisonment, together with a large fine, namely (Connell and

Sutherland, 1978): many people were left uninsured when Fire, Auto and Marine fell; the integrity of the London insurance market had to be protected; and the swindle was gigantic.

The sentence was upheld on appeal.[2] Similarly, Markus, the principal in the Agrifund conspiracy was sentenced to seven years imprisonment, later reduced to five. Others, such as Grunwald, who was responsible for the State Building Society scandal, were also sentenced to long terms of imprisonment. However, it can be argued, that cases of this character are exceptional. In any *cause célèbre*, the accused is at risk of a heavy penalty. Prosecutors argue strongly that in the ordinary run of cases, courts are frequently unduly lenient. Even in a *cause célèbre*, the court may not impose a custodial sentence. John Bloom was sentenced to a fine of £30,000, the court evidently subscribing to the not uncommon view that although he had done wrong, he was basically the prisoner of a rapidly deteriorating business situation.[3]

The Criminal Statistics certainly suggest that sexual offences and robbery are more likely to attract custodial sentences than offences of fraud and forgery, but it cannot be said that they are of great value for the purposes of close analysis.[4] 'Fraud by company director' could hardly be called a closely controlled category, nor does the appellation 'company director' tell one much about the offender. Various frauds are brigaded together, yet courts may treat some much more harshly than others. No information is given concerning the length of suspended or custodial sentences, nor is separate information given concerning the status of persons as first offenders or recidivists. On the other hand, information is given concerning the type of sentence employed, and it is interesting that in fraud or white-collar offences a fine or imprisonment is commonly imposed, while other measures such as community service orders are used more readily in respect of other property offences. This suggests both that courts are prepared to be merciful in other cases, and that the age distribution of such offenders is younger than fraud offenders.

Quite different in character is D.A. Thomas's work (Thomas, 1979). This relies on sentences upheld in the Court of Appeal, and thus contains information about the length of sentences together with an indication of those factors which the sentencing court considered to be important. It suffers from the limitation that it is founded upon what the Court of Appeal is prepared to uphold, and thus may not represent accurately the sentencing pattern of trial courts. It is, however, of considerable value as disclosing maxima, and also very often the values which courts invoke in sentencing.

Thomas's work does not suggest that serious cases of fraud are treated lightly by the courts. He notes, for example, that deliberately planned long-firm fraud attracts sentences of up to five years imprisonment. In one such case, where the appellant acquired control of a reputable company which he then used as a vehicle for long-firm fraud, sentence was reduced on appeal from nine years to five years imprisonment on the basis that the fraud was not an unusually severe long-firm fraud. Shorter sentences of three or two years were imposed in cases where the business began honestly, but the proprietors turned to fraud to maintain the solvency of a business that was hopelessly under-capitalised. It is in this category that, one suspects, there may be a consistent pattern of leniency by the courts. Planned frauds on finance houses similarly have been visited by sentences of five years imprisonment. These are cases in which automobile dealers have foisted false hire-purchase agreements on finance houses. By contrast, frauds to obtain mortgages where there was an intention eventually to repay have been dealt with by sentences of twelve months imprisonment, and again one would expect lower courts to afford instances of greater leniency. Organised cheque frauds have attracted sentences of five to seven years imprisonment.

Tax evasion, too, tends to be severely punished, at least by the higher courts. There is plenty of evidence that prison terms are commonly imposed for sustained tax evasion. The Parliamentary debates record, for example, that J. Murphy Co. and its susbsidiary, J.M. Piling were fined £575,000 in connection with payments to labour-only sub-contractors, and three executives were not only fined, but given jail sentences.[5] In *Reg.* v. *Francis*,[6] where the accused concealed business receipts, avoided payment of £1,612 and then went to ground for twelve years, a sentence of imprisonment was reduced, but the accused was still required to serve a sentence of three months imprisonment. In another case, involving an accountant convicted of defrauding the revenue over a ten-year period, a prison sentence of two years and a fine of £5,000 were imposed.[7] It seems clear enough that whatever may be general public attitudes towards tax evasion, the courts are prepared to react with some severity. This may well be due to their knowledge that only flagrant cases are prosecuted. Such leniency as exists in the system is exercised in respect of the decision to prosecute.

As one might expect, impressions of leniency found upon lower court decisions, in respect of frauds which, for one reason or another, have not attained the status of a *cause célèbre*. One would expect a sentencing pattern somewhat different from that in the Court of

Appeal, for it is, after all, the most severe sentences which tend to be appealed against. Such data as we have suggests that fraud offences are not sentenced stringently. With the exception of Dr. Levi's sentencing study, the data is fragmentary, however. The register of proceedings maintained internally by the Department of Trade, and similar information kept by the D.P.P., certainly afford striking examples of leniency. Department of Trade records indicate that short-term imprisonment is often invoked where a bankrupt manages a company without leave, and this is coupled with a disqualification order under section 187 of the Companies Act 1948. Sometimes, the prison sentence is suspended. Fraudulent trading often attracts a disqualification order, but the courts do not always impose a prison sentence, whether custodial or suspended, or a fine. Indeed, in 1979, in only one case was imprisonment ordered, for fifteen months, coupled with a disqualification order for four years. In two cases, a Community Service Order was imposed. Offences of failing to return accounts were invariably fined.

It could be argued that these were not serious cases, although the Department of Trade would not agree with that description. As one might expect, the D.P.P.'s records show a pattern of greater severity. They include cases like the Israel-British Bank where sentences of five and four years imprisonment were initially imposed upon the principals. Other cases of conspiracy to defraud, the circumstances of which do not appear from the records made available to me, show far lower sentences. For conspiracy to defraud by operating an insolvent company, sentences of two years and twelve months imprisonment respectively were imposed on the principals. Theft of company shares valued at £100,000 attracted a sentence of three years imprisonment. On the other hand, charges of forgery and corruption resulted in suspended sentences, and a conspiracy to obtain property by deception resulted in a fine.

Provincial cases show, overwhelmingly, the use of imprisonment, whether custodial or suspended, by the courts. In only one case was a fine alone imposed. In most cases involving companies, a disqualification order was imposed. Table 18.1 shows the range of sentences imposed by provincial courts, the longest of which was a sentence of six-and-a-half years imprisonment imposed for conspiracy to defraud, fraudulent trading and theft. Details of the offence and the offender were not shown on the material to which I had access. It seems clear, however, that multiple charges of fraud, and especially cases involving conspiracy to defraud, attract sentences of three years and upwards. There are, inevitably, exceptions to this generalisation but their significance ought not to be exaggerated.

Nor ought the tentative nature of what is said here to be overlooked; the records which I have seen are obviously incomplete, and no proper sentencing study has been done in respect of them. There is, indeed, a certain scepticism in some quarters as to whether any pattern could ever be discerned. It is a pessimism which is, in my opinion, misplaced. At present, one is left with conflicting impressions. Are courts in the provinces more severe than the Central Criminal Court? Or were the few cases there, in some of which leniency was exhibited, explicable on grounds personal to the offender. At present, one cannot say.

TABLE 18.1. Provincial Courts: Length of Sentence in Fraud Cases 1979

Offence	Imprisonment (months)			Imprisonment suspended (months)	
	0–12	12–24	24–60*	0–12	12–24
Conspiracy to steal or obtain by deception			2	1	
Obtaining pecuniary advantage by deception					
Fraudulent trading		1	2		1
False accounting	1				
Theft Act 1968, s. 20(2), procuring execution of document	1	1		1	
Theft		2	1		1
Conspiracy to defraud	1	1	3		
Obtaining by deception	2				
Forgery					
Conspiracy to pervert justice		1			

*Compiled from information supplied by the Director of Public Prosecutions

Dr. Levi's findings on sentencing long-firm frauds indicate that principals' sentences in highly organised frauds range from nine years imprisonment to one year with an average sentence of 2.82

years. The most commonly occurring sentence is eighteen months, and 50 per cent of principals are sentenced to no more than two years. All the figures are, he concludes, below the tariff norm found in Court of Appeal cases. All his figures derive from the Central Criminal Court (Levi, 1980). Where the accused slipped into crime as a result of business pressures, particularly a lack of liquidity, a sentence of less than twelve months immediate imprisonment was generally given. Dr. Levi concludes that judges as well as police distinguish between someone who has committed a criminal act and someone who is regarded as a real criminal. He concludes that, in the former case, the fraud is only one auxiliary aspect of the man to be sentenced, whereas in the latter it is taken as representative of him. On the other hand, previous criminal conduct was not regarded as particularly relevant to the way in which the offender was categorised. I have heard others express similar views.

My findings on sentences passed on bankrupts are broadly similar (Leigh, 1980b). Immediate sentences of imprisonment were imposed for some theft and deception offences, but the accused's record was relevant, especially where it was a record with theft and deception offences. The number of such offences for which the offender was convicted in the instant case was the single most important factor. A grave view was taken of repeated instances of a bankrupt obtaining credit, because this seemed to evidence a criminal system or a readiness to flout the restrictions of the Acts. Where such factors were absent, and in particular where there appeared to be a descent into crime, for example by endeavouring to cope with a liquidity crisis by the unauthorised sale of vehicles on hire-purchase, Crown Courts imposed suspended sentences of imprisonment, while magistrates' courts often fined the offender. The same basic distinctions as those noted by Dr. Levi operated. Indeed, they operate in very large cases. We have noted that the court, in sentencing John Bloom to a fine of £30,000 arising out of false accounting charges in respect of Rolls Razor Limited, expressly refrained from imposing a sentence of imprisonment because it felt that the crimes were the product of desperation rather than wickedness.

At present one can only comment tentatively about the leniency or otherwise with which fraud offenders are dealt. Leniency is not a matter dictated by courts alone. Some maxima are unduly low as the result of a legislative choice. For example, until the Companies Act 1980 the maximum penalty under section 54 of the Companies Act 1948 was a fine of £100. The maximum penalty for fraudulent trading was only two years imprisonment. The penalty for failure to keep proper books was a fine, and it was not until the Companies Act 1976 that it became possible to charge the offence on indictment, thus putting the accused in peril of two years imprisonment. Dr. Hadden was right to question, apropos SUITS, whether the penalties for defective accounts should not be much higher (Hadden, 1980). Happily, the defect was remedied earlier, but historically some penalties were decidedly low. The puzzle is to know why this should be so. In the case of section 54, the prohibition, though directed against looting, is, as we have seen, apt to catch transactions which do not injure the company and are unlikely to do so. Its very breadth, and its status as an offence in which neither intent to defraud nor recklessness need be shown to convict, would militate against the provision of a severe penalty. Similarly, the vice struck at by fraudulent trading was no doubt serious, but narrowly conceived. No one sought at the time of its enactment to extrapolate a general principle of fraud from it. The original sentence of two years imprisonment, maximum, might be sufficient to deter controllers of companies from fraudulently filling up debentures. Neither section was intended, it is submitted, to serve the purpose of a general fraud section, nor does either have implications for the level of sentence to be awarded in cases of consipracy to defraud. English law lacks a general fraud provision.

Are courts lenient otherwise, and why? The importance of factors personal to the offender, such as those which have been mentioned above, should not be overlooked. But there are cases, and prosecutors and police do not lack examples with which to regale the researcher, where penalties which seem strikingly low were imposed in fraud cases. If these are more than striking instances, and Dr. Levi's study lends support to the notion that they are, several factors may be offered in explanation. In the first place, these are not crimes of violence. Very long sentences, a few striking exceptions apart, are usually imposed upon violent offenders whose personalities are such that a repetition of violence is likely.[8] Only very serious frauds will attract similar sentences and they, too, may well strike the sentencer as evidencing a durable tendency to offend again.

Secondly, one must take account of the criminal's previous record. A number of fraud offenders may not have a criminal record. That does not mean that they are ingenues; they may well be experienced fraud offenders, and have links with other forms of crime. There is an obvious danger today of organised crime. But a sentencing court cannot sentence a person on supposition. It must treat a first offender as such, and it must have regard to the policy, embodied in statute, which specifies that imprisonment should be the last resort for a first offender.[9] One ought not to expect a long sentence of imprisonment unless the crime is a grave one.

Thirdly, it must be recognised that whether a sentence is severe or not is a matter of subjective judgement. So, too, is the severity with which the crime is regarded. It is, no doubt, inevitable that views should be coloured by the sentences meted out to other criminals. After all, the existence of a sentencing tariff is premised upon a rough view of the deserts of offenders who commit particular types of offences. But the process of comparison must be inhibited by a failure to articulate reasons for ranking offences for the purpose of sentence. Furthermore, there are few sentencing studies in Britain which would enable one to say with any exactitude what principles are actually applied by sentencing courts, how much weight is given to mitigation and to personal circumstances, and whether distinctions are drawn between different patterns of conduct within the same offence. Theft can, for example, be committed in several modes. I, for one, am not persuaded that crude comparisons between offences meted out to white-collar criminals and others are particularly helpful.

Much of the writing on white-collar crime is American. It reflects certain assumptions which American scholars make about the pattern of business crime in America. One tacit assumption appears to be that all business crime can be dealt with together for the purposes of analysis. Another stresses the high social class of offenders (Geis, 1978). From that base, arguments in favour of class bias are erected as explanations for lenient treatment throughout the system. It is not clear that such assumptions are valid for Britain. Both Levens, who studied white-collar offenders in England, and Professor John Spencer found that the guilty were not captains of industry, but solicitors, haulage contractors, struggling clerks, and the like (Levens, 1964; Spencer, 1968). Spencer concludes that we cannot say that dishonest businessmen should be seen as a major threat to society. In any event, even were accused persons drawn from the same social milieu as the judges, one would have to ask whether, in fraud cases favouritism is likely to operate at a sub-conscious level. Such a result seems improbable.

On the other hand, violations of legislation forbidding trade with Rhodesia, or certain categories of currency offences, may well be found on examination to benefit from a tacit judicial view, doubtless widely shared, that the accused, while guilty, were not true criminals. It probably is the case that even crimes such as false accounting, where they appear to be isolated unlawful incidents of an otherwise lawful business enterprise, will benefit from leniency.

But this result as we have already noted, is apt to reflect the exigencies of a system of tactical compromises. Any comment in the present state of knowledge must be tentative, but one should be wary of stressing any supposed rapport between offender and judge as an explanation for lenient sentencing patterns. Many accused are adventurers. Not all adventurers succeed in British society, and more than one figure has attributed his failure to the entrenched conservatism of British society.

Another characteristic of the American system that makes the translation of arguments difficult is the tendency there to impose very long sentences against certain categories of offenders (Ogren, 1973). This circumstance makes arguments about disparity more pointed, for if crimes involving theft from the person and appreciable but not gross violence attract very long sentences, substantial, but much shorter sentences are bound to engender suggestions of favouritism. These arguments become still more forcible if some categories of offence attract very short sentences, as is the case with tax and anti-trust offences, but not with respect to securities fraud (Leigh, 1979). That consideration is not so evident in Britain, and in any event, both here and elsewhere, sentencing studies ought surely to break down offences within the white-collar crime group, if such there be, before engaging in broad generalisations. Allegations of favourable treatment for the fraud offender cannot be investigated until there is basic agreement on values, including agreement on grading quite different offences for severity, but also comparative research sufficient to enable the student to evaluate the various factors which weigh in the sentencing process.

Criminal Bankruptcy

Criminal bankruptcy affords another recourse for cases other than those of violence to the person. It enables a Crown Court before which the offender is convicted to make such an order if the aggregate of loss or damage, not attributable to personal injury, of the offence for which the offender is tried and any other relevant offence or offences exceeds £15,000. 'Relevant offence' means another offence of which the person is convicted in the same proceedings or an offence taken into consideration in determining his sentence. This latter criterion is strictly applied. A court may, if the accused formally admits guilt, take into account previous offences admitted to, but for which he has not formally been tried or convicted, in setting sentence in the case before the court. Thereafter, the accused cannot be tried for the earlier offence.[10] Only offences formally taken into account may be considered in determining whether the £15,000 limit is reached.[11] If there is a contest between invoking this machinery and the desirability of bringing sample charges only, the latter consideration governs.

The D.P.P. as Official Petitioner must determine whether to bring a criminal bankruptcy petition. He looks to the amount and accessibility of the accused's assets, and the degree of public concern about the case.[12] The Official Receiver acts as trustee of the accused's property. Other debts may also be proven in such a bankruptcy. A victim of fraud is thus enabled to claim for civil redress in criminal proceedings. This is an unusual pattern in English criminal procedure, though there are provisions for civil compensation in certain other enactments.[13] The fact that the Official Petitioner can take proceedings should enable criminals, particularly frauds, to be divested of their gains to the benefit of some of those at least who they have injured. But the proceedings do not give the victim of crime an advantage over the rogue's ordinary creditors. If he proves to have insufficient assets to satisfy all his creditors, each will have to settle for a share in the estate. This simply reflects the operation of ordinary rules of bankruptcy. The prudent rogue arranges either to transfer his assets to his wife well in advance of any wrong-doing, or salts it away abroad where it cannot be traced.

Disqualification Orders

In many European countries, disqualifications are extensively used. Persons convicted of crime are disqualified from pursuing certain trades and professions, and even from driving a motor vehicle. (Société Internationale de Oefense Sociale, 1969; Levasseur, 1975). Such orders are sparingly used in Britain, being provided for only under company and insolvency legislation.

The Companies Act 1948 contains two disqualifications. The first disqualifies an undischarged bankrupt from taking part in the management of a company without the leave of the court.[14] The second is directed towards fraud. Section 188 of the Companies Act 1948 enables a court to make an order that any person who has been convicted on indictment of any offence in connection with the promotion, formation or management of a company, or any person who, it is discovered on a winding-up, has been guilty of an offence of fraudulent trading or of any fraud in relation to the company, or in breach of his duty to the company, shall not, without the leave of the court, be directly or indirectly concerned or take part in the management of a company for such period not exceeding five years, as may be specified in the order. Breach of the section is punishable with a two-year term of imprisonment if the offender is convicted on indictment, or, on summary conviction, to a term not exceeding six months imprisonment, or a fine, or both.

In cases of fraud involving companies, the court is usually asked to make a disqualification order and it generally does so for the full five-year period. The section is not, however, as useful as it should be. It is limited in some important respects. The offender must actually be convicted on indictment.[15] It is not enough that he is suspected of having committed such an offence, nor even that he has been stringently criticised for fraudulent conduct in a Department of Trade Inspectors' report. Such a report does not even raise a *prima facie* inference against him. No disqualification may be based upon a foreign criminal conviction or order, however serious its nature. Nor may a conviction for fraud not in connection with a company be used as the basis for an order. This was stringently criticised in *Roadships Limited.* The Inspectors suggest that for some serious crimes of dishonesty, there should be an automatic disqualification. At present the legislation '...permits men to be directors of public companies when by reason of convictions involving dishonesty they are patently unfit so to serve' (Report, 1976, p. 50).

More serious still is the fact that as the law now stands, the period of disqualification starts from the date of sentence.[16] If, therefore, the offender is sentenced to a term of imprisonment of more than five years, the disqualification may hardly bite. Even if a shorter term of imprisonment is passed, the order may have only a short time to run after the offender's release from prison. The Company Law Committee recommended, twenty years ago, that the disqualification should run from the expiry of the sentence (Cmnd. 1749, 1962, para. 85(c)). Furthermore, the penalty for breach of an order is low, and it is often used simply as a make-weight or additional count in a prosecution for fraud.

The Companies Act 1976 enables the court to impose the like disqualification where a person has been persistently in default in relation to the delivery of documents to the Registrar.[17] Persistent default may be conclusively proven by showing that in the five years ending with the date of the application, he has been adjudged guilty, either on the same or on different occasions, of three or more defaults in relation to such requirements. No account may be taken of convictions before the Act came into force and its operation is therefore prospective only. The machinery could be very effective; the Department of Trade has adopted a vigorous prosecution policy for failure to return documents, one purpose of which is to enable it to secure disqualification orders in the future.

Section 9 of the Insolvency Act 1976 provides for the disqualification of persons who have, repeatedly, been directors of insolvent companies. The criteria are difficult to paraphrase, but, briefly, it must be shown first that the person concerned is or has been a director of an insolvent company in liquidation, secondly that he was, within five years of the date when the instant company went into liquidation, a director of another such company which has gone into liquidation, and thirdly that his conduct as director of any of those companies makes him unfit to be concerned in the management of a company. The court has a discretion whether to make the order and it is incumbent upon it to form a judgement as to the person's suitability to participate in management. This provision is buttressed by a power in the Secretary of State to require a liquidator or former liquidator of any company to furnish him with information and to produce or permit access to the company's books for the purpose of determining whether to make an application for a disqualification.

The section requires that at least one of the companies involved must have gone into liquidation after the coming into force of the Act. The provision is thus prospective in operation. It is certainly a potentially important innovation. The disqualifications thus imposed are not restricted to cases involving fraud. Nevertheless, failure to submit returns and documents can be deliberate, done to cloak a fraud, and repeated bankruptcies may evidence not just ineptitude, but fraudulent conduct, or at least conduct of so questionable a character that the person involved should not manage a company. The danger of fraud and prejudice to creditors in both cases is sufficient to justify the coverage achieved by the section and its application to all companies and not just to public companies.

Enforcement of disqualification orders has always posed problems. Until the 1976 Companies Act there was no obligation on the Registrar of Companies to keep a register of disqualification orders. Obviously, the Department of Trade kept an internal record. Now a publicly available register is provided, which should facilitate enquiries by creditors and prospective creditors of the company. Entries should , however, be keyed in to a fingerprint register. Some problems will inevitably persist. Bankrupts do engage in the management of companies, hiding behind their wives or other nominees. It is not uncommon for such a person to purport to be an employee or a consultant. Ascertaining and proving the true situation may be difficult, and sometimes impossible, for it must be remembered that a wife is not a compellable witness against her husband.[18] Persons subject to fraud disqualifications also conceal their status as managers, and—not uncommonly—the truth only emerges after a further, general, fraud investigation. In such a case, as we have noted, breach of the disqualification order is used as a make-weight only. These inefficiencies are, as we have elsewhere remarked, inevitable in a free society, in some measure at least (Leigh, 1980a).

Conclusion

We have concentrated upon the fine, imprisonment, criminal bankruptcy, and disqualification orders. English law is much richer in dispositions than this, and if we have not discussed other alternatives it is because they seem not to be applied in fraud cases in any great measure. In any event, good standard accounts of the sentencing system can be consulted (Cross, 1975). We have not considered the peculiar position of companies as criminally responsible entities. It is a general principle of English law that companies are criminally responsible for most crimes (Leigh, 1969, 1977). Not infrequently, both the directors of a company and the company itself are convicted of an offence. Indeed, the directors' liability clauses discussed in connection with directors' duties are drafted with just this principle in mind. So wide is the rule, that directors who conspire to cheat the Revenue, for example, render the company liable in respect of their acts even though it is in some measure also a victim.[19]

In some cases, especially of omission, where one cannot locate the person who allowed a forbidden consequence to occur, there can be no doubt that such liability is necessary.[20] Furthermore, in respect of much legislation, a supervisory duty must be imposed on management through rendering the company liable. There is no difficulty about the punishment: almost all offences, save murder and treason, are punishable with a fine.[21] But in English law the fine is the only generally available penalty against the company. Our system does not provide for dissolution of a company, nor for the systematic use of publicity against it, although that would be possible, and is done elsewhere (Leigh, 1977a). Furthermore, in large fraud cases there does not seem to be much to be gained from prosecuting the company, though this is conventionally done. It may be that in some cases formal proof fails against the officers, or some of them, so that a corporate conviction enables a conviction to be pronounced and an indirect penalty imposed on directors by fining the company, but it has not yet been established that corporate liability is an indispensable sanction in such circumstances as these.

References and Notes

1. See *Criminal Statistics (England and Wales) 1978*, Cmnd. 7670, Tables 8.1 and 8.11. On attitudes to burglars, see *Rex* v. *Phillips* (1947) 32 Cr. App. R. 47.
2. *Reg.* v. *Savundranayagam* [1968] 1 W.L.R. 1761 (C.A.).
3. *The Times*, 11 October 1969.
4. *Criminal Statistics (England and Wales) 1978*, Cmnd. 7670.
5. Sess. 1976–7, 931 H.C. Deb. (Vth Ser.) col. 1626.
6. [1979] Crim. L.R. 261.
7. *The Accountant*, 26 January 1978 (vol. 178), p. 99.
8. For example *Reg.* v. *Arrowsmith* [1976] Crim. L.R. 636; *Reg.* v. *MacFarlane* [1977] Crim. L.R. 49; *Reg.* v. *Cunningham* [1976] Crim. L.R. 694; *Reg.* v. *Jones* [1977] Crim. L.R. 234.
9. Powers of Criminal Courts Act 1973, s. 20.
10. *Rex* v. *Syres* (1908) 1 Cr. App. R.172.
11. *Reg.* v. *Anderson* [1978] A.C. 964.
12. D.P.P., *Evidence to the Royal Commission on Criminal Procedure* (1979), para. 164.
13. For example, Theft Act 1968, s. 28 (restitution orders), but these are not made where title to property is seriously disputed; *Reg.* v. *Ferguson* [1970] 2 All E.R. 820.
14. Companies Act 1948, s. 187.
15. *Hastings and Folkestone Glassworks Ltd.* v. *Kalson* [1949] 1 K.B. 214.
16. *Reg.* v. *Bradley* [1961] 1 W.L.R. 398.
17. Companies Act 1976, s. 28.
18. Criminal Evidence Act 1898, s. 1(d).
19. *Rex* v. *I.C.R. Haulage Ltd.* [1944] K.B. 551.
20. *Alphacell Ltd.* v. *Woodward* [1972] A.C. 824.
21. Criminal Justice Act 1948, s. 13.

We have seen that extraterritorial problems bedevil the investigation and prosecution of fraud offences. Persons whom it is desired to investigate remain abroad, and so out of the reach of Department of Trade investigators. Persons whom it might be desired to call as witnesses at trial similarly decline to return voluntarily. Rogues commit schemes of fraud abroad and return, sometimes, immune from trial because no part of the offence was committed within the United Kingdom. Rogues who have committed crimes in this country flee abroad, hoping to take advantage of either a lack of power to secure their return, or at any rate the cumbersome nature of extradition procedures. As Professor Tiedemann has noted, it is grotesque that international crime can overflow borders, while bureaucratic delays and obstacles impede co-operation between tax and customs authorities, the police, and public departments (Tiedemann, 1974). Furthermore, Britain's position in the E.E.C. now means that she cannot consider the financial interests of the E.E.C. as involving only the affairs of a foreign jurisdiction.

Faced with these problems, governments and international institutions have begun to reconsider problems of international co-operation of which extradition is but one aspect. Other aspects include territorial competence, recognition of foreign penal judgements, the exchange of dossiers for trial, and the like. In one respect there has been no fundamental re-assessment. International police competence hardly exists. Co-operation among forces must take account of sensitive questions of national sovereignty, and law enforcement operations can only be conducted in any given country by that country's law enforcement officers acting on the basis of their own laws (Bossard, 1980). Not all have departments specialised in complex fraud cases. Nor can British police exercise powers of arrest, search and seizure on behalf of a foreign police investigation. Indeed, in a Hong Kong case, the court points out that the police cannot even show documents and exhibits seized for the purpose of an investigation within the colony to a foreign police force with whose investigation it was co-operating.[1] If this latter limitation applies in Britain, and nothing suggests that it does not, investigations could be substantially impeded. Dr. Rider points out that, in any event, information will pass clandestinely. Even if this is tolerable, and blatant subversion of legal restrictions surely cannot be, it is inefficient because it depends on personal relationships between officers of different forces (Rider, 1980). It is apparent that powers need to be extended. There also appears to be room for fuller co-operation in international frauds between forces, acting within their lawful powers.

Extradition

This is the term used to denote the surrender by one state of a fugitive criminal to the authorities of another state, the requesting state. Among the countries of the Commonwealth, the procedure is governed by the Fugitive Offenders Acts. There is a simple procedure which applies in respect of the Republic of Ireland. Extradition to foreign states depends upon the Extradition Act 1870 as amended by subsequent legislation, and treaties with the particular countries concerned. There is a broad similarity of approach between the U.K. Extradition Act 1870 and the Fugitive Offenders Act 1967, but there are also important differences of detail.

Extradition involves the arrest of a suspected fugitive criminal on warrant.[2] The suspect is brought before a magistrate who must determine whether there are grounds upon which to order the return of the fugitive. He is to hear and determine the case in the same manner and have the same jurisdiction and powers as though the accused were brought before him charged with an indictable offence in England and Wales.[3] He must hear any evidence to show that the crime is not an extradition crime, or that the alleged offence is of a political character, a question which need not trouble us here.

If there is evidence which would justify the accused's committal for trial he is committed to prison; if not, he is released.[4] If he is committed, he has fifteen days in which to bring *habeas corpus* to have the committal reviewed. The powers of the court on *habeas corpus* are wide. It may review the sufficiency of evidence for committal:[5] whether the offence comes within the Act or the Treaty; whether the offences in the two jurisdictions correspond; whether it is sought to return him for trial on a different offence than that alleged; and whether extradition is sought for a political crime. There have been cases in which the applicant has alleged that a request, ostensibly for his return to face fraud charges, has been motivated by a desire to settle political scores.[6] In that case the court must review the matter. The court cannot refuse to return a fugitive simply on vague grounds of natural justice; one of the bars to extradition contained in the Act must apply.[7]

A person who is surrendered by the United Kingdom to another state may only be tried there on charges proved by the facts on which the surrender is granted, and our authorities are subject to the same inhibition.[8] This does not, however, prevent facts additional to those contained in the deposition being given at trial.[9] Whether an absolute restriction on trial of this sort is desirable has been questioned (*London Capital Group Limited*, 1977, p. 3). Under fugitive offenders legislation it can be relaxed by agreement of the state to which the request is made.[10] The two most troublesome problems in the area of commercial fraud are, first, the question whether the offence for which surrender is requested is an offence listed in the Extradition Acts or the Treaty (as embodied in a Statutory Instrument) and, if so, whether the ingredients are the same in both jurisdictions (the problem of mutuality) and, secondly, whether the particular extradition arrangements preclude the surrender of its own nationals by the requested state to the requesting state.

The list of offences contained in extradition legislation and treaties is fairly wide. From the earliest treaties entered into after 1870, to the present time, the lists have included fraud by bailee, banker, agent, director or public officer of any company.[11] Bankruptcy offences are also included. In the Anglo-United States Treaty of 1972, apparently not yet implemented, false accounting is included, as are false statements and fraud by a company director.[12] It is apparent that as our extradition treaties with foreign states are renewed, the opportunity is taken to extend the list. The process is one of piecemeal reform, and many treaties are old. Even though the Victorian treaties were remarkably comprehensive, there is no doubt that gaps in the coverage exist, particularly in relation to intangibles, computer data, and the misuse of confidential information. Indeed, some of these also reflect weaknesses in domestic law. Revenue offences are excluded. This is undesirable within the circle of the E.E.C., and the Council of Europe's draft extradition convention has been completed by an additional protocol making it possible to include tax offences as extraditable offences.[13]

The problem of mutuality also affects fugitive offenders legislation. Its basis is the consideration that British public policy does not countenance that a person should be surrendered for trial elsewhere on charges which would not be available had the acts been committed within the United Kingdom.[14] Mutuality also extends to problems of territorial jurisdiction, so that it must be shown not only that the accused committed the crime, but also that had he been charged with the crime in England an English court would have been bound to conclude that it had territorial jurisdiction to try the case.[15] Substantial similarity of offences is all that is required as between the two jurisdictions.[16] However, problems can readily arise in commercial fraud cases. As Lord Wilberforce in *Tarling's* case noted, the court must display considerable agility of mind. It must translate the actual charge laid into terms of English law and consider whether the offence would be sufficient to warrant trial on that equivalent offence.[17] In that case it had to endeavour to fit an elaborate complex of facts into English legislation which was largely inapplicable to deal with them. The facts may, for example, have fitted the Singapore offence of criminal breach of trust, but seemingly they did not readily fit the English offence of theft, nor were the facts such as would have given an English court jurisdiction had the accused been charged with the crime in England (Smith, J.C., 1979b). Plainly, the requirement of mutuality can cause problems in commercial fraud cases which stray outside the well-worn pathways of theft and obtaining by deception.

The second problem, already cited, is that extradition arrangements with some states preclude the surrender of their nationals. When this occurs, the United Kingdom will not surrender its nationals to the foreign state. An example is afforded by the Anglo-German Extradition Treaty of 1960, Article IV of which precludes such return. Similar inhibitions exist under the treaties with Italy[18] and Switzerland, though the Anglo-Swiss Treaty expressly stipulates that Switzerland will itself prosecute the offender under Swiss law.[19] Under other treaties the countries concerned generally reserve the right not to extradite their nationals, but there is no bar to doing so and the United Kingdom tradition favours such extradition. Countries which generally refuse extradition of their nationals often, like Switzerland, stand ready to prosecute them for at least some of their acts committed abroad. Nevertheless, there can be little doubt that bars to extradition founded on national status inhibit enforcement of the law in an area which increasingly is beset by problems of crimes committed across national boundaries, (Schultz, 1967).

The structure of the Fugitive Offenders Act 1967 is somewhat different. It applies to the United Kingdom in relation to most Commonwealth countries and they, for their part, have passed counterpart measures. Basically, the scheme provides for the return of persons accused or convicted in a designated Commonwealth country for an offence listed in the Schedule to the Act and punishable with imprisonment for twelve months or more. The general restrictions on return are similar to those which obtain in relation to extradition. Like extradition, mutuality poses problems, and it is doubtful whether the list of offences is sufficiently up-to-date. Paradoxically, a former measure, the Fugitive Offenders Act 1881, was wider, in that surrender could be granted in respect of any offence committed in Her Majesty's Dominions and punishable with twelve months imprisonment. The evolution of the Common-wealth, and its ability to comprehend regimes of different sorts with values which were not always shared in common, made a move to a structure akin to that which applies as between foreign states a practical necessity. In one respect, however, no problem arises, for countries which have adopted the same structure as that in the 1967 Act will extradite their nationals. Furthermore, with the consent of the requested state it is possible to try a surrendered fugitive on charges other than those for which he was surrendered. Such a consent can be given at any time before the trial commences.[20]

Surrender from Ireland, which, as will have been noted, stands in rather a special relationship in these matters, is governed by the Backing of Warrants (Republic of Ireland) Act 1965. This provides for the endorsement of warrants issued by courts in the Republic by magistrates in England. The warrant must be for an indictable offence or for one punishable on summary conviction with six months imprisonment or more. This obviously comprehends most criminal offences. The procedure is subject to the requirement of mutuality. It does not apply to political offences, offences under military law, or to offences concerning taxation, customs and excise duties, or exchange control. Unlike extradition, the magistrate may make an order on affidavit evidence endorsing the warrant, whereupon the suspect may be held for return without a further hearing. He has, however, fifteen days to bring an application for *habeas corpus* to show that a bar to his return applies. The procedure is thus simple and swift.

There seems every reason why the procedures applicable to Ireland should be followed in respect of offences arising within the E.E.C., subject always to reservations about political and military crimes. The existing procedure has been castigated as cumbersome, repetitive and redolent of delay (*London Capital Group Limited*, 1977, p. 3). Machinery for return under warrant would be easy and fast. Such a system could not, perhaps, be made fully comprehensive mutually, given constitutional inhibitions to the return of their citizens in Germany and Italy. It may be that problems of mutuality would still remain. But the list of extraditable offences could be extended to include tax offences, and a partial reform would be better than none.

Britain ought also to reconsider the rule forbidding extradition of its nationals to states which will not extradite their nationals. Whatever view other states may take of public policy, and whatever constitutional limitations they may be subject to, there seems no reason why Britain should hesitate to return its nationals for trial in a foreign jurisdiction, provided that the requirement of substantial mutuality of offences is met, that there is *prima facie* evidence of the person's involvement in crime and that we have confidence in the administration of justice in the foreign state. Any such procedure could be made subject to the discretion of the Home Secretary. Neither should treaty machinery always be necessary. Unilateral arrangements apparently work well elsewhere.[21] One's only substantial doubt is whether the adoption of such a rule might not subject the British government to blackmailing pressure from states with authoritarian or unpleasant governments. At present, because extradition requires a treaty, there can be no question of yielding to pressures.

Territorial Competence

The basis of English criminal jurisdiction is territorial. Some element of the crime must be located on English soil. Other countries are sometimes readier to try their nationals for crimes committed abroad. This is particularly marked in the case of states which refuse to extradite their nationals, although it is said that jurisdiction is not merely a complement to the impossibility of extradition (Schultz, 1967). But in Britain, with a few exceptions such as terrorism, piracy, murder and genocide, which are also treated as exceptions in other countries, so that there is a fair measure of agreement on the point, the principle of territoriality applies. This obviously inhibits the control of fraud. Marine fraud presents notorious problems. If a Liberian-registered oil carrier is scuttled in the Atlantic by a Greek crew, the Greek or Liberian courts may well have jurisdiction, but British police and courts do not, even though the effect of the crime may be felt here as a loss covered by the London insurance market. But traditionally, such an effect alone does not found jurisdiction.

Several reasons have been advanced for the territoriality principle. Classically, it was thought that only by trying the case in the country where the crime was committed could the ends of retribution and deterrence be properly served (Herzog, 1963).

Another reason is that adherence to territoriality helps to prevent a conflict of jurisdictions; it is clear which country has the best right to try the matter—that of commission, because there the authorities can best detect the crime and present it to an appropriate court (Schultz, 1967). Yet another reason is that a country, by asserting jurisdiction to try persons for offences against its laws committed abroad, may bring its public policy into conflict with that of other states. This was evident when the United States sought to compel United Kingdom subsidiaries of American firms to disclose commercial documents relevant to American anti-trust enforcement. The response was a United Kingdom statute enabling a British minister to forbid such disclosure.[22] An even wider measure has just been enacted, not only enabling a minister to direct that information be not supplied, but also providing that exemplary damages awarded by foreign civil courts shall not be enforceable in Britain. [23] British courts, where necessary, recognise that foreign subsidiaries of British companies stand in a similar relationship to their own government.[24]

Even on a technical level, where there are no political overtones, very difficult problems can arise. Suppose for example that a state, Erewhon, tries one of its nationals for a crime committed in Utopia. Suppose, further, that it fails for want of proof. If the law of Erewhon accords with that of most states, a second trial in its courts would be precluded by the double-jeopardy principle. Can Utopia then try the case? It may, after all, have been in a better position to do so all along. The answer seems to be that many nations would consider that they had to recognise the foreign penal judgement to the extent of precluding a further trial on it. Utopia might take the traditional view that jurisdiction depends on territoriality, that its own interests were more vitally engaged than those of Erewhon, and that comity ought therefore to have led Erewhon to decline jurisdiction. There are, therefore, sound policy reasons for a restricted rule of jurisdiction.

Fraud cases have forced English courts to depart in some measure from the territorial principle, although they have insisted that no such departure is intended. It is the case that our courts will not sit upon frauds committed entirely abroad by British nationals or residents. Thus a conspiracy to commit a fraud abroad is not triable here.[25] Nor, apparently, is a deception made from England which results in property being obtained abroad subject to the jurisdiction of English courts, but the status of this principle is in doubt.[26] But whether a fraud is entirely committed abroad depends upon whether any one of its elements can be located here, a question whose answer depends in part upon the definition of the offence and in part upon the acts done. Some extensions are uncontroversial. For example, an overt act sufficient to support a conspiracy to forge documents, or to defraud, takes place in a jurisdiction to which the documents are sent, as well as that from which they emanate.[27] Similarly welcome, is the rule that a secondary party to a crime committed in England may be tried here, even though he was not present when the crime was committed.[28]

The first real indication that the courts were prepared to reconsider the territoriality principle came in *Treacy* v. *D.P.P.*[29] The ratio of the case is narrow, namely, that the offence of uttering a blackmail letter is complete when it is posted. But Lord Diplock went further, to inquire into the bases of jurisdiction. According to Lord Diplock, there is no reason why persons who, from outside England, have done acts which cause harm to persons in England, and which are crimes here, should not be tried in English courts. Criminal jurisdiction ought only to be limited by notions of comity, and comity gives no right in a state to insist that a person may with impunity do physical acts within its own territory which have harmful consequences to persons within the territory of another state. It cannot complain in international law if the state in which the harmful consequence occurs punishes the malefactors involved. Injustice need not arise from dual, or in some frauds multiple jurisdiction, because the accused can raise a plea in bar of trial in respect of prior proceedings before a foreign court.

Lord Diplock has pursued the effect doctrine further in other cases, in one of which at least he has been followed by others of their Lordships who, seemingly, have not appreciated the extent to which the rules have been altered.[30] Others simply extended the notion of a sufficient act. In some cases, even an act of a preliminary character will found jurisdiction.[31]

The most elastic approach to territoriality is to be found in *Secretary of State* v. *Markus*, the Agrifund case,[32] which involved a scheme not unlike the Livestock Marketing scheme. A company was formed in London for the purpose of organising the sale of shares in an investment trust created in Panama. Visits were made to prospective investors in West Germany who were shown brochures by agents who forwarded application forms and completed powers of attorney to London, together with money or money's worth. When the money was lodged in the company's Swiss bank account, the applications were processed in London.

The accused was charged under section 13 of the Prevention of Fraud (Investments) Act 1958 with conniving at a company inducing persons to invest money by false representations concerning the honesty of the scheme and the redeemability of investments in it. He was convicted and he appealed. The question of jurisdiction was acute since neither the statements nor prospectuses were made in England. Only the processing was done here. Lord Diplock solved the problem thus: the accused was charged with a 'result' crime; one had therefore to ask whether any part of the forbidden result occurred in England. That result is the taking part by the victim in the arrangements, consequent upon the fraudulent inducement. Anything that a person does to enable him to participate in, or receive profits or income in respect of, the scheme constitutes taking part in the arrangements, and a person may take part through the agency of another. A nexus therefore existed, sufficient to found jurisdiction. Viscount Dilhorne dissented.

Lord Diplock's analysis is both subtle and practical, given the impossibility of returning the accused to West Germany. But the territorial principle, while extended in recent years and applied flexibly, has by no means been abandoned. In the *Tarling* case, for example, their Lordships declined to hold that the Singapore courts would have jurisdiction over certain charges of criminal breach of trust and fraud. On the former counts this was partly on the ground that there was no evidence to show the commission of wrongful acts in Singapore, and on the latter, partly it would seem, on the basis that loss occasioned to a Hong Kong subsidiary of a Singapore company was not a loss occurring in Singapore from which jurisdiction could be premised.[33]

It is obviously desirable that the question of jurisdiction be looked at afresh. There is, surely, a need to move away from territoriality as the sole nexus of jurisdiction in fraud cases. The question of result is obviously important. Perhaps we should be asking broader questions: whether the Realm is associated in any significant way with the fraud, or whether jurisdiction should not be asserted where steps, innocent in themselves, are taken in Britain as part of a scheme to perpetrate a fraud elsewhere. It would seem reasonable for English courts to take jurisdiction, subject to exceptions arising from comity. Certainly, there have been indications that jurisdictional rules might be reconsidered in respect of frauds arising in the E.E.C.[34]

Transfer of Proceedings

In some jurisdictions and under a Council of Europe Convention, arrangements are made for the transfer and allocation of criminal proceedings.[35] The fact that a fraud may have been committed in several states may lead to a multiplicity of jurisdictions having the right both domestically and according to international law to try the rogues concerned. But some states may be more substantially involved than others, and a particular state may in fact provide the most convenient forum for trial. It may be easiest to mount an effective prosecution there, to secure witnesses, documents, and the like. Of course, formal arrangements are not necessary to resolve such problems. They can be dealt with on an *ad hoc* basis. But the advantage of dealing with the matter by a convention is that it helps states to co-ordinate their policies and to work to uniform rules, in particular the rules of double jeopardy. It also helps to expedite investigations, since delay arising from uncertainty concerning which state will ultimately take jurisdiction is at least minimised.

These problems have in fact had a preliminary discussion in Britain in connection with an E.E.C. proposal concerned with the safeguarding of Community funds.[36] The case both for extended jurisdiction provisions and for the transfer of proceedings was fairly strongly made. It is also clear that the project will be opposed by those who see it as yet another step down the road to supra-nationalism.[37] Hence it cannot be said that such a step is likely in the near future. There is the further problem that no detailed study seems to have been undertaken concerning whether obstacles flow from English or Scottish criminal procedure, and if so, how these might be surmounted. Members of the government of the day did not think that civil liberties considerations posed particular difficulties, but this view depends upon the acceptance that safeguards existing in the domestic laws of our European partners, though somewhat different from our own, nevertheless maintain the same balance between the citizen and the state.

The Effect of Foreign Penal Judgements

Another area which has been developed on the Continent is the effect to be given to foreign penal judgements. A profound difference has always been acknowledged between recognition which gives a negative effect to such judgements, for example barring prosecution on the double-jeopardy principle, and recognition which gives positive effect to them. In English law a foreign penal judgement would probably be recognised for the former purpose.[38] But English courts will not enforce the penal laws of a foreign jurisdiction.[39] According to conventional notions of sovereignty, no state can require the courts of another to enforce the judgements of its courts (Association Internationale de Droit Pénale, 1963). There are, however, ways in which account can be taken on a discretionary basis of foreign penal judgements without infringing United Kingdom sovereignty, and without obliging British courts to give effect to judgements emanating from countries whose standards of justice we are unsure of or condemn (Kunter, 1968).

It should, for example, be possible to refuse a dealer's licence in securities to a person who has been convicted of fraud within the E.E.C., or in the United States, Canada, Australia or New Zealand, to name but a few countries in whose legal systems we have confidence. Equally, it should be possible for a court to order that a person be disqualified from participating in the control or management of a secondary bank, or insurance company, or even a trading company, where he has been convicted of an offence of fraud or dishonesty before a foreign court. Indeed, it might be possible to give effect not only to the penal judgements of some foreign jurisdictions, but also to the orders of appropriate administrative agencies. Had this rule applied in the past, Dr. Savundra's Belgian conviction could well have prevented him from operating here.

At present, nothing prevents self-regulatory agencies from taking account of foreign determinations, provided that they are given access to the information. Some governmental bodies could also reach judgements on the fitness of persons to manage on this basis. It would be preferable if the criteria were specified and the powers bestowed by statute. A court, in order to make a disqualification order on a foreign judgement or order, would need statutory powers; the Stock Exchange would not, so far as it simply wished to warn members against dealing with certain individuals, but statutory powers could be more safely employed. Once again, however, the subject is one which has not been developed in Britain.

Exchange of Information

Such potential as there may be for giving domestic effect to foreign penal and administrative judgements depends, obviously, upon information about them reaching the authorities of self-regulatory bodies. Even within Britain, there are problems concerning the dissemination of information. Self-regulatory bodies are in even greater difficulties than the police, and they do not have access to criminal records; nor, apparently, do foreign agencies always co-operate with them (Rider, 1980). Some method is necessary for channelling information to both governmental and self-regulatory agencies, some of which will have to be regarded as statutory protégés.

A further facility for the provision of information derives from provisions which permit British courts to take the evidence of witnesses on request, for the purpose of criminal proceedings before foreign courts.[40] Such provisions are common in the laws of most states. British courts can assist foreign courts, but because of the oral nature of our procedures British authorities cannot take full advantage of the reciprocal procedures permitted by foreign laws. It is a dogma of criminal evidence that no power exists to take evidence by commission in criminal proceedings, for in principle an accused always has the right to see and cross-examine the witnesses against him.[41] English law does permit the admission of written statements from Scotland and Ireland in committal proceedings, but this does not extend to trial,[42] nor do other, minor exceptions to the principle of oral evidence. Yet, in other common law jurisdictions, for example the United States, documents can be authenticated abroad on commission for the purpose of criminal proceedings.[43] In some Commonwealth countries, for example India and Canada, the evidence of witnesses can be taken abroad on commission, and the transcript read to the jury. The machinery appears to work well, in the interests of the prosecution and the defence, and its adoption should be considered here (Beullac, 1966).

If, as we shall argue, there is room for a reform of criminal procedure by means of which a range of matters could be admitted in evidence without the support of oral testimony by a witness in person, the facility could become much more significant. Even now, there is a need to facilitate the production of foreign financial documents. It would be absurd to perpetuate a rule which requires such production through a witness who may well have little else to depose to, save formal matters concerning its making and custody. Various other proposals have been suggested in recent years, as some continental jurisdictions at least, grow closer together. European conventions concern the transfer of prisoners, the service of process, attendance of witnesses and experts, and—potentially most useful—the transfer of criminal records from one state to another.[44] Again, these are matters from which Britain appears to have stood aloof.

References and Notes

1. *A.G. for Hong Kong* v. *Ocean Timber Transportation Ltd.* (1978) no. 86 (unrep.).
2. Extradition Act 1870, ss. 7 and 14.
3. *Ibid.*, s. 8.
4. *Ibid.*, s. 10.
5. *Reg.* v. *Brixton Prison Governor, ex p. Armah* [1968] A.C. 192; *Tarling (No. 1)* v. *Government of Singapore* (1980), 70 Cr. App. R. 77.

6. For example, *Reg.* v. *Governor of Pentonville Prison, ex p. Teja* [1971] 2 All E.R. 11.
7. *United States of America* v. *Atkinson* [1969] 3 W.L.R. 1074.
8. Extradition Act 1870, s. 19.
9. *Reg.* v. *Aubrey-Fletcher, ex p. Ross-Munro* [1968] 2 W.L.R. 23.
10. See *Reg.* v. *Boog* (1974) 23 F.L.R. 417.
11. For example, the Anglo-Belgian Treaty of 29 October 1901, Treaty Series no. 7 of 1902; Anglo-Swiss Treaty of 26 November 1880 appended to Clarke (1903).
12. *Extradition Treaty Between the Government of the United Kingdom of Great Britain and Northern Ireland and the United States of America* (1972), Cmnd. 5040.
13. *International Tax Avoidance and Evasion*, Council of Europe, Press Release, R(80)3 (25.2.80).
14. *Reg.* v. *Brixton Prison Governor, ex p. Gardner* [1968] 1 All E.R. 636; *Reg.* v. *Governor of Pentonville Prison, ex p. Elliott* [1975] Crim L.R. 516.
15. *Reg.* v. *Governor of Pentonville Prison, ex p. Khubchandani, The Times L.R.,* 14 February 1980.
16. *Re Budlong* (1980) 130 N.L.J. 90.
17. *Tarling (No. 1)* v. *Government of Singapore* (1980) 70 Cr. App. R. 77 at pp. 107–88.
18. Treaty of 5 February 1873 between Her Majesty and the King of Italy for the Mutual Surrender of Fugitive Criminals, Art. III.
19. Anglo-Swiss Treaty for the Mutual Surrender of Fugitive Criminals, of 26 November 1880.
20. *Reg.* v. *Boog* (1974) 23 F.L.R. 417 (Aus.); *Reg.* v. *Crux and Polvliet* (1971) 3 C.C.C. (2d) 427 (Brit. Col).
21. For example, Canada, Extradition Act, R.S.C. 1970, c. E-21, Pt. II, ss. 35–40; Fugitive Criminals (Special Extradition) Act, 383 of 1977 (Malaysia).
22. Shipping Contracts and Commercial Documents Act 1964 s. 2.
23. Protection of Trading Interests Act 1980.
24. *Lonrho Limited* v. *Shell Petroleum Co. Ltd.* [1980] 1 W.L.R. 627 (H.L.).
25. *Board of Trade* v. *Owen* [1957] A.C. 602 at p. 625; *Tarling (No. 1)* v. *Government of Singapore* (1980) 70 Cr. App. R. 77.
26. *Reg.* v. *Governor of Pentonville Prison, ex p. Khubchandani, The Times* L. Rep., 14 February 1980.
27. *Reg.* v. *Governor of Brixton Prison ex p. Rush* [1968] 2 All E.R. 316.
28. *Reg.* v. *Robert Millar Ltd.* [1970] 2 Q.B. 54.
29. [1971] A.C. 537.
30. *D.P.P.* v. *Stonehouse* [1978] A.C. 807.
31. *Reg.* v. *Doot* [1973] A.C. 55.
32. [1976] A.C. 35.
33. *Tarling (No. 1)* v. *Government of Singapore* (1980) 70 Cr. App. R. 77, and see dissent on this point by Viscount Dilhorne at p. 124. The majority of their Lordships do not deal with the issue.
34. Sess. 1977–8, vol. 952 H.C. Deb. (Vth Ser.), cols. 1491 *et seq.* (Sir M. Havers).
35. European Convention on the Transfer of Proceedings in Criminal Matters, Council of Europe, Strasbourg, 1972.
36. E.E.C. Document No. R/204/76; and see Commission of the European

Communities COM (76) final, Art. 2, chapter II, which provides for the conditions of transfer.

37. Sess. 1977–8, vol. 952 H.C. Deb. (Vth Ser.), col. 1496 (Mr. Enoch Powell); for government views, see col. 1493 (Mr. Brynmor John).
38. *Treacy* v. *D.P.P.* [1971] A.C. 537 at p. 562 *per* Lord Diplock.
39. *Government of India* v. *Taylor* [1955] A.C. 491.
40. Evidence (Proceedings in Other Jurisdictions) Act 1975 s. 8(2).
41. *Reg.* v. *Upton St. Leonard's (Inhabitants)* (1847) 10 Q.B. 827.
42. Criminal Justice Act 1972, s. 46.
43. 18 United States Code, ss. 3491–4.
44. European Convention on Mutual Assistance in Criminal Matters, Council of Europe, Strasbourg, 1959; it now contains a protocol on tax matters.

PART V

CONCLUSION

20 Some Suggested Reforms

Throughout this book there appear references to reforms which if adopted would, I submit, enable us better to prevent, detect and punish fraud. Many of these involve amendments to the details of criminal or civil law. Some are of capital importance, in particular the vexed questions which arise in respect of the protection of intangibles. *Tarling's* case alone ought to convince us that there is a range of undesirable conduct which is not adequately covered by the present law of theft, which founds on appropriation.[1] Other questions concern the law of criminal procedure, in particular access to financial records. Happy must be the California policeman who can obtain a warrant to secure a print-out from a computer (Whiteside, 1979, pp. 46–7). The veneration with which the privacy of financial records is regarded in this country is startling. It is also undesirable.

Other considerations relate to the management structures of companies and the redress of abuses, and the reform of administrative procedures, for example in the licensing of dealers in securities. It is not my intention to rehearse all these matters yet again. I propose, rather, to concentrate upon the reform of institutional arrangements for the regulation of commercial affairs and the prosecution of crime. Any excursus into law reform must take account of certain characteristics of the British system of control. Powerful inhibitions to change exist, deriving partly from a pervasively conservative attitude to institutions and procedures, and partly from a want of financial resources.

We have seen that the control of fraud in Britain is a task which falls upon both governmental and self-regulatory bodies, the latter—private bodies—performing essentially governmental functions. Being the product partly of deliberate decision, partly of evolution, the system of control is fragmented; there is no single government department charged with overseeing the commercial life of Britain, let alone the prevention and punishment of fraud and other dishonest commercial practices. It is doubtful whether any such body could be devised, or whether any sensible person would wish it to be. At the same time, fragmentation and lacunae in the

structure of powers could be minimised, and the unhappy consequences which arise from them mitigated. The division of competence
between different regulatory agencies acting in related areas, but on
different terms, with different powers and sometimes with imperfect
co-operation among them, needs to be reviewed. So too, do aspects
of the procedures which they operate.

None of this is particularly controversial, provided that it is stated
in suitably abstract terms. When practical proposals emerge for
discussion, extreme positions are sometimes taken. The City values
a flexible system in which rules for doing business are not minutely
confining, and in which self-regulation permits the rapid adaptation
of standards. At one extreme, it is manifested in the notion that all
governmental interference in the setting of rules and working of
institutions is wrong, apt only to blunt the competitive spirit in one
area at least where it has functioned well. On the other side of the
debate are ranged various shades of opinion. Some critics call for
the nationalisation of financial institutions; others see avoidable
imperfections in the volunteer system which, they believe, could be
minimised by closer governmental intervention.

Successive governments have adopted a cautiously evolutionary
approach. They have been reluctant, partly on financial grounds, to
alter the fundamental characteristics of the system. They have
responded to pressure, partly by tightening up the regime of
company, insurance and banking law, and partly by encouraging
the development of self-regulatory agencies. On balance, governments have considered that self-regulation works well and that its
efficiency and cheapness either could not be duplicated by a
government agency or could only be duplicated at excessive cost,
and with an undue measure of rigidity.

This emphasis is also a feature of the report of the Wilson
Committee (Financial Institutions Committee, 1980). Stressing
non-statutory regulations as the appropriate dominant mode, the
report concludes that regulation by City institutions should continue, but that the regulatory activities of such institutions should be
made publicly accountable through a review body with wide and
open responsibilities, and composed both of civil servants and
outsiders. Non-statutory regulation by the City institutions which
deal with particular cases, should be open, fair and effective. The
report rejects the notion of a British Securities Exchange Commission, partly on the grounds that it would be a constitutional novelty
of a sort which would be difficult to assimilate. It concludes, rightly,
that the American system also contains a substantial element of

self-regulation and that, in the result, the differences between the American and British systems are differences of degree.

This is, of course, true, and affords a useful starting point for analysis. But it is, alas, where the Committee ended. As a result, no attempt was made to deal with details of the regulatory system, or the question whether any further detailed accommodations between self-regulation and statutory regulation were required. Such matters are no doubt for the Joint Review Body, as remodelled. It does seem clear that the present mixture of governmental and self-regulatory controls will continue, although the balance will no doubt alter. Governments have not been eager to embrace the adoption of ambitious new agencies, and the Committee's report must, for the present, weigh decisively against such change.

In relation to fraud in the strict sense, successive governments have been parsimonious and unimaginative. Germany and France have acted, both to reformulate the law, and to provide institutional support for the police and other agencies engaged in the control of fraud. Britain has dawdled. Rules of law have, it is true, been changed, provided that the alteration was technical and no charge upon public funds was implied. But such changes left difficult contemporary problems unredressed. Radical changes, whether of an institutional or doctrinal character, have seldom occurred.

It seems reasonable to conclude that immediate change to the fragmented prosecutions system, if such it be, is unlikely. It may be that the Royal Commission on Criminal Procedure will suggest sweeping changes, but I would guess that the prosecutions system is likely to remain pretty much as it is, with no national prosecution service, but with an augmented Director of Public Prosecution's office, and reliance at the local level on prosecuting solicitors. Police fraud squads will, I assume, continue to be composed and operate much as they have in the past. The Scottish system is, of course, one of public prosecutions functioning under the aegis of the Lord Advocate.

In criminal investigation, a major problem is that of drawing together the various elements of the system into an effective working whole. In part, as this concerns the referral and allocation of cases, the problem is one of ensuring that instances are brought to the attention of the police and the Department of Trade by self-regulatory agencies. In relation to investigation and prosecution, the problem is one of devising procedures so that the expertise which is scattered throughout the system can be welded into an effective working whole.

Difficulties are exacerbated because there is no umbrella under which these matters can come. There is no national prosecutions service. To centralise control in the Director of Public Prosecution's office would in any event be cumbersome where the matter fell outside the normal processes of investigation and prosecution. He is, otherwise, not in a central position. It is here that a companies commission, like that of New South Wales, appears attractive. That commission enables expertise in several disciplines, including accountancy, to be concentrated. It smooths liaison between inquiry procedures, and investigation and prosecution. It prosecutes indictable matters arising from its own investigations, and it disposes of police as well as Inspectors. It also has oversight, like the American SEC, of stock exchanges and licensed dealers in securities (New South Wales, Corporate Affairs Commission Report, 1979). Lacking a bureaucratic home of this sort, one must adapt, endeavouring to devise something better than a mere set of *ad hoc* responses, useful though those might be. In respect of investigation and prosecution, we might borrow ideas from the machinery created in West Germany to deal with complex fraud cases (Leigh and Hall Williams, 1979; Romer, 1974–5). There, special prosecution units are organised within the *Länder* ministries of justice. Teams of police, business managers, accountants and lawyers, all of whom have specialist training, prepare cases for prosecution.

The West German system has a number of advantages. The specially trained policemen develop the case in conjunction with persons from other disciplines. If questions arise concerning the acceptability of business and accounting practices, or the reasons for which matters were recorded in a particular way by a company, the business manager or *Wirtschaftsreferent* can not only make the necessary explanations, but also investigate the matters himself, ultimately making a report to the court on the matter. He is able to direct the accountants concerning matters to be investigated in detail. The prosecutor, who also is specially trained, directs the investigation. He thus can indicate which avenues ought to be explored, and which can be ignored. He is able to shape the case for trial. Because all such prosecutors are specialists, the file is never in the hands of a generalist who must acquaint himself with matters of an unfamiliar character.

The West German system could not be reproduced here in any exact form. Its relevance lies in the example which it gives of teamwork. Such teamwork should be attainable here. The numbers of very large company frauds are relatively small. It should be possible to institute, perhaps by Home Office circular, a procedure whereby all serious cases would lead to planning and allocation meetings between the Fraud Squad, the Department of Trade and the Director of Public Prosecutions (whose staff would need to be augmented somewhat). At such a meeting the needs of the investigation would be assessed. An officer of the D.P.P. would be invested with the duty of overseeing the investigation with a view to preparing the case for trial. He would, therefore, afford the necessary focal point, and the police could come to him for guidance. He could arrange with the Department of Trade, or with a company inspector if one were active in the case, for accounting expertise. Similarly, the Director's office should be able to call upon the City institutions for advice, in particular for comment about doubtful transactions, and even for help in the investigation of share dealings. Counsel could as now, be instructed at an early stage.

Such a system should conduce to smoother and better-informed investigations. It would also, one hopes, conduce to a more adventurous attitude towards the investigation and prosecution of fraud. Practices which appear to be criminal in some of their manifestations at least, for example window dressing, might be more readily perceived to be crime, and more vigorously tackled, if accountants were available as part of a team to explain the significance of practices to investigators, and to comment to the police and the Director's personnel concerning the integrity of explanations given of such phenomena. If somewhat longer postings to the Fraud Squad could be secured, greater advantages deriving from specialisation might be achieved. Similarly, teamwork could be fostered in provincial centres by the adoption of standing machinery in appropriate prosecuting solicitors' offices. If, of course, national or regional prosecuting services were to come about as the result of the forthcoming report of the Royal Commission on Criminal Procedure, specialisation and concentration might be more readily and effectively secured.

There is, as we have noted, a need for a proper chambers jurisdiction for complicated criminal cases. But, unlike the existing machinery, it should have compulsory features. Both prosecution and defence should be invited to concede facts and should be obliged to do so, save where disputed questions of admissibility and relevance are in issue, or where the circumstances surrounding the making of documents, for example, bear upon their cogency or provide a context which affects inferences to be drawn from them. It should be possible to adduce a wide range of documents without necessarily calling a witness, and the same rule could apply to documents obtained abroad under letters rogatory. There is every reason why an accused, or the prosecution, should have the facility to test genuinely disputed and disputable matters; there is nothing to be said for perpetuating a system in which admissions are not made not because there is genuine dispute about formal evidence or the admissibility of documents, but simply because one side or the other hopes that the other side will fail formally to prove a matter.

Similarly, there should be compulsory machinery for the production of reports and exhibits to the defence. Much is done now, of course, on an informal basis between counsel, and there is thus a wide, conventional measure of disclosure. But a formal rule to serve as a backstop would not come amiss. Matters such as particulars could also be dealt with routinely at this stage. What is suggested is compulsory machinery to isolate disputable issues, making provision for the others before trial with a consequent saving of time and expense, and to provide for wide disclosure in order to ensure that issues are developed smoothly at trial without disruptions caused by allegations of unfair tactics, and to narrow the essential issues to be litigated.

There is, indeed, a good deal to be said for a rule which would require the defence to disclose documents and exhibits, and to indicate its principal lines of defence. Under the present rules, this applies to matters concerning a defendant's mental condition only. Both sides at present should give forewarning of difficult issues of law to be raised at trial, and this should be made compulsory so far as the percipience of counsel extends. This, obviously, suggests drastic changes to accepted modes of procedure, which would by no means be easy to enforce. One would, however, expect the Bar to adapt if the rules were made under express statutory authority, and if obedience to them were the subject of judicial exhortation. No doubt further sanctions could be devised; it might be possible, for example, to penalise counsel personally in costs. But it is probable that vigorous judicial insistence on obedience to such procedures would suffice.

Jury trial, as we have noted, is of doubtful value in fraud cases. Both acquittals and convictions may stem from an imperfect assimilation of evidence. Yet jury trial is strongly embedded in English law, and pleas for its restriction have not been greeted with enthusiasm. A possible reform would be to permit waiver of jury trial by the accused, in favour of trial by judge alone. This is provided for under the Canadian Criminal Code for a wide range of offences.[2] It is also possible under the United States Federal Rules of Criminal Procedure and in the laws of a number of the States (Goldstein and Orland, 1974, pp. 1123–5). To the extent that accused persons chose non-jury trials, trials of complicated fraud cases might be expedited, and a better informed verdict reached. There seems no reason to suppose that accused persons would never choose this route. That would not correspond to the Canadian or American experience (Laskin, 1969; Kalven and Zeisel, 1966). A substantial proportion of all serious cases are tried by a judge alone in those jurisdictions, at the accused's election, and this, of course, reduces pressure on the jury list.

We have noted criticism of sentencing policies. To the extent that undue leniency depends on low maxima set by legislation, there is a clear tendency towards greater severity, particularly under company law. Maximum penalties are being increased, and, equally important, more offences are being made triable both summarily and on indictment. For the rest, the task is rather one of inducing courts to take fraud more seriously by stressing its undesirable aspects, than seeking to remedy the situation by desperate measures such as the enactment of minimum penalties. In any event, if there is a judicial instinct which favours the use of the least force necessary to deter, it ought to be applauded.

But it would be idle to pretend that undue leniency has no bad results. Police and prosecutors, although expected to act in a detached and dispassionate fashion, do regard a substantial sentence as setting a seal of approval on their work. They are apt to regard their work as devalued when a very lenient sentence is passed in a serious case. The public must question the values which the legal system reflects when serious cases are dealt with leniently, or are not prosecuted because, in the eyes of the authorities, no worthwhile sentence is likely to result. These, as we have noted, are factors which affect what might be thought of as second-rank frauds. It would be desirable to foster measures which would enable self-regulatory agencies to play a fully effective role in the prevention of fraud and in the wider regulation of the market.

There is, I think, a strong case for making the Stock Exchange and the Take-Over Panel statutory protégés, and to bring them and the City policy-making bodies partially under the aegis of government. In saying this, I do not advocate the end of self-regulation. But additional powers should be bestowed upon the City institutions, and the government should have supervisory powers over them, as have the SEC in the United States and the New South Wales Companies Commission. I have hitherto remarked that this may come about as a result of entry into the E.E.C. A directive requires member states to nominate the national authority competent to decide on the admission of securities to official listing, and provides for a right to apply to the courts concerning a refusal to list a security or a discontinuing of such listing.[3] This seems to premise an administrative recourse from a public agency, or at least an agency invested with statutory powers, from whose decision an appeal exists.

In evidence to the Financial Institutions Committee, the Department of Trade took the view that statutory powers could not be given to a body which was not answerable to Parliament.[4] The Committee accepted this. Certainly, there would have to be responsibility, at least in so far as functions were underwritten by statute, through a sponsoring Ministry, such as the Department of Trade. That alone would probably suffice to cause the self-regulatory agency and the Department to regard the bestowal of statutory powers as a poisoned chalice. Much, however, could be left to self-regulation, and, given the possibility of judicial recourse in questions of listing, the responsibility of Ministers and the range of matters for which they would be answerable would be few. To the extent that political embarrassment is a valid consideration, the possibility of it would be minimal.

The bestowal of statutory powers would, as the EEC directive envisages, conduce to widespread co-operation among regulatory agencies. It would then, surely, be able to provide material gathered by Interpol and national forces on the criminal records of directors of companies applying for listing. The Stock Exchange now asks for such information from applicants, but it lacks the power to check the veracity of replies. Under statutory powers, the City institutions might be able to enforce the production of documents and the attendance of witnesses, even against third parties.

In America, the SEC can exercise control over members of self-regulatory agencies and can exercise an appellate jurisdiction over the disciplinary decision of those bodies. In Britain the Department of Trade controls licensed dealers in securities, and vets the rules of self-regulatory bodies whose members deal in securities. In respect of other self-regulatory agencies, it could, perhaps, prove useful to invest the Department with augmented powers. It should review, with all self-regulatory agencies, the rules and procedures which they adopt, the types of hearings being held and the sanctions being imposed. It should have the power to proceed against persons who refuse co-operation with the self-regulatory agencies, if necessary by approaching the courts for the invocation of contempt procedure. It should have full powers to order investigations after the event, where such matters as profit forecasts are shown to be thoroughly inaccurate, or where there appeared to be reason to think that the integrity of a take-over bid was suspect, but the transaction has been concluded. Although, at present, the Take-Over Panel endeavours to ensure this at the time, its follow-up machinery is not wholly effective. It would, one hopes, review the question of when investigations should be commenced, and it should have power to investigate whenever there is reason to think that the City panel was imposed upon.

One thinks of take-overs such as that involving Gilgate Holdings, where, apart from allegedly concealing the purchase of shares, the bidders ought, in the Panel's opinion, never to have bid at all, because they lacked the financial means to carry out their bid. At the end of the day, the offending individuals undertook to pursue certain measures 'which might possibly at some future date realise for shareholders some indeterminate value for their investment in Gilgate'.[5] It is good to have a strong statement from the Panel that certain individuals who acted in concert should bid for St. Piran, a mining and property company, but how effective the Panel's decision will be in that case must depend on the willingness of the parties criticised to complete a bid, and upon their financial resources.[6] Admittedly, the Department of Trade is investigating the company. But it would be more useful, for example, if the Department had a wide power to investigate following a complaint from a self-regulatory agency, and if it had power, either on such complaint or on its own motion following an investigation, to ban persons from acting in the securities market, or from acting in the management of companies, permanently or temporarily. Such a ban could be premised upon breach of the self-regulatoy agency's rules regarding transactions, or upon failure to assist in an investigation. Indeed, it ought, under such a scheme, to be possible to ban financial institutions from acting for banned individuals and companies. The SEC, for example, has power to prevent certain companies from acting in the American securities market, and can order that dealers in the United States be forbidden to act for them. This has had a salutary effect (Leigh, 1979).

Because the regime suggested would be statutory in part, either the Department of Trade or the self-regulatory agencies should be able to take full advantage of the facilities available at governmental level for obtaining information from abroad. The SEC and the Ontario Securities Commission not only maintain data banks, but actively seek information from foreign sources for regulatory purposes. As reference bodies, the self-regulatory agencies should have the status, and the governmental powers in reserve, to enable them to play a full part in regulation. One would expect that in time, close working relationships between the agencies, and with the Department of Trade and the police would evolve. These are, of course, already a feature of regulation in Britain, but the system might be expected to evolve further. What is wanted is to enhance the best features of the system, not to destroy it.

Any suggestion must, of course, recognise certain inherent limitations to powers which may prove to be wholly or partially insurmountable. The foreign dimension is bound to prove troublesome. For example, even if adequate investigation machinery were to be devised for insider trading, it would be difficult to penetrate the façade of a Swiss bank or Liechtenstein Anstalt to discover the true identity of bidders. Even where traditional crime is involved and no absolute rule of bank secrecy precludes international co-operation, it can be difficult to trace the source and destination of funds which criminals have sought to launder by passing them through financial institutions or using them in legitimate trade (Rider, 1980). Moreover, sanctions are not easy to devise. Measures such as freezing shares harm the innocent and are at best short-term expedients. Bank accounts cannot be frozen on mere suspicion. For some classes of transactions it may be possible to suggest long-term remedies, for example divestiture and restitution of shares. But these are incidental to fraud.

The existing system of control has been vigorously attacked at one sensitive point by both the Council for the Securities Industry and the Law Reform Committee of the Bar. That is in relation to company investigations. The objections to the slowness of procedures and to the willingness of Inspectors to comment extensively on the character of persons appearing before them have, as we have seen, been partly met by the government. The government has not, however, acceded to pleas to set up standing internal machinery for investigations, nor has it elaborated natural justice requirements beyond the statement already contained in its notes to Inspectors. Above all, it has not agreed to suggestions either that reports should not be published, or that animadversions on the conduct of persons under investigation should be wholly eschewed.

It is of course true that allegations of unfairness have come to the fore in recent years, and that, as Sachs L.J. noted in *Re Pergamon Press Ltd.*,[7] there were no such allegations in earlier years. That circumstance is not necessarily persuasive. The Company Law Amendment Committee of 1945 advocated the wide powers which now apply because the original machinery, which could only be set in motion by a substantial proportion of shareholders, was ineffectual (Cmd. 6659, 1945, paras. 145–56). There were thus few cases in which such issues could arise. The tensions inherent in the present inspection system derive from the different purposes which inspections fulfil. If the sole purpose were that of criminal investigation, speedy, confidential reports, would be the ideal; if its purpose were solely to inform shareholders, a dry factual account would suffice.

The inspection system is not, however, for the sole purpose of informing shareholders, nor ought it to be thought of as primarily a facility for the prosecution of offences. It has wide public purposes, and of these, the most significant is that of informing the public concerning the nature and integrity of financial and commercial practices in circumstances where their integrity appears to be open to serious question. The rash of secondary banking cases affords an example of this. The need to inform shareholders of companies of the manner in which their company is being managed is a secondary consideration. So too, is the obtaining of information with a view to prosecution. The historic emphasis has changed, from informing the members of a private body, to obtaining and evaluating information in the general public interest.

While inspections are no doubt useful in some cases of prosecution, many prosecutions begin as a result of information obtained under section 109 of the Companies Act 1967, while others commence at an early period after an informal report and long before the full report is ready. There has, as we have noted, always been doubt whether the full panoply of a departmental inspection is the best way of developing complicated fraud cases for trial. But the fact that the machinery exists may have blinded us to other avenues for reform. As already stated, there is evidence that although in some cases the compulsory examination of witnesses and the production of documents assists in mounting a police investigation, and a later prosecution, in other cases it actually impedes police work. We have remarked that some Inspectors are reluctant to involve the police closely with their work lest witnesses, fearing prosecutions, will fail to co-operate in the investigation. In some cases the police are obliged to wait until Inspectors have interviewed a witness before doing so, and transcripts of witnesses' evidence are sometimes not focused in a way that the police find helpful, nor placed in a context which helps in criminal investigation.

Accordingly, where there is no general public interest to be served, corporate irregularity might well be left to the ordinary processes of the civil or criminal law. In major cases of fraud or mismanagement, shareholders would continue to derive an incidental benefit from inspections. In advocating this, I do not overlook that the Department of Trade may bring civil proceedings on behalf of a company, following an investigation. Instances of this, however, are too few to have a general regulatory effect, and it is doubtful whether the Department would be able, on account of a lack of resources, to intervene more frequently than it does at present. Tactically, it is better that the Department concentrate its efforts. It is, for example, valuable that it can and will move to safeguard assets of a firm which has engaged in defrauding the public. It is better equipped to perform that task than it is for providing general civil redress for members of companies. The latter activity could, more generally, come within the competence of large, institutional shareholders, if they will act. But, plainly, we are faced with unavoidable imperfections, and difficult choices must be made.

It is not, however, necessary now, nor should it be so in the future, to premise a civil order to wind-up and freeze assets upon an elaborate Inspector's report. This can be done on the basis of information obtained under informal investigation procedures, or otherwise. Formal machinery may help to surmount problems of evidence, but it is not necessarily required as a trigger for action. In fact, the investigation provisions may have blinded successive governments to the need to confer wider powers upon the police. The police alone cannot examine witnesses compulsorily or gain ready access to financial records. The Department of Trade and the Inland Revenue can. Whether or not the investigation system is restricted, there is a need to extend police powers to deal with fraud. Wide and sensible search and seizure powers and the use, under safe-guards, of electronic surveillance, and the adoption of better investigation techniques, are all needed. Our perception of the issues ought not to be dominated by the company inspection machinery; equally, its present significance as a repository of powers must be admitted, as must the political difficulties of securing additional powers to the police.

Of wider matters, such as the terms in which reports are couched, I venture only a few observations. If inspections are to inform the public, they will necessarily have to be published. They will not convey their information if they are just a dry narrative. Nor, if any sort of meaningful discussion is to ensue, can they avoid making judgements. Lawyers underrate the importance of inspections in setting standards; accountants do not. No doubt, character assassination should be avoided, but from Inspectors' reports we can learn something about issues relevant not only to business studies but to criminology as well, in particular the influence which a corrupt management exerts over all levels of an enterprise. Inspectors have passed harsh judgements on characters in City dramas; they were not always wrong to do so, nor are their comments to be seen simply as yellow journalism emanating from a superior, and privileged, source. In the end, there must be exposure and evaluation. There is a financial demi-monde to whose members the solace of anonymity ought not to be extended. Those whose conduct is squalid ought better to amend it, then to complain of its exposure.

But these conclusions are not intended to argue either against changes in the inspection system, nor to serve as an apologia for cases in which Inspectors may have overstepped the mark. They are, instead, an argument for openness, and, while in favour of increasing police powers, for the maintenance of institutions which enable fraudulent and improper conduct to be exposed and evaluated. Prosecution is, of course, the aim to which much effort must be directed. But the difficulties of prosecution are such, and the need to maintain faith in the integrity of the financial and commercial system is such, that a bundle of institutions and procedures is needed. Faith in the integrity of the institutions and practices of commerce and finance underlies all developed economic systems. It is certainly crucial to capitalism. If the public is to have confidence in the system, fraud must be controlled. Otherwise, there will be fewer small investors, more corruption, more manipulation, less attention paid to the interests of proprietors, creditors and workers in companies, and less solid achievement. To that end, improved civil, criminal and administrative procedures are necessary, and there must be available a public searchlight which can, where necessary, probe into dark corners.

At the time of the Lynskey Tribunal, an inquiry into governmental corruption, H.T.F. Rhodes, in his comments on the machinations of Sydney Stanley, the villain of the piece, concluded, rather optimistically, that Stanley's financial conjuring tricks were nothing more 'than the end-product of a financial system which has become increasingly divorced from productive acts', a system which, Rhodes thought, was being terminated by social evolution (1949, p. 91). If that conclusion now seems naive, it seems so because it both overestimates the perfectability of the human character and underestimates, indeed ignores, the vital commercial significance of an honest and efficient financial sector. Aware as we must be of the importance of that financial sector to Britain's prosperity, we cannot afford to be complacent about its regulation.

References and Notes

1. *Tarling (No. 1)* v. *Government of Singapore* (1980) 70 Cr. App. R. 77.

2. Criminal Code, Canada, 1970, C-34, s. 484. Canada early provided for non-jury trial in restraint of trade cases; see 52 Vict., c. 4, s. 1. In the province of Alberta, an accused may elect for non-jury trial for any offence.

3. *Council Directive* of 5 March 1979, co-ordinating the conditions for the admission of securities to official stock exchange listing, Official Journal, 16.3.79, no. L 66/21.

4. Wilson Committee, Second Stage Evidence, vol. 5, *Department of Trade*, pp. 30–1 (1979).

5. 'Panel censures three Gilgate directors', *The Times*, 15 March 1980.

6. 'Takeover Panel rules on St. Piran', *The Times*, 2 April 1980.

7. [1971] Ch. 388.

Postscript

·

In the short time since the manuscript of this book was delivered to the publishers, there have been important developments in the field of commercial fraud and its control.

The most significant fraud case has been that of Lord Kagan who admitted four charges of theft from his company and three of falsifying accounts. He was imprisoned for ten months on each charge, to run concurrently, and disqualified from taking part in the management of companies for three years (*The Times*, 13 December 1980). There are also reports of meat frauds, involving lorries ostensibly carrying offal, which on inspection proved to be carrying prime beef. *The Sunday Times* (8 March 1981) suggests that the fraud was carried on with intent to manipulate E.E.C. levies and subsidies on meat imports and exports. The technique is described on pp. 67–8 of this book. Attitudes towards tax fraud continue to vary: while Customs and Excise are clear that V.A.T. frauds should be regarded as criminal, the Law Society, in a report to a committee which is reviewing the tax system, argues that such conduct should no longer constitute a criminal offence (*The Observer*, 8 March 1981).

The most significant development is the Companies (No. 2) Bill 1981, which is pursuing an irregular course through Parliament. It is impossible to give a detailed analysis of the measure since it is not certain what exactly it will contain when it finally reaches the statute book. It will certainly contain measures relevant to the control of fraud, and the outlines of these can be given here.

The Bill proposes to improve the provisions for investigations and inquiries. It will enable the court to order an investigation at the instance of the company as well as the shareholders, and this may be done by ordinary rather than special resolution of the company. It proposes on the other hand to increase dramatically the security for costs which could be demanded before commencing an investigation from £100 to £5,000 or such other sum as the Secretary of State may order. This will, if enacted, serve as a means by which recourse to the inspection machinery may be discouraged.

The Bill also deals with the difficult problem of access to books and documents. Inspectors who consider that a person other than a director or officer is or may be in possession of information concerning the affairs of a company would be able to require that person to produce books and documents in his possession relating to the company or other body corporate, and to give all reasonable assistance with the investigation. This is welcome, and probably meets the criticism in Inspectors' reports that it is impossible to force a person to give information about a company which is not a holding or subsidiary company of the company under investigation, but which is a company in which the same controlling figure has a substantial shareholding (see pp. 167–8). On the other hand, it would be possible to obtain access to directors' bank accounts where these are thought to contain details of pertinent transactions, for example emoluments or contracts which should have been disclosed in the company's accounts. The powers proposed with respect to directors' bank accounts would not extend to investigations into share ownership. Those provisions, however, extend beyond powers to investigate persons financially interested in the company, or persons able to influence materially its policy to any other person who the Inspector believes to have information relevant to the investigation.

Section 111 of the Companies Act 1967 prohibits the disclosure of information obtained from investigations under that Act, save for certain limited prosecutions or other legal proceedings. The Bill proposes to make such information available to Inspectors conducting formal investigations for the purpose of cross-examining witnesses. The purposes for which disclosure may be made would be simplified and extended to enable the Secretary of State to exercise his functions under the Companies Acts, the Prevention of Fraud (Investments) Act 1959, the Insurance Companies Act 1974, and the Insolvency Act 1976. Disclosure could be made to the Law Officers, the Director of Public Prosecutions, any constable and any procurator-fiscal. This would not, however, enable disclosure to be made for the purpose of any criminal prosecution whatever.

The Department of Trade, in exercising its powers to investigate cases where it appears to the liquidator in a voluntary winding-up that any present or past officer of a company has committed a criminal offence in respect of it, would be able to exercise all the powers available to Inspectors under the general company inspection machinery.

Substantial improvements are proposed to the provisions applying to the disqualification of directors. A director would be liable to disqualification in respect of any indictable offence in connection with the promotion, formation or management of a company, or where he appears to have been persistently in default of his obligations concerning the making of reports under the Companies Acts, or where in the course of winding-up he appears to have been guilty of fraudulent trading, whether convicted or not, or has otherwise been guilty of any fraud in relation to the company or has been in breach of his duty to it. It would be possible to disqualify a director who had been guilty of any summary offence concerning the return of documents to the Registrar. A court would be empowered to disqualify such a director if, during the five years ending with the date of conviction, he had had made against him or had been convicted of not less than three default orders and offences of the sort mentioned in the Act. In the case of a summary offence or breach of order, the maximum period of disqualification would be for five years; in the serious cases it would be for fifteen years, a period long enough to meet criticisms of the existing machinery.

The offence of fraudulent trading would be reformed to the extent of making it apply whether or not the company had been or was in the process of being wound up. The offence would thus look more like a general fraud provision than it does at present, but it would still apply only to bodies corporate and not to all forms of business organisation. The offence under s. 54 of the Companies Act 1948, so extensively dealt with in this book, would be recast, maintaining a wide prohibition, but enabling loans for innocent purposes including, presumably, share support during a take-over. The original draft was rather nebulous in its terms and, at the time of writing, it is impossible to predict what its final form will be.

Finally, complicated clauses have been introduced to deal with concert parties, a phrase which refers not to the London Mozart Players, but to coalitions which build up shareholdings covertly with a view to facilitating a take-over, or to gaining control through a later swoop upon the market. It is again unclear what final form such provisions will take; the original proposals were obscurely drafted.

At present, enterprises which wish to do business under a name which is not that of the person or company carrying it on must register the name in the Registry of Business Names. This has long worked imperfectly, and the present government intends to abolish rather than to improve it, despite complaints from a number of sources that to do so would facilitate fraud. It appears that the government will prevail.

Sundry other matters should be noted. The continuing saga of St. Piran produced bitter complaints from Lord Shawcross that the voluntary system of regulation in the City requires support from the government by wielding statutory controls where necessary. In that case, Lord Shawcross complained, the government wrongly declined to follow the advice of its Inspectors to move for the winding-up of the company. It is noteworthy that Lord Shawcross treated as unrealistic the government's suggestion that private shareholders might bear the cost of applying to the court (*The Times*, May 2 1981). Similar comments came from the chairman of the Council for the Securities Industry (*The Times*, May 8 1981). One cannot but wonder whether the government is not entering a phase of extreme *laissez-faire* in defiance alike of the dictates of history and common sense.

This book has been critical of prosecution policies which it described as timid. On the other side of the ledger should be noted cases in which the courts have signally demonstrated the problems involved in prosecuting these cases especially where accounting evidence conflicts. Thus, one trial arising out of the London and County Securities Group was halted by the trial judge firstly because some of the accused could not safely be convicted on the evidence, and secondly because, window dressing was not thought to be dishonest at that time if not done 'overwhelmingly'. It would, Talbot J. stated, be unsafe to try to pinpoint the degree of criminality in the minds of certain of the accused (*The Times*, October 4 1980). Then, in the British-Israel Bank case, convictions were overturned on the grounds that the judge had misdirected the jury (*The Times* Law Report, January 12 1981). The Court of Appeal concluded that the defence had not been given adequate particulars, that the prosecution case was presented in an unduly complicated fashion, that it was overloaded and unselective, and that the summing up was so diffuse as to confuse the jury. Seldom can the problems alluded to on pp. 260–63 of this book have been more clearly illustrated. On the other hand, in further London and County Securities proceedings, one director at least has pleaded guilty to considerable thefts and forgeries (*The Times*, February 28 1981).

For the first time, directors have been banned for being in persistent default of reporting requirements under the Companies Acts ('Three Gilgate directors banned', *The Times*, 14 March 1981). Secondly, and most important, in *In re St. Piran Ltd.*, *The Times* Law Report, July 10 1981, Dillon J. held that a contributory who moves to wind up a company may rely on the report of Departmental Inspectors to the same extent as the Secretary of State could on a petition presented by him. Such a report is not mere hearsay, because Inspectors act in a statutory fact-finding capacity, and it would be nonsensical if the court could not take the report into account in deciding whether to make a winding-up order. The respondent may of course bring evidence to challenge the report. This decision again extends markedly the potential ambit of control over fraud and misconduct in relation to companies.

Important developments have occurred concerning sentencing. In *Reg.* v. *Bibi*, [1980] 1 W.L.R. 1193, the court noted that sentences should be kept as short as possible consistent with the protection of the public interest, and deterrence and punishment of the offender. In *Reg.* v. *Murray*, (1980) 71 Cr. App. R. 379, the court distinguished between a man who engaged in deception in an endeavour to shore up a failing business and a person who deliberately engages in a long-firm fraud. In the former case, a short-term prison sentence may be appropriate, while the latter conduct merits a substantial prison term. Finally, the relative severity of courts in tax evasion cases is underlined by K. Deane, 'Tax Evasion, Criminality and Sentencing the Tax Offender', *Brit. J. Criminol.*, Vol. 21, January 1981, pp. 47–57.

The Royal Commission on Criminal Procedure, *Report*, 1981, Cmnd. 8092, did not, indeed, make specific recommendations concerning prosecution machinery in fraud cases. It did, however, recommend a power to search for evidence, which would extend to searches for papers and business records (paras. 3.40–44). A similar suggestion is advanced on pp. 229–30 of this book.

JULY 1981

Bibliography

Books

American Law Institute (1961), *Model Penal Code, Proposed Official Draft*, Philadelphia, Pennsylvania, The American Law Institute.

———(1972), *Federal Securities Code, Tentative Draft* vols. 1–3 and Reporter's Revision.

ARGENTI, J. (1976), *Corporate Collapse, the Causes and Symptoms*, London, McGraw-Hill.

ARNOLD, T.W. (1937), *The Folklore of Capitalism*, New Haven, Connecticut, Yale University Press.

BALDWIN, J. and McCONVILLE, M. (1979), *Negotiated Justice*, London, Martin Robertson.

BALDWIN, J. (1979), *Jury Trial*, London, Martin Robertson.

BERLE, A. and MEANS, G. (1936). *The Modern Corporation and Private Property*, New York, The Macmillan Company.

BORRELL, C. and CASHINELLA, B. (1975), *Crime in Britain Today*, London, Routledge & Kegan Paul Ltd.

BORRIE, G. and LOWE, N. (1973), *The Law of Contempt*, London, Butterworth & Co. Ltd.

CAMPBELL, D. (1979), *The Investigation of Fraud*, 2nd ed., Chichester, Barry Rose Ltd.

City Company Law Committee (1976), *Insider Trading*, (unpublished).

CLARKE, SIR E. (1903), *The Law of Extradition*, 4th ed., London, Stevens & Haynes.

Combined Committee of Accountancy Bodies (1980), *Auditing Standards and Guidelines*.

COMER, M. (1977), *Corporate Fraud*, Maidenhead, McGraw-Hill Inc.

CONKLIN, J. (1977), *'Illegal But Not Criminal': Business Crime in America*, Englewood Cliffs, New Jersey, Spectrum Book S-450.

CONNELL, J. and SUTHERLAND, J. (1978), *Fraud: The Amazing Career of Dr. Savundra*, London, Hodder & Stoughton.

COOPER, V. (1974), *Students' Manual of Auditing*, 2nd ed., London, Gee & Company Ltd.

CORNISH, W. (1968), *The Jury*, London, Allen Lane, The Penguin Press.

COSSON, J. (1971), *Les Industriels de la Fraude Fiscale*, Paris, Editions du Seuil.

COSSON, J. (1979), *Les Grands Escrocs en Affaires*, Paris, Editions du Seuil.

CREW, A. (1913), *The Law Relating to Secret Commissions and Bribes*, London, Sir Isaac Pitman & Sons.

CROFT, R. (1975) *Swindle! A Decade of Canadian Stock Frauds*, Toronto, Gage & Co. Ltd.

CROSS, SIR R. (1975), *The English Sentencing System*, 2nd ed., London, Butterworth & Co., Ltd.

DEL MARMOL, C. (1936), *La Faillité en Droit Anglo-Saxon*, Paris, Librarie Générale de Droit et de Jurisprudence.

EDWARDS, J. (1964), *The Law Officers of the Crown*, London, Sweet & Maxwell Ltd.

FLETCHER, G. (1978), *Rethinking Criminal Law*, Boston, Mass., Little, Brown & Co.

FLORENCE, P. (1961), *Ownership, Control and Success of Large Companies*, London, Sweet & Maxwell Ltd.

FRIEDMANN, W. and GARNER, J. (1970), *Government Enterprise*, London, Stevens & Sons.

GEIS, G. and MEIER, R. (eds.) (1977), *White-Collar Crime*, New York, Free Press.

GOLDSTEIN, A. and ORLAND, L. (1974), *Criminal Procedure*, Boston, Mass., Little, Brown & Co.

GORDON, G. (1978), *Criminal Law*, 2nd ed., Edinburgh, W. Green & Co.

GOTLEIB, C. and BORODIN, A. (1973), *Social Interests in Computing*, New York, Academic Press Inc.

GOWER, L. (1969), *The Principles of Modern Company Law*, 3rd ed., London, Stevens & Sons.

——(1979), *The Principles of Modern Company Law*, 4th ed., edited by L. Gower, J. Cronin, A. Easson and Lord Wedderburn, London, Stevens & Sons.

GRIEW, A. (1978), *The Criminal Law Act 1977*, London, Sweet & Maxwell Ltd.

HADDEN, T. (1968), *The Control of Company Fraud*, London, P.E.P., vol. xxxiv, Broadsheet 503.

HAILSHAM, Lord (ed.) (1973), *Halsbury's Laws of England*, 4th ed., vol. 1, London, Butterworth & Co. Ltd.

HAMPTON, C. (1977), *Criminal Procedure*, London, Sweet & Maxwell Ltd.

JUSTICE (1972), *Insider Trading*, London, Justice.

——(1974), *A Companies Commission*, London, Justice.

KALVEN, H. and ZEISEL, H. (1966), *The American Jury*, Boston, Little Brown & Co.

KELLENS, G. (1974), *Banqueroute et Banqueroutiers*, Brussels, Dessart et Mardaga.

KROPOTKIN, P. (1968), *Memoirs of a Revolutionist*, New York, Grove Press Inc.

LASKIN, HON. B. (1969), *The British Tradition in Canadian Law*, London, Stevens & Sons.

Law Commission (1974), Working Paper No. 56, *Conspiracy to Defraud*, London, H.M.S.O.

LEIGH, L.H. (1969), *The Criminal Liability of Corporations in English Law*, London, Weidenfeld & Nicolson.

—— (1975b), *Police Powers in England and Wales*, London, Butterworth.

——(1980), ed. *Economic Crime in Europe*, London, The Macmillan Press

——and HALL WILLIAMS, J.E (1979), *The Management of Prosecutions in Three European Systems*, (unpublished).

LEVENS, G. (1964), *A Study of the Occupational and Social Mobility of White-Collar Criminals after their Discharge from Prison*, (unpublished).

LOEFFLER, R. (1974), *Report of the Trustee of Equity Funding Corporation of America*, Report to the United States District Court for the Central District of California, 31 October 1974.

MAGNUS, S. and ESTRIN, M. (1978), *Companies Law and Practice*, 5th ed., London, Butterworth & Co. Ltd.

MAIR, W., Wood, D. and DAVIS, K. (1976), *Computer Control and Audit*, 2nd ed., Altamonte Springs, Florida, The Institute of Internal Auditors.

MALIK, P. (1978), *Criminal Court Handbook*, 16th ed., Lucknow, Eastern Book Co.

MANNE, H. (1966), *Insider Trading and the Stock Market*, New York, The Free Press; London, Collier-Macmillan Ltd.

MARTING, J. (1973), *Security, Accuracy and Privacy in Computer Systems*, Englewood Cliffs, New Jersey, Prentice Hall Inc.

MATHIJSEN, P. (1975), *A Guide to European Community Law*, 2nd ed., London, Sweet & Maxwell Ltd.

NOKES, G. (1967), *An Introduction to Evidence*, 4th ed., London, Sweet & Maxwell Ltd.

NORTHEY, J.F. and LEIGH, L.H. (1980) *Introduction to Company Law*, 2nd ed., London, Butterworth & Co. Ltd.

OUGHTON, F. (1971), *Fraud and White-Collar Crime*, London, Elek Books.

PATERSON, W. and EDNIE, H. (1972), *Australian Company Law*, Sydney, The Law Book Company.

PEARCE, F. (1976), *Crimes of the Powerful*, London, Pluto Press Ltd.

PENNINGTON, R. (1979), *Company Law*, 4th ed., London, Butterworth & Co. Ltd.

PONCET, D. (1977), *La Protection de l'Accusé par la Convention Européene des Droits de l'Homme*, Geneva, Librairie de l'Université, Georg & Cie, S.A.

RAW, C. (1977), *Slater Walker: An Investigation of a Financial Phenomenon*, London, Coronet Books, Hodder & Stoughton.

RAW, C., PAGE, B., and HODGSON, G. (1971), *Do You Sincerely Want To Be Rich?*, London, Penguin Books Ltd.

RHODES, H. (1949), *The Lynskey Tribunal*, Leigh-on-Sea, Essex, The Thames Bank Publishing Company Ltd.

RIDER, B. (1980), *The Promotion and Development of International Co-operation to Combat Commerical and Economic Crime*, London, Commonwealth Secretariat.

ROSSUM, R. (1978), *The Politics of the Criminal Justice System*, New York and Basel, Marcel Dekker Inc.

SAMPSON, A. (1977), *The Arms Bazaar*, London, Hodder and Stoughton.

SCHWABE, W. and BRANSON, G. (1914), *A Treatise on the Law of the Stock Exchange*, 2nd ed., London, Butterworth & Co. Ltd.

SEIPEL, P. (1973), *Computing Law*, Stockholm, Liber Forlag.

SLATER, J. (1977), *Return To Go*, London, Weidenfeld & Nicolson.

SMITH, J.C. (1979a), *The Law of Theft*, 4th ed., Butterworth & Co. Ltd.

—— and HOGAN, B. (1978), *Criminal Law*, 4th ed., Butterworth & Co. Ltd.

SOCIÉTÉ Internationale de Défense Sociale (1969), *Les Interdictions Professionelles*, Milan, Cujas.

STEFANI, G. and LEVASSEUR, G. (1977), *Procédure Pénale*, 10th ed., Paris, Dalloz.

STREET, H. (1979), *Freedom, the Individual and the Law*, 4th ed., London, Penguin Books Ltd.

TAYLOR, I., WALTON, P. and YOUNG, J. (1975), *Critical Criminology*, London, Routledge & Kegan Paul Ltd.

THOMAS, D. (1979), *Principles of Sentencing*, 2nd ed., London, Heinemann Educational Books Ltd.

TIEDEMANN, K. (1975), *Die Verbrechen in der Wirtschaft*, Hamburg, Rohwalt.

TURNER, J. (1964), *Russell on Crime*, 12th ed., London, Stevens & Sons.

WADE, H. (1978), *Administrative Law*, 4th ed., Oxford, Clarendon Press.

WHITESIDE, T. (1979), *Computer Capers*, London, Sidgwick & Jackson.

WILCOX, A. (1972), *The Decision to Prosecute*, London, Butterworth & Co. Ltd.

WILLIAMS, G.L. (1961), *Criminal Law, The General Part*, 2nd ed., London, Stevens & Sons.

———(1963), *The Proof of Guilt*, 3rd ed., London, Stevens & Sons.

———(1978), *Textbook of Criminal Law*, London, Sweet & Maxwell Ltd.

Articles

ANON. (1960), 'Control of non-governmental corruption by criminal legislation', *University of Pennsylvania Law Review*, vol. 108, p. 848.

ANON. (1975), 'Il Colloque de l'OIPC-Interpol sur les activités frauduleuses internationales', *La Revue de Science Criminelle*, 1975, no. 1, pp. 262–3.

ANYANGWE, C. (1978), 'Dealing with the problem of bad cheques in France', *Criminal Law Review*, 1978, pp. 31–42.

ASHE, T. (1979), 'Supervising the banks', *New Law Journal*, vol. 129, pp. 1160–2.

Association Internationale de Droit Pénal, 'Les effets internationaux de la sentence pénale', *La Revue Internationale de Droit Pénal*, 1963, pp. 205–67.

BENNION, F. (1979), Letter, *New Law Journal*, vol. 129, p. 1215.

BEULLAC, R. (1966), 'De l'intérrogatoire à l'étranger en matière pénale,' *La Revue du Barreau*, vol. 26, pp. 591–603.

BOSSARD, A. (1980), 'The ICPO-Interpol and international police co-operation', *The Police Journal*, vol. 53, no. 2, pp. 124–7.

BOYLE, A. (1978), 'Company law and the non-executive director—the U.S.A. and Britain compared', *International and Comparative Law Quarterly*, vol. 28, pp. 487–509.

BRAITHWAITE, J. (1979), 'Transnational corporations and corruption: towards some international solutions', *International Journal of the Sociology of Law*, vol. 7, pp. 125–52.

COFFIELD, J. (1967), 'Fraud and the Inland Revenue', *New Law Journal*, vol. 117, p. 221.

Committee on Federal Regulation of Securities (1977), 'Foreign payments legislation', *Business Lawyer*, vol. 32, pp. 1901–23.

CONWAY, B. (1976), 'The Stock Exchange investigates...', *Investors' Chronicle*, January 9, 1976.

DAVIS, A. (1975), 'Computer security and you', *Accountancy*, vol. 86, September 1975, pp. 80–4.

DAVISON, I. H. (1978), 'The role of the audit committee', *The Accountant*, vol. 179, pp. 290–4.

DELMAS-MARTY, M. (1977), '"Le delit des initiés", va-t-il changer la bourse?', *Recueil Dalloz Sirey*, 1977, pp. 91–6.

——— (1980), 'White-collar crime and the E.E.C.', in L. H. Leigh (ed.), *Economic Crime in Europe*, London, The Macmillan Press Ltd.

——— and TIEDEMANN, K. (1979), 'La criminalité, le droit pénal et les multinationales', *La Semaine Juridique, Edition Commerce et Industrie*, no. 1, January 1979, 12900.

DEVINE, A. (1976), 'How independent are auditors?', *Accountancy*, vol. 87, December 1976, pp. 49–51.

ELIASBERG, W. (1951), 'Corruption and bribery', *Journal of Criminal Law* (U.S.A.), vol. 42, pp. 317–31.

ELLIOTT, N. (1975), 'Joint audits—from three viewpoints: accountant's view', *Accountancy*, vol. 86, June 1975, pp. 34–6.

FERAUD, H. and SCHLANITZ, E. (1975), 'La coopération policière internationale', *La Revue Internationale de Droit Pénal*, 1974, pp. 475–8.

FINER, M. (1966), 'White-collar crime', in H. Klare and D. Haxby, *Frontiers of Criminology*, pp. 46–9, Oxford, Pergamon Press.

GLAZEBROOK, P. (1970), 'Some further comments on the working paper on forgery', *Criminal Law Review*, 1970, pp. 554–9.

GRIEW, E. (1975), 'Two law reform working papers on fraud', *Criminal Law Review*, 1975, pp. 70–81.

HADDEN, T. (1980), 'Fraud in the city: enforcing the rules', *The Company Lawyer*, vol. 1, pp. 9–16.

HARE, D. (1974), 'The need for new anti-corruption laws in local government', *Public Law*, pp. 146–74.

HERMANN, D. (1977), 'Criminal prosecution of United States multinational corporations', *Loyola University Law Journal*, vol. 8, pp. 465–98.

HERZOG, J. (1963), 'La VIIIe Congrès international de droit pénal', *La Revue Internationale de Droit Pénal*, 1962, pp. 353–80.

HOLMES, G. (1976), 'Roadships Ltd.—yet another lesson for auditors', *Accountancy*, vol. 87, December 1976, pp. 52–5.

HOPKINS, R. (1979), 'Section 54: the Slater Case and proviso (a)', *New Law Journal*, vol. 129, pp. 1089–92.

HUISKAMP, J. (1980), 'Definition, scope and importance of international tax avoidance', *Abstract*, Council of Europe, Strasbourg, Press Release, R[80] 3, 25.2.80.

INSTONE, R. (1978), 'Inspectors, investigations and their aftermath', *Journal of Business Law*, 1978, pp. 121–8.

JAMES, L. (1962), 'Bribery and corruption in commerce', *International and Comparative Law Quarterly*, vol. 11, pp. 880–6.

KUNTER, N. (1968), 'Disqualifications and other consequences of foreign criminal judgements', in *Aspects of the International Validity of Criminal Judgements*, Strasbourg, Council of Europe.

LEIGH, L. H. (1975a), 'The Law Commission's conspiracy to defraud: working paper no. 56', *Modern Law Review*, vol. 38, pp. 320–28.

—— (1977a), 'The criminal liability of corporations and other groups', *Ottawa Law Review*, vol. 9, pp. 246–302.

—— (1977b), 'Policy and Punitive Measures in Respect of Economic Offences', in *12th Conference of Directors of Criminological Research Institutes*, Strasbourg, Council of Europe, 1977.

—— (1978), 'Il controllo della criminalita economica: l' esperienza Britannica', in C. Pedrazzi (ed.), *Comportamenti Economica E Legislazione Penale*, Milan, Revista Della Societa.

—— (1979), 'Securities regulation: Problems in relation to sanctions' in *Proposals for a Securities Market Law for Canada*, vol. 3, pp. 513–624, Ottawa, Minister of Supplies and Services.

—— (1980a), 'Aspects of the control of economic crime in the United Kingdom', in L. H. Leigh (ed.), *Economic Crime in Europe*, London, The Macmillan Press Ltd., pp. 15–38.

——— (1980b), 'Crimes in bankruptcy', *Ibid.*, pp. 106–208.

LEIGH, L. H. and TEMKIN, J. (1975), 'The vice of section 16: a review of the Criminal Law Revision Committee working paper, section 16 of the Theft Act 1968', *Modern Law Review*, vol. 38, pp. 186–92.

LEIGH, M. (1977), 'The challenge of transnational corporate wrongdoing to the rule of law', *Department of State Bulletin* (U.S.A.), vol. 74, no. 1926, pp. 642–8.

LEVASSEUR, G. (1975), 'Réformes récentes en matière pénale due à l'école de la défense sociale nouvelle', in *Aspects Nouveaux de la Pensée Juridique, Recueil d'Études en Hommage à Marc Ancel*, vol. 2, Paris, Éditions Pedone.

LEVI, M. (1980), 'The sentencing of long-firm frauds', in L.H. Leigh, (ed.), *Economic Crime in Europe*, London, The Macmillan Press Ltd., pp. 57–77.

LOSS, L. (1970), 'The fiduciary concept as applied to trading by corporate "insiders" in the United States', *Modern Law Review*, vol. 33, pp. 34–52.

MANNHEIM, H. (1937), 'Trial by jury in continental law', *Law Quarterly Review*, vol. 53, pp. 388–412.

NEEDHAM, C. (1979), 'Recovering the profits of bribery', *Law Quarterly Review*, vol. 95, pp. 537–56.

NEPOTE, J. (1978), 'International Crime, International police co-operation, and the ICPO-Interpol', *The Police Journal*, vol. 51, pp. 125–35.

OGREN, R. (1973), 'The ineffectiveness of the criminal sanction in fraud and corruption cases; losing the battle against white-collar crime', *American Criminal Law Review*, vol. 11, pp. 959–88.

OWLES, D. (1978), 'Auditors' responsibilities', *The Accountant*, vol. 178, pp. 730–1.

PRENTICE, D. (1976), 'Wallersteiner v. Moir: the demise of the rule in Foss v. Harbottle', *The Conveyancer and Property Lawyer*, vol. 40, pp. 51–65.

PUECH, M. (1974), 'Surveillance du marché boursier et droit pénal', in *Mélanges en l'honneur de Daniel Bastian*, Paris, Librairies Techniques, pp. 211–40.

QUINNEY, R. (1975), 'Crime control in capitalist society', in I. Taylor, P. Walton and J. Young, *Critical Criminology*, London, Routledge and Kegan Paul Ltd.

REGAN, D. and MORRIS, A. (1969), 'Local government corruption and public confidence', *Public Law*, 1969, pp. 132–52.

RENSHALL, M. (1978), 'Qualified audit opinions—are there too many?', *The Accountant*, vol. 178, March 23, 1978, pp. 383–5.

RIDER, B. (1978a), 'Changes in company law—directors' private transactions', *New Law Journal*, vol. 128, pp. 1138–40.

——— (1978b), 'The law of insider trading', *Journal of Business Law*, 1978, pp. 19–29.

——— and HEW, E. (1977), 'The regulation of corporation and securities laws in Britain—the beginning of the real debate', *Malaya Law Review*, vol. 19, pp. 144–74.

——— and HEW, E. (1978), 'The role of the City Panel on Take-overs and Mergers in the regulation of insider trading in Britain', *Malaya Law Review*, vol. 20, pp. 315–43.

ROBINTON, M. (1953), 'The British method of dealing with political corruption', *Political Science Quarterly*, vol. 68, pp. 109–24.

RODDAM, P. (1977), 'Auditors and computers', *The Accountant*, vol. 177, pp. 168–9.

ROMER, J. (1974), 'De la criminalité économique et de sa répression par la création de parquets centraux', *La Revue de Droit Pénal*, 1974–5, pp. 227–35.

RUDOFSKY, J. (1978), 'Not an unqualified success', *Investors' Chronicle*, December 1, 1978.

SCHOTLAND, R. (1967), 'Unsafe at any price: a reply to Manne', *Virginia Law Review*, vol. 53, pp. 1425–78.

SCHULTZ, H. (1967), 'Competence des juridictions pénales pour les infractions commises à l'étranger', *La Révue de Science Criminelle*, 1967, pp. 305–38.

SEALEY, L. S. (1974), 'Companies inquisition—twentieth-century style', *Cambridge Law Journal*, 1974, pp. 225–6.

SEIFMAN, R. (1977), 'The plea bargaining process, trial by error', *New Law Journal*, vol. 127, pp. 551–3.

SHYLLON, F. (1969), 'The corruption of corruptly', *Criminal Law Review*, 1969, pp. 250–58.

SIGLER, J. A. (1974), 'Public prosecutions in England and Wales', *Criminal Law Review*, 1974, pp. 642–51.

SMITH A. T. H. (1977), 'Constructive trust in the law of theft', *Criminal Law Review*, 1977, pp. 399–403.

—— (1978) 'Criminal misuse of cheque cards and credit cards', 1978, *Journal of Business Law*, pp. 129–40.

SMITH, J. C. (1979b), 'Theft, conspiracy and jurisdiction: Tarling's Case', *Criminal Law Review*, 1979, pp. 223–9.

SPENCER, J. (1968), 'A Study of incarcerated white-collar offenders', in G. Geis (ed.), *White-Collar Criminal, The Offender in Business and the Professions*, New York, The Free Press.

STEVENSON, R. (1977), 'The SEC and foreign bribery', *Business Lawyer*, vol. 32, pp. 52–73.

STUART, R. (1967), 'Law reform and the reform of the law of theft', *Modern Law Review*, vol. 30, pp. 609–34.

SUTHERLAND, E. (1940), 'White-collar criminality', *American Sociological Review*, vol. 5, no. 1, pp. 1–12.

TERRY, A. (1979), 'Interpol grapples with the computer criminals', *Sunday Times*, December 23, 1979.

TIEDEMANN, K. (1974), 'La criminalité socio-économique: aspects internationaux et de droit comparé', *La Révue de Science Criminelle*, 1974, pp. 749–63.

—— (1980), 'Antitrust law and criminal law policy in Western Europe', in L. H. Leigh (ed.), *Economic Crime in Europe*, London, the Macmillan Press Ltd.

TRICKER, R. (1979), 'The independent director', *C.B.I. Review*, vol. 30, pp. 19–29, Winter 1978–79.

WALLER, R. (1978), 'Security and computers', *The Accountant*, vol. 178, pp. 500–1, April 13, 1978.

WHEATCROFT, P. (1979), 'Are companies inflating their concrete assets?', *Sunday Times*, November 25, 1979.

WILL, I. (1980), 'Management and the police', *Management Today*, January 1980, pp. 56–61.

WILLIAMS, B. RHYS (1978), 'Why companies need audit committees', *Investors' Chronicle*, February 17, 1978.

YONTEF, M. (1979), 'Insider trading in Canada', in Department of Consumer and Corporate Affairs, *Proposals for a Securities Market Law for Canada*, vol. 3, pp. 615–718, Ottawa, Minister of Supplies and Services, Canada.

Command Papers

(by serial and date)

Cmd. 2657 (1926), *Report Of The Company Law Committee*, Chairman Sir W. Greene, London, H.M.S.O.

Cmd. 6659 (1945), *Report Of The Company Law Amendment Committee*, Chairman Lord Justice Cohen, London, H.M.S.O.

Cmd. 7617 (1949), *Report Of The Tribunal Appointed to Inquire Into Allegations Reflecting On The Official Conduct Of Ministers Of The Crown And Other Public Servants*, Chairman Mr. Justice Lynskey, London, H.M.S.O.

Cmd. 9474 (1955), *Royal Commission On The Taxation Of Profits And Income*, Chairman Rt. Hon. Lord Radcliffe, London, H.M.S.O.

Cmnd. 1749 (1962), *Report Of The Company Law Committee*, Chairman Lord Justice Jenkins, London, H.M.S.O.

Cmnd. 5012 (1972), *Report of the Committee on Privacy*, Chairman Rt. Hon. Kenneth Younger, London, H.M.S.O.

Cmnd. 5281 (1973), *Report Of The Committee On Property Bonds And Equity-Linked Life Assurance*, Chairman Sir Hilary Scott, London, H.M.S.O.

Cmnd. 5636 (1974), *Prime Minister's Committee On Local Government Rules of Conduct, Conduct In Local Government*, Chairman Lord Redcliffe-Maud, vol. 1, *Report Of The Committee*, London, H.M.S.O.

Cmnd. 6068 (1975), *Report Of The Commissioner Of Police For The Metropolis 1974*, London, H.M.S.O.

Cmnd. 6524 (1976), *Royal Commission On Standards Of Conduct In Public Life*, Chairman Rt. Hon. Lord Salmon, London H.M.S.O.

Cmnd. 6584 (1976) *The Licensing And Supervision Of Deposit-Taking Institutions*, London, H.M.S.O.

Cmnd. 6893 (1977), *Amendments To The Prevention Of Fraud (Investments) Act 1958, A Consultative Document*, London, H.M.S.O.

Cmnd. 7291 (1978), *Changes In Company Law*, London, H.M.S.O.

Cmnd. 7455 (1979), *Commissioners of Her Majesty's Customs and Excise, Report 1978*, London, H.M.S.O.

Cmnd. 7473 (1978), Board of Inland Revenue, *121st Report, For The Year Ended 31 March, 1978*, London, H.M.S.O.

Cmnd. 7557 (1979), *Gray's Building Society, Investigation Under Section 10 Of The Building Societies Act 1962*, Report by I. H. Davison F.C.A. and M. S. Smith Q.C., London, H.M.S.O.

Cmnd. 7580 (1979), *Report Of The Commissioner Of Police For The Metropolis 1978*, London, H.M.S.O.

Cmnd. 7937 (1980), *Report Of The Committee To Review The Functioning Of Financial Institutions*, Chairman Sir Harold Wilson, K. G., London, H.M.S.O.

House of Commons and House of Lords Papers (by Session)

H. L. 80, H. C. 133 (1971–2), *Report Of The Tribunal Appointed To Inquire Into*

Certain Issues In Relation To The Circumstances Leading Up To The Cessation Of Trading By The Vehicle And General Insurance Company Limited, Chairman Mr. Justice James, London, H.M.S.O.

H. C. 48 (1977–8), *Report Of The Committee Of Inquiry Appointed By The Minister Of Overseas Development Into The Circumstances Which Led To The Crown Agents Requesting Financial Assistance From The Government in 1974*, Chairman His Honour Judge E. S. Fay, Q.C., London, H.M.S.O.

Board of Trade Company Investigation Reports

(Including items under Department of Trade and Industry and Department of Trade, arranged by date)

Board of Trade (1957), *Investigation Into The Affairs Of The Gordon Hotels Limited*, Investigation Under S. 164 Of The Companies Act 1948, Report by S. Melford Stevenson Q.C. and D. V. House, F.C.A., London, H.M.S.O.

—— (1958), *Investigation Into The Affairs Of Hide & Co. Limited*, Interim and Final Reports by N. J. Skelhorn Q.C. and Sir W. S. Carrington, F.C.A., Investigation Under S. 164 Of The Companies Act 1948, London, H.M.S.O.

—— (1961), *Investigation Into The Affairs Of Eglinton Hotels (Scotland) Limited*, Report by J.O.M. Hunter Q.C. and T.C. Currie, F.C.A., Investigation Under S. 164 Of The Companies Act 1948, London, H.M.S.O.

—— (1966), *Cadco Developments Limited, Royal Victoria Sausages Limited, Royal Victoria Wholesale Meats Limited*, Investigation Under S. 165(b) Of The Companies Act 1948, Report By R.O.C. Stable Q.C. and H.O.H. Coulson F.C.A., London, H.M.S.O.

—— (1968), *Town Centre Properties Limited and Star Explorations Limited*, Investigation Under S. 165 Of The Companies Act 1948, Report by M. M. Wheeler Q.C. and C.E.M. Hardie, C.B.E., F.C.A., London, H.M.S.O.

—— (1968), *Livestock Marketing Company Limited, Western Livestock Producers Limited, Highland Livestock Producers Limited, Northern Livestock Producers Limited, Southern Livestock Producers Limited, Agribusiness Limited*, Investigation Under S. 165 (b) Of The Companies Act 1948, Report By Sir Norman Skelhorn, K.B.E., Q.C., and Sir William Lawson, C.B.E., B.A., F.C.A., London, H.M.S.O.

—— (1971), *Report On The Affairs of Internationl Learning Systems Corporation Limited, And Interim Report On The Affairs Of Pergamon Press Limited*, Investigation Under S. 165 (b) Of The Companies Act 1948, Report by R.O.C. Stable Q.C. and Sir R.G. Leach, C.B.E., F.C.A., London, H.M.S.O.

—— (1971), *Pinnock Finance Company (Great Britain) Limited And Associated Companies*, Investigation Under S. 165(b) Of The Companies Act 1948, Report by B. Wigoder Q.C. and P. Godfrey, F.C.A., London, H.M.S.O.

—— (1972), *Hartley Baird Limited*, Investigation Under S. 172 Of The Companies Act 1948, Report by J.B.R. Hazan Q.C., T. Harding, F.C.A., and A.M. Troup B.A., London, H.M.S.O.

—— (1972), *Further Interim Report On The Affairs Of Pergamon Press Limited*, Investigation Under S. 165(b) Of The Companies Act 1948, Report by

R.O.C. Stable Q.C. and Sir R.G. Leach, C.B.E., F.C.A., London, H.M.S.O.

—— (1972), *E. J. Austin International Limited*, Investigation Under S. 165(b) Of The Companies Act 1948, Interim Report by J. L. Eley Q.C. and D. Garrett, F.C.A., London, H.M.S.O.

—— (1973), *Report On The Affairs Of Maxwell Scientific International (Distribution Services) Limited; Robert Maxwell & Co. Limited, And Final Report On The Affairs Of Pergamon Press Limited*, Investigations Under S. 165(b) Of The Companies Act 1948, by R.O.C. Stable Q.C. and Sir R.G. Leach, C.B.E., F.C.A., London, H.M.S.O.

—— (1974), *First Re-Investment Trust Limited, Nelson Financial Trust Limited, English And Scottish Unit Trust Holdings Limited*, Investigations Under S. 165(b) Of The Companies Act 1948, Interim Report by D. C.-H. Hirst Q.C. and R.N.D. Langdon F.C.A., London, H.M.S.O.

—— (1975), *The Australian Estates Company Limited, First Re-Investment Trust Limited, Nelson Financial Trust Limited, English And Scottish Unit Trust Holdings Limited*, Investigations Under S. 165(b) Of The Companies Act 1948, Second And Final Report by D.C.-H. Hirst Q.C. and R.N.D. Langdon F.C.A., London, H.M.S.O.

—— (1975), *Bernard Russell Limited*, Investigation Under S. 165(b) Of The Companies Act 1948, Report by D.A.L. Smout, M.A., LL.M.,and B. E. Basden, M.A., F.C.A., London, H.M.S.O.

—— (1975), *Blanes Limited (now named Black Arrow Group Limited)*, Investigation Under S. 165(b) Of The Companies Act 1948, Report by D. A.L. Smout, M.A., LL.M., and B. E. Basden, M.A., F.C.A., London, H.M.S.O.

—— (1975), *Ardmore International Film Studios Limited (formerly New Brighton Tower Company Limited)*, Investigation Under S. 165(b) Of The Companies Act 1948, Report by J. Corbett and R. Turnbull, London, H.M.S.O.

—— (1976), *Lonrho Limited*, Investigation Under S. 165(b) Of The Companies Act 1948, Report by Allan Heyman Q.C. and Sir William Slimmings, C.B.E., C.A., London, H.M.S.O.

—— (1976), *Roadships Limited (formerly known as Ralph Hilton Transport Services Limited)*, Investigation Under S. 165(b) Of The Companies Act 1948, Report by B. A. Hytner Q.C., and I.A.N. Irvine F.C.A., London, H.M.S.O.

—— (1976), *The Vehicle And General Insurance Company Limited*, Investigation Under S. 165(b) Of The Companies Act 1948, Report by T. M. Eastham Q.C. and R. T. MacPhail M.B.E., C.A., London, H.M.S.O.

—— (1976), *London And County Securities Group Limited*, Investigations Under S. 165(b) and 172 Of The Companies Act 1948, Report by A. M. Leggatt Q.C. and D. C. Hobson M.A., F.C.A., London, H.M.S.O.

—— (1977), *London Capital Group Limited (Formerly British Bangladesh Trust Limited)*, Investigation Under S. 165(b) Of The Companies Act 1948, Report by M. Sherrard Q.C. and I. H. Davison, F.C.A. London, H.M.S.O.

—— (1977), *Edward Wood & Company Limited; Skibben Winton Construction Limited*, Investigations Under S. 165 Of The Companies Act 1948, Report by D. J. Clarkson Q.C. and K. A. McKinlay C.A., London, H.M.S.O.

—— (1978), *Court Line Limited*, Investigation Under S. 165(b) Of The

Companies Act 1948, Final Report by J. P. Comyn Q.C., D. S. Morpeth T.D., B.Com., F.C.A., and J. Hamilton M.A., London, H.M.S.O.

―――― (1978), *Electerminations Limited (In Liquidation) (formerly known as APT Electronic Industries Ltd.)*, Investigation under S. 165(b) Of The Companies Act 1948, Report by A. J. D. McCowan Q.C. and A. P. Humphries F.C.A., London, H.M.S.O.

―――― (1978), *Kuehne & Nagel Limited*, Investigation Under S. 165(b) Of The Companies Act 1948, Report by Dame Rose Heilbron D.B.E. and S. D. Samwell, F.C.A., London, H.M.S.O.

―――― (1979), *Larkfold Holdings Limited*, Investigation Under S. 165(b) Of The Companies Act 1948, Report by D. J. Nicholls Q.C. and E. K. Wright M.A., F.C.A., London, H.M.S.O.

―――― (1979), *Ashbourne Investments Limited*, Investigations Under Sections 164 and 172 Of The Companies Act 1948, Report by Robin Auld Q.C., Hobart Moore F.C.A., and Ian Glick, London, H.M.S.O.

―――― (1979), *Peachey Property Corporation Limited*, Investigation Under S. 165(b) Of The Companies Act 1948, Report by R. J. Kidwell Q.C. and S. D. Samwell F.C.A., London, H.M.S.O.

―――― (1979), *North Devon Railway Company Limited, Words In Action Limited*, Investigation Under S. 165(b) Of The Companies Act 1948, Report by A. Belchambers and A. Howarth, London, H.M.S.O.

―――― (1979), *The Barnstaple and Ilfracombe Railway Company Limited*, Investigation Under S. 165(b) Of The Companies Act 1948, Report by A. Belchambers and A. Howarth, London, H.M.S.O.

―――― (1979), *Ferguson & General Investments Limited (formerly known as Dowgate & General Investments Limited); CST Investments Limited*, Investigations Under S. 165(b) Of The Companies Act 1948, Report by Joseph Jackson Q.C. and Kirkpatrick L. Young, T.D., F.C.A., London, H.M.S.O.

――――(1980), *Ozalid Group Holdings Limited*, Investigations Under Ss. 165(b) and 172 Of The Companies Act 1948, Report by Neil Butter Q.C. and B.A. Kemp, F.C.A., London, H.M.S.O.

Other Government Publications

Central Statistical Office (1979), Studies In Official Statistics, No. 34, C.S.O., *The Ownership Of Company Shares, A Survey For 1975*, Erritt, M.J., Alexander, J., and Watson, A., London, 1975.

Committee To Review The Functioning Of Financial Institutions, 1978–80, Chairman, Sir Harold Wilson, K.G., Second Stage Evidence: Vol. 2, *Insurance Company Association*, Vol. 4, *The Stock Exchange; The Bank of England*, Vol. 5 *The Department of Trade*, London, H.M.S.O. 1978–80.

Department of Trade (1979), Bankruptcy, *General Annual Report For The Year 1978*, London, H.M.S.O.

―――― (1977), *Companies in 1976*, London, H.M.S.O.

―――― (1978), *Companies in 1977*, London, H.M.S.O.

―――― (1979), *Companies in 1978*, London, H.M.S.O.

Foreign and Commonwealth Office (1978), *Report On The Supply Of Petroleum and Petroleum Products to Rhodesia*, T. H. Bingham Q.C. and S. M. Gray, F.C.A., London, H.M.S.O.

Home Office (1969), *Consolidated Circular To The Police On Crime and Kindred Matters*, London, H.M.S.O.

—————— (1978), *Evidence To The Royal Commission On Criminal Procedure*, Memorandum No. VIII, *The Prosecution Process*, London, H.M.S.O.

Law Commission (1973), *Report On Forgery And Counterfeit Currency*, Working Paper No. 55, London, H.M.S.O.

—————— (1974), *Conspiracy to Defraud*, Working Paper No. 56, London, H.M.S.O.

Foreign Government Publications

Australia New South Wales (1979), *Report Of The Corporate Affairs Commission For The Year Ended 31 December 1978*, Sydney, The Government Printer.

Canada (1965), *Report Of The Commissioners For Uniformity Of Legislation*, Ottawa, Information Canada.

France (1978), Commission De Révision Du Code Pénal, 1978, Projet Définitif De Code Pénal, Livre 1, *Dispositions Générales*, Paris, La Documentation Française.

Interpol (1974), *Report Of The Second Symposium On International Fraud*, St. Cloud, 9–12 September 1974 (unpublished).

United Nations (1978), *Draft International Agreement To Prevent And Eliminate Illicit Payments In International Commercial Transactions*, UNESCO Document No. E/1978/115.

United States (1971), *Final Report Of The National Commission On Reform Of Federal Criminal Laws*, Washington, United States Government Printing Office.

—————— (1973), *Multinational Corporations*. A Compendium Of Papers Submitted To The Subcommittee On International Trade Of The Committee On Finance Of The United States Senate, 93rd. Congress, 1st Session, Washington, United States Government Printing Office.

Table of Cases

Index